THE DISCOURSE OF NEGOTIATION

STUDIES OF LANGUAGE IN THE WORKPLACE

Edited by

ALAN FIRTH

Aalborg University, Denmark

PERGAMON

U.K.	Elsevier Science Ltd, The Boulevard, Langford Lane, Kidlington, Oxford OX5 1GB, U.K.
U.S.A.	Elsevier Science Inc., 660 White Plains Road, Tarrytown, New York 10591-5153, U.S.A.
JAPAN	Elsevier Science Japan, Tsunashima Building Annex, 3-20-12 Yushima, Bunkyo-ku, Tokyo 113, Japan

First edition 1995

Library of Congress Cataloguing in Publication Data

The discourse of negotiation : studies of language in the workplace / edited by Alan Firth.
p. cm.
1. Interpersonal communication. 2. Negotiation in business.
I. Firth, Alan.
P94.7.D57 1994
302.2--dc20   94-17002

British Library Cataloguing in Publication Data

A catalogue record for this book is available from the British Library

ISBN 0 08 042400 7

Printed and bound in Great Britain by Galliard Printers Ltd,
Great Yarmouth

PREFACE

This book has its origins in a 3-day research symposium held at Aalborg University, Denmark, 11-13 May, 1992. Entitled 'Negotiations in the Workplace: Discourse and Interactional Perspectives', and attended by over 100 academics from 11 countries, the symposium was a truly international and interdisciplinary event, reflecting the relevance and importance of 'negotiation' throughout the social sciences. At Aalborg the attempt was made to marshall the special interests of a group of scholars for whom 'negotiation' had hitherto remained of largely peripheral interest; these were scholars of discourse analysis and language-in-social interaction, researchers that people the departments of linguistics, anthropology, sociology, and communications in our universities and colleges. Although the term 'negotiation' appears in numerous studies in discourse analysis, pragmatics, and language-in-social interaction, its use has been mainly metaphorical and incidental; somewhat surprisingly, 'negotiation' has rarely been studied and investigated as a discourse-based *activity* in its own right. The brief communicated to the presenters at the symposium was intended as a form of 'corrective' to this state of affairs, the task being to explore, through analyses of naturally occurring materials culled from 'workplaces', negotiation as a *discourse phenomenon*; i.e., an activity of social decision making undertaken in and through situated, interactive language. The motivations behind this can be traced to three perceived omissions and imbalances in extant literature. First, whilst 'negotiation' has attracted considerable scholarly attention over the last three decades, there is a striking paucity of work undertaken on the actual discourse — i.e., the *language in use* — of negotiation. Second, overwhelmingly in the literature, 'negotiation' is equated with a formal *event*, temporally and spatially bound, where the event concerned is prototypically linked with the affairs of unions and management, trade or diplomacy; rarely has negotiation been studied as an activity that pervades myriad social contexts and interpersonal encounters. And third, existing literature is dominated by studies of simulated negotiations conducted within laboratory settings. Consequently, little is known of negotiation as it occurs in real-life contexts. Based on detailed analyses of aspects of negotiation activity occurring in a wide range of 'real-life' workplace settings, the studies in this book, selected from the presentations at the Aalborg symposium, represent a collective attempt to redress these perceived imbalances and omissions.

This book walks a seldom trodden (research) path, and by so doing contributes to and extends existing (though embryonic) knowledge of negotiation as a discourse-based, communicative process. We may hope that the work reported here advances our understanding of the phenomenon of negotiation in particular, and of social interaction in general, for the activity of negotiation is a pervasive feature of social life. Furthermore, the book aims to provide scholars and students with insight into the researchable potential of detailed, transcript-based studies of the discourse of actual negotiation, and by so doing encourage and stimulate further work of this nature; certainly much remains to be done in the area. Finally, the work collectively endeavours to shed light upon a tenebrous terrain: the interactional foundations of modern workplaces — those multivarious and variegated settings in which large numbers of the population spend their daily lives. These are indeed tall orders, and as such the present volume constitutes what we may hope will be if not an inaugural then at least an early and substantive attempt to establish a discourse and interactional perspective on the study of negotiation.

In addition to acknowledging my gratitude to the participants at the Aalborg symposium, whose contributions, professional commitment, and discussions during the symposium made for a highly successful and intellectually stimulating event, sincere thanks are due to the Danish Council of Social Science Research, and the Department of Languages and Intercultural Studies, Aalborg University. Both bodies generously provided funding for the symposium. Thanks are also due to the symposium coordinator, Bente Vestergaard, and her assistants Jennifer Burke and Charlotte Nielsen. Throughout the compilation of this book I have been thankful of the patience and cooperative spirit of the individual chapter authors. I acknowledge my indebtedness to two scholars who have directly influenced my work and interests in negotiation discourse. First, Jack Bilmes, and second, Douglas Maynard. Both have undertaken exemplary work on negotiation discourse, much of which has provided the research impetus for a number of the studies in this collection.

The Department of Languages and Intercultural Studies at Aalborg University granted me leave time to complete the work undertaken here, and the Department of Sociology, University of York, U.K., provided me with access to research and administrative facilities as well as a conducive research climate; I am most grateful to both departments. During the book's production I have benefited from the skill and professionalism of Chris Pringle and Tom Merriweather at Elsevier Science in Oxford. Finally, a huge thanks to my wife, Marianne, for her continued and unfailing support; and to Tim, who didn't complain too much when his father 'urked'.

Alan Firth
York, January, 1994

CONTENTS

I. Theoretical Considerations

II. Negotiation in Intraorganizational Encounters

III. Negotiation in Commodity Trading

IV. Negotiation in Professional-Lay Interactions

LIST OF CONTRIBUTORS

Bell, D. V. J. Department of Political Science, Faculty of Environmental Studies, York University, 4700 Keele Street, North York, Ontario, Canada M3J 1P3

Bilmes, J. Department of Anthropology, University of Hawaii at Manoa, Honolulu, HI 96822, U.S.A.

Boden, D. Department of Sociology, Lancaster University, Lancaster LA1 4YL, U.K.

Button, G. Xerox EuroPARC, 61 Regent Street, Cambridge CB2 1AB, U.K.

Firth, A. Department of Languages and Intercultural Studies, Aalborg University, Havrevangen 1, DK-9100 Aalborg, Denmark

Fredin, E. Department of Communication Studies, Linköping University, S-581 83, Linköping, Sweden

Huisman, M. Department of Dutch Linguistics, Faculty of Arts, Free University of Amsterdam, De Boelelaan 1105, 1081 HV Amsterdam, The Netherlands

Jones, K. Department of East Asian Studies, The University of Arizona, Tucson, AZ 85721, U.S.A.

Linell, P. Department of Communication Studies, Linköping University, S-581 83, Linköping, Sweden

Marriott, H. E. Department of Japanese Studies, Monash University, Clayton, Victoria 3168, Australia

Mazeland, H. Department of Language and Communication, Rijkuniversiteit Groningen, P.O. Box 716, 9700 AS Groningen, The Netherlands

Schasfoort, M. Department of Dutch Linguistics, Faculty of Arts, Free University of Amsterdam, De Boelelaan 1105, 1081 HV Amsterdam, The Netherlands

Sharrock, W. Department of Sociology, Faculty of Economics and Social Studies, University of Manchester, Oxford Road, Manchester M13 9PL, U.K.

ten Have, P.   Department of Sociology, Faculty of Political and
                Socio-cultural Sciences, University of Amsterdam, Oude
                Hoogstraat 24, NL 1012 CE, Amsterdam, The Netherlands

Torode, B.   Department of Sociology, University of Dublin, Trinity
                College, Dublin 2, Ireland

Wagner, J.   Institute of Language and Communication, Odense University,
                Campusvej 55, DK-5230, Odense M, Denmark

Walker, E.   Department of Psychology, University of Stirling, Stirling
                FK9 4LA, Scotland, U.K.

Wheatley, J.   Secção Autónoma de Communicação e Arte, Universidade de
                Aveiro, 3800 Aveiro, Portugal

TRANSCRIPT NOTATION

The audio- and video-recorded materials analysed in this book are transcribed according to the following notations, developed mainly by Gail Jefferson (for a more detailed account of the notations, see Atkinson and Heritage 1984:ix-xvi). The notations, widely used by Conversation Analysts, are a continually evolving set of symbols designed to capture the interactional qualities and nuances of speech delivered in real-time.

Symbol	*Represents*
yes (1.5) me too	Figures in rounded brackets represent inter- and mid-turn silences, hand-timed in 10th's of seconds.
yes (.) me too	Period in rounded brackets are 'micro-pauses' of less than 0.2 seconds.
yes (**)	Unrecoverable speech; the number of asterisks represent the number of unrecovered syllables uttered.
yes ((clap)) me too	Double rounded brackets contain relevant contextual information, added by the transcriber.
ye::s: me too	Colons represent lengthened vowel or consonant sounds; the number of colons show the relative stretch of sound.
yes .hh me too	Lower-case h's preceded by period indicates audible inhalations. These are inserted into the turns where they occur.
yes me too hh::	Colons following h's show audible exhalations; these symbols are also inserted into turns where they occur.

ye(hh)s me too	H's encased in rounded brackets indicate aspirated sounds.
it's v<u>e</u>ry odd	Underlined letters indicate emphasis.
it's VERY <u>O</u>DD	Capitalized letters indicate that the utterance/word is enunciated louder than surrounding speech.
not <u>ALL</u> (.) no	Underlined, capitalized utterance/word shows emphatic stress, enunciated louder than surrounding speech.
I think so.	A period indicates falling tone.
I think so, do you	Comma denotes tone group boundary
do you think so?	A question mark indicates rising intonation; this symbol is not necessarily coterminous with a question.
do you ↑think so↓	Particularly animated rising and falling shifts in intonation are indicated by, respectively, upward and downward pointing arrows.
I think so °yes°	Degree signs encapsulate talk that is quieter than surrounding talk.
she said >who me<	'Greater than' and 'less than' symbols encapsulate speech that is delivered at a markedly quicker pace, relative to surrounding talk.
I think- I think so	A single dash following a word or letter(s) indicates an abrupt cut-off in the flow of speech.

A I agree=

B =me too — Equals signs show latched speech, where the turn or utterance is followed without a perceptible pause by the next turn or utterance.

A ⌈well I said
B ⌊yes — Utterances starting simultaneously are indicated by double left-hand (square) brackets.

A she's ⌈right
B   ⌊huh mm⌋ — Overlapping utterances are marked by single (square) brackets; the left-hand bracket shows where the overlap began; the right-hand bracket shows where the overlapped speech is terminated.

A → I think so — Horizontal left-to-right arrows preceding lines of transcript draw the reader's attention to aspects of the analysis being developed in the text.

SECTION I

THEORETICAL CONSIDERATIONS

CHAPTER 1

INTRODUCTION AND OVERVIEW

ALAN FIRTH

Negotiation is ubiquitous. As a formal, problem-solving *event*, the paradigmatic industrial, legal, and diplomatic negotiation figures prominently in the news media, while as an *activity of social decision making on substantive matters*, it often goes unnoticed, sometimes even to participants, yet regularly and routinely occurs in myriad interpersonal encounters in innumerable social settings.[1] This book is unlike the majority of existing research on negotiation. Whereas research rarely considers the communicative processes of negotiation, and overridingly conceptualizes negotiation as a decontextualized formal event, our point of departure takes negotiation to be a *discourse-based* and *situated* activity, an activity that is interactionally constructed in concrete social settings. Although communication is recognized to be a crucial feature of negotiation (cf. e.g. Lewicki and Litterer 1985, Putnam and Roloff 1992), the ways in which communication is *accomplished* have been overwhelmingly glossed over or taken for granted rather than described in detail. For example, Sawyer and Guetzkow (1965:479) observe that "the core of

My thanks to Jack Bilmes and Douglas Maynard for valuable comments on a previous draft of this chapter.

3

what is generally taken as the central process of negotiation [is] reciprocal argument and counter-argument, proposal and counterproposal in an attempt to agree upon actions and outcomes mutually perceived as beneficial". Unfortunately, *how* such things as arguments, counter-arguments, proposals and counter proposals — aspects that are prototypically proffered as defining characteristics of negotiation — are interactionally accomplished, how they arise in and articulate with the unfolding discourse process, how they are linguistically structured, and what consequences follow upon them, remains largely unresearched. By describing these and other aspects of negotiation in detailed ways, and by focusing specifically on negotiation in concrete, 'real-life' settings, this book endeavours to redress some serious imbalances.

The book has been compiled in an attempt to better understand (1) how negotiation is undertaken through *discourse* — here interpreted as the situated *use* of language-in-interaction,[2] (2) how negotiation as an *activity* is both contingent upon and constitutive of context,[3] and (3) to elucidate the discourse-interactional foundations of a particular range of settings wherein negotiation activity is a routine occurrence: the modern workplace[4] (cf. Collins 1981, Maynard 1989, Boden 1994). While some of the studies contained here are based on negotiation activity as it occurs in encounters explicitly characterized as 'negotiations', most examine negotiation that is implicitly embedded or woven into the fabric of work practices characterized in other ways. Such practices include 'meetings', 'talks', 'interviews', 'consultations', 'presentations' and 'inquiries'. The studies have been compiled in the belief that negotiation activity, as a pervasive and fundamental aspect of sociation, is a microcosm within which multiplex and often delitescent features of social interaction may be discovered and profitably examined. As such, the book has a dual task: to advance knowledge of negotiation as a discourse-based activity, while contributing to a greater understanding of the complex social processes underpinning human discourse.

1. NEGOTIATION AS EVENT AND ACTIVITY

In order to gain insight into negotiation as an activity, it will be useful initially to focus briefly on negotiation as an event. At the time of writing, potentially life-saving, 'high-level' formal negotiation *events* are taking place. In these cases, negotiation activity *coalesces* with the event. For example, brokered by the European Union, Bosnian Muslims, Serbs, and Croats have been (at least ostensibly) attempting to sue for a peaceful settlement for several months now; no mutually acceptable decision to desist fighting has yet been reached. Consequently, hundreds of people have been killed or injured, and towns across Bosnia reduced to rubble. The decision to resolve the military conflict cannot be unilaterally imposed or dictated, however; it must be *mutually* agreed to. Yet while the parties share interests in a cessation of the conflict, other interests are opposed. It is the interplay of opposing and shared interests (the latter seemingly the more dominant) that compels the warring sides to engage in formal negotiations. This they do in attempts to reach a mutually acceptable agreement on *how* to resolve the conflict.

Similarly, Israelis and Palestinians are currently attempting to negotiate peace, and South African political leaders are negotiating the conditions of their participation in upcoming elections. Here too, the matters being negotiated — peace and participation in elections — cannot be unilaterally declared or imposed, but must be mutually agreed to and collaboratively managed. In all cases, then, it is the acknowledged and socially accomplished elements of mutuality and reciprocity, where parties' actions and decisions are *interdependently* entwined, that allow for a multilateral shaping of outcomes.[5] Neither party, as Rubin and Brown (1975:3) put it,

> "can hope to satisfy his individual needs and interests without in some way taking account of the fact that his relationship with the other is one of mutuality and interdependence".

Characteristic contextualizing features of formal negotiation events are that they are undertaken on the basis of a prespecifiable task (e.g. to arrange terms of exchange), engaged in on others' behalf, often protracted, commonly preceded by written agendas, summarized in minutes and reports and, if successful, properly concluded with the signing of declarations, agreements, contracts, etc. Judging by the numerous public (media) statements preceding and following formal negotiations, it would appear that the 'negotiation' epithet mobilizes a cultural awareness of what constitutes appropriate behaviour during the event. Hence, although it has proven difficult for social scientists to specify what a negotiation behavioural 'prototype' might consist of, participants do seem to evince commonsense understandings of what negotiation events entail or purport in behavioural terms. For example, on 8 January 1991, days prior to the commencement of the Gulf War, the then U.S. Secretary of State, James Baker, arrived in Geneva to meet his Iraqi counterpart, Tariq Aziz. Given, amongst other things, that face-to-face bilateral diplomatic meetings held in Geneva are normally labelled as 'negotiations', Baker was prompt to assert that the meeting would be "a communication and not a negotiation". The 'communication' was that, in order to avert a military confrontation with NATO forces, Iraq must withdraw immediately from Kuwait. NATO's position, said Baker, was "non-negotiable". Such vernacular usage furnishes evidence for an implicit understanding of what type of activity 'negotiation' entails and expects, and is regularly found in (public) media statements preceding and following high-profile negotiation events. Predicated on onlookers' commonsense understanding of the negotiation-communication distinction, Baker's statement implies, of course, that NATO's ('non-negotiable') decision to commence combat in the event of non-withdrawal could not be compromised during the subsequent meeting. The Iraqis were not being negotiated with; they were presented with a predetermined and *immutable* decision.

Such implicit, commonsense understandings of the kind of behaviour negotiation events entail may also be made explicit *during* encounters. This is particularly the case when conduct is out of line with expectations. For example, in his transcript-based study of plea bargaining discourse, Douglas Maynard (1984) reported that one of the plea bargainers had reacted to the other party's actions by complaining — during the encounter — that 'this isn't plea bargaining' (op. cit.:116). Maynard showed that the perceived transgression of acceptable behaviour centred on a party's failure to display a willingness to in some way accommodate opposing interests in order to reach a decision *collaboratively*.

But as an *activity* of social decision making, where decisions on substantive matters are properly made conjointly, negotiation is not restricted to formally-defined events. In countless social settings, negotiation activity is a regular and routine occurrence, free from media attention. Outside formal negotiation events, such activity is typically perfunctory, evanescent, often extempore, frequently does not directly engage the interests of people other than those involved, and is sometimes neither recognized nor explicitly labelled — as 'negotiation' — by the people implicated in it (Tedeschi and Rosenfeld 1980). This latter factor may have important, though as yet unresearched, implications for the way people behave, interpret and interact during the activity of social decision making. When interaction is devoid of the formal 'negotiation' epithet, yet the goal is to make mutually acceptable decisions on a collaborative basis, it is pertinent to ask such questions as: how do the discourse and interpretive processes compare with negotiation activity in formally-defined events? And more generally: in which type of interactions, over what kinds of matters, and how, does negotiation activity arise?

As the collection of studies in this book suggests, the activity commonly occurs in offices, committee rooms, marketplaces, consultancy rooms, shops, used car lots, and on the telephone. In short, in myriad social settings where people interact. Here, as in the high-profile negotiations of international diplomacy and industry, people engage one another in *a communicative attempt to accommodate potential or real differences in interests in order to make mutually acceptable decisions on substantive matters,* matters that ostensibly cannot or will not be decided upon unilaterally, but rather as a conjoint arrangement. While the substantive matter to be decided upon may often be specifiable beforehand, on occasions it may be unclear prior to engagement, being often discovered, specified and defined *during* interaction. Viewed in these terms, and in contrast to the literature's prevailing view of negotiation (cf. e.g. Gulliver 1979:xiii, Putnam and Roloff 1992:3), the activity is not *of necessity* predicated on pre-existent and mutually recognized competitive or conflictual grounds. Similarly, outside the formal event, negotiation activity is not contextualized by 'disputants' (cf. Chatman, Putnam and Sondak 1991:139), nor by a mutually recognized disagreement between negotiators voluntarily relating for the purpose of jointly resolving their differences, as formal negotiations have often been described. Although disagreements and various other forms of conflict *may and often do arise during* negotiation activity (cf. Grimshaw 1990), these are neither necessary preconditions nor obligatory reasons for the activity.

As the Bosnian negotiations make clear, the outcomes of negotiation activity are seen to be properly and qualitatively dependent upon the contributions of the parties involved. Both parties legitimately exert formative influence on the outcome, though not necessarily in equitable measures. Clearly, however, as many of the studies in this volume show, although the requirements for a mutually acceptable outcome would appear to furnish the interactants with a 'goal' or 'task' that globally informs their collective actions, it is not only the acceptability of putative 'final decisions' that is the locus of negotiation activity. In quite implicit ways, negotiation activity implicates the discourse process itself, revolving around such things as the acceptability of categories used to describe objects or concepts, and the veridicality of facts, reasons or assessments. Negotiation on these processual and more covert features have profound effects on final outcomes and definitive arrangements.

But rather than arranging the cessation of wars or the ramifications of election participation, for most people negotiation activity pertains to such quotidian matters as deciding upon holiday destinations, delegating housework, arranging terms of loan repayments, establishing entitlements to welfare benefits, defining acceptable working conditions and job responsibilities, and agreeing upon courses of treatment, the acceptability of salaries, remunerations, and prices. In many ways such instances of negotiation are both the substance and sustenance of sociality, their researchable import apparent in the way the activities shed light upon those areas and aspects of the culture (or sections within it) that are perceivedly and warrantably conjoint — *negotiable* — assemblages. They may arise in institutionally-defined activities such as 'plea-bargaining' sessions, 'job interviews', 'inquiries', producer-retailer 'talks', interdepartmental or professional-lay 'meetings', or, indeed, in encounters formally and explicitly characterized as 'negotiations'. But negotiation activity may also be implicitly (and sometimes covertly) woven into the fabric of everyday activities such as 'having dinner', 'going shopping', or 'just talking'. While such instances of negotiation do not normarily attract outsiders' attention, they are nevertheless activities through which people collectively shape, structure, organize and understand their working and/or domestic lives.

2. NEGOTIATION AS COMMUNICATION

Although communicative interaction is the quintessence of negotiation, there is nevertheless a veritable dearth of studies that address the discursive and interactional nature of the phenomenon, let alone reproduce and examine transcripts of recordings of negotiation. In addition, remarkably few studies have hitherto been based on 'real-life' instances of negotiation; studies of simulated encounters predominate. In the majority of existing research, language has been ignored, or relegated to the status of a manipulable independent variable, on par with, though no more significant than, variables such as the negotiator's behavioural disposition (e.g., Cole 1972), negotiating tactics (e.g., Siegel and Fouraker 1960), and the disclosure of specific types of information (e.g., Lewicki and Litterer 1985). Where language is made the object of attention, it is most frequently subjected to the dictates and strictures of categorization and statistical analyses via inductive coding schemes (e.g., Donohue, Diez and Hamilton 1984, Neu 1988), where many of the interactional and contextual features of negotiation activity are lost. This has resulted in an impoverished view of negotiation as a cultural and interactional phenomenon. For, as Barley (1991:190) notes,

> "even though ... culturally embedded micro-processes are likely to shape
> the tenor and outcome of negotiations, aside from work by a handful of
> scholars ... they have been completely ignored by researchers who study
> bargaining and negotiation in organizational contexts".

Similarly, in their introduction to a recent compilation of negotiation studies, Putnam and Roloff (1992:5) observe that: "Although social interaction is a central element in bargaining, much of the extant literature and many theoretical perspectives are insensitive to the role that communication plays in negotiation". Rather than examine in detail the interactional processes and contextual embeddedness of negotiation, the major task for researchers has been to predict or explain *outcomes*. The following observation, made almost twenty years ago by Walcott, Hopmann and King (1977:203), still rings true today:

"Though negotiation is essentially verbal interaction, the bulk of empirical literature concerning it does not deal directly with words. Much of the work on bargaining behavior has dealt with nonverbal interaction, such as the choosing of rows and columns in a Prisoner's Dilemma Matrix. In many other studies, verbal behavior has been permitted, but it has not been recorded or analyzed systematically ... [W]hat is measured is the *outcome* of that interaction (agreement, attitude change, etc.), not the content or patterning of the interaction itself (emphasis in orginal)".

What we might call 'end-result' research prevails, as Zartman's (1975:70) injunction also serves to illustrate: "A theory of negotiations", he contends, "is a set of interrelated causal statements which explain how and which outcomes are chosen".

In this book, no encompassing 'theory of negotiation' is attempted; neither does the book focus specifically on outcomes, their causes, efficacy or desirability. Such tasks must properly be left for others. Rather, each chapter is concerned with interactionally significant aspects of negotiation activity, i.e., those features of linguistic interaction that are demonstrably relevant for and produced by the participants themselves. The features described are in a variety of ways occupied with mutual decision making on a matter of substance, including the acceptable price of commodities, the suitability of a vacation 'package', the contents of a memorandum, a person's entitlement to social benefits, the adequacy of legal advice, the acceptability of pay increases and the appropriacy of medical treatment. Taken together, the studies here contribute not so much to a 'theory' of negotiation, but more to a detailed simulacrum of negotiation as a dynamic, unfolding activity of social decision making. *The discourse of negotiation* should not be equated with 'the theory of negotiation'. Rather, the book captures and methodically explores a congeries of language-based actions that in systematic, orderly and describable ways pursue (though sometimes fail to achieve) a mutually agreeable outcome. *How* that outcome is conjointly assembled through situated, interactive discourse is the focus of this book.

By restricting the focus to negotiation activity as it regularly and perfunctorily arises in a wide range of modern (industrial, bureaucratic, and service) work settings, the essays collected here attempt a rarely undertaken task: to explore and describe in detailed ways the discourse and interactional characteristics of negotiation as a socially constructed, reflexively context-shaped and context-shaping activity. This is accomplished mainly by recourse to close analyses of *transcripts* of actual, 'real-life' instances of negotiation. In all but two of the book's fourteen chapters (discounting the present chapter), each author's point of departure is close-grained transcripts of audio- or video-recordings of negotiation activity. Transcript analyses are prevalent in a number of approaches to discourse study (cf. Schiffrin 1994), and are a defining feature of work in ethnomethodological conversation analysis (e.g., Atkinson and Heritage 1984,

A. Firth

Drew and Heritage 1992), an approach to discourse which several of the chapter authors have adopted. Although surprisingly little of such work has been hitherto directed to the study of negotiation, over the last two decades an accumulating body of transcript-based work on casual conversations, interviews, emergency calls, court proceedings and doctor-patient interaction (amongst others) has established that not only is interactive discourse delicately yet systematically composed in extraordinarily intricate ways, but that it is also eminently describable. Transcripts can be difficult to read, and are always very time-consuming to prepare in a form that straddles accessibility to the reader and faithfulness to the source. However, done well, they grant the analyst-observer access to a level of detail that is unsurpassed, opening up the intricacies of interactive discourse to repeated, careful and precise observation. Basing analyses on reproduced transcripts thus represents a methodic attempt to establish a close relationship between data and their analyses. For the reader, the reproduced transcripts mean that the analyst's observations on and descriptions of the data materials are not merely to be taken 'on trust' as a result of inaccessibility of the materials. Rather, transcripts allow for the possibility of directly evaluating and reexamining the materials as they are being subjected to analysis (cf. Heritage and Atkinson 1984:2-5).

3. RESEARCH ON NEGOTIATION

Research on negotiation, and its cognate, *bargaining*, is truly voluminous.[6] Over the last three decades in particular, the study of negotiation has witnessed a dramatic upsurge of scholarly attention. The area is presently characterized by diverse disciplinary approaches, a wide accumulation of conceptual, empirical, and experimental materials, differing theoretical emphases and goals, numerous analytical methodologies, and both disparate and overlapping findings (see Zartman 1989a:241).

The terms 'negotiation' and 'negotiate' have gained widespread currency throughout the social sciences. In many cases, 'negotiation' is used *metaphorically* (and thus often encapsulated in scare-quotes), to stress that the essential nature of a phenomenon is not stasis or fixity, but its contingent mutability, its situated emergence, and its intersubjective interpretation — each symbiotically accomplished through interactive processes. For some sociologists (e.g. Berger and Luckman 1967, Strausss 1978), negotiation extends to all areas of social life, since social order itself is a ceaseless, *negotiated* process, where — the argument goes — all forms of human interaction ineluctably and incessantly entail 'negotiated' interpretations, meanings, goals, roles, decisions, arrangements and outcomes. For Michel Foucault (e.g. Foucault 1972), one of this century's most influential historians, a perennial issue was the dichotomy between predetermined socio-historical and economic conditions of existence and its emergent, 'negotiated' properties. The social psychologist Rom Harré (1993:132) has recently emphasized the need for his discipline to attend to the 'negotiation of social identities or personas'. And throughout the language studies of sociolinguists, sociologists, and anthropologists, the metaphorical use of the term 'negotiation' is prevalent, particularly in research into the interactional and pragmatic dimensions of language use. Here, context (Goodwin and Duranti 1992, Kendon 1992), utterance meaning (Bilmes 1992b), interpretations (Dore and McDermott 1982), interactional 'frames' (Streek 1983), topics (Gumperz 1982:6), turn-taking (Fairclough 1992:146), and code (Heller 1982) are commonly perceived not as predetermined, unilaterally accomplished or fixed entities, but as emphatically *negotiable* phenomena, in the sense of being dynamic, socially determined, contingently mutable, and emergent within the symbiotic processes of human interaction.

But the most substantial body of work on negotiation conceptualizes the term as the descriptor of a problem-solving encounter. In this case, negotiation is overridingly studied as the sanctioned locus of *corporate conflict resolution.* Typical instances are commercial, industrial, and diplomatic negotiations, wage- and collective-bargaining sessions, and arms control negotiations. In the present volume, our understanding of 'negotiation' — as a pervasive activity of social decision making on substantive matters — steers a middle course between two poles: the metaphorical use of the term highlighting the interactionally contingent nature of language-in-use, and the understanding of negotiation as a formal problem-solving event. In this way, insights, concepts, and methodologies from both the metaphorical and event 'poles' of research inform the studies contained here.

In terms of research output, the areas from which the bulk of materials and theories on negotiation has emerged are economics, game and bargaining theory, political science, anthropology, and social psychology. Within these disciplines, scholars have largely sought answers to questions integral to their respective fields of inquiry. For example, economists turn to negotiation and bargaining as the source of insight into bilateral monopoly and oligopoly; game theorists focus on bargaining in the construction of rationalistic models of decision-making; anthropologists examine negotiations to account for culture-bound methods of conflict resolution, and social psychologists describe the effects of contextual variables on the negotiator's behaviour.[7]

The picture of existing research is one of theoretically distinct, though thematically contiguous, approaches to negotiation. For expository purposes, research may be collapsed into five overriding orientations, which collectively account for the large majority of existing work. These orientations may be termed *prescriptive, abstract, ethnographic, experimental* and *discourse.* While prescriptive orientations are represented in the main by practising, or former, negotiators, and are largely aimed at a (trainee) managerial readership, the four remaining orientations aim at an academic and research audience. Abstract orientations are characterized by the implementation of hypothetico-deductive methodology; ethnographic orientations typically utilise 'interpretive' research procedures; experimental orientations are characterized by the implementation of 'positivistic' methodological practices undertaken on simulated negotiations; while discourse orientations most commonly utilize coding schemes in an attempt to account for the micro details underlying negotiation processes. In terms of research output and concentration of scholarly attention, the most substantial volume of work has emanated from studies adopting either abstract or experimental orientations. These orientations are represented largely by studies within the fields of economics, political science and social psychology. In the following section, each of the five orientations will be reviewed briefly in turn, though main emphasis will be afforded discourse-oriented research.

3.1. Prescriptive Orientations

A *prescriptive* orientation is represented by the popular writings of former, or practising, (and usually North American) negotiators who attempt to enlighten their readers on '*how* to negotiate' (see, e.g., Fisher and Ury 1981, Mastenbroek 1989, Griffin and Daggart 1990, Salacuse 1991, Sunshine 1990). The target of such work is overridingly the practising negotiator, manager or salesperson. Practical, strategic advice is given in order that the reader may develop an effective negotiating 'style'. The advice given attempts to be highly concrete in nature, and is generally couched in a prohibitive and prescriptive terminology, underpinned by anecdotal evidence from actual negotiation events (see Groth 1992). Fisher and Ury (1981), for example, proffer four maxims as 'keys' to successful negotiating method, while Salacuse (1991) lists "seven elements in a global deal". Fisher and Ury (op. cit.: 11) contend that their maxims "define a straightforward method of negotiation that can be used under almost any circumstance". The maxims are as follows: (1) separate the people from the problem, (2) focus on interests, not positions, (3) generate a variety of possibilities before deciding what to do, and (4) insist that the result be based on some objective standard. To a large extent, prescriptive-oriented writings have been discarded by academic researchers [see, e.g., Janosik's (1987) criticisms]. The major reason for this is the generally impressionistic and anecdotal character of the writings. Lampi (1986:22) has argued, however, that the significance of such work should not be underestimated, for the prescriptive literature, she argues, "influences in-field negotiations through corporate training schemes based on their teachings ... [resulting] in 'better' and 'more successful' negotiations, which are then the subject of research".

3.2. Abstract Orientations

In almost direct contrast, *abstract* oriented work — as typified by economics-based bargaining models — is rigorously theoretical. Though highly abstract and constructed on the basis of hypothetico-deductive theory, the conceptual richness and logical sophistication of the models has resulted in wide-ranging theoretical utility. Young (1975) proposes that the most influential economics-based models are von Nuemann and Morgenstern's (1944) 'Game Theory', and by Zeuthen's (1930) 'Bargaining Theory'. In the formulation of the deductive models of both approaches, a number of restrictions, or 'parameters', are applied by theorists. For example, variables are controlled or eliminated, a range of problems are abstracted away, and outcomes are fixed prior to bargaining. Clearly, then, the relationship to real-world negotiations carried out by real-world people is highly tenuous. However, Gulliver (1979:43) claims that the obvious gulf between reality and theory may allow us to gain insight that might otherwise be overlooked.[8]

Game theory is characterized by deductive reasoning, simplifying assumptions, and a rationalistic conception of the negotiator, or 'player'. Major efforts are concentrated on providing a theoretical framework which can predict determinate *outcomes*. Built around 'games' [e.g.,'prisoner's dilemma' and 'chicken; see Rubin and Brown (1975:19-35)], the framework is thoroughly idealized and hypothetical. Players are assumed to possess 'perfect' information, to make error-free calculations, and to behave independently and rationally in accordance with logical principles. The premise of such logic and rationality is an assumed motivation to *maximize* individual 'payoffs'. The resolution of conflict via negotiation and bargaining is thus seen in terms of a 'zero-sum' (i.e., win-lose) scenario.

In contrast, bargaining theory formulates problems in real-world (economic) terms. These include wage-bargaining encounters and buyer-seller bargaining. Bargaining models also differ in other respects. First, there is a focus on non-zero-sum or 'mixed-motive' situations; thus a range of outcomes (the so-called 'contract-zone') is postulated. Second, models attempt to take temporality into account by showing that bargainers converge over time through a process whereby offers and counteroffers are exchanged. Third, a dynamic element is incorporated into the theoretical framework: models emphasize the importance of the formation of expectations about others' behaviour, the influence of individual dispositions, and the individual's rate of learning.

However, such variables are determined *before* negotiations and bargaining begin; they are not viewed as either 'locally'-produced during bargaining or retrospectively determined. In addition, the 'payoff' function of bargaining models is assumed to remain stable over time. That is to say that a contract-zone exists, is specifiable in advance, and remains stable throughout the course of the negotiation. The overriding aim of bargaining theorists remains, like that of game theorists, the prediction and determination of outcomes *a priori*. The difference here is that the task is attempted by taking account of a wider range of hypothetical variables. But this fact aside, niggling problems are inherent in the status of the variables, particularly when such work is applied to the study of naturally-occurring negotiations. First, it is unclear to what extent negotiators themselves are aware of, or influenced by, temporality, risks, delays, and the possible future actions of opposing bargainers. Second, it is unknown how variables arise from, and thus form, the emerging context.

3.3. Ethnographic orientations

The third orientation can be characterized as *ethnographic*. Relying mainly on first-hand field observations and post-negotiation interviews, this work involves the description of actual cases of (real-life) negotiations (e.g., Druckman 1973, Ikle 1964, Stein 1989, Gulliver 1979, 1988, Zartman 1975; see also Maynard 1984: chap.2). The ethnographic orientation is evident in the large number of field-based 'case studies' of negotiations, the best known of which is Douglas's (1957, 1962) study of four private sector negotiations. The working assumption for Douglas's work — perhaps the first negotiation study to be based on transcribed recordings — and other ethnographic studies is that individual negotiation events are not idiosyncratically structured, but rather that they bear generalizable similarities. The major aim is to provide an account of the nature of the similarities. Gulliver's (1979:64-65) premise is thus typical of ethnographic approaches to negotiations; he writes:

"My working hypothesis is that there are common patterns and regularities of interaction between the parties in negotiation irrespective of the particular context or the issues in dispute (emphasis deleted)".

According to ethnographically-oriented work, the most prominent feature of negotiations is that they proceed through specifiable, ordered, and generative phases. Phases are variously identified as shifts in emphases, negotiating purpose, or behavioural disposition (for a recent review of this work, see Holmes 1992). The identification of phases allows for the construction of theoretical models of varying complexity. Douglas (1957), for example, identified three phases which she claimed characterized successful labour-management negotiations: (1) establishing the bargaining range, (2) reconnoitering the bargaining range, and (3) precipitating the decision-reaching crisis. Marsh (1974) identifies five stages of (commercial) negotiation 'proper' (i.e., minus the 'planning' stages), those being (1) the opening, (2) the review of the opening, (3) the follow-up, (4) identifying the bargain, and (5) concluding the bargain. This phase-development emphasises two features of so-called 'successful' negotiations: first that changes occur over a period of time in negotiations, and second that the changes move from explicit disagreement over positions to mutual engagement in problem-solving activity. In contrast to Douglas's three-phase progression and Marsh's five, Gulliver's (1979) model is more complex, consisting of eight phases. These are as follows: (1) search for an arena (i.e., deciding on the physical location of negotiation); (2) composition of agenda and (working) definition of issues; (3) establishing maximal limits to issues; (4) narrowing the differences; (5) preliminaries to final bargaining; (6) final bargaining; (7) ritual affirmation; (8) execution of the agreement. Throughout this phase-based progression, Gulliver (op. cit.) argues, negotiations proceed as exchanges of information, leading to 'learning' and concomitant alterations in expectations.[9] His 'cyclical model' attempts to account for such processes.

Closely related to claims of phase progressions, researchers adopting other theoretical approaches have postulated that negotiations and bargaining progress through a series of *interaction sequences.* The most basic pattern, Maynard (1984) found in his discourse-oriented study of plea bargaining interaction, is the 'proposal-alignment/nonalignment' sequence. That is, according to Maynard, plea bargaining negotiations, at their most fundamental level, proceed in terms of a two-part sequence: (1) a party formulates a proposal while (2) the opposing party either accepts or rejects the course of action contained in the proposal. In actual performance, Maynard found, the basic sequence undergoes considerable elaboration. Analyses led to the conclusion that plea bargaining interaction reveals sequences which follow one of three patterns. Hence, following a proposal, the opponent will either: (1) unilaterally align himself with the proposal, (2) nonalign himself, whereupon exchanges of 'positions' ensue, resulting in one party 'conceding', or (3) seek a compromise.[10] These findings are similar to Ikle's (1964). Working within social exchange theory, he discusses a 'logical' tripartite choice-pattern continually facing the negotiator: (1) accept the opponent's proposal, or (2) discontinue negotiating without agreement, or (3) try to improve 'available' terms through further bargaining. Pruitt's (1981) experimentally-oriented 'Strategic Choice Model' reflects a parallel view of the progression of negotiations. Negotiators, he notes, can pursue agreement either by *conceding unilaterally,* or engaging in *competitive behaviour,* or by adopting *coordination* strategies. Landsberger's (1955) experimental study also suggests that negotiation success is determined by the extent to which groups pass through a series of problem-solving stages. Successful negotiating groups, Landsberger suggests, are those which deal *in turn* with problems of 'orientation', 'evaluation', and 'control'.

Similarly, the view that formal negotiations proceed from initial antagonism to coordinated agreement has been propounded by many researchers (e.g., Schelling 1960, Douglas 1962, Gulliver 1979, Kochan 1980, Morley and Stephenson 1977, Pruitt 1971). The analogue seems to be movement from disorder to order; indeed, "the whole process of negotiation", claims Gulliver (1979:114), "is, in one sense, the gradual creation of order". Negotiation order is obtained through a jointly accomplished process of *incremental convergence*, where initial disagreement over positions leads to gradual coordination and 'mutual accommodation' (see Schelling 1960:102).

Moerman (1988:87-100), amongst others, has criticized traditional anthropology and ethnography for failing to explicate the relevant actions which allow for comprehension of how social activities are constructed. That is to say that descriptions seldom extend to the reproduction of observable-reportable phenomena; hence the reflexive way in which *discourse* simultaneously forms and is formed by context is not made an empirical issue. Thus, without details of the communicative processes of negotiations, and denied access to transcripts and recognition procedures, the reader is left in a position where he must simply take the descriptions offered 'on trust'. Gulliver's (1979) work is a case in point. For despite the elegance of his 'cyclical model' of negotiation, and despite his intuitively appealing arguments in favour of viewing negotiations as 'learning' encounters, his efforts, like so many other ethnographic descriptions of negotiations, founder on language and discourse.

3.4. Experimental Orientations

The fourth orientation is *experimental*. This work is characterized by the study of simulated negotiation and bargaining encounters,[11] the majority of which has been carried out by social psychologists adopting methodology based on a 'positivistic' paradigm of hypothesis testing, verification and replication of findings, and the quantification of data analyses. Attempts are made to identify and quantify causal relationships and assess the effects of contextual (i.e. 'independent') variables on negotiating and bargaining activity. Such variables include the bargainer's behavioural disposition (e.g., Cole 1972), preordained tactics (e.g., Siegel and Fouraker 1960), visual accessibility of the negotiating parties (e.g., Lewis and Fry 1977), and the disclosure of specific types of information (e.g., Lewicki and Litterer 1985). The importance of cataloguing cause and effect relationships between dependent and independent variables inevitably results in researcher manipulation. For this reason, the majority of social psychological work has been directed to the study of simulated, laboratory-based negotiations.

For social psychologists, the negotiation event is an obvious locus of study. Besides its practical, real-world importance, "negotiation claims the attention of social psychologists because it highlights a pervasive *conflict* between individual needs and group allegiances" (Morley and Stephenson 1977:128, emphasis added). Thus the researcher confidently expects to gain insight into a range of features relating to individual behaviour. These might include competitiveness, cooperation, the functioning of small groups, the development of motives, and the resolution of social conflict. In a sense, negotiating and bargaining encounters provide the 'base elements' of the discipline, and it is with this assumption in mind that social psychologists set about the task of examining negotiation activity within simulated negotiation events. The task has extremely broad appeal; so much so that studies undertaken from social psychological perspectives constitute the bulk of the negotiation research literature. Indeed, Druckman (1977) contends that a new sub-discipline has emerged within the behavioural sciences: 'the social psychology of negotiation', and notes that one of two general approaches are adopted by social psychologists: either a *discipline-oriented* or a *phenomenon-oriented* approach. The former utilizes the (simulated) negotiation event in order to study theories relevant to social psychology (e.g., utility theory, influence theory, coalition theory, the nature of motives), while the latter approach utilizes social psychological theories and methodology to gain insight into negotiating activity per se.[12]

In virtually all cases, Rubin and Brown (1975) report, games (e.g. 'prisoners' dilemma' and 'chicken') developed by game theorists had been employed.[13] The games provide both a lexicon and a standardized framework for laboratory-based experiments, while concepts and theories from the abstract models allow testable predictions to be made about the results the negotiations might yield.[14] Researchers are thus in a position to systematically manipulate independent variables, undertaken with one of two concerns in mind: either to measure the effects of specific independent variables, or to identify the type of bargaining outcome and the effectiveness of the path towards the outcome. Variables include the number of trials, availability of communication between parties (e.g., free vs. restricted), incentives (e.g., points, imaginary and real money), and motivational orientation (e.g., 'be cooperative', 'be competitive'). Effectiveness is usually measured in terms of one (or a possible combination) of three 'metrics'. First, the time it takes the parties to reach agreement, second the amount of cooperation/ competition displayed by the parties, and third the magnitude of outcomes obtained.

However, while the laboratory setting allows the researcher to control for a range of testable variables, experimental negotiations inevitably suffer in the realm of realism. A gulf thus emerges between real-life and simulated negotiations. And there is, as yet, a paucity of studies contrasting real-life and experimental data.[15] Very few experiments contain what Morley and Stephenson (1977:127) identify as the central ingredients of real-life negotiations: "principles, pragmatics, personalities and the past". As Pruitt (1981:12) concedes, many of the fundamental characteristics of experimental negotiations are "unusual in professional negotiation": 'negotiators' share a similar background and culture (being in most cases North American college students), time is severely compressed, past and future relations between the parties are minimal or non-existent, negotiators are instructed to adopt specific behavioural dispositions, priorities and rewards are specified rather than freely chosen, communicative modalities are limited to the spoken, and negotiations are sponsored by an authority figure — the researcher.

Recently, some researchers have sought to alleviate these problems by employing practising negotiators in laboratory-controlled simulations [see, e.g., Fant (1989) and Grindsted (1989)]. Nevertheless, despite some painstaking attempts to authenticate real-life encounters, the product as a whole retains distortions. For example, a number of features are inevitably abstracted away (e.g., 'corporate' responsibility, past relations, putative future dealings, and accountability), while others (e.g., time and location constraints) are falsely imposed. As a result, progression has been somewhat piecemeal. "Islands of theory" (Druckman 1977:17) have emerged without clear linkages to processes, settings, and concepts. As Druckman observes, "Extant paradigms are limited in scope and provide a structure only for the analysis of selected problems" (Druckman op. cit.:34).

3.5. Discourse Orientations

Over the last decade and a half, a growing amount of work has emerged which focuses specifically on the discourse processes of negotiation. While the goal of this work is to uncover and describe the interactional bases upon which the many facets of negotiation activity are constructed, the bulk of the work falls into two categories, each predicated upon quite distinct ontological assumptions and methodological practices. The first and most substantial body of work in this orientation has been the implementation by communication scholars and social psychologists of *coding* schemes. The second contains micro-analytic work based on *transcript analyses*. In the main, the impetus for transcript-based work is provided by the theoretical assumptions and methodology developed by conversation analysts (e.g. Sacks 1992a,b; Sacks, Schegloff and Jefferson

1974, Heritage 1984a:chap. 8). Let us consider the two categories briefly in turn.

3.5.1. *Coding Schemes*

Negotiation researchers who utilize coding schemes characteristically stress that communication is "an outgrowth of mental processes" (Chatman, Putnam and Sondak 1991:143). This view is important since it underpins the tendency to perceive communication as the product of atomic individuals who, in negotiations, contribute to a process of tactical move and counter-move. The progression of discourse is thus predicated on the coordinated efforts of strategically-motivated individuals. Accordingly, research has been directed to specifying tactical patterns or sequences created by negotiators' 'moves' or 'acts' (Putnam 1985:228). These interlock to form the discourse structure of the negotiation.[16] The majority of this work has been undertaken by communications scholars (see the reviews in Putnam and Poole 1987, Putnam and Roloff 1992). In the main, communication scholars gravitate towards an individual-centred rather than interaction-centred view of communication. Analytic focus is directed to the individual's actions (strategies, tactics, moves) rather than what is collectively accomplished through interdependent action.

A number of pre-existing coding models have been used or modified by researchers with specific interests in the processes of negotiations, Bales's (1950) model being the most common. On the whole, however, only two models, namely Morley and Stephenson's (1977) 'Conference Process Analysis' (CPA), and Hopmann and Walcott's (1977) 'Bargaining Process Analysis' (BPA), have been refined through programmatic use. Models are constructed on the assumption that negotiation discourse can be broken down into recognizable periods, phases, units, 'moves', or 'acts'. Often researchers apply existing category schemes in their analyses of data (e.g. Neu 1988, Hinkle, Stiles and Taylor 1988). In other cases category schemes are invented, sometimes preceding, sometimes following, data collection. In terms of the former, the units or categories of analysis are partly determined by the nature of the data the researcher expects to collect and partly by research goals. Donohue (1981:277), for example, asserts that "the category scheme must be relevant to the context or situation that is being examined, or focused upon", which seems to imply that the researcher should be clear about what type of setting he is faced with *before* being faced with it. In Donohue's case this was an apparently simple matter, witnessed by his declaration that his study "will focus on distributive bargaining given the predominance of this situation in formal bargaining settings" (op. cit.:273-274). In other cases, where categories are invented *post hoc*, the analyst confronts the data and is putatively able to 'recognize' (and therefore categorize) the participants' actions and/or intentions (e.g. Manusov, Cody, Donohue and Zappa 1994).

But recognizing speakers' intentions is only one of several methods deployed to isolate and categorize discourse units. Morley and Stephenson (1977) account for six different unit types in their review of the literature; these include: temporal units (arbitrary time intervals), transactional units (uninterrupted speech bursts), psychological units (the expression of a single thought), categorical units (defined in terms of a system of categories to be used), and, finally, hybrid units (a combination of elements of the above). Along with the task of dividing discourse into units, the researcher must also map each unit onto a set of categories. Bales's (1950) Interaction Process Analysis model (IPA), for example, contains twelve categories, with each unit corresponding to a 'complete simple thought'.[17] Hopmann and Walcott's BPA II consists of thirty-three categories, separated into six 'clusters' of bargaining functions: strategic, substantive, persuasive, affective, task, and procedural. Morley and Stephenson's CPA has three dimensions along which each unit must be categorized; these are 'mode', 'resource', and 'referent'. The mode dimension indicates *how* information is exchanged, resource indicates the *function* of the information, and the referent dimension indicates who is being *talked about*.

Data are gathered in the form of transcribed recordings of (most often simulated) negotiations, after which trained observers code behaviour. Unfortunately, transcripts are rarely reproduced in published studies [though Morley and Stephenson's (1977) study is one notable exception]. Once coding is complete, quantitative analyses (e.g., 'factor analysis': Neu 1988; temporal segmenting and word counts: Donohue, Ramesh and Borchgrevink 1991; lag sequential analyses: Manusov et al. 1994) are carried out on the data. On the whole, analysts seek to test specific and predetermined hypotheses [e.g. meaning in negotiations is conveyed through structure, Neu 1988; certain action types are followed by specific other types, Manusov et al. op. cit.)]. Putnam and Jones (1982:274-275) report that coding schemes yield consistent findings regarding cooperative and competitive behaviours. In particular, they note, cooperative bargainers elicit reactions from their opponents, make proposals after a settlement is imminent, initiate many proposals, use more soft than hard tactics, and make more references to self and others than to party identity. Competitive behaviours consist of threats, put-downs, irrelevant arguments, and retractions. Donohue (1981:285) discovered that "individuals using tactics with greater attacking power relative to their opponents were more successful negotiators". Donohue, Diez, and Hamilton (1984), in using a coding scheme to compare simulated and real-life negotiations, concluded that more attack sequences were used in real-life settings than in the simulated negotiation settings.

The findings gathered are used for a variety of purposes. For some, they allow generalizations to be made about negotiating activity which in turn allows for the prediction of outcomes; for others they permit comparisons of negotiating behaviour in different types of settings; yet other researchers seek out the effectiveness of specific tactics. The findings are also claimed to be of practical benefit, as Donohue (1981:285) contends: "When ... information becomes visually displayed, the researcher can use it as a training tool to diagnose tactical competence".

There are, however, a number of methodological and epistemological problems associated with coding schemes, some of which can be mentioned briefly. To begin with, due to the proliferation of schemes and the potentiality of an ever-expanding number of categories, utilizing an existing model often proves to be problematic. Morley and Stephenson (1977:188) note that it is "extremely difficult to use many of the systems outlined in the literature, unless one has been specially trained by the authors concerned". This situation is related to the fact that, since models are constructed on the basis of a specific data corpus and *a priori* hypotheses, they are generally devoid of firm theoretical grounding. A further difficulty relates to observer reliability when coding language into units or acts. Longabaugh (1963:333), for example, found that "the chief cause of unreliability was act omission by one or the other of the observers". This points to a more deep-rooted problem, namely that of attempting to deploy an essentially static or unifunctional framework to analyse actions that are likely to be (1) multifunctional and (2) determined not at the moment of speaking but subsequently — in the emerging discourse (cf. Bilmes 1992a). Thus, as Putnam and Poole (1987:573) concede,

> "communicative statements do not fit neatly into discrete categories of ... bargaining [...] Messages perform multiple functions through a variety of verbal and nonverbal cues, a given utterance may serve both distributive and integrative goals simultaneously".

Yet even in the light of such misgivings, it would appear that the predilection for specifiable, predetermined categories is retained; the added proviso is that categories ought to accommodate conflicting 'goals' and message functions. They therefore suggest that

> "Adopting the view that messages serve a variety of functions that can fulfill contradictory goals might yield more insights about bargaining interaction than does a reliance on discrete, dichotomous categories (ibid)".

What, then, does coding actually entail? First, in order to segment language into behavioural 'units', each observer must not only assume that he or she shares the participants' knowledge of the linguistic code and the concomitant communicative conventions, but also knowledge of the participants' negotiating dispositions (e.g., cooperative/integrative or competitive/distributive). For example, in one study, a change of topic by a negotiator assumed to be adopting a 'distributive' disposition was coded as an 'attacking' move, as topic change was adjudged to demonstrate that the 'competitive' negotiator was attempting to exert *control* (Donohue 1981:278). Consequently, in order to make sense of what he or she reads or hears, the observer has to presuppose insight into the negotiators' motives and intentions. Moreover, once the segmenting has been carried out by attending to the surface (i.e., phonological, syntactic and semantic) characteristics of the utterance in question, the observer must decide not only what utterances mean, but also what they 'do' — albeit within the confines of a delimited set of categories. This entails being able to select one meaning per utterance, being able to distinguish between the illocutionary force and perlocutionary effect of utterances, separate 'questions' from 'assertions', 'persuasive behaviour' from 'strategic behaviour', 'threats' from 'demands', and more. The 'accuracy' of the coder's assessments is accounted for in terms of statistically significant tests of 'observer reliability'.[18]

Yet while research utilizing coding schemes has produced some suggestive findings, it is arguable that the theoretical and methodological thrust of the approach ultimately underplays the very phenomenon it sets out to describe — the interactional and processual character of communication. As Manusov et al. (1994:14) recognize in their coding study, both the category scheme itself and the predetermined hypotheses impose a rigid analytical framework around the data, with the result that analysts are at best obliged to overlook important features or are at worst effectively rendered blind to them. For when coding practitioners propound the view that the meaning of an utterance is somehow categorizable and specifiable — at its moment of utterance — they do not allow for the possibility that meanings of utterances *can be* ephemeral and malleable, in that utterance meanings are socially constructed.[19] Extrapolating from this, coding analyses are driven by an *etic* (or outsiders') metric of analytical saliency or relevance, rather than an *emic* (participants') processual metric. Emphasis is thus placed on verification (of, e.g., hypotheses) rather than discovery.

For example, Donohue (1981:274) informs us that, in his coding scheme, "each utterance is taken at face value in that its role in the negotiation is determined immediately and not at some future point in the interaction". Findings in conversation analysis suggest that this conception of utterance meaning is fundamentally flawed. Indeed, a great deal of research has demonstrated the difficulties — and in some cases the impossibility — of making accurate (observer-based) assessments of meaning on the basis of the surface features of utterances alone (see, e.g., Bilmes 1992a, Goodwin 1986, Levinson 1983:288-293, Schegloff 1977, Streek 1980).[20] Indirectly, these scholars have highlighted the limitations of applying *a priori* categories to utterances made in interaction without taking account of the accomplished sequential placement of the utterances. Research has shown how the function or meaning of an utterance is *locally* determined (1) by its placement in the *sequential (discourse) context* (cf. Schegloff and Sacks 1973:299) and (2) in the way it is socially corrigible in the subsequent, unfolding discourse. As Bilmes (1986:133) puts it, "an utterance has a horizon of possible meanings"; at the moment of encoding, utterance meaning can be indefinite and therefore potentially multifaceted and transient. Yet the sequential organization of talk allows for meanings to be socially determined and hence capable of revision in the light of subsequent utterances (see also Gumperz 1982:154, Grimshaw 1987). Although this feature of talk has been amply demonstrated by conversation analysts, the majority of coding researchers are apparently either unaware of or oblivious to the methodological consequences of such findings.

3.5.2. *Transcript Analyses*
As noted, the majority of coding-based work emanates from communication scholars, in which case a great deal of the research undertaken demonstrates a strong ontological and methodological affinity with social psychology and its emphasis on the individual's mental calculus (strategy, motive, intention, tactic, etc.). Transcript analyses of negotiation discourse, on the other hand, have been undertaken largely by interactional sociolinguists and conversation analysts, in which case it is not so much the individual's cognition that is of interest, but rather the individual's competent *social membership*, a membership that is accomplished interactionally through locally ordered discourse practices. Utilizing (and reproducing) detailed transcripts of actual, real-life instances of negotiation, these scholars attempt to uncover, in the minutiae of interactive talk, the meaningful, socially-accomplished features and interactionally-achieved structures of negotiation discourse. As yet, such studies are relatively few in number.

In transcript analyses, the analyst eschews *a priori* judgements on participants' intentions, dispositions, roles, or the efficacy of 'strategies' or 'tactics'; nor does the analyst impose category schemes on the transcribed materials. Instead, attention is drawn to features of social interaction that are demonstrably *made* relevant by the participants themselves *during* the interactional process. 'Interactional relevance' is thus seen as a contingent and dynamic aspect of linguistic interaction, made visible, sustained or transformed by participants in the way they differentially 'orient to' — and thus construct — the unfolding context. In other words, analytic impetus is provided more by 'bottom up' considerations emanating from the collected data materials than by the imposition of 'top down' constructs and predetermined research goals. Ideally, then, aspects of the discourse become analytically salient (and therefore describable) because participants render them salient in their construction and management of the interactive process.

Amongst negotiation scholars working within the confines of a narrower research remit, one that specifies a need to contribute to an encompassing theory of negotiation, we might anticipate the view that findings made in transcript-based studies appear inconsequential, piecemeal and lacking in overall coherence. Two reasons behind this impression are: (1) the relatively small number of existing studies adopting the transcript-analtyic perspective, and (2) that transcript analyses have tended to be social-interaction oriented, directed to uncovering features that are endogenous to the interaction, rather than exogenously imposed as a result of the researcher's interest in negotiation per se. Certainly transcript-based studies do not (yet?) aspire to the construction of an overall 'theory' of negotiation, although findings may contribute indirectly to such a theory. And yet, arguably, it is to transcript-based studies that one must turn in order to find the most detailed descriptions of negotiation as a locally managed discourse activity.

Some of the earliest transcript analyses of negotiation are Bilmes (1981) and Maynard (1982a,b; 1984). The point of departure for these and other studies is detailed transcripts of (audio or video) recordings of naturally-occurring instances of negotiation activity. Bilmes studied social decision making in a task-based discussion in the Federal Trade Commission, focusing particularly on the way discourse was used to demarcate and contingently adjust individual opinions in order to reach a socially acceptable outcome. Maynard's work on negotiation activity in plea bargaining uncovered a (participant) oriented-to and interactionally-achieved two-part 'bargaining sequence'. Showing that the basic two-part sequence was "at the root" of activity recognizable as plea bargaining, Maynard described how participants were able to elaborate the sequence in *systematic*, and hence describable, ways. The bargaining sequence, as Maynard puts it, is thus

> "a fundamental unit of social organization [...] Systematic procedures
> for leading into, elaborating, and exiting from the sequence relate it to
> other components of negotiation, such as discussion, argument,
> justification, counterproposing ... and so on (1984:103)".

Other transcript-based studies adopting this interactional perspective include Francis's (1986) study of an industrial negotiation [based on Douglas's (1962) transcripts], Garcia's (1991) work on divorce mediations, and Firth's (1994) study of commodity trading. Francis (1986) demonstrates how entities such as 'parties' and 'issues' are accomplished and emergent in the talk, rather than fixed and predetermined. Garcia's (1991) study shows how, in the way talk is interactionally organized, mediators are able to minimize arguments and promote agreement in order to assist parties in their attempts to reach a mutually satisfactory outcome. Firth's (1994) study of a trading negotiation focuses on the resourcefulness of 'accounts' (justifications and excuses), and shows that accounts are produced systematically and then probed contingently and collaboratively by the participants in their attempts to reach a mutually acceptable (sales) agreement. In each of these studies, negotiation activity is viewed as a situated accomplishment, locally and socially achieved on an unfolding, turn-by-turn basis.[21]

The methodology and ontological assumptions behind the majority of transcript-based studies originate in conversation analysis (CA), an approach to language and social action founded three decades ago by Harvey Sacks (e.g. Sacks 1992a,b) and developed in his collaborations with Emanuel Schegloff and Gail Jefferson (see, e.g., Schegloff and Sacks 1973, Sacks, Schegloff and Jefferson 1974, Schegloff, Jefferson and Sacks 1977). From its 'home base' of naturally-occurring, adult conversation, a large number of CA studies have been produced, each attempting to describe in detailed ways the methods and resources with which conversationalists accomplish 'ordinary' talk (for recent overviews, see Goodwin and Heritage 1990, Drew and Heritage 1992). Although CA views casual conversation as the primordial site of sociality, and thus the 'bedrock' on which other forms of talk (e.g. interviews, cross-examinations) are based, a recent and sustained trend within CA has been to focus not only on *non-casual* talk — i.e., talk displaying participants' orientations to 'institutionalized' activities such as news interviews, emergency calls, and doctor-patient consultations — but also on the way talk and setting mutually configure. Almost impercetibly, analytic emphasis has shifted from the description of sequences in casual conversation (turns, repair, 'preference', pre-sequences, adjacency relations), to the ways in which (institutionalized) tasks, mandates and roles configure the interactional management of talk, talk which simultaneously reveals, confirms and sustains its institutional moorings (cf. Maynard 1991).[22]

An important methodological practice in CA emanates from the view that institutionalized forms of talk are contingent 'transformations' or 'adaptions' (see Zimmerman 1988, Zimmerman and Boden 1991:15-17) of casual conversation. This is the practice of contrasting 'institutionalized' features and sequences with comparable sequences from mundane conversations in order to explicate the putative transformations (see, e.g., Greatbatch 1988, Drew and Heritage 1992:38). Unfortunately, as Drew (1990) has observed, a good deal of such work has been directed to the study of institutionalized settings where turn-taking systems within those settings are highly constrained and stylized (e.g. courtrooms, classrooms, news interviews). What is required, and is now beginning to emerge (see, e.g., Drew and Heritage 1992), is that the CA perspective be brought to bear on a much wider range of social settings and activities, ones "in which there is no ... formal constraint on turn-taking, and therefore in which the distinctiveness of the discourse, as compared to conversation, is not to be found in stylized sequential patterns" (Drew 1990:31). CA's concentration on a relatively narrow range of settings and activities in part explains the paucity of CA-based studies undertaken on negotiation. Somewhat surprisingly, given the prevalence of formal negotiation events and the pervasiveness of negotiation activity, surprisingly few CA studies have focused on negotiation as an activity in its own right. Fortunately, however, several of the studies contained in this volume go some way towards filling the lacuna.

4. NEGOTIATION ACTIVITY IN WORKPLACES

An undercurrent running through the studies contained here is that negotiation occurs not as a decontextualized activity, but as an activity that is skillfully and often indiscernibly woven into the fabric of work practices. Largely as a result of the proliferation of experimental studies of negotiation, overridingly in the negotiation literature the phenomenon has been implicitly treated as an isolated and disjunctive event, undertaken in a kind of temporal and organizational vacuum, somehow removed from, rather than embedded within, its location of occurrence (cf. Barley 1991). In this collection, negotiation activities are simultaneously constituted by and constitutive of working practices within concrete settings.

How, then, are negotiation activities visibly embedded into working practices? The studies contained here suggest that this is achieved in a variety of ways, the most prominent of which is that the activity is demonstrably carried out in response to the exigencies of a work-related task, the completion of which entails arriving at a decision on a substantive matter. Negotiation activity articulates with work practices in the way parties display the activity's connectedness with and relevance for tasks occurring before, during, and after the current spate of interaction. Two methods by which this is achieved is in the way the parties — through their discourse actions — display an awareness of the *reasons for* the current activity, as well as the implications of decisions made during the current activity for future undertakings. Negotiation activity does not 'just happen'. In systematic, orderly ways it emerges from the work context, a context which reflexively furnishes the activity's import and a rationale for engagement. The prototypical components of negotiation activity — the suggestions, proposals, counterproposals, refusals, reasons, etc. — are embedded into the discourse, systematically arising out of sequentially structured actions. This means, for example, that proposals or counterproposals are produced, 'designed' and made recognizable as a result of their accomplished sequential placement. Once produced, an action or utterance establishes a 'conditional relevance'[23] on what occurs subsequently — in the next turn or series of turns. And throughout its sequential progression, the content of talk reveals parties' (sometimes conflicting) perceptions of contextually 'normal', appropriate, inappropriate and challengeable behaviour and values. Talk itself is thus a 'running index' of its contextual embeddedness, simultaneously confirming, transforming and, indeed, accomplishing, the selfsame context.

The studies have been arranged into four sections. Section I, which includes the current chapter, provides an overview of theoretical and conceptual considerations surrounding the study of negotiation as a discourse activity. Sections II-IV are divided into types of encounters that broadly characterize the work contexts wherein the analysed negotiation activity arises. Thus the studies in Section II are concerned with negotiation in *intra*-organizational encounters. Section III contains studies of negotiation in international commodity trading, and Section IV negotiation as it occurs in an array of professional-lay interactions. The aim of such a division is to initiate, in an empirically defensible manner, an exploration of the reflexive relationship between negotiation discourse on the one hand, and work practices and work contexts on the other. That is, while work tasks, working relationships and various 'institutional mandates' (cf. Maynard 1984:12) configure and inform the way discourse is produced, interpreted and managed, the constraints and resources inherent in discourse clearly exert an influence on how the tasks themselves are conceptualized and perceived to be properly undertaken. The studies here represent a collective attempt to answer questions such as: To what extent, and how, do certain types of work tasks and work contexts relate to the way those tasks are undertaken through discourse? How do discourse processes lend shape to and aid in the recognition of work tasks? And what is the relationship between work settings, work activities and negotiable matters? Clearly not all aspects of working practices are negotiable — at least not in the way 'negotiation' is understood in this volume — but clearly many facets are: why is this the case? How can detailed, situated studies of discourse cast light upon this and other important questions?

Throughout the last seventy years, beginning perhaps with Malinowski's (1923) notion of 'context of situation', sociolinguists, ordinary language philosophers, anthropologists and sociologists have emphasized — and in more recent times empirically demonstrated — that language is a context sensitive phenomenon. What this means in essence is that people are *contingently* sensitive to who they relevantly are, where they are, what they are attempting to do, and what is expected of them (cf. e.g. Levinson 1979, Duranti and Goodwin 1992). Moreover, such sensitivity, though ordinarily tacit, is differentially and ceaselessly made manifest in social actions — discourse included. Locally invoked knowledge of settings, tasks, relationships and roles is selectively revealed in aspects of negotiation activity. This contextual knowledge furnishes resources for parties' assessments of, amongst other things, *what* is and what is not legitimately negotiable, as well as *how* something is negotiable. While on most occasions such assessments are likely to be shared, occasions also arise where the assessments are not shared. And as we shall discover, each alternative has implications for the way negotiation activity is socially managed through discourse.

4.1. The Studies

In Section I, Bell's chapter (ch.2) deals with concepts central to our concerns. In discussing 'the workplace', 'negotiation', and 'analysis', Bell sensitizes us to the theoretical utility and broad conceptual sweep of each term. His major task is to consider how a micro-analytic perspective on negotiation discourse — specifically, the perspective of conversation analysis (CA) — might be deployed in an attempt to extend his own 'Political Linguistics', an approach to language study that is centrally concerned with the concepts of *power*, *influence*, and *authority* — concepts that for Bell (and others, e.g. Bacharach and Lawler 1981) lie at the heart of negotiation activity in formal negotiation events. In its transcript-based analyses of the sequential organization of talk, CA insists that notions such as power, influence and authority (PIA) are relevant to the analysis only when they are rendered salient by participants in their orientations to them. For CA, then, such notions are *locally* relevant and *locally* produced. While subscribing to this position, Bell also argues that non-transcript materials — namely pre- or post-negotiation interview data — are potentially useful for shedding light on aspects of PIA that may not be made manifest in transcripts (e.g. strategies, motives and intentions). The crucial next step, of course, is to have Bell's recommendation put to the test. This will be necessary in order to demonstrate whether, and how, the concerns of Political Linguistics and the assumptions and methodology of CA can be fruitfully combined and empirically applied to the study of negotiation discourse.[24]

Section II brings together five studies concerned with negotiation in *intra*-organizational encounters. In different ways, these studies highlight the fact that employees are increasingly compelled to perform complex tasks on a collective basis. It is during such tasks that negotiation activity frequently arises. Bilmes's (ch.3) study of a four-person meeting in the U.S. Federal Trade Commission demonstrates how, through discourse, traditional hierarchies are blurred, opinions shared, and differing interests accommodated in the pursuit of a collectively arrived-at decision. Analyzing a single transcript segment, he demonstrates how a *compromised agreement*, rather than representing the 'in-between point' of initially-stated positions, emerges and takes recognizable shape in and through interaction. This is accomplished in the way the parties closely monitor and contingently respond to each other's positions as those positions unfold. Bilmes introduces the notion of 'response priority' — a pragma-linguistic concept relating to inferential processes. This concept would appear to provide valuable insight into how argumentative and negotiation discourses are constructed. As such it deserves further empirical investigation, not least into how 'response priority' is context- and activity-sensitive.

The materials for Boden's chapter (ch.4) are extracted from internal meetings held in a hospital, a TV station and a department within a university administration. It is in the talk of such meetings that parties subtly pursue their own (work-related) interests and yet, through instances of what Boden calls 'verbal synchronicity', make mutually acceptable decisions. Boden points up the importance of bracketing out assumptions about negotiation in order to see the "fine structural elements out of which it is constructed". In particular, she focuses on *persuasion* as a constituent of negotiation activity, and looks at how persuasive discourse is composed, noting especially the role of 'reformulations'. She shows that, when making a proposal, the proposer is able to monitor how the proposal is being received and, within a fraction of a second, deftly reformulate it in such a way as to significantly alter not only the proposal itself but also the interactional 'footing', i.e., "the alignments we take up to ourselves and the others present as expressed in the way we manage the production or reception of an utterance" (Goffman 1981:128). Such reformulations serve the purpose of attempting to arrive at a mutually acceptable decision.

The related phenomenon of *formulations* is the focus of Walker's chapter (ch.5). This study focuses on negotiation activity as it occurs in a formal (union-management) negotiation event. A 'formulation' is an utterance that summarizes the sense or gist of prior talk. Walker proposes that, in her data materials, formulations that arise during 'concessionary phases' in the negotiation are resolution-implicative: "they are used as a device for initiating concessionary activity, thereby providing an opportunity for the two sides to reach agreement". Because the parties in these materials are cognizant of the conflictual foundations upon which their interaction is constructed, formulations are almost invariably oriented to as making a tendentious interpretation of prior talk. This study thus furnishes strong evidence that the formal 'negotiation event' epithet — implying pre-existing conflictual positions — permeates and informs the discourse and interpretative processes of interaction. Walker finds that concession-seeking formulations are of two types: 'optimistic' and 'pessimistic'. 'Optimistic' formulations are oriented to (by the parties involved) as being strategically motivated and implicitly pursue a mutually acceptable offer: in providing a formulation, the speaker selects to extract and focus on a particular implication of prior talk. This is understood to be tendentiously designed to indicate what the speaker can agree to. In highlighting this hitherto unresearched phenomenon, Walker is not only making a substantive contribution to the study of negotiation discourse; she is also able to demonstrate how analysts may approach *strategy* as the product of a social-discursive process, rather than — as is usually the case — a psychological one.

Whereas the preceding studies in this section indicate that negotiation is the legitimate and frequently engaged in activity through which decisions are made conjointly, Jones (ch.6) introduces the intriguing possibility that in some cases negotiation may be eschewed, even viewed with apprehension. Arguing that this view is prevalent amongst the Japanese, Jones accounts for her observation by invoking (her own) cultural knowledge of Japanese social practices, noting that "subordinates are not expected to negotiate over whether they will obey a superior's orders". Jones is concerned to show how parties' best interests can be served by *concealing* or 'masking' the fact that their joint activity is, in essence, negotiation. The analysed data are two Japanese academics, one of whom is more senior in job status than the other. In their interaction, the participants "work to mask their negotiation because admitting that a negotiation was underway would have entailed violating at least two cultural ideals — the ideal of harmony and the ideal of hierarchy". Although the junior party is demonstrably attempting to secure the other party's agreement, the methods used to do so — invoking a joking discourse style, refraining from expressing overt disagreement, etc. — ensure that the interaction is afforded a 'harmonious' rather than a conflictual appearance. Moreover, by not producing an explicit proposal or suggestion, negotiation activity is rendered opaque. However, while this study usefully identifies a seldom-described phenomenon — the way agreement on a matter is sought without being overtly pursued — one is tempted to suggest that Jones may have overstated her case in arguing that such 'masking' occurs solely as the result of *Japanese* norms of interaction. For the factor contended to obviate overt negotiation activity — the need for consonous interpersonal relations — surely also applies in non-Japanese (including occidental) cultures (cf. e.g., Brown and Levinson 1987; also ten Have, this volume).

The final chapter in this section distinguishes itself from other studies in the collection by its metaphorical use of the term *negotiation*. Button and Sharrock's (ch.7) chapter is thus concerned with negotiation in a very broad sense. Their task is to examine the relationship between the formal representations of software development that are portrayed in development methodologies and guidelines, and the actual work of software development as it is 'negotiated' in the situated activities and interactions of a group of software engineers. This chapter is an ethnomethodological study of work (for programmatic statements on such studies, see Garfinkel and Wieder 1992), and is concerned with the idea of an 'achieved' or 'negotiated' order, a notion that has affinities with Strauss et al.'s (1964) symbolic interactionist research. The methodology adopted in the chapter is ethnographic: Button and Sharrock rely upon first-hand observations and field notes for their descriptions of the 'negotiated' work practices. The study makes a number of revealing observations relating to how parties jointly, artfully (and at times cunningly!) overcome externally imposed constraints — a requirement continually facing employees, though one which is perhaps especially acute in large bureaucratic organizations. For researchers with specific interests in (negotiation) discourse, the chapter's contribution lies in its detailed depiction of working practices and its pregnant observations on the negotiable nature of those practices. As such, the chapter provides a solid foundation upon which more discourse-oriented studies can be undertaken. For it is of central importance that scholars also attempt to pinpoint precisely *where* and describe *how* the 'negotiated order' is, in fact, actually negotiated through interactive *discourse*.

The three studies comprising Section III are each concerned with negotiation amongst buyers and sellers engaged in international commodity trading. Firth (ch.8) examines negotiations between Danish (cheese) sellers and wholesale importers in the Middle East. The negotiations (labelled as such by the participants) are conducted via telephone. Firth claims that the telephone negotiations exhibit stable patterns of discourse structure, and that the calls can be described in terms of a 'gross organizational structure' (cf. Torode, this volume). Through the conjoint management of discourse, the calls take on the appearance of being compact and to-the-point; they are also overwhelmingly single-topic encounters. In early sections of the calls, parties 'get to work' by locating the 'problem' at hand. The problem is then accounted for, whereupon the account is contingently probed and incrementally 'unpacked'. These actions inform and precede the exchange of substantive offers and proposals. It is through such sequences of talk that the parties cumulatively display a mutual desire to resolve the 'problem' *during the call itself*. This is seen most clearly in the way argumentative talk is minimized, and in the rapid-fire manner in which offers and counteroffers are exchanged in a here-and-now attempt to reach agreement. Firth's chapter, like Wagner's (ch.9), makes a contribution to the nascent study of negotiation discourse and communication technologies. Not only does the chapter provide insight into how an interaction characterizable as negotiation is discursively structured from beginning to end, it also demonstrates how the *medium* exerts an influence on the way discourse and social actions are managed. As such, the study lends itself to much-needed comparative research, most clearly perhaps to that which explores how and why other (telephone) negotiations, in different types of workplaces, are discursively structured.

Wagner (ch.9) looks at technical problem-solving in telephone interactions involving Danes and Britons, and Danes and Belgians. Drawing upon written correspondence materials also, he attempts to test the applicability of Firth's (1991) sequentially-oriented definition of 'negotiation activity'. Wagner makes some percipient observations, particularly in relation to the way parties' work practices inform interpretations of 'problems' and 'solutions'. The observation that, in his materials, parties engaging in negotiation activity do not appear to have to agree to the precise nature of a problem before attempting to solve it, is important, not least when contrasted with more logical and abstract models of problem-solving behaviour. His findings also lead him to question the generalizablity of Maynard's (1984) and Firth's (1991) notion of 'alignment' [the origins of which can be traced to Goffman (1974)] as the demonstrable 'end goal' of negotiation activity. The 'solution' of a technical problem does not, it would appear, call for the parties to be 'aligned' in the way Maynard's plea bargaining negotiators and Firth's commodity traders are. In some work contexts involving certain types of activities, it would appear that parties may disagree about the nature of the problem facing them and about the solution to the problem (and hence remain 'misaligned'), and yet still — by relinquishing the need for mutual acceptability — be able to reach a solution (see Wagner's 'Case 3').

Whereas the two preceding chapters in this section do not directly investigate matters surrounding the international, or cross-cultural, element in their materials, it is this element that constitutes Marriott's (ch.10) focus of interest. Relying on transcripts and post-negotiation interview materials, Marriott analyses a face-to-face business meeting involving a Japanese buyer and an Australian manufacturer/seller. Her main focus is 'discord deviance', an experiential notion referring to those almost intangible elements of interaction that lead participants to feel intuitively that 'something about the interaction is not right', without usually being able to specify what that 'something' is. Hence, Marriott attempts to investigate the way *socio-cultural norms* of interaction impinge upon and surface in linguistic activity during a cross-cultural encounter. She examines 'discord deviance' in relation to three communicative factors: content, form, and medium (cf. Hymes 1972), and reports, amongst other things, that the Australian seller experienced considerable 'discord' as a result of unclarities as to the overall purpose of the encounter. Whereas the seller saw the meeting as the legitimate locus of negotiation activity — wherein proposals and suggestions (etc.) could be made and discussed — to the Japanese buyer the primary purpose of the meeting was one of information-gathering. Such skewed expectations remained tacit throughout the interaction, though were traceable in the discourse. They resulted in 'discord', particularly on the Australian's part. Now while one may question the felicity of the 'deviance' notion, particularly its pejorative connotations and implied reliance on a 'base' or 'unmarked' (preferred?) form of behaviour, and while the appropriacy of referring to 'repairs' and 'corrections' as 'deviance' is debatable given its prevalence in all forms of interactive talk (see Schegloff, Jefferson and Sacks 1977), Marriott's study nevertheless casts light upon an area of considerable importance: the study of discourse and interaction in intercultural negotiation events, particularly in relation to socio-cultural norms. If expectations and assessments of appropriate (discourse) behaviour are culturally acquired, then it is reasonable to assume they are differently acquired and differently made manifest (cf. Gumperz 1982a,b). What are the consequences of this for the discourse produced in negotiation activity? Marriott's study highlights some implications — for the patterns of linguistic interaction and for international trade.

The fourth and final section of the book concerns negotiation activity in professional-lay interactions. In each of the five chapters comprising this section, negotiation activity arises as an expedient, contingent and embedded part of various professional-client interactions. Each study shows professionals (travel agents, civil servants, general practitioners, consumer advisors, advertising executives) and 'clients' engaging one another in demonstrable attempts to arrive at an outcome that can be seen to accommodate and represent both parties' interests. In the chapter by Mazeland, Huisman and Schasfoort (ch.11), the travel agent attempts to reconcile the customers' wishes with regard to a desirable vacation 'package' with the packages the agency has available for sale. When these (potentially conflicting) interests are reconciled, the parties arrive at a mutually acceptable vacation arrangement. In their analyses, the authors focus on *categorizations* relevant to the activity under examination. These include destination, types of accommodation, and persons (e.g. child/adult). Though 'categorizations' are culturally-available inferential resources, they are also quintessentially *locally* deployed and interpreted; as the authors put it, the sales person "not only has to find out which categories are essential for or constitutive of the wishes of the customer. When she has discovered them she may also try to adapt them to the possibilities the agency has in its assortment". Mazeland, Huisman and Schasfoort insightfully describe two ways in which locally relevant categories are discursively deployed ('scaling up' and 'attribution transfer') in the interaction as part and parcel of the work of attempting to discover and then agree upon a suitable and sellable vacation package.

Linell and Fredin (ch.12) examine social worker-client interactions occurring in Swedish social welfare offices. They observe that negotiation arises over a range of matters, both substantive (e.g. the amount of social benefit entitlements to be paid out) and processual (e.g. the applicability of descriptive concepts used to categorize clients and their circumstances); of course, the latter has direct bearings on the former, since entitlements are ascertained on the basis of one's status, circumstances, etc. It is negotiations over such processual matters that is of interest to the authors here. They note that "[t]here is an intrinsic, and highly significant, relation between outcomes and category of definitions in negotiation activities". There is, then, a certain amount of flexibility inherent in the bureaucratically-imposed categories and the client's actual life circumstances ('realities') as instantiations of the categories. Linell and Fredin not only show that it is this flexibility that provides the basis for negotiation, they also explicate *how* the negotiations are undertaken.

In his analyses of General Practitioner-patient consultations, ten Have (ch.13) found that negotiation activity may arise when the physician recommends a course of treatment (a 'disposal') to a patient. ten Have observes that, on some occasions, such recommendations are *formatted* in such a way as to signal and invite negotiation, thus signalling, in the way a disposal is discursively constructed, that the disposal is inherently mutable and tentatively 'offered'. However, despite the physician's formatting, patients displayed a passivity vis-à-vis the 'proposed' disposal, and invariably declined to take up the implicit invitation to openly 'negotiate' its appropriacy and acceptability. The author suggests that the choice of format is responsive to locally determined case characteristics, including the extent of the physician's confidence in the diagnosis, patients' contributions, and whether the disposals are medical or have social implications for the patient. In terms of the 'proposal' format, ten Have observes that "[the] proposal is to cure the symptoms, rather than the disease which is as yet accounted for. The 'proposal' strategy may function as a way to co-opt the patient's acceptance of this less satisfactory solution". Direct comparisons can be made between this study and Jones's (ch.6), particularly in the way that mutual agreement is sought in implicit, almost furtive, ways. Whereas Jones proposes that culturally learned norms of (Japanese) interaction (in this case: do not question superiors' decisions) obviated overt negotiation, ten Have finds that a congeries of interaction-based features appear to exert an influence on whether or not a decision was displayed as negotiable. But in light of the fact that it is invariably the physician that signals the negotiable quality of a decision, and given that patients decline to 'negotiate' regardless, perhaps we are led to search in other areas as an explanation for this, and one suspects that the area might encompass culturally learned norms of interaction.

Torode (ch.14) analyses in its entirety a single telephone call made to a consumer advice 'helpline'. Similar to Firth (ch.8), Torode proposes that the call can be seen to be discursively organized in terms of a gross structure of adjacently related actions. In the sense that both parties to the call — the advisor and the advice-seeking member of the public — search for mutual agreement as to the practical course of action which the caller can best pursue, the call can be seen to contain instances of negotiation activity. Torode makes the point that although the advisor recommends the caller to "see if you can negotiate" with the store, the call itself is a negotiation, since the advice given is oriented to as being a mutable and incomplete 'offer'. As Torode puts it, "in the way they actually practice negotiation together on the helpline, they display to one another how the negotiation with the store may have been done in the past and might be done differently in the future". This chapter is particularly important for our concerns in the way it uncovers and explicates negotiation activity that is embedded within other encompassing task-oriented work practices.

The final chapter in the book is Wheatley's (ch.15) study of negotiation activity in document design presentations. Wheatley's methodology is eclectic; he uses a speech-act-based coding scheme and 'topic-type analysis' to "describe an oriented-to generic pattern in the unfolding social activity". In the materials examined, it is claimed that negotiation activity occurs at well-defined points in the discourse, specifically in the topic type 'visual presentation'. It is in these topic type phases, Wheatley shows, that the client is afforded the opportunity to evaluate the designer's work. In the event of negative evaluations of the work, negotiation activity arises. This entails making one or more proposals for changes, followed by counterproposals, agreement, etc. What is negotiable in this material is the appropriacy of the proposed designs, a negotiability that is sequentially and topically ordered and accomplished. Similar to Torode's (ch.14) finding — that 'advice' is oriented to as being negotiable — Wheatley suggests that the designs are oriented to as being tentative and mutable 'offers'. This work has strong methodological affinities with Sinclair and Coulthard's (1975) functional, 'exchange structure' approach to the analysis of discourse, and, as some commentators (e.g. Levinson 1983, Taylor and Cameron 1987) have argued, deploys categories whose relevance to the participants is likely to be more by accident than design. However, it would appear that the analytic power of the model is increased when it is applied to highly structured and predictable types of activities, and in this sense Wheatley's data materials seem to lend themselves favourably to this type. By incorporating 'emic' (i.e. participant-relevant) aspects of interaction into his analyses, Wheatley is also engaged in extending the exchange structure model in the direction of interactive, participant-oriented discourse.

NOTES

1. Negotiation as a formally- and explicitly-defined event and negotiation as an activity are not mutually exclusive: negotiation activity — the jointly constructed process of social decision making — may, and most often will, occur in negotiation events.

2. The term 'discourse' has been used in several different ways in language study (for useful discussions on this, see van Dijk 1985, MacDonell 1986, Fairclough 1992). Uses include the description of a hierarchically-ordered 'level' of language, namely language 'above the sentence' (e.g. Harris 1951); extended samples of spoken dialogue (in contrast to written 'texts'); a genre or language style (e.g. 'newspaper discourse', 'advertising discourse'); and the situated use of language-in-social-interaction — the sense adopted in this book.

3. The view that discourse is *simultaneously* contingent upon and constitutive of context is articulated in numerous approaches to the study of language-in-interaction. For example, Gumperz (1982a) and his associates (Gumperz 1982b, Auer and Di Luzio 1992) examine the *contextualizing* function of interactive discourse, while ethnomethodologists (e.g., Garfinkel 1967, Heritage 1984a) are concerned

with the methodological ways in which social actions — including discourse — ongoingly render context 'accountable' (observable-reportable). Conversation analysts (e.g., Schegloff 1991, Drew and Heritage 1992) hold that while context exerts an influence on how talk is produced and interpreted, the selfsame context is endogenously and dynamically constructed through the talk; as Heritage (1984a:242) puts it, talk is both 'context-shaped' and 'context-renewing'. Goodwin and Duranti (1992) provide a lucid overview of research which adopts a reflexive perspective on the discourse-context relationship.

4. In this volume, 'workplace' is used as a cover-term for an array of organizational settings and insti-tution-related activities, where at least one party to the activities is in paid employment as a repre-sentative of an organization. Workplaces are usually though not necessarily coterminous with institu-tional settings. For example, although a telephone call between a member of the general public and a Consumer Advisor (see Torode, this volume) does not occur in one-and-the-same 'work' environment (the call is being made from a private home), the call is nevertheless conceptualized as a work-based activity in the sense that one of the interactants is demonstrably 'at work'— both in the physical-setting (work*place*) sense and in the activity sense.

5. Walton and McKersie's (1965:35) oft-cited definition of 'negotiation' emphasizes the defining role of interdependence. Thus negotiation is "the deliberate interaction of two or more complex social units which are attempting to define or redefine the terms of their interdependence".

6. In the literature, 'bargaining' is often used in a narrower sense than 'negotiation'. 'Bargaining' thus frequently refers to a specific set of actions (e.g. bids, proposals, counterproposals) occurring within the more encompassing frame of 'negotiation' (e.g. Cross 1969, Gulliver 1979). Gulliver (1979:71) propounds that "Bargaining consists of the presentation and exchange of more or less specific propos-als for the terms of agreement on particular issues". In some studies, though, 'negotiation' and 'bargain-ing' are used synonymously (e.g. Rubin and Brown 1975:2), and often interchangeably (e.g. Schelling 1960).

7. A bibliography of studies of negotiation and bargaining would fill volumes. For an indication of the extent and breadth of such studies, see the overviews provided by Bacharach and Lawler (1981: chap. 1), Gulliver (1979:chap. 2), Putnam and Poole (1987), and Putnam and Roloff (1992). Brenneis (1988) has compiled a useful overview of studies on language and disputing, including negotiation. For an indication of the volume and diversity of studies of negotiation and bargaining undertaken in social psychology alone, see Druckman (1977), Morley and Stephenson (1977:chap. 3), Putnam and Jones (1982), and Putnam and Poole (1987).

8. Thus Gulliver (1979:43):

> "[T]he inducement is to reexamine the assumptions and prescribed limitations made
> by game and bargaining theorists. In so doing, it is possible to come to an improved

understanding of some of the components of actual negotiations when, in real-life conditions, those limitations do not obtain and the assumptions cannot be made".

9. Gulliver (1979:70) writes:

> "[The negotiating] parties give each other information, directly and indirectly. Each engages in learning about the other, about himself, and about the possibilities and impossibilities of their common situation. Negotiation is a process of discovery. Discovery leads to some degree of reorganization and adjustment of understanding, expectations, and behavior, leading (if successful) eventually to more specific discussion about possible terms of a final, agreed outcome".

10. Maynard (1984:173) revealed that "The negotiations in each of our fifty two cases fit one of the three patterns".

11. For useful overviews of this orientation, see Magenau and Pruitt (1979), Pruitt (1981) and Druckman (1977).

12. In actuality, the premise upon which this dichotomy is based is fallacious. For in defining the very research problems to be investigated, 'phenomenon-oriented' researchers are guided by a 'discipline-oriented' outlook.

13. In subsequent research, 'games' have been developed specifically for empirical research into bargaining; see the review of such games in Rubin and Brown (1975:20-31).

14. Kelley and Schenitzki (1972:299), for example, saw their study as one of the "pioneering experimental forays into the thickets of 'economic' conflict and resolution". Of their working method they write:

> "Principles and theories from economics provided the specifications for the bargaining task as well as contrasting predictions about the results the negotiations would yield. The setting and methods of the social psychological laboratory were employed to test these predictions and social psychological concepts (e.g., level of aspiration, rivalry, cooperativeness, communication) were introduced to account for departures from the predicted results (ibid.)."

15. Certainly many experimental researchers acknowledge the need for closer links with field-based work, pointing out that until firmer links are forged, experimentally-based theories remain preliminary. Thus Pruitt and Lewis (1977:188): "We believe the laboratory provides a heuristic setting for the development, clarification, and testing of concepts. But in the broader sense, theory development requires the constant interplay of both laboratory and field methodologies. Hence, our theory should best be viewed as preliminary, subject to the refinements that additional laboratory *and* field research will provide" (original emphasis). See also similar comments by Brown (1977:295-296).

From some experimental perspectives, contrasting experimental and real-life negotiations will not necessarily lead to revealing findings. Experimental researchers are, of course, aware that differences exist between both sets of data; in many cases, however, theoretical interests do not extend to the discovery of linkages between sets. Such a disposition may well be explained in terms of methodological isolationism, in part induced by financial and time constraints. Gulliver (1979:61, fn. 16) chastizes the social psychological approach for its unwillingness to confront real-life data, arguing that "many theorists are simply unprepared to go out and collect real-life data, preferring the secure coziness of the study or laboratory". Some studies do attempt to contrast simulated and real-life negotiations. See, e.g., Brehmer and Hammond (1977), Donohue et al. (1984), Hopmann and Walcott (1977), and Morley and Stephenson (1977).

16. For recent reviews, see Gibbons, Bradac and Busch (1992), and Chatman, Putnam and Sondak (1991).

17. For the sake of illustration, Bales's (1950) twelve categories are as follows:

1	shows solidarity	7	asks for orientation
2	shows tension release	8	asks for opinion
3	agrees	9	asks for suggestion
4	gives suggestion	10	disagrees
5	gives opinion	11	shows tension
6	gives orientation	12	shows antagonism

18. A number of linguistic and speech act approaches to discourse contend with parallel analytical hurdles. It would appear, however, that communication scholars working with coding schemes in the analysis of negotiation discourse are unfamiliar with the closely-related work undertaken by linguists (e.g., Labov and Fanshel 1977, Sinclair and Coulthard 1975, Burton 1980, Edmondson 1981) and speech act theorists (e.g., Searle 1979). Sinclair and Coulthard's (1975) linguistic model, for example, based on segmenting language into predetermined units (e.g., 'act', 'exchange', 'move', 'inform', 'initiate'), is also predicated on the assumption that speech is divisible into mutually exclusive, predetermined categories. Lampi (1986) has attempted to utilize a modified version of Sinclair and Coulthard's (1975) model in her analysis of a real-life negotiation. For critiques of linguistic models, see Levinson (1983:286-294) and Taylor and Cameron (1987 ch. 4). For an interaction-oriented critique of Searle's (1979) speech act theory, see Streek (1980).

19. Such a view is far from novel; over sixty years ago, Volosinov ([1930] 1973:93) wrote:
"Utterance ... is wholly a product of social interaction, both of the immediate sort as determined by the circumstances of the discourse, and of the more general kind, as determined by the whole aggregate of conditions under which any given community of speakers operates".

20. This is not to deny that *participants* attribute intentions in their interpretations of utterances;

however, for conversation analysts, such attributions are topics, but not tools, of analysis.

21. Adopting a somewhat different approach (i.e. Hallidayan), though utilizing negotiation transcripts, O'Donnell (1990) was concerned to uncover how the components of 'power' and 'solidarity' are realized in the way discourse is structured.

22. Some (e.g., Maynard 1984:55-6; Moerman 1988; M.H. Goodwin 1990; Bilmes 1992, 1993a) have identified a need to incorporate directly into their analyses ethnographic information about settings and tasks in order to explicate the activity/setting-talk relationship. There is, though, some debate as to the form such an incorporation should take, as well as the extent to which ethnography (or knowledge of social structure, or culture) can complement CA, and vice versa (for representations of differing views on this, see, e.g., Cicourel 1992, Wilson 1991, Schegloff 1991). Moerman (1988) propounds what he calls 'culturally contexted conversation analysis', an approach that calls for the analyst to draw explicitly upon his cultural knowledge of settings and activities in order to both understand *and* explicate the local significance of conversational actions. The need for such an approach would appear to be increased when the analyst is faced with the description of talk wherein he cannot unproblematically assume an isomorphic relationship between his and the participants' pragma-linguistic competence, or between his and their knowledge of the talk-related activity.

23. 'Conditional relevance' is a conversation-analytic term that refers to the way the production of one utterance or action establishes expectations and therefore a 'relevance' upon anything that occurs in the turn 'slot' that follows. Thus whatever comes to be said in the 'slot' will be inspected for its relevance to the preceding action. If a second action fails to occur, it is *noticeably absent*; if some other (first) part occurs it will be heard where appropriate as a preliminary to the doing of the impending second part, the relevance of which is not lifted until it is directly attended to or aborted by the announced failure to provide some preliminary action [see Schegloff (1972a:363-364) and Levinson (1983:306)].

24. In a similar vein, Grimshaw (1990:chap. 13) provides a thorough and insightful discussion on why and how the 'variables' of power and affect should be incorporated into the analysis of discourse.

CHAPTER 2

NEGOTIATION IN THE WORKPLACE: THE VIEW FROM A POLITICAL LINGUIST

DAVID V. J. BELL

1. INTRODUCTION

My work on negotiation arises from an interest in 'Political Linguistics' — a theoretical approach that I developed nearly twenty years ago in an attempt to make sense of the concepts *power, influence,* and *authority*. The approach conceptualized these relationships as involving language and communication 'strategies' for affecting others' values and behaviour. This chapter suggests some theoretical and methodological issues regarding the study of negotiation that emerge from the political linguistics perspective, and comments on possible implications for conversation analysis. It begins with some terminological clarification.

This paper was first presented at the Conference on "Negotiation in the Workplace" held at Aalborg University, Denmark, May 11-13, 1992. In revising it, I have benefited from comments and criticisms offered by Harry Arthurs, Barbara Falk, Alan Firth, Tamara Johnson and Stephen Weiss; and from the comments of other members of the Negotiation Workshop at York University, to whom a revised version was presented in February, 1993. Kim Arnold provided helpful bibliographic assistance. For its many remaining imperfections, I bear full responsibility.

2. DEFINING THE WORKPLACE: SOME ISSUES AND COMMENTS

The phrase 'negotiation in the workplace' suggests a particular negotiation 'site' that is easily distinguished from the 'non-workplace'. But what is the workplace? This question is less straightforward than it seems. Nor is a ready answer available from the usual sources. For example, neither the Oxford English Dictionary (OED) nor the 1993 'New Shorter Oxford English Dictionary' have entries on 'workplace'.

The 'workplace' is a modern notion. The concept of work has roots that go back past the middle ages, however. The OED suggests that the concept 'work' was used in its present connotation in Middle and even Old English. Definition number four in the OED is "action involving effort or exertion, directed to a definite end, espec. as a means of gaining one's livelihood; labour, toil; [one's] regular occupation or employment". Under this definition, examples are found from the 9th century and later. Yet work took on meanings in the early industrial period that would have associated the workplace primarily with the factory or the shop.

This focus is far too narrow today, as we quickly realize when we attempt to identify the *non*-workplace. For example, we might expect that workplace negotiation excludes politics and especially international politics. Yet people work in and for governments. Indeed, in many countries governments are the largest single employer. These sites are (for them) their workplace. Similarly we might expect that family settings are excluded. But there is much work done in the family (housework for example) about which considerable negotiation often takes place. Furthermore, some of the work of the family that for years went unrecognized — i.e. daycare — is being done 'professionally' outside the family in the new workplaces (e.g. daycare centres) that have sprung up in advanced industrial societies. Finally, leisure would appear by definition to fall outside the scope of this discussion particularly because the original root of the term 'negotiation' is '*neg otium*' literally *not leisure*. Yet the 'leisure industry' is one of the most important areas of growth in recent years. So perhaps the workplace *is* everywhere. 'Negotiation in the workplace' could embrace nearly any negotiation setting.

3. NEGOTIATION

The term 'negotiation' has had an interesting history. As mentioned, its Latin roots (*neg* — not, and *otium* — leisure, i.e., *business*) identify its origin in the marketplace, where it referred to the process of haggling in the barter or sale of goods. In the early modern period (late 16th century) it came to be used in the sphere of politics to refer to talk between princes and rulers (Bell 1988). Its present connotations embrace a wide spectrum of settings and issues, ranging from collective bargaining in the workplace to the loftiest reaches of what has been called 'summit diplomacy'.

3.1. Definition of Workplace Negotiations

What counts as 'negotiation' in the workplace? We use the term *negotiate* in many contexts. We negotiate a raise. We negotiate where we will go out for lunch. We negotiate our way out of a conflict that has led to a bitter dispute. If we have done someone a number of favours, perhaps volunteering to serve on a time-consuming committee, or agreeing to participate in a lengthy review exercise, we will have built up a large number of "negotiable credits" that we can later 'cash in' by asking a favour(s) of them. In short the term negotiation, or its derivatives, is applied to a wide range of speech interactions in the workplace. But not all.

Negotiation is not coextensive with speech or discourse but is a subset of it.[1] At its core, negotiation implies conflict, cooperation, and talk. Parties to negotiation share some objectives, disagree on others, and (for the time being at least) attempt to resolve their differences and/or firm up their agreements through discussion. The term negotiation presupposes a particular type of communication that involves an element of 'bargaining' or perhaps conflict and mediation. Walton and McKersie (1965:3, quoted in Weiss and Stripp 1985) defined negotiation as " . . . the deliberate interaction of two or more complex social units which are attempting to define or redefine terms of their interdependence". Weiss adds to this notion the criteria of both common and conflicting interests, mutual movement, and the goal (but not guarantee) of reaching an agreement. Casse (1981:152) defines negotiation as "a process in which one individual tries to persuade another to alter ideas or behaviour; a process in which at least two partners with different needs and viewpoints try to reach agreement on matters of mutual interest" (Adler and Graham 1987:213).

4. THE POLITICAL LINGUISTICS APPROACH

This latter definition resembles closely my characterization of political linguistics as the use of language and communication to change values, beliefs, attitudes and behaviour (Bell 1975, 1977, 1988).[2] Thus negotiation entails politics, i.e. the deliberate use of communication to change outcomes.

Political linguistics attempts to unpack the notion of how people are able, through speech and communication, to affect the behaviour, values and attitudes of others. It distinguishes three dominant modes of political action language: power, influence, and authority. *Power* is the use of sanctions that may be either positive (inducements) or negative (punishments). In a *power statement* the speaker purports to be capable of manipulating the contingent outcomes that will affect behaviour. The paradigm of a power statement is, "If you do X, I (we) will do Y", where X or Y may be either positive or negative. Examples include the following: "If your job performance doesn't improve, I will have to fire you". "If you do a good job, I will give you a raise". "If you don't agree to our demands, we will go out on strike". The force of such statements is obvious. But we need to take account of a second form of political communication, namely *influence*. In influence communication, the speaker is not purporting to be able to affect directly the positive or negative contingent outcomes that will reinforce behaviour. Instead the user of influence merely *predicts* certain contingent outcomes that will follow from certain types of behaviour. The paradigm of an influence statement is, "if you (I, we) do X, you (I, we) will experience Y" or "if you do X, he, she, or they will do Y". Examples here include, "Better be careful. If the boss catches you goofing off once more, he'll fire you". "If we get this report done by next Friday, we'll get a nice bonus". "If we don't offer them at least 5%, they'll walk". The third concept central to the political linguistics approach is *authority*. The paradigm of an authority communication is "Do X" or "I hereby do X". Authority statements typically take the form of orders, instructions, directives, pronouncements, commands, rules etc. Examples include, "Pack up your personal items. You're fired". "I am hereby authorizing a $1,000 bonus". "Remove the picketers". Authority is usually found in highly institutionalized settings. Its effectiveness depends on the listener's belief in certain "credenda" or articles of faith affirming an obligation to *accept* authoritative statements in specified situations from specified persons with respect to specified issues. (In the absence of the requisite set of beliefs, authority must revert to strategies of either influence or power to gain compliance.)

That most students of negotiation are insensitive to these distinctions — particularly between power and influence — is noted by Weiss (1991:33):

> "... research on negotiations' communicative behaviour has traditionally been limited in scope to 'offers' and 'threats' with relatively few studies of the subtle ways Americans and other negotiators shape relationships ...".

It is of course true that negotiation frequently involves the use of power language by the contending parties, who attempt to bargain by making promises, providing incentives, threatening punishments, or withholding rewards. It is this aspect of negotiation that can be (partially) captured in game theoretic analyses of "pay-off matrices", and other approaches that relate negotiation to the language of threats and promises. But negotiation is far more complex than power-based models allow. Furthermore, parties other than the disputants themselves play a role. Increasingly negotiation involves advisors on the one hand, mediators on the other. Yet some scholars try to apply power-based models to all aspects of negotiation. For example, Carnevale's article on "Strategic Choice in Mediation" carefully analyses the range of "strategies available to the mediator" in terms of four possible choices:

> "*integration*, which involves efforts to find a solution within the region of common ground; *pressing*, which involves efforts to reduce the set of management alternatives; *compensation* which involves efforts to enhance the set of agreement alternatives; and *inaction*, which involves letting the disputants handle the conflict themselves" (Carnevale 1986: 42).

Each of these strategies rests on tactics that require the use of power as I have defined it. Reference is made to log-rolling, cost-cutting, compensation, threats, guarantees, expanding the resources, direct payment, and so on. Almost entirely absent from Carnevale's analysis is an informed discussion of influence strategies. A moment's reflection makes clear, however, that power is not all that 'counts' in negotiation, particularly for mediators. Yet Carnevale pays little attention to mediators' invaluable influence skills e.g. persuading the protagonists to change the way they see their opponents, or to reinterpret their own and/or the other's demands and positions. Typically such efforts require the skilful use of the language of *influence* rather than power or authority.

In a more balanced discussion of this issue, Kolb notes that (most) mediators are not in a position to issue orders or instructions.[3] Nor can they make threats and promises. Their task is to change perceptions, "to influence parties into rethinking their positions ... and into modifying their positions in order to achieve some sort of compromise" (Kolb 1985:12). This task requires special skills and tactics. The mediator may, for example, attempt to gain credibility as an expert on the 'facts' with regard to both the existing dispute and other disputes that can be invoked to cast a different light on the immediate controversies.

Mediators need effective interpersonal skills and often "establish rapport by creating an impression of intimacy and friendship" (Kolb 1985:19). Mediators attempt to define or redefine many aspects of the negotiation. They may insist that a particular move is very positive, a sure sign of progress. Mediators frequently try to take responsibility for positive steps. All of this use of influence requires careful management or self image in order to create favourable impressions. Thus Kolb (1985:11) declares that "[w]hat direct and indirect influence mediators have emanates from their person, their reputation and skills, and the parties' ongoing assessment of them during the case".

The same is true of those who advise the contending parties about how best to achieve their objectives in a negotiation. Advisors are influence politicians par excellence. Their value derives from their ability to appear credible predictors of the actions of others and the outcomes of alternative strategies and tactics. As Zartman (1989b:243) points out, academics' concern with prediction mirrors that of policy makers, and helps explain why academics are often sought after as policy advisors: "The Academics' question 'What causes A?' is the mirror image of the policy-makers' question 'What will happen if I do B?' and the same as the latter's question 'How can I help bring about A?'".

In short, analysis of negotiation must, I would argue, focus not only on what the contending parties say to each other, but also what they say to other interested parties who are involved as advisors, or mediators, beneficiaries or benefactors of the outcome to negotiation. In the case of collectivities (such as management and labour) the process of negotiation is typically placed in the hands of a small team that represents — and is ultimately responsible to — the collectivity. The team usually designates a chief negotiator, and other members of the team serve in an advisory and/or consultative role.[4] The team may be under the authority of another group (for example a board of management or an executive of the union) who can issue binding directives (in the language of authority) to the negotiating team, constraining its ability to make offers and threats. And so the political linguistic analysis of negotiation requires attention to the full range of linguistic strategies — not only power, but also influence and authority as well.

If formal negotiation in the context of collective bargaining evinces the full range of political linguistics strategies, what about the highly informal negotiations that take place in everyday interactions in the workplace? If anything, these relationships are equally complex. They entail a wide spectrum of communication behaviour, enlivened and expanded by a whole range of non-linguistic communication. Students of communication estimate that in a face to face encounter, as much of 60% - 80% of the communication occurs non-verbally. Relevant factors include voice tone, facial expression, relative placement (e.g. sitting or standing), distance, and 'body language' (Fast 1971). Students of negotiation must be sensitive to these factors in their efforts to understand the dynamics and outcome of face-to-face negotiations (Rosenthal, 1988, Garcia 1991).

5. THE CONVERSATION ANALYTIC APPROACH

Conversation analysis (CA) is a methodology (derived from ethnomethodology) for undertaking detailed analyses of talk-in-interaction. It requires video or audio recording of 'naturally occurring' speech interactions that are transcribed using a notation system developed in large part by Gail Jefferson (see, e.g., Atkinson and Heritage 1984:ix-xvi). Attention is given to many details of speech, including turn-taking, pauses, 'gaps', overlaps, mispronunciations, voice tone and inflection, laughter, etc. Analysts use the transcript (informed where necessary by referring back to the tape itself) to analyze and "explicate how conversation actually works as an accomplished achievement of the participants" (Firth 1993). Conversation analysts have developed a model to account for the mechanisms, structures and patterns of turn-taking in everyday conversation (Sacks, Schegloff and Jefferson 1974). Relying on inferences that can be corroborated in the 'data' of the transcript, CA attempts to unravel the mysterious process by which mutually intelligible conversation takes place among interactants. Several theoretical assumptions underpin the CA approach:

1. Interaction is *structurally organized*;
2. Contributions are *contextually oriented*;
3. *All details* of interaction are (potentially) important;
4. The structure and the contributions are *describable phenomena*;
5. 'Ordinary' talk situations inform 'extraordinary' talk situations (Heritage 1984, Firth 1993).

This latter assumption is very important. Much of the corpus of CA research focuses on 'mundane' everyday conversation in the belief that there are recognizable and predictable structures common to all types of 'naturally occurring' conversation. CA holds that these natural structures form the interactional *bedrock* on which other forms of speech interaction — including, presumably, negotiation — take place. Conversation analysts believe further that careful analysis can reveal the underlying 'rules' of ordinary conversation and that this knowledge will illuminate non-ordinary forms of talk which deviate from these rules. Stated differently, socialized interactants learn how to participate in everyday conversation. This is no simple matter. Not everyone learns the rules of conversation and is able or willing to act upon them. Some people are rude or awkward or socially incompetent in everyday conversation. In extreme cases, inability to participate in 'normal' conversation is taken as a symptom of mental illness. The 'machinery of interaction' is rather complex, and reflects sophisticated shared understandings about how to exchange various greetings, offers, questions, what constitutes interruption, acceptable forms of (non) verbal 'feedback', etc.

How does all of this relate to the political linguistics approach? First, CA provides through the transcript usable data that can be analyzed to discover the presence and effect of the language of power, influence or authority. This immediately presents a challenge.

Political linguistics assumes that the observers' perspective needs checking against that of the participants with respect to both meaning and interpretation ("I meant to assure him, but I said the wrong thing and instead made him feel worse". "She came across like an arrogant, self-righteous know-it-all"). The question is one of methodology and practicality. Ideally one would want to supplement an analysis of transcripts with a 'debriefing' of participants to check their perceptions. Adherents of CA distrust the accuracy of these *post hoc* discussions, however. As one CA practitioner put it, "I'm only interested in what people actually say and do during a negotiation, not in the nice stories they tell about it afterwards".[5] Stated differently, "...CA avoids stipulating what negotiators *'really' intend* or *'really'* mean. Instead focus [rests] on the interactional manifestations that participants take to be indicative of intentions" (Firth 1991:43).

On this methodological issue, CA and PL are opposed.[6] The CA position is fully defensible. Conversation is sequentially organized. Interactants respond to what they see and hear, especially in the previous speaking turn. They cannot respond to unexpressed thoughts or uncommunicated feelings, nor to distant aspects of context or reputation. Their behaviour is comprehensible only in terms of what has been 'locally produced' in the course of the conversation. The conversation analyst must in the first instance seek clues and explanations in the transcript, in the verifiable record of what was 'introduced' by the various interactants *in the course* of their conversation (see, though, Moerman 1988).

The PL position starts from a slightly different premise. While acknowledging that 'local production' is extremely important — that to actually exercise power, or influence, or authority, normally requires communication-in-interaction — the literature of political science nevertheless recognizes that political control is sometimes achieved through tacit rather than explicit means (Bell 1975:33-34). One notable formulation of this insight is Carl Friedrich's "rule of anticipated reaction", first enunciated in 1941. According to this rule, political actors sometimes adjust their behaviour *in anticipation of a probable response* from another political interactor. Friedrich illustrated this by pointing out that some congressional legislation fails even to be seriously proposed in anticipation of a likely presidential veto. More mundane examples come easily to mind however. Indeed, in one sense we all constantly shape or refine our comments based on an implicit anticipation of how they will be received by others. We seldom 'blurt out' the first thing that comes into our mind. Is it reasonable therefore to give some credence methodologically to post hoc interviews in which the analyst tries to determine what forms of *tacit political relations* were effected through anticipated reaction on the part of negotiators? The answer depends in part on how important a role power, influence, or authority *differentials* seemed to play in the case being analyzed.

A different though related form of tacit political control is conceptualized in the notion of "non-decisions" introduced to the political science literature by Bachrach and Baratz (1970). In this view, focusing too much attention on what gets discussed leads analysts to ignore what gets suppressed or forced off the agenda. Again, the illustrations are drawn from formal decision-making settings (councils, legislatures) but the point may be generalizable to other settings, including negotiations. Some proposals simply are unthinkable and will never come up in negotiation. How topics and issues get so completely marginalized becomes a challenging puzzle for analysis. The answer may (or may not) be retrievable through post-hoc interviews of interactors.

These important caveats aside, CA does provide an ideal methodology for analyzing 'political talk' to discover the role of the language of power, influence and authority in interaction.

But what is political talk? Talk where there is an important presence of PIA? According to PL, politics *is* talk. But is all talk political? In one sense yes. If we define politics as the use of language/communication to affect others, all talk is political. By its very nature, the talk of others — *all* such talk and its nonverbal accompaniment — affects those who are within its ambit. Talk is the adhesive of social connection. We learn from infancy how to understand (or at least interpret) the talk of others and how to talk back to them. Our talk is sequentially related to their talk. Conversation is a mutual dance in which both (all) interactants take part. To 'ignore' the talk of others is a prime symptom of autism.

All talk therefore affects others. All talk is therefore political in the broadest sense of the term. But some talk is more political then others. The language of PIA is highly political, and reveals intentions to change other's behaviour.

When do people use the language of PIA? What reaction does it engender? CA provides (perhaps uniquely) a methodology for answering this question. The faithful finely-grained analysis of negotiation transcripts would permit a careful indication of the use of political linguistic strategies. Clearly, in most instances, the use of threats, warnings, promises, predictions etc. is surrounded by much *other* talk. One might hypothesize that explicit power, influence or authority communications constitute a critical point in negotiation when matters are brought to a 'crunch'.

Whatever the circumstances, CA will reveal the (apparent) effects of PIA statements on subsequent talk. What type of confirmation or acknowledgement occurs? How does the level of conflict or cooperation change? What type of 'mitigation' accompanies the use of PIA? (Weiss 1988). Are 'accounts' typically offered or demanded? (see, e.g., Firth this volume).Using a political linguistics approach, one might also broaden the focus beyond the detailed analysis of actual interaction to consider the broad strategies for negotiation used by each participant. One way in which negotiation (especially 'important' negotiations where the stakes are relatively high) differs from everyday 'mundane' conversation is in the extent to which it is planned in advance. In preparation for a negotiating session, participants often try to anticipate and to some extent program what 'line' they will take. In effect they develop a 'game plan'. Sometimes they rehearse or role-play the entire negotiation, perhaps, 'scripting' certain key statements, or at least reviewing the main points they wish to make and anticipating counter-arguments to the other side's case. Certain interpersonal negotiations — such as those between parent and child or teacher and student; and common negotiation settings — such as returning merchandise to a store (cf. Torode this volume), or requesting a raise — have been formularized in various handbooks of interaction (Parent Effectiveness Training; Teacher Effectiveness Training) or in such interaction pedagogies as "assertiveness training", which prescribes negotiation tactics and techniques for "handling" difficult interpersonal negotiations.

In negotiation as in sports, having a game plan does not guarantee that one can implement it or use it to control the course and outcome of play. The other side has its own strategy, one aspect of which may include anticipating and nullifying the effects of the opponent's strategy. Interaction occurs rapidly and often requires instant action or reaction that will inevitably require departures from the strategy or script. Negotiators, no matter how thoroughly briefed, prepared or rehearsed, must invariably improvize. CA records and analyses the details of improvization that are manifest in the 'local production' of negotiation. How can we study the strategy that informs the participants? In the case of individuals, some sort of interview (prior to and/or after negotiation) would be required. In the case of group negotiations, strategy sessions (including relevant 'briefing papers') are themselves (in principle) accessible and analyzable using CA methods and insights.

6. THE ROLE OF CULTURE AND LANGUAGE

The political talk that takes place during negotiation interaction — the *speech* — must be understood in relation to the underlying political culture — the available symbols and widely shared meanings that constitute the *language* of political interaction.

Negotiation is quintessentially a linguistic act. It involves the use of language to cajole, persuade, threaten, induce, drive, blackmail, intimidate, and flatter. These are the familiar 'weapons' employed at the bargaining table and in everyday life.

Negotiation's outcome is also a linguistic act. The object of negotiation is almost always to arrive at a written agreement of terms and conditions: some kind of formal resolution, a declaration, a treaty, a collective agreement, and so on. Each of these outcomes involves careful use of 'language', a term that acquires special meaning in labour negotiations, for example when the parties speak of putting "new language" in the collective agreement.

Those who share a culture by definition share mutual understandings about the meaning of various forms of verbal and nonverbal expression, and are thus usually able to comprehend each others' utterances and to correctly decode their nonverbal communication. Individuals from different cultures, however, may systematically miscommunicate, sometimes with disastrous consequences. Much of the pioneering work on the problems of cross-cultural communication and negotiation were carried out by the anthropologist Edward Hall, whose landmark study entitled *The Silent Language* was written in part to help businessmen from the United States in their dealings with associates in Latin America and elsewhere. Since that time the literature on cross-cultural communication for business has ballooned and is now voluminous (see, e.g., Weiss 1993). It has been parallelled by a smaller but nevertheless insightful literature on cross-cultural communication in international politics (see, e.g., Cohen 1990 and 1987). But in societies like Canada and the United States which have large numbers of recent immigrants and other minorities who have retained elements of their native culture, the problem of cross-cultural communication exists in the office, the classroom, the campus, and the factory. These problems pose serious challenges to managers and employees alike. Rosalie Tung (1988:218) concludes her chapter on international business negotiations with the following comment:

"... a theoretical paradigm of international business negotiations such as the one posited in this paper can assist our understanding of cross-cultural phenomenon [sic] by examining how people from different cultural backgrounds interact under varying sets of contextual environments and negotiation contexts, and how these in turn determine the strategies that will be pursued. Such findings can facilitate the identification and prescription of management practices that can be effective in organizations comprising of employees from more than one nationality. Given the increasing multiethnic composition of the U.S. workforce, this is an important consideration in improving organizational effectiveness for most companies".

7. LANGUAGE, FRAMING, AND THE TRANSFORMATION OF DISPUTES

Language has a crucial impact on disputes that give rise to negotiation. In order for disputes to be transformed into formal complaints that can be negotiated in one way or another (including judicial litigation), a special kind of awareness must be created, along with a capacity to articulate complaints in an appropriate form. The fascinating issue of the *Law and Society Review* in 1980-81, discussed this phenomenon and made important contributions to its analysis. For example, Festinger, Abel, and Sarat pointed out that disputes are "social constructs" that only become recognized and reacted to if they are transformed from an "unperceived injurious experience" into something that can be *named* and thereby identified as a particular injurious experience. Once it has been named, this experience can now be *blamed* on some individual or organization which is held to be at fault. "By including fault within the definition of grievance, we limit the concept to injuries viewed both as violations of norms and as remediable". The final stage in the transformation of disputes is to move from naming and blaming to *claiming*: identifying a remedy which is sought from the perpetrator of the injurious experience.

Mather and Yngvesson expand on this analysis by describing various ways in which rephrasing affects the perception of and response to disputes. Sometimes this involves *narrowing*, which they describe as "the process through which established categories for classifying events in relationships are imposed on an event or series of events, defining the subject matter of a dispute in ways which make it amenable to conventional management procedures". Alternatively the dispute may be changed through *expansion*, which involves "rephrasing in terms of a framework not previously accepted by the third party". Whichever transformation occurs, the discourse into which the dispute gets phrased "strengthens the position of those whose interests and values are represented in that discourse". This latter point helps them link the interaction between the disputants to the broader social context which includes "publics and audiences, allies of the disputants, lawyers and other spokesmen [sic], as well as third parties and the disputants themselves". With regard to formal litigation, these interests serve well lawyers and paralegals. As Mather and Yngvesson point out, "a need to rephrase a dispute into the official language of law restricts the disputing arena to those who can understand and use the language or can hire someone to act on their behalf" (Mather and Yngvesson 1980-81:791).

Negotiations with regards to conflicts and disputes can arise if and only if conflicts get 'transformed' through a process of naming, blaming and claiming.

There is a growing awareness of workplace conflicts related to inequalities of power. Some forms of these conflicts, particularly those reflecting racism or sexual harassment, have generated new vocabularies and new institutions devoted to negotiated settlements of grievances and complaints. These new developments are indicative of the "culture shift" (Inglehart 1990) that has occurred in advanced industrial societies and has transformed values and actions across a wide sphere of social institutions.

The new discourse surrounding *sexual harassment* — a term that scarcely existed as little as ten or fifteen years ago — testifies to the way in which language change and social change overlap and reinforce each other, and affect the transformation of disputes, with obvious consequences for negotiation. The very appearance of the term sexual harassment testifies to the cultural shift that has occurred. The discourse has helped victims of harassment *name* their injury, and go on from there to *blame* the perpetrator and *claim* an appropriate remedy. At York University in Toronto, a special organization was put in place to deal with sexual harassment. The purpose of this Centre is to respond to complaints from students, staff, or faculty that involve sexual harassment. It has developed a negotiation methodology for this purpose. The first objective is to talk about the complaint and then to give an opportunity for the parties involved, if possible, to resolve the matter through negotiation. The Centre attempts to decentralize this phase by having a responsible individual in the unit where the complaint originated convene a meeting of the two parties (if they so desire) to talk about the problem and how they would like to see it resolved. If this first stage of informal discussion fails, or if either party is uncomfortable attempting this kind of informal resolution, the Centre has other more formal responses available to them including ultimately a quasi-judicial proceeding. Clearly all of this is a form of negotiation that requires skills initially of mediation and ultimately of a more forensic nature. As individuals become more aware of their rights, and as the social complexity and cultural plurality of the workplace increase, inevitably organizations of this kind will become even more important and widespread. The existence of Centres for Sexual Harassment and other rights-based complaints reflects the importance of cultural change in society as a whole and a particular kind of political cultural development among individual members of society.

The issue of naming and defining sexual harassment is carefully taken up in the York University SHEACC brochure:

"What is Sexual Harassment?
Sexual harassment can be defined as:
1. Unwanted sexual attention of a persistent or abusive nature, by a person who knows or ought reasonably to know that such attention is unwanted,
   or
2. Implied or expressed promise or reward for complying with a sexually oriented request,
   or
3. Implied or expressed threat of reprisal, in the form either of actual reprisal or the denial of opportunity, for refusal to comply with a sexually oriented request,
   or
4. Sexually oriented remarks and behaviour which may reasonably be perceived

to create a negative psychological and emotional environment for work and study.

Sexual harassment can include behaviour such as:
- unnecessary touching or patting
- suggestive remarks or other verbal abuse
- leering at a person's body
- compromising invitations
- demands for sexual favours
- sexual assault

In other words, sexual harassment can be either psychological or physical. Or it can be a combination of both elements.

Gender Harassment is Sexual Harassment

Gender harassment also creates a negative environment for scholarship and research. Gender harassment consists of derogatory or degrading remarks which are directed towards members of one gender group or one sexual preference group. Most often, women and homosexuals are the targets for these discriminatory remarks".[7]

8. THE IMPORTANCE OF CONTEXT

It is my belief that successful analysis of negotiation in the workplace requires some understanding of the context within which it takes place. Context has at least two aspects: extra-institutional and intra-institutional. In studying the extra-institutional context, we begin with the recognition that each workplace is situated in a wider societal context. It is surrounded, in other words, by a series of larger settings within which it is 'nested'. Depending on the nature of the negotiation, these extrainstitutional contexts may be very important to what is taking place in the workplace. This is obvious in the case of wage settlements negotiated during a recession or during a period of rampant inflation. The external setting may be equally important with respect to non-wage issues such as harassment which reflect wider social trends and current issues.

I contend also that the intrainstitutional environment is important. Each workplace has in some respects a distinctive "normative order" (Arthurs 1985) that will affect the nature of conflict, constrain the type of cooperation, and have an impact on the process of negotiation itself. As an observer of the workplace setting one must attempt to understand this normative order and see it through the eyes of the interactants who live it as part of their daily working existence.

Context, it would appear, can be studied either directly or indirectly. To look at it directly involves the use of various quantitative and non-quantitative descriptors of the context, or analysis of secondary accounts of experts, journalists, informants, etc. It is equally important, however, to examine the context indirectly by looking at how the parties to a negotiation describe and comprehend the context within which they see themselves situated. One would examine in particular how they 'frame' a dispute or issue for clues about how they characterize contexts.

Interactants' approach to negotiation is affected by what Barbara Gray calls the *frame* that they apply to the conflict or dispute that they are attempting to resolve. These frames, which are language based and frequently involve the use of metaphor, in effect translate context into meaning and interpretation. The way interactants frame a negotiation reveals what aspects of the context they have deemed of greatest significance. The frame also helps them select an appropriate linguistic strategy for handling the dispute. (Note the link here to the notion of 'scripts'.) Gray and her colleagues regard frames as significant for every aspect of negotiation. They have put special emphasis on the following six types of frames:

"Substantive frames define what the dispute is about.

Outcome frames represent the disputants' preferred solution.

Loss-Gain frames are interpretations of the conflict that focused primarily on the risks or benefits associated with various outcomes.

Aspiration frames expressed the disputants' *needs or interests*.

Characterization frames are labels applied to other disputants, to the self or to the relationship.

Process frames depict the negotiators' expectations about how the negotiation will or should proceed" (Gray, Purday and Bouwen 1990: 9-10).

Context alone is insufficient to explain negotiation. We require an *interactional* (as opposed to a dispositional) approach. Here the techniques of conversation analysis have yielded the most interesting and exciting results.

Practitioners of CA are very aware of the need to take context into consideration. Zimmerman (1988:417) points out that the "autonomy principle" — which he characterizes as "a commitment to the investigation of social interaction as a distinctive domain with its own organization ..." — requires that CA take "a cautious stance regarding the issue of the connection between conversational interaction and the so-called larger contexts of social action".

The emphasis on local production or "local determination" entails two consequences for the CA treatment of context. First, emphasis is placed on the sequential context of the conversation itself, i.e. the way in which preceding statements shape or influence what follows (Zimmerman 1988:423, Duranti and Goodwin 1992:29). Second, the "external" context may be made manifestly "relevant" by being invoked into the conversation. Therefore CA would give special credence to elements of external context that are so implicated by the interactants themselves.

9. SUMMARY AND CONCLUSION

1. Negotiation entails linguistic interaction. It must be analyzed with a sensitive appreciation of how humans interact to affect each others' values, beliefs, and actions. These issues are central to the political linguistics approach.

2. I have argued that it is important to identify all the relevant 'parties' to a negotiation. In addition to the protagonists a number of other parties may be closely involved. These include principals (on whose behalf the negotiators are working); advisors (to principals or their proxies); third parties, who may be either mediators, conciliators, arbitrators, or in the perspective of some, meddlers. The relevant 'talk' in negotiation includes not only what the negotiators say to each other but what they say to those other parties. In broadening the focus of relevant conversation, I am aware that it may be impossible to find data in appropriate form for conversation analysis. This constitutes one of the limitations of that particular methodology, but it should not deter us from attempting to form and describe the bigger picture.

3. In trying to look at the text of negotiation, the methodology that is used will depend on access. Naturalistic direct observation is preferable, particularly when it is accompanied by the possibility of getting tapes and transcripts of the negotiation. These texts can be analyzed according to the notions of power, influence, and authority developed in the political linguistics approach. This type of analysis can complement the other analytic questions asked by conversation analysts.

4. All negotiations take place in a context which can be described in relation to formality, power, conflict, cooperation, and so on. The structural context within which negotiation

takes place can have a profound impact on the course of negotiation as well as their outcome. An important aspect of learning a culture entails learning about structures and contexts. We learn how to behave, including what to say and what not to say in a particular setting. This point applies with special force in the case of negotiations.

5. We can also observe the various 'frames' used by interactants and look especially for attempts to change the frames.

6. But the text alone is not everything. We must recognize the importance of nonverbal communication. We must also pay attention to the 'subtext' or hidden agenda — What are the parties really after? What's really driving them? Similarly, there may be a 'pretext', i.e. an excuse to initiate an action for other reasons. We should attempt to uncover negotiation strategies. Researchers must be aware of cultural differences between various parties and the possibility of miscommunication that may result. But even those who share a culture may fail to understand each other. We need therefore to explore with those involved their view of what they were trying to 'say' (intention) and how they made sense of what others said (interpretation). I recognize that this may lead to distortions because of wilful or unconscious twisting of experience and false reporting by respondents.

7. Finally, there are at least two types of 'language' that are important to negotiation. There is a language of understanding and a language of interaction. The former is linked to a culture of rules and assumptions (i.e., a normative order). It affects us in a very profound way. It provides available frames, metaphors, scripts (i.e. 'ways of knowing') that may prevent our seeing options and developing new understanding. On the other hand, the language of interaction is the language we use to communicate in an attempt to change actions and values of others. We *use* it but sometimes we are its prisoners as well. An interesting point of convergence between those two senses of language appears when we use the language of interaction to change the understandings: to suggest new frames and metaphors, to develop new scripts. This is the essence of what has been called 'track two diplomacy' in the international setting, what might simply be described in political linguistic terms as the use of influence rather than power in a negotiation interaction (Bell 1988).

NOTES

1. A broader conceptualization of negotiation underlies 'negotiated order theory', which emerged out of symbolic interactionism (cf. Button and Sharrock this volume). This approach "focuses upon the

social construction of interpretive framework, which help the various actors make the adjustments and adaptations required to get their daily work completed" (Day and Day 1977:134). In this perspective, all interaction involves the "negotiation of meaning" among interactants.

2. Like the term politics, negotiation can be seen as an "essentially contested concept" (Connolly 1974). Its meaning is a source of conflict and controversy that defies simple resolution by definitional fiat. How negotiation is defined depends on an underlying set of assumptions, implies a certain perspective on the social world, and has implications for a host of related ('cluster') concepts. Given these concerns, our attempt to define negotiation is itself a political exercise. Our assertions must be explained and justified in relation to wider theoretical assumptions and perspectives.

3. Garcia (1991) describes a role for mediators that involves considerable use of authority in the form of strict rules for disputing and frequent use of authority statements by mediators to bring the disputants back "into line" and enforce the "rules" for interaction.

4. The members of the 'team' may communicate with each other in ways that entail the use of language other than influence. The whole issue of communication between negotiation team members is worth exploring.

5. This remark was made by Paul ten Have during discussion at the Aalborg Conference. The view he expressed is well represented in the literature, for example in Zimmerman (1988:418):

> "The order found in conversational materials is not imposed by the analysts' use of a priori conceptual schemes or coding categories, but discovered [...] Order is not sought by soliciting participants' accounts of their conversational behavior, for what this solicits is their beliefs about ways of talking. It is found in the ways they go about methodically solving problems and addressing issues posed by the situated, turn-by-turn management of conversational interaction".

6. Zimmerman (1988:418) does discuss the potential use of "non text-based sources" (including post hoc participant interviews) in an attempt to "warrant" (i.e. validate) the many "references" about meaning and interpretation conversation analysts must inevitably make.

7. Since its establishment, the Centre has investigated an increasing number of complaints, which have risen from 51 in 1986-87 to 201 in 1991-92. In that year the Centre reported receiving an average of 25-30 calls per day.

SECTION II

NEGOTIATION IN INTRAORGANIZATIONAL ENCOUNTERS

CHAPTER 3

NEGOTIATION AND COMPROMISE: A MICROANALYSIS OF A DISCUSSION IN THE UNITED STATES FEDERAL TRADE COMMISSION

JACK BILMES

1. INTRODUCTION: THE EXCHANGE

This chapter puts forward a notion of negotiation as a situated and locally developed process. It suggests that the outcomes of negotiation and even the nature of compromise cannot be adequately understood in terms of pre-existent variables, such as the interests and bargaining positions of the negotiators, but is emergent from the negotiating process itself. It attempts, through an intensive analysis of a single exchange, to show how the participants get from suggestion to opposition and argument, and from there to a decision that can be said to represent a compromise. Although such things regularly happen,

The research on which this paper was based was supported by the National Science Foundation (Grant BNS 8103583). I would like to express my gratitude to the officials and staff members of the Federal Trade Commission who aided me during the period of my research here. This chapter has benefited from the comments of Charles Goodwin, Alan Firth and Alan Howard.

their very regularity may cause us to overlook how it is that they come about and the kind of work that it takes to make them happen. (See Firth 1991, especially Chapter 2, for an excellent and extended discussion of the sort of talk-centred analytical approach that I am attempting here.)

We will examine one exchange which occurred during a meeting in a division of the Federal Trade Commission. At issue was the content of a memorandum which was to be sent from the division to the Office of the Director of the Bureau of Consumer Protection. The Bureau, as the members of the division called it, supervised the work of the division. The memo described the charges and evidence against the XYZ loan company, and suggested what orders to the company might be issued and what penalties might be assessed. Only if the Bureau approved the memo could the division go ahead and negotiate with the company as to what orders it would agree to and what penalties it would pay. If no agreement with the company could be reached, or if the Bureau and Commissioners would not approve the agreement, the case would go to court.

The case had been developed and the memo written by two of the division attorneys, Judy and Mary, with the supervision of Paula, their immediate supervisor. Paula's supervisor was Ben, and Ben's was Helen, the head of the division. Diagramatically, then, the relevant organizational hierarchy was:

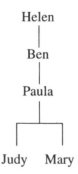

At this particular meeting, Ben was offering his views on the memo for the first time. Later, Helen would join the meeting, discuss the issues with them, and give her instructions for modifying the memo. At the point when the exchange quoted below takes place, Helen had not yet entered the room.

The central charge against the company is that it discriminated against women by refusing to consider alimony and child support payments in processing loan applications. There were also, however, three subsidiary charges. One of those charges, the one under discussion in our exchange, is that the company illegally asked applicants about their marital status. The memo includes the charge and an order to desist, but no penalty. There has been some discussion of the charge, whether it is provable, and whether the company's actions were in fact illegal under the circumstances. Ben has finally agreed that the charge is provable and the company's actions illegal, but he still has reservations:

FTC (S—10/7) [1]

1	Ben	...but one of the things you're gonna have to do is see if you can find some legislative history (1.0) saying that this section (1.0) was intended to allow them to make (1.0) inquiries (1.0) where it's necessary for security and that's it. (1.0)
2	Mary	We:ll okay (1.0)
3	Ben	Okay? (2.5) I- i- ysee- It would just make it a who:le lot stronger.=I'm not saying that if we can't find out (1.5) that that that we can't go ahead with it althou:gh (1.0) y'know I don't know how Helen's gonna feel about it but I know that that's a problem. an' an' y' you need to really (1.5) address it. (3) plus it (.) y'know the other thing is y'know (1.0) given what the rest of the case is about assuming (1.5) y'know (1.0) an' an' an' given what the rest of the case is about (1.0) and the fact that we don't (2.0) u:h (1.0) that we don't want um: (1.0) penalties (1.0) for this if it's gonna be an issue: (0.5) sorta who cares (1.0) y'know if it's gonna hold the whole case up (1.0) why wo- why would (we) ca ⌜re
4	Paula	⌞(Well) (.) I know wh- I- I'll tell you why I care.=Would you like to know Ben why I care (1.5) Becau ⌜se
5	Ben	⌞Why (do) you care. You're not divorced
6	Paula	hhh ·hhh ⌜ hhh ((nasal))
7	Ben	⌞ huhhuh ⌜ huh ((subdued laugh))
8	Paula	⌞ (That's right) and I'm the guilty liberal. I- I'm one of those guilty single (1.0) people. (1.0) u:m (2.5)
9	Ben	Try ⌜ ing to protect your sister.
10	Paula	⌞I-
11	Ben	⌜⌜ ((laugh))
12	Paula	⌞⌞ ((laugh))
13	Paula	Ri(h):ght (0.5) that's right.
14	Ben	((laugh)) Th(h)at's a little (low down). ·hhh

15   Paula   U:h (3) for the deterrence value: (.) of having this in an order
               (0.5) If creditors (.) don't a:sk (1.0) and don't have the
               information (1.0) then they can't (.) intentionally discriminate
               on the basis of marital status ·hh If they have the information
               (1.0) then we have to con- then- we are put to: (.) a much
               greater burden: as an enforcement agency (.) in determining
               whether or not they've used it illegally.=

16   Ben   =(It will happen) if the deterrence: (.) if you: charged them ten
               thousand dollars for each time we were able to (.) and no
               deterrence if it's issued in (a consent order) (1.0) Nothing. (1.0)

17   Mary   So why don't we charge 'em. (1.0) I don't have any
               problem ⌜ with (not charging)

18   Ben   ((to Paula))
                     ⌞ You know that. I mean it's just another piece of
               paper (4.5)

19   Paula   I have to believe that my work is meaningful ⌜ because (*)

20   Ben   ⌞ No I- I- I- I just-
               I just- I just don't think (1.0) me:rely having it in as a provision
               in a consent order (.) has any impact beyond the company.=I
               think that this will have an impact on the company (.) and that
               might be a reason to put it in (.) because (1.0) a- as we suspect
               that this is a pretty (0.5) y'know wi:despread problem I mean (.)
               y'know (.) y- you're dealing with XYZ (1.0) and it's a pretty big
               company. I mean that might make it worth putting it in

21   Judy   Well if it's not p- worth putting in without penalties then I'ds- I
               would- say: let's: get penalties f(h)or it particularly
               if ⌜ the feeling generally is that (.) (penalties aren't) high enough.

22   ?   ⌞ Well-

23   Ben   I mean- (1.0) and the- and the- the problem is that that (0.5) that
               (0.5) the benefit to the creditor here:: (1.5) well (1.0) (won't)
               talk about the benefit to the creditor (now) but (1.0) the injury
               (.) to the consumer here is sli:ght (.) but the difficulty of
               detection as we've already found ou:t (1.0) is very very very
               difficult (.) and that that (1.0) that merits (.) at least a (.)
               nominal civil penalty (1.0) y'know ten thousand dollar⌜s

2. SEQUENTIAL STRUCTURE

We begin with Ben's objections in turn 3. He starts by conceding in a very tentative way that the charge may be viable even without background on legislative intent, but it is clear that he has misgivings. Then, after a three second pause, he proceeds to make an argument against including the charge, culminating with "why would we care". One question that is relevant in the light of what happens later in the exchange is whether he is in fact arguing against including the charge or is suggesting that the charge be bolstered by the inclusion of penalties. This second interpretation is given some credibility by an exchange that took place earlier in the discussion:

> Ben   Then th- the other issue is how much of a penalty
> (1.5)
> Paula Well ⌈ as I recall in the memo you weren't requesting=
> Ben   ⌊ (*)
> Paula =any penalties for this violation isn't that right
> Judy   That's right
> (1.5)
> Paula Yeah ar- um and we got to that because we decided (1.0) there's no evidence that they actually used it to (1.0) discriminate
> Ben   I mean is this this would be like the first time that we've ever gone after somebody for knowingly violating the act without asking (for penalties)
> Paula We:ll u:h we can deal with how to do tha:t when we plead the case (1.5) I mean ⌈ (I'm not)

In this exchange, Ben appears to be suggesting that perhaps a penalty should be added to the charge. Is it possible that he is doing the same thing in turn 3? Paula, in turn 15, clearly does not take him to be making such a suggestion. Rather, she sees him as advocating that they drop the charge altogether, and she therefore stresses the importance of the charge rather than defending the absence of penalties.[2] Furthermore, it appears that her interpretation is more or less required by the form of his objection in turn 3. He presents no-penalties as a "given" and as a "fact" and as only one among three reasons or conditions for dropping the charge. (The other two are that the charge somehow does not fit with or is not integral to "the rest of the case" and that inclusion of the charge may "be an issue" and "hold the whole case up" [because their organizational superiors may raise objections]. In contrast to the first two reasons, which are presented as givens, holding-the-whole-case-up is foregrounded. The form in which it is presented

— "If it's gonna hold the whole case up" — offers it, in contrast to the other two reasons, as a possible topic for argument, or rather as the least taken-for-granted of the three. Ben has already argued or at least implied that inclusion of this charge *would* be an issue. Earlier in the discussion, Ben mentioned that Helen and the Director of the Bureau would have problems with the interpretation of the law embodied in the charge.) If he had wanted to imply that with no penalties the charge was not worth including, and that therefore penalties should be added, he would not have mentioned two other reasons for dropping the charge, or he would have foregrounded the absence of penalties. At least, this is the line of reasoning that a hearer would use in interpreting the implications of his utterance. The form of his utterance makes it clear what he is suggesting, and Paula interprets it accordingly. There is nothing in his further talk to suggest that he rejects Paula's interpretation.

Of special interest is the way he completes turn 3: "sorta who cares (1.0) y'know if it's gonna hold the whole case up (1.0) why wo- why would (we) care". The expression "who cares", although it has the form of a question, implies that "I don't care, this is unimportant". As such, it is a rather strong thing to say. Ben mitigates "who cares" with "sorta". He then goes on to "downgrade" with "why would we care", inviting the others to give reasons and suggesting that he still has an open mind on the subject. "Why would we care" is less provocative than "who cares".[3] Coincident with this downgrading of his opinion is an upgrading of the accompanying reason, from "it's gonna be an issue" to "it's gonna hold the whole case up". By weakening his stance and strengthening his reason, he may leave himself somewhat less open to attack.

Paula cuts into his last word with "(Well) I know mo- I- I'll tell you why I care. Would you like to know Ben why I care (1.5) Because". She responds to "why would we care", but in a personal way rather than simply by giving reasons. She then aggravates the confrontational tone of her response by asking, with a sarcastic lilt, if he would like to know why she cares. After a 1.5 second pause during which Ben does not respond, she begins her reasons with "because". Thus, whereas Ben downgrades from a more to a less confrontational style, Paula, in her turn, does the opposite. This creates a tense moment. As it appears that Ben is not going to respond, Paula begins to offer her reasons, but Ben cuts in on the first word with a joking comment. The joke is placed to deal with a situation that has become delicate and uncomfortable.[4]

The exchange that follows (turns 5-14) appears itself to be somewhat forced and uncomfortable, but I will not attempt any analysis of it here. In turn 15, Paula returns to her reasons for caring. She does this with a clause that makes no sense as a continuation of the immediately prior turns: "U:h (3.0) for the deterence value: of having this in an order". Turn 15 is very clearly a continuation of turn 4. It picks up a logical and topical connection to turn 4 as a response to turn 3. "For" in turn 15 substitutes for her earlier "because" (in turn 4); it has the same function — introducing a reason — but takes a different grammatical construction. ("Because" was grammatically matched to Ben's "Why would we care". Also, turn 15 reinstates the more technical style of discourse used by Ben in turn 3.[5] The joking episode is thus marked off, within the ongoing talk, as a conversational unit. In beginning in this way, she is presuming that the others have recognized (or will recognize) the joking as a *side sequence* (Jefferson 1972) rather than a new topic superceding the old, and that they have continued to grasp the loose thread of the earlier talk. She mentions deterrence, and then goes on to give her reasons as to why one might want to deter such behaviour.

Ben, in his reply (turn 16), fixes not on her reasons for finding the charge important but on her goal of deterrence. He says that without a penalty there will be no deterrence.[6] He pauses for one second, receives no response, and adds "nothing".[7] He evidently has a strong point here, and he pursues a response from Paula. When one makes an assertion and receives no response to it, one way to elicit a response is to repeat or re-emphasize the assertion, as Ben does with "nothing".[8] There follows a further pause of one second, and then Mary speaks (turn 17), offering what I will call (with reservations to be explained later) a compromise. She says "So why don't we charge 'em. (1.0) I don't have any problem with not charging". "Charge" here does not mean to include the charge in the memo, but rather to attach a penalty to the charge. Mary is using the term as Ben has used it in the previous utterance, when he speaks of charging them ten thousand dollars (for each provable violation).

Ben interrupts her on the word "problem", redirecting his remarks to Paula, continuing his pursuit of a response to his argument ("You know that. I mean it's just another piece of paper"). Although Mary has spoken loudly and clearly and has completed her proposal before Ben interrupts, he ignores what she has said. Sometimes, the act of ignoring requires special interactional work. But a suggestion, because it requires a certain kind of response, provides the resources for its own ignoring. Simply by not responding to the suggestion, Ben has observably ignored it.[9] In effect, he insists that there is an unfinished piece of interactional business that must be dealt with first. Mary is placed in the position of having spoken out of turn. Her recognition of this fact is indicated by the four and one half second pause after Ben's turn 18. During this pause, Mary refrains from reiterating her proposal. She allows the interactional business between Ben and Paula to reach completion.[10]

Suggestions have their interactional moments. Mary's suggestion is ignored when it occurs, even though it is "reasonable" at that point. A short time later, the same suggestion is attended to and accepted. Although Mary has not succeeded in gaining recognition for her suggestion, she has not necessarily acted clumsily or out of turn. There is a certain finesse in what she has done. It is true that Ben is in the process of trying to elicit a response from Paula, and has not yet succeeded in doing so. But he has made his assertion, paused, reiterated, and paused again. Paula's failure to reply may suggest that she has no adequate counterargument. Mary's proposal, while taking account of the force of Ben's point, would, if successful, relieve Paula of the discomfort of having to explicitly concede that point. With this in mind, we might see Mary's proposal as carefully placed and tactfully designed.

Ben's turn 18 is clearly a continuation of turn 16 rather than a response to Mary's suggestion. He is once again insisting on a response from Paula. Paula's response ("I have to believe that my work is meaningful because (*)"), after a long pause, is dramatic, in part perhaps because it is a profession of faith in what has up to now been a game of logic. I will deal with turn 19 in detail in the next section, but there are certain observations that we might make immediately about the form and placement of the utterance. Paula's "I have to believe" is a kind of transformation of Ben's "You know" in turn 18. What she "knows" is countered by what she "has to believe". And she responds to Ben's statement about her by making another statement about herself. A similar exchange takes place later in the discussion:

> Ben   We:ll (1.0) it's not very compelling
> Paula   We:ll
> Ben   To me at least (1.5)
> Paula   You never liked sex and marital status cases anyway

In this exchange, Ben's statement about himself is followed by Paula's statement about him.

I think that we can also give some analytical force to the characterization of turn 19 as "dramatic". I don't know how to get a technical grasp on the content, although it seems that when someone implies that you are threatening her sense of identity she has said something dramatic. Let us consider instead the sequential aspects of turn 19: One piece of sequential evidence, of course, is that Ben's reply is somewhat disjointed and that he backs down. More interesting is the pause that precedes Paula's utterance. Drama is not simply a property of utterances but of sequences. It seems to me that it is possible to construct a sequence in such a way that whatever occurs at point X will be dramatic — the drama of utterance X, that is, may be largely or entirely an outcome of the sequence-so-far, regardless of the nature of utterance X. The pause that precedes Paula's turn 19 is unusually long (4.5 seconds). Moreover, it is especially pregnant for at least two reasons. One is that Ben has been relentlessly pursuing a response. The other is that it is a space where Mary is withholding a repeat of her suggestion, which Ben has ignored. We might say that it is a very intense pause, a dramatic moment which will culminate with whatever it is that Paula ends up saying, and in that sense whatever she ends up saying is inherently dramatic.

The beginning of Ben's response to Paula's turn 19 shows some disfluencies that indicate discomposure ("N<u>o</u> I- I- I- I just I just I just don't think"). He goes on to make a point that mitigates his own argument and justifies Paula's position. Inclusion of the charge, even without a penalty, will deter at least one large company (because if XYZ violates the order it will be subject to penalties). Thus, it appears that Paula's turn 19, despite the fact that it offers no logical counterargument, has been effective. Judy then (turn 21) reinstates Mary's proposal, and Ben accepts the proposal.

In making her proposal, Judy begins with "Well if it's not p- worth putting in without p<u>e</u>nalties", ignoring the fact that Ben had just said that it might be worth putting in without a penalty. The word "if" is sometimes used to preface a pure hypothetical, as in a geometry theorum. There are a couple of examples of this usage in turn 16. It can also be used to introduce counterfactuals: "If that were true, we'd all be dead". But in turn 21, "if" is being used to grant the validity of Ben's point about there being no deterrence without penalties. "If" is being used here to mean something like "Now that it is established that...". It is apparent that "let's get penalties" is an actual and not a contingent suggestion; this is shown by the fact that it is bolstered by another consideration (the feeling is that penalties are not high enough) which is not hypothetical. (Although the second consideration is also introduced with "if", the fact that organizational authorities felt that penalties were not high enough was established and accepted earlier in the conversation. Thus, the second occurrence of "if" in this utterance is a very clear instance of the use of "if" to introduce an accepted fact.) Since "it's not worth putting in without penalties" is a premise for an actual suggestion, Judy has indicated that she accepts that penalties are necessary. In turn 23, Ben does not defend his point further, but rather picks up on Judy's suggestion. This is consistent with the notion that he considers that his original point (no deterrence without penalty) has been accepted. We have passed on from discussing whether no-deterrence-without-penalty is true to discussing what to do about it.

3. "I HAVE TO BELIEVE THAT MY WORK IS MEANINGFUL"

I will try to demonstrate that Paula's (turn 19) — "I h<u>a</u>ve to believe that my work is meaningful because (*)" — constitutes a crucial moment in the discussion, and not simply, or even primarily, because of its evident impact on Ben, resulting in his concession in turn 20. For the moment, though, let us put aside the question of just how and why turn 19 is crucial, and consider certain other aspects of Paula's utterance.

It struck me that the expression "I have to believe that my work is meaningful" is intensely "cultural" in the sense that, in many non-Western cultures, it might sound bizarre or even incomprehensible. People might ask "What do you mean by that?" or "Why do you have to believe that?", or perhaps they would understand but still find it an odd thing to say. In fact, even within our own culture, such expressions seem to be limited to, or at least more common in, certain segments of the population.

In considering the cultural context of Paula's statement, there are a number of matters, aside from social and cultural distribution, that might be examined. First, what are the sorts of things of which Americans might plausibly say "I have to believe that"? I will return to this question shortly. Second, we need to examine the concept of work and the expression "my work". Perhaps Paula could have said "my job" instead of "my work", but it would not have sounded quite right, or at least not as right. A job is something that one has to do or that one does for money. "Work" can, of course, mean merely labor, but, as Paula uses the term, it is something that is recognizably tied to her sense of herself as a person. Especially for people in creative and intellectual professions, "their work" constitutes for them an important part of who and what they are, and not just their means of making a living. The contrast with "work" in this usage is not play or leisure or idleness or unemployment, but aimlessness, alienation, and anomie. When the word is used in this way, it seems natural to associate it with the word "meaningful". If one's work is not meaningful, then it is merely labor for which one is paid. It is possible that not only these sorts of sentiments about work but even the use of the word "meaningful" is associated with social and educational position.

These details are speculative, to be sure, but it seems fairly certain that "I have to believe that my work is meaningful" is not the sort of statement that might appropriately be made by just anyone in any occupation or social status in any culture. Reflecting further on this, I began to wonder just what sorts of things people in our culture might plausibly "have to believe". One presumes that there is a sort of inventory of such things. Let us first specify that we are talking about expressions where "have to believe" is taken to indicate faith and psychological need, as against "I have to believe it because the evidence is overwhelming", and as against flippant or trivial usages, such as "I have to believe that those are the most beautiful shoes in the world". Paula's statement is recognizably of the first type, implying commitment and need.

If, then, there is a class of things of which one might plausibly say, "I have to believe that", what is the nature of that class, what members does it have besides "my work is meaningful"? In other words, in the expression "I have to believe that X", what sort of an object is X? This seemed to me to be an interesting and worthy question, one that might throw some light on the FTC conversation as well as on other matters. I decided as a first step to see what I could get from a questionnaire. I asked a class of twenty three undergraduate students to complete a sentence beginning "I have to believe that...".

Of the twenty-three answers, nine dealt with God or religion, five with purpose or meaning (of what one is doing or of life itself), three with the existence of good and evil. Thus, it appears that there are culturally typical categories of statements and topics in regard to what one "has to believe", even though many of these statements may not elicit universal agreement.[11] (A typical characteristic of such statements may be that they are not provable.) Moreover, Paula's turn 19 fell into one of these categories. While her statement may have been startling in its sequential context, there was nothing surprising about what it was that she had to believe. Ben's first word in turn 20 is "no". As is made apparent by the rest of his utterance, he is not saying "no, you don't have to believe that your work is meaningful", but "no, I wasn't implying that the charge (or your work) is meaningless". (See Bilmes 1992b, for an extended discussion of utterance-initial "no".) I take it that her colleagues would find Paula's sentiments proper and unremarkable, and that these sentiments do not in themselves account for the dramatic quality of her utterance. But her statement's status as a kind of emotional truism gives it power as an argumentative move — it cannot readily be contradicted.

Nevertheless, it is my contention that with this very move Paula loses the argument. The problems with turn 19 are not with its content as such but with its sequential logic and with its status as a type of talk. The problem with its logic is that it implies that Ben has been suggesting that her work is meaningless. This would seem to follow directly from the assumption that turn 19 is relevant to the previous talk. That is, one (the generalized hearer) begins by (tentatively) assuming the relevance of turn 19 to Ben's prior utterances and then seeks a proposition that relates the two, thus demonstrating relevance.[12] One such proposition — the only plausible one given what Ben has actually said and the context of argument — is "You have implied that my work is meaningless". Turn 19 is clearly said in opposition to Ben's priors. We might posit a hearer's maxim: If you can hear a response to a contradiction as disagreeing, hear it that way. In any case, her utterance clearly takes issue with a (supposed) implication that her work is meaningless.

Ben might have responded to turn 19 by attacking her deduction: Just because this particular charge as it stands is ineffective does not mean that your work in general is meaningless. Rather than making a direct attack on her logic, however, Ben responds with a claim that he has been misunderstood: He was merely saying that the charge will not have any impact beyond the company itself. (This contradicts what he said earlier about "no deterrence" and "just another piece of paper".) Thus, the problem with turn 19, as indicated by Ben's response, is not that the conclusion does not follow from the premise but that Paula has misunderstood the premise. This, in turn, allows him to back down on his argument that it is not worthwhile to include the charge as it stands.

It will not be apparent how the discussion in the last paragraph supports the claim that, with turn 19, Paula has lost the argument. If anything, the opposite conclusion is supported. Ben might have exploited an apparent fault in her logic and thereby gained an argumentative advantage, but he did not do so. It will be seen, then, that the problem with Paula's logic, as initially stated, is only a problem-in-theory. It is clear, I think, that Ben could have plausibly responded that he had not claimed that her work was meaningless, only that this particular charge was meaningless without a penalty, but that was not in fact his response. There is no evidence that this problem-in-theory was a problem for the participants in this conversation or that it actually affected the course of the interaction.

The second problem, though, has a more palpable interactional reality. It is a problem with turn 19 as a "type of talk". As I mentioned earlier, turn 19 does not belong to the rational, logical, empirical type of discourse that they have been engaged in up to this point. It is not about what is known, or what can be inferred or deduced, but about what Paula "has to believe". It is not about the effectiveness or practicality of policy decisions, but about Paula's needs and, in common parlance, her sense of identity. In order to give analytical force to these observations, I must introduce the concept of *response priority*, derived from an early formulation of what Harvey Sacks called "preference" in a 1972 lecture. I will say that, if X is the first priority response, then any response other than X (including no response) implies (when it does not explicitly assert) that X is not available or is not in effect, unless it is being withheld. That is, when X does not occur, it is specifically "not there". So, to take a simple example, upon the occurrence of an invitation, acceptance is the first priority response. If A invites B, say, to dinner, and B does not reply (or does not reply relevantly), A is likely to understand that B has refused, or is going to refuse, or at least has some problem with, the invitation. Because acceptance is first priority, the absence of a relevant response to the invitation is heard specifically as the absence of acceptance rather than as the absence of refusal.

Response priority need not involve meaningful silence: Refusals of invitations can be done on stronger or weaker grounds. In American culture, at least, to refuse an invitation on the grounds that it would be inconvenient to the invitee to accept (say, he might have to travel across town) is a relatively weak excuse. On the other hand, to refuse on the grounds that the event to which one has been invited occurs at the same time as one's brother's funeral is quite strong. Strong excuses have first priority. (In the expression "Is that the best excuse you can come up with?", there is an assumption that you have offered the strongest excuse that you have, that that is in fact the best excuse you can come up with.) Therefore, if one gives weak grounds for refusing an invitation, it may be inferred that stronger grounds are not available. The reverse is not true; the fact that one has given strong grounds does not imply that weaker grounds are absent. (The concept of response priority is explained at greater length in Bilmes 1993b.)

I would suggest that, in the context of a logic-oriented argument, such as the one which is taking place in our excerpt, and particularly in this institutional setting, a logical refutation of one's opponent's point, or logical support of one's own, is the first priority response.[13] Somewhat more precisely: In at least some social-cultural situations, when one has been contradicted with an apparently powerful argument, logical counterargument is first priority. What Paula does instead is to cite her psychological needs as a reason for not accepting Ben's argument. She does not offer any logical reason for finding his stance wrong or her own right. By not giving a first priority response, she leaves herself open to the inference that she has no such response available, that she has, as a matter of logic, lost the argument.[14] This interpretation is reinforced by the fact that she has waited so long to respond, suggesting that she has had trouble finding an adequate answer. (That is, I take it that her long silence would be so understood by the participants themselves.)[15] It has been suggested (Sacks 1987, Pomerantz 1984b) and widely accepted in the conversation analytic literature that agreeing responses are produced without delay, whereas disagreements are typically delayed. This does not appear to be the case in the context of argument (Bilmes 1988, Kotthoff 1993), and is certainly not typically true in my transcripts of argument among attorneys in the FTC. In these transcripts, disagreement is frequently produced without delay. Therefore, Paula's nonresponses and delays would not be seen as indicating a reluctance to disagree. They would, as I have suggested, very likely be seen as indicating that she is having trouble finding an appropriate argument with which to contest Ben's point.

What we have in this exchange is in fact nested response priorities. When one is contradicted, the first priority response is some form of disagreement. To fail to resist or disagree may produce the impression that one has accepted the other's argument. But given that one produces an oppositional response, and in so doing shows that one has not accepted the other's argument, the nature of that response may be examined to determine whether it constitutes a logical counter, which is first priority, or merely expresses a reluctance, on some nonlogical grounds, to accept the other's point. Paula has not accepted Ben's argument, but she has allowed the inference that she cannot find logical grounds to oppose it.

We might note that, in theory at least, it could be otherwise. Perhaps we will discover that in some other culture the first priority response to a contradiction is to plausibly claim that one has a strong personal motivation to believe that one's interlocutor is wrong. To offer such an answer would not lead to the presumption that one did not have a logical refutation available, but to offer only a logical refutation would lead to the inference that one had no personal motivation to believe that the other was wrong. For such a priority ordering to exist, perhaps arguments from need-to-believe would have to be considered more convincing than pure logic.

Returning to turn 19, can we ground the claims regarding priority ordering in the discussion itself? It is clear from Ben's response that turn 19 has not been ineffective. Indeed, if we knew only what preceded turn 19, and Ben's response to it, without knowing the content of turn 19 itself, we might suppose that Paula had made a strong logical point. Therefore, Ben's response does not in itself appear to support my analysis of turn 19. It is in Judy's turn 21 — "Well if it's not p- worth putting in without penalties then I'ds- I would- say let's get penalties f(h)or it particularly if the feeling generally is (**) high enough" — that the analysis is supported. Judy ignores Ben's concession entirely. That is, whereas he, in turn 20, discovers a reason for including the charge (without penalties), she takes it as more or less settled that Ben's previous argument has been correct, that the charge is "not worth putting in without penalties".[16] She goes on to suggest adding penalties, even though Ben has already seemingly acquiesced to including the charge without penalties. Apparently, she has concluded that the argument is closed, that Paula has no way of refuting Ben's point. If Paula had had such a refutation at hand, she would have used it. By not using the first priority response, Paula allows the inference that she has no such response available. It is to be noted that Judy had not held this position from the beginning. Judy was one of the team that wrote the memo, and had never before suggested that this charge should have a penalty attached to it.[17]

The reader may have noticed that, in connection with Paula's turn 19 — "I have to believe that my work is meaningful" — and Ben's response thereto, there are certain obvious lines of discussion that I have avoided. The dramatic nature of turn 19 derives at least in part from Paula's sudden display of vulnerability. She appears to be appealing to Ben to back off his logic and not press his argument. This in turn raises issues about the kinds of relationship and identity work that is going on here, the interpersonal uses of logic within such a frame, etc. Paula might even be seen as threatening Ben that their relationship was at stake. Certainly, she is insisting that something important to her is at stake. In thinking about turn 19, I found myself repeatedly coming up with formulations based on identity, relationship, values, face, and such. The use of such concepts, however, seemed to lead into a kind of open-ended, intuitive, overly flexible analysis, only loosely connected to the data. These concepts are part of a modern commonsense vocabulary that must, because of the general everyday uses to which it is put, be quickly and easily applicable to a wide range of situations. I am certainly not denying the significance of emotional and "interpersonal" aspects in this interaction, but I do not know how to deal with them in a technical way, except perhaps by dressing up commonsense observations in psychological jargon. Still, Paula's turn 19 was clearly a pivotal moment in the discussion, and that fact required some recognition in the analysis. I have tried to achieve this using a structural and cultural rather than a psychological approach.

We have been able to set Paula's turn 19 into a larger analytical frame and to explain thereby the outcome of the discussion. More specifically, we have been able to understand how it is that Paula is taken to have lost the argument (which is not to say that she has been unsuccessful in the negotiation). Does it therefore follow that Ben has won, or even that he has achieved a compromise?

4. NEGOTIATION AND COMPROMISE

In connection with their consideration of the charge, there seem to be three possible positions: 1. Include the charge without penalties, i.e., let the memo stand as is. 2. Drop the charge. 3. Include the charge, but add penalties. Paula appears to favour (1), Ben (2). That is certainly the way each understands the other's position. (3) is offered by Mary and Judy and accepted by Ben and eventually, after some initial resistance, by Paula, as a "compromise". In what sense, we may ask, is (3) a compromise? In negotiation, a compromise might seem to have two characteristics. First, it is not identical to either party's stated initial position, and, second, it is somewhere "between" the parties' stated initial positions, that is, for each of them it represents an outcome that is preferable to what the other party initially offered. If an employee is demanding a raise of $100 and the employer is offering $50, then $75 is a compromise, whereas $25 is not. The point that I wish to make in regard to this matter is that it is not at all clear that the final outcome of this negotiation represents a compromise according to the second criterion. Or, to put it more accurately, its nature as a compromise is emergent from the actual course of events, rather than being apparent from the mere knowledge of the parties' initial positions. It is not at all clear that, if Paula and Ben had been asked to rate their preferences before the discussion began, they would each have made include-charge-with-penalty their second choice. In fact, when Ben "backs down" in turn 20, he does not offer charge-with-penalty as a compromise. This is all the more striking in that Mary has already suggested such a solution. Instead, he qualifies his own position in such a way as to yield to the outcome preferred by Paula.[18]

If Paula's initial position had been include-charge-with-penalty, then include-charge-without-penalty would have presented itself as an obvious compromise, that is, it would have been seeable as a compromise position simply from a knowledge of the participants' initial positions. Charge-without-penalty is, in one respect at least, "between" charge-with-penalty and drop-charge. We cannot, however, necessarily suppose that Ben would have made this "compromise" his second choice if Paula's initial position had been charge-with-penalty. Unlike a simple negotiation over money, the considerations here are multi-dimensional. Ben might feel that a charge without a penalty is in principle to be avoided, making charge-with-penalty his second choice. The point is that, even for this hypothetical situation, we have no way of knowing from their initial preferred outcomes what their second choices would have been.

Ben's position in turn 3 is to maximally weaken the charge by dropping it altogether. Paula's position moves up the strength-of-charge scale, by including the charge in the case but demanding no penalties. The strongest position, advocated by neither, is to include the charge and demand penalties. Since Paula is in a middle position, adding penalties might be her second choice, but then so also might dropping the charge. One would not suppose, though, merely from a statement of their most-preferred outcomes, that Ben would select include-charge-with-penalties as his second choice, that is, one would not suppose that he would go directly from the maximally weak outcome to the maximally strong. (On the other hand, as I pointed out in the last paragraph, it is quite possible that it would have been his second choice.) What makes charge-with-penalties a compromise position is not the nature of their initial positions but the progression of the negotiation.

I have already shown that Paula takes Ben's turn 3 as a suggestion to drop the charge rather than to add penalties, and I have argued that this interpretation is reasonable and perhaps even necessary. She accordingly shapes her reply to stress the importance of including the charge rather than the importance of not charging penalties. This, in turn, makes it appear that, for her, the addition of penalties would be preferable to the dropping of the charge. At least, she has committed herself strongly for including the charge, but has not made a strong argument against penalties.[19] What we need to see here is that her emphasis on preserving the charge, in contrast to a possible emphasis on not having penalties, does not necessarily indicate that she "really" holds the one as more important than the other. Rather, that emphasis follows from the nature of her utterance as a response to Ben's turn 3. The effect, though, is to leave her more committed on the one point than on the other, and to leave addition of penalties available as a "compromise".

But her argument has an obvious weak point, and Ben pounces on it. Instead of maintaining his three-point argument against the charge, or countering her argument as to the importance of the charge, he addresses himself to the matter of deterrence which she has raised. A charge without penalties will not deter. He wins this argument, in that Paula apparently has no way to refute it. He pursues a response relentlessly, until Paula in effect concedes by producing a response which, despite its cultural plausibility, is not first priority. Just as Paula's response in turn 15, arguing for the importance of the charge, has been shaped by Ben's turn 3, Ben's response to Paula's turn 15 is determined by an easy point of attack that she leaves open. The focus is now on deterrence, and to that there is an obvious solution. Thus, the argument as it develops leads almost inevitably to Mary's and Judy's suggestion to add penalties. This is the solution to the weak point that Ben has found in Paula's argument, a point whose importance has been emphasized by Ben's pursuit of a response. The proposed compromise may be acceptable to Paula, since she has focussed on the importance of including the charge, and to Ben, since he has stressed the importance of penalties in achieving deterrence. The other two of Ben's original points (that the charge does not support the rest of the case and that it may hold the case up) are lost, and any arguments that he may have disputing the significance of the charge go unexpressed.

If we wanted to credit Paula with unusual brilliance in negotiating, we might say that she had used a kind of logical judo to manoeuvre Ben into this stance. However, to judge from the talk that immediately follows Ben's acceptance of the "compromise", she is not, at least at first, satisfied with the idea of adding a penalty. She protests at first that there is no harm (and therefore no justification for a penalty), but then finds that there is harm (and therefore presumably accepts the notion of adding a penalty). Of course, at this point, she is thoroughly outnumbered, the three others having already accepted the idea of adding penalties. If Ben's original suggestion had been (understood as) "add a penalty" rather than "drop the charge", it is entirely conceivable that Paula would have constructed her reply as an argument against including a penalty and that the subsequent discussion would have gone in a very different direction. For one thing, add-a-penalty would not have been available as a compromise.

Let me try, briefly, to generalize from these circumstances. Say that P_t is the set of propositions that a person, A, would be willing to accept about a particular topic at some particular time (for example, the statements that Paula would be willing to accept regarding the illegally-asking-marital-status charge). Any utterance that A makes on the topic will be selected from P_t. B's prior utterance on the topic will influence A's selection of a proposition from P_t. (At the same time, B's utterance may be constitutive of P_t, in the sense that what B says may bring about a change in P_t. There is no pre-existing and stable standard of acceptabiliby.) When A states a particular proposition as true, A has made a commitment. Each commitment is an obstacle to some line of negotiation. One can push against the obstacle and perhaps overcome it, but other lines have now become easier to pursue. The more strongly and the more recently a commitment has been expressed, the more formidable the obstacle. On the other hand, expressed propositions can also influence further talk by presenting argumentative opportunities, as does Paula's reference to deterrence. When A's utterance, U, offers an opportunity, and B takes advantage of that opportunity, other aspects of U which B might otherwise have opposed may escape comment. This leaves open lines of possible negotiation and compromise which might otherwise have been closed. I will not pursue these matters further, except to note that the notions of commitment and opportunity might provide bases for a general interactive model of negotiation.

Finally, let us return to Ben's "Who cares" (in turn 3). Recall that he downgrades the provocativeness of this question-opinion to "Why would we care". Nonetheless, Paula is provoked and replies in a challenging manner. He has evoked from her not merely an argument but an expression of personal commitment — "I care". Her sense of personal commitment is expressed again, and elaborated, in turn 19 — "I have to believe that my work is meaningful". The decision, it seems, is based not only on reasons, but on a demonstration of caring by the participants. In an earlier paper (Bilmes 1981:269), also set in the Federal Trade Commission, I wrote:

> "The participants are all operating with the same set of relevant values.
> Presumably, if they share all the relevant information which they possess,
> they will, as rational beings, arrive at identical decisions. But the matter
> is far too complex for this presumption to hold. Consensus will not be
> reached in this way. Rather, the problem is to define individual positions
> and then to negotiate a decision. Participants may sway each other with
> rational-sounding arguments, but the individual decision processes cannot
> be made wholly public and uniform. In the end, the crucial questions are
> not "What do we know about the matter at hand?" and "What is a rational
> decision?", but rather "What is the position of each participant?" and
> "What decision can we agree to?".

In the light of the analysis presented in this chapter, we can see that it is not enough to know the position of each participant — we must also take into account the degree of demonstrated commitment to that position. And to ask what decision can be agreed to may be misleading if it is understood merely as a matter of determining each participant's "bottom line". To look at the matter this way leaves out of consideration the interactional contingencies that determine what an agreement might possibly look like.

NOTES

1. I am using a standard system of transcript notation (see Button, Drew, and Heritage 1986) with one elaboration. Rather than using empty parentheses for unintelligible (to the transcriber) speech, I have indicated the approximate duration of that speech with asterisks, one for each half second.

2. In understanding this piece of talk, the analyst works "backwards", from Paula's response to (her understanding of) the meaning of Ben's prior utterance: Paula stresses the importance of the charge rather than defending the absence of penalties. Therefore, she must have heard Ben as advocating that they drop the charge. In her response is an implicit interpretation of Ben's utterance.

3. This discussion, and the microanalysis of talk in general, sometimes relies on a presumed congruence between analyst's and reader's understanding of the language. The nature of linguistic competence is, for the most part, beyond the bounds of the conversation analyst. The presumption of congruence can at times become uncomfortable. In claiming that "who cares" is more provocative than "why would we care", I am at least approaching the limits of what can be asserted as a premise for rather than an object of the analysis. That is, I am not entirely certain that every competent member would have to hear this the way I do.

4. Conversationalists do not simply put jokes wherever there is an opportunity for humor. The occurrence of jokes is patterned by other factors. They are used, for instance, to relieve tense or embarrassing moments. Earlier in the discussion, we find this exchange:

Ben	Well- y'know- y' ya sąy that but I mean I if I were a counsel I could come back
	and say well (1) y'know we may have decided that she wouldn't qualify: on
	her own for seven hundred dollar: we may have been: thinking she may not
	she may not qualify on her own for seven hundred dollars but (1) ah w wd i-
	if she was married she may be able to get a cosigner: an' qualify for more.
Paula	An' you made that determination as soon as she asked as soon as you asked
	her name ⌈because that's (*) marital status
Ben	⌊As soon as I saw that she was a woman (I already decided ⌈ she) (*)
Judy	⌊ R- right
	yes (th(h)s) ((laughs))

Paula has found a flaw in Ben's argument. He replies with a joke which, in effect, concedes the very point that he was disputing.

5. I owe this latter observation to Charles Goodwin.

6. It should be noted that Ben's argument hinges on a cultural assumption about the bases for business decisions. It is assumed that businesses will not be influenced merely by being made aware that some practice is illegal, that is, by merely normative considerations. There must be a penalty. (See Bilmes 1985, Bilmes and Woodbury 1991, on normative versus economic approaches to consumer law enforcement.) This assumption is not challenged in the ensuing discussion.

7. I have deliberately refrained from placing analytically significant pauses on separate lines in the transcript. Although doing so would perhaps be heuristically useful in presenting the analysis, it would also tend to "stack the deck" in favor of the author and be an obstacle to those who might otherwise see alternate interpretations of the data. For somewhat similar reasons, I do not give sepa-

rate lines to between-turn pauses. This practice tends to leave the impression that such pauses are somehow different from within-turn pauses that are not given their own line, that a between-turn pause somehow calls for, and necessarily results in, speaker change, whereas a within turn pause does not. That a particular pause results in a new speaker taking the floor is a contigent matter — the original speaker might have begun to talk again. It might be more justifiable to give every pause that occurs after a transition-relevance point (Sacks, Schegloff, and Jefferson 1974) its own line. I have chosen instead to treat all pauses the same in the transcript.

8. Pomerantz, in her article "Pursuing a Response" (1984a), describes several techniques for eliciting responses to what one has said, including dealing with no response by changing one's position. Oddly, she does not mention the technique that Ben uses here, which is to demand a response by insistently reasserting his point. We cannot, I think, deal with this repetition as an attempt to clarify what he was saying (another technique mentioned by Pomerantz.)

9. For a relevant discussion of ignoring, see Goodwin and Goodwin (1990), especially pages 101-107.

10. This episode indicates the normative power of one of the conversational turn-taking rules proposed by Sacks, Schegloff and Jefferson (1974): "If the turn-so-far is so constructed as to involve the use of a 'current speaker selects next' technique, then the party so selected has rights, and is obliged, to take the next turn to speak, and no others have such rights or obligations, transfer occurring at that place" (704). (They may have made their point too powerfully — see Power and Martello 1986.) Ben's tactic is thus something more than an exercise of his authority as Mary's organizational superior. It is grounded in interactional norms for speaking.

11. Graduate student responses on this exercise tended to be more diverse and idiosyncratic and more based on purely cognitive and logical criteria. Frequently, they seemed to be talking about what they had to believe on the evidence (e.g., "I have to believe that I will die someday") rather than what they needed to believe to maintain a sense of well-being. Their answers were not necessarily unrealistic in the sense that no one would actually say such a thing, but they were clearly offered in a very different spirit from Paula's "I have to believe that my work is meaningful".

12. This is an adaptation and simplification of Labov (1972: 300).

13. An observation on the power of such "language games": I overheard a discussion in which academic A made an analytical point. Academic B offered a contrasting anaysis. When A began to defend his point, B said, "I'm not going to argue with you." A replied, "You *have* to argue," and B did. It is A's reply that is of interest here, in that it indicates that they were playing a language game with known rules.

14. I am not insisting that she in fact did not have a refutation at hand. Perhaps she deliberately chose this mode of response when others were available to her — she does, after all, get Ben to back down. But, in doing so, she allows the inference that she cannot refute Ben's point.

15. It could be argued (with some credibility, I think) that Paula's turn 19 was a response not only to Ben's most recent point but to what she perceived as his generally obstructive position. This would not affect the point that logical refutation is the first priority response. It is also relevant that this was not at all the usual way that Paula, or any of the other (male or female) attorneys in the Division, argued. In this sense, Paula's turn 19 was very clearly "deviant".

It could also be argued that gender differences are relevant to this exchange — men's ways of speaking versus women's ways of speaking. This could be so even though Paula did not habitually use this style of argument. But this does not negate the fact that the lawyerly language game of logic provided a frame for understanding the implications of her utterance.

16. There is one sense in which it might be argued that she has not entirely ignored Ben's concession. The fact that he has shown himself willing to modify his stance may encourage her in offering her alternative. (I owe this observation to Alan Firth.)

17. It has been suggested to me that Judy, in turn 21, is merely mediating the disagreement by suggesting a compromise. Paula would get something — the charge would be included in the case — and Ben would get something — penalties would be attached to the charge. It might be noted, though, that Ben has not actually suggested that penalties be added, and, judging from his turn 20, this is not what he was aiming at. More importantly, if Judy were merely offering a compromise, she could have done so without conceding Ben's point. She might have said something on the order of "How about if we include the charge but attach penalties to it?", which is similar to what Mary said in turn 17. There was no need for her to concede that the charge is not worth putting in without penalties.

18. We might go further and ask if this, in the end, actually represents a compromise in the view of the participants. They do not actually call it a compromise. It gives Paula a part of what she wants and at the same time concedes the power of Ben's point, so, in terms of the dynamic of the argument, if not of their initial positions, it is a compromise. Nevertheless, I can find no way to demonstrate from the evidence of the discussion that the participants understood the Mary/Judy proposal to be a compromise, although I feel confident that they would agree that that is what it was.

19. In the exchange under examination, she makes no argument at all against penalties, but earlier in the discussion she indicated a preference for no penalties.

CHAPTER 4

AGENDAS AND ARRANGEMENTS: EVERYDAY NEGOTIATIONS IN MEETINGS

DEIRDRE BODEN

1. INTRODUCTION

Most negotiation, in business, politics and even love, is first and foremost a talk-based activity. It may be anticipated by documents, speeded by telex or fax, and summarized in bound reports or wedding rings, but the *process* of negotiation is a talk-based and thereby inherently communicative and linguistic process. This chapter explores the fine-grained structure of negotiation in everyday business meetings. Using conversational data recorded in a variety of organizations, internal meetings within firms are used as a grounded way of examining the 'blow by blow' enactment of routine interdepartmental and interorganizational arrangements. In a practised and precise manner, achieved through the turn-by-turn structure of the meeting, social actors stake out positions and provide accounts in such a way as to mediate the demands of others. Earlier meetings, past accommodations, and present contingencies merge in the interactional intensity of face-to-face exchange. In the process, everyday accounts and arrangements provide a fine interactional grid through which work colleagues from different departments and firms filter their own organizational agendas.

Language-in-action thus provides a moving image of the essential *structuring* of social life. A negotiation process is sedimented into larger and larger layers of interconnected, multiplex elements that form the apparently solid conditions of next actions for actors, and those 'outcomes' of negotiations social scientists tend to study.

Negotiations can thereby be viewed as *sequentially* structured rather as determined by relations of power, influence or overarching strategy. The process is temporally ordered; as such, any starting position, however strong or calculated, is mediated by the interactional elements of talk as it unfolds.

The 'unfolding' quality of negotiation is the focus of this chapter. But an important caveat is in order. Ethnomethodologists have long insisted on the 'accomplished' rather than 'negotiated' nature of social order. This emphasis is grounded in an ethnomethodological 'indifference' to labels, which is to say an avoidance of *a priori* assumptions about the specific nature of social organization. To propose that certain activities constitute 'negotiation', or 'bargaining', or 'conflict resolution' entails clear assumptions about the goals, intentions and even presuppositions of the social actors involved (e.g. Putnam and Jones 1982). They, in turn, are assumed to adopt strategies, follow gameplans, engage in manoeuvres, score points, or fall into traps as they pursue these goals or follow through on their intentions. For the ethnomethodologist, such otherwise reasonable descriptions of behaviour contain within them a core research problem, namely that, in providing these social science definitions, the labelling process may actually mask far more illuminating and accurate descriptions of human conduct. Moreover, in a rush to explain 'why' actions may be taken, the fine details of 'how' they are organized slips from view. In the process, the essential phenomenon of interest may be lost. Negotiation researchers recognize the interactional nature of the activity (e.g. Donohue 1981, Donohue, Deitz and Stahle 1983), but what is recommended here is a further step: to bracket out assumptions about 'negotiation' in the interests of observing *how* interaction constitutes the context and conditions of these basic exchanges.

2. EVERYDAY MEETINGS IN ORGANIZATIONS

In the analysis that follows, I draw on a larger study (Boden 1994) of everyday talk in a variety of organizational settings. These are not formal or official settings explicitly labelled as 'negotiation'. The original research addressed a very general ethnomethodological interest in how people get work done in organizations and the ways in which talk structures these essential everyday activities, what I have called the *business of talk*. People in such everyday work settings talk all day, every day, and, in many consequential ways, talk *is* the work (see Gronn 1983, 1985). Much of the talk is on telephone calls and in meetings, although it is through corridor chat, quick lunches, and hanging out in office doorways that the essential flux of information and mood is conveyed. Since rapid transfer and absorption of information are critical to the success of modern organizations, talk is an essential mode and medium through which the goals, decisions and overall direction of any organization are achieved. Formal negotiation may indeed take place in sales encounters, union bargaining sessions, boardroom battles, legal disputes and so on, but the business of the day is conducted *and* resolved through ordinary, everyday talk (e.g. Firth 1994).

For the current discussion, meetings in two hospitals, a travel agency, a local TV station and a department within a university administration will be used to explicate some of the interactional devices through which organizational actors pursue a variety of agendas. As these local agendas are fitted together and 'meshed' with those of others, often distant from the immediate interactional setting, they also significantly sustain recursive activities that constitute the organization across time and space. The collaborative yet divergent goals of different teams, departments and firms are achieved in an interactional dance whose steps and stages are paced across many meetings and telephone calls, rather than in a single or formal negotiation. This entails, in turn, flexibility, cooperation and accommodation which, layer upon layer, smooth the way to larger goals. It also involves organizational actors in an elaborate spatio-temporal network that itself must be constructed, connected, arranged and rearranged.

When, for instance, a group of hospital administrators were planning cost-cutting strategies in a large urban research facility, their own schedules had to be carefully meshed to fit into a stream of meetings with physicians and hospital staff:

Extract 1 : Hospital Meeting

```
1     Lucy      Now! y'kno:w Ba:rb'ra's gonna be (0.2) g- go::ne
2               (0.8)
3               for the week a:fter next?
4     Mary      Oka::y ┌ So you ┐
5     Lucy             └ No::w- ┘
6               (0.4)
7     Mary      The last week in Ju:ne, firs' week in July type
8               o::f=
9     Barbara   =Yeah=
10    Mary      =th ┌ i::ng? ┐
11    Barbara       └ Yeah, ┘ overlap.
12    Mary      Over ┌ la:p? ┐
13    Barbara        └ Yeah ┘. From Ju:ne twenny-seventh to July
14               (.) fifth.
15    Lucy      So, ┌ now- ┐
16    Mary          └ May ┘ be thissiz somethin' we can get done
17         →     ne::xt week?
```

```
18    Barbara   I thi::ink so (.) ⌈ yeah.⌉
19    Lucy                       ⌊ Sure ⌋ we ⌈ ca:n,      ⌉
20    Mary                                 ⌊ W'd be ⌋ goo::d
21    Lucy      Just because we're- w- I'm going to uhm- u::h-
22              going away (.) the next two weeks=
23    Barbara   =Okay
24    Lucy      And the first meeting is coming- coming up quickly ...
              ((continues))
```

Scheduling arrangements are routinely accomplished as ways of both facilitating or shaping later meetings, those meetings being further occasions on which diverse organizational agendas can be pursued, merged, changed or subverted. Here, a closely collaborative strip of talk achieves the task of exchanging information and identifying a workable timetable. Lucy's opening (Now!) marks a subtle topic transition from materials being reported by Barbara to series of similar meetings scheduled for August. These fiscal specialists need to have informal meetings to devise specific cost-cutting ideas based on a recent analysis of hospital statistics and an ongoing cost analysis being conducted by Barbara's department. Timing and positioning are critical in all organizational activities, none less than when costs are to be cut in favourite areas and on favoured turfs. Their own meetings must be slipped in ahead of the August gatherings just so that they can present a united and persuasive front to the physicians and nursing staff who will otherwise resist changes in their own practices. For this delicate reason, Mary hopes the necessary work can be fitted into their shared schedules "next week" (line 17), before Barbara's July 4th week of holiday. Their own discussions lay down the conditions of later more formal 'negotiations' of considerable importance to the hospital.

Meetings provide an essential environment in which information can be transmitted and, in many organizations, critically updated (Boden 1994). While telephone calls provide for constant mini-updates, meetings are necessary to get key personnel all looking at the same problem at the same time. The simultaneity is important to decision-making and also to the fine-grained process of negotiating stages of a project or agreement. Organizational actors invest a great deal of time and energy ensuring the 'right people' see each other at the 'right time', and this issue of synchronicity has recently begun to interest major theorists and researchers of management and organizational structure (e.g. March 1988, Stinchcombe 1990). Rapidly changing external conditions mean that many organizations need to be quite effective in keeping different units in touch and in tune with each other.

In another cost-cutting discussion, at another hospital, we can see this continuous updating of both understanding and information in action. Here, the Chief of Physicians (Hal) is presenting recent cost-related interventions his staff have made on routine laboratory tests to Paul, from the hospital's Finance Department. At issue is a discussion of costs versus revenue:

Extract 2 : Hospital/2 Finance Meeting

1	Hal	... Y- <u>your</u> bu:dget is based on <u>charges</u>, I mean you take a look at
2		<u>rev</u>enues
3	Paul	Hmhmm
4	Hal	And when revenues <u>fa:ll</u>? (0.5) you make ad<u>just</u>ments for it. You
5		don't ma:ke adjustments for <u>co::sts</u> first. (0.6) You know what
6		I mean- you don't say=
7	Paul	=(I do.)
8	Hal	NO, no, no, but- but- let me jus' say that if- that if <u>you:</u> (0.7) I
9		mean if you say yer ex<u>pe::nses::</u>
10		(1.0)
11	Paul	average out
12	Hal	A <u>hundred</u> dollars inna <u>lab</u>'ratory and you're getting a
13		<u>hun</u>dred an' ten dollars in <u>rev</u>enue, arright?
14	Paul	Hmhmm.
15	Hal	And revenues fall to a hundred an'five do:llars- you don't say:
16		We::ll, c- costs <u>really</u> weren't a hundred, I mean- let's readjust it
17		down t'<u>real</u> dollars (0.3) <u>you</u> don't do <u>tha:t</u>. You say <u>look</u> we're
18		living onna revenue- onna <u>rev</u>enue base. Bud gets are <u>built</u>=
19	Paul	Mm,
20	Hal	=up that way, an' <u>that's</u> what <u>we</u>'ve do:ne. <u>So</u>, ra:ther than
21		saying: well it's no s::ense in takin' out a BVRL because it only
22		co:sts a <u>nickel</u>
23		(0.7)
24		<u>We</u> say there's <u>sti:ll</u> a sense taking it out because we're cha:<u>rg</u>ing
25		(.) five dollars for it. And in the- in the <u>rev</u>enue discussion (.)
26		twenny thousan' versus <u>fif</u>teen thousand?
27	Paul	(Hmhmm)
28	Hal	It <u>means</u> so:mething to the doctor to change his behavior. (0.8)
29		Arright?
30	Paul	Hmhmm.
31	Hal	Now it <u>ma:y</u> not mean as much to <u>you</u> in terms of a <u>c</u>ost
32		function, but in <u>fa:ct</u> (.) the <u>lab</u>'ratory has built their <u>BUDGET</u>!

```
33          up on revenue? not on cost. (0.4) Arright?
34  Paul    Well, that's not exactly- that's not really true: (.) though, because
35          we- we have looked- y'know we've done efficiency studies t'see
36          ho:w (.) many hou:rs it takes to run some of these te ⌈ :sts ⌉
37  Hal                                                           ⌊ No- ⌋
38          I know ⌈ that ⌉
39  Paul            ⌊ So  ⌋ that's- tha:t's the way that we bu:dget
40          ⌈ (for various percentages 'n tha:t) ⌉
41  Hal     ⌊ But- but- you still- but you- look ⌋ look- and again WE: use a
42          cost-of-charge (0.2) figure (0.2) for the laboratory of- let's say
43          eight point se:ven (0.8) when we ta:ke ou:t a BVRL (0.3) we
44          don' kno:w whether that's a point ni::ne or a point o:ne
45          (0.9)
46          Arright, we don't go: into tha::t detail ...
            ((continues))
```

Here too hospital adminstrators in several departments are engaged in creating an environment in which doctors can be persuaded to eliminate unnecessary costs — in this case, unneeded laboratory tests. But the issue, at this stage, is one of examining and contrasting two different approaches to calculating budgets and, more centrally, of resolving *ways of thinking* about conventional categories such as costs and revenue. *Built in* to this discussion are important ideological differences between finance-driven analysis and an analysis based on the day-to-day practices of the hospital staff and departments. The 'negotiation' is thus internal yet, in these days of cost-constraints on all manner of health care systems, significantly related to huge external pressures *and* consequences. *How* local actors instantiate these very real conditions of action will have equally real longterm consequences far beyond this particular moment in this particular hospital.

In this extract, Hal, a doctor by training and Chief of Physicians, is attempting to persuade Paul, an accountant responsible for longrange fiscal planning, of recent work in calculating hospital costs in ways that make sense to doctors. Their discussion is congenial and collaborative as may be seen for the quick, close-ordered fitting of turns, lack of long pauses or intrusive overlap, and general efforts at comprehension and cooperation located at the level of talk. Hal uses this brisk exchange to produce a series of contrastive formulations of accounting practices interactionally designed to produce alignment on the costs/revenue issue. In this extract, taken from well into his persuasive discussion, he is in the middle of explaining how, by elimination of a cheap lab test, even a small reduction in costs can be used to show doctors ways of reducing costs in general. *His* agenda, ultimately, is related to the needs and performance of physicians. The local logic of this strategy is embedded in his sequential presentation of the idea. In lines 4-6 he is outlining the finance department's revenue-based approach. "You know what I mean" he invites Paul, who echoes softly "I do" in yet another contrastive with "you don't say" (lines 5-7). Hal has framed his argument several minutes earlier in the meeting with: "The problem of course in dealing with fi:nance people is you turn the charge-cost argument arou:nd all the time" (not shown here). In our extract, he is expanding this point, stage by stage, iteratively constructing his argument. This, as we shall see below, is an essential procedural strategy in the production of persuasion and thus of the sequential accomplishment of negotiation.

Notice several recurrent verbal ploys used by Hal to draw Paul into his logic. He produces multiple formulations and reformulations, 'braced' together with such conversational objects as "I mean" (e.g. lines 1, 6, 8 and 16) and contrasts these position statements with other possible 'meanings':

Extract 2a : partial repeat

28	Hal	→	It <u>means</u> so:mething to the doctor to change his behavior. (0.8)
29			Arright?
30	Paul		Hmhmm.
31	Hal	→	Now it <u>ma:y</u> not mean as much to <u>you</u> in terms of a <u>c</u>ost
32			function, but in <u>fa:ct</u> ...

Intersubjectivity is an essentially sequential phenomenon. It involves the continuous updating stressed by the ethnomethodologists. It takes constant interactional work in a manner revealed by conversation analysts. That work, in turn, constitutes the organization as a practical and workable place in which doctors, accountants and administrators make many meanings merge. Cutting out a single lab test may not make a great deal of sense in the longrange agendas of the finance department but, Hal is suggesting, if it helps doctors to change *their* understandings and thus behavior, then multiple agendas can be made to merge and quite disparate goals can seem as one.

Hal trades on the divergent organizational agendas of hospital staff to build a kind of conversational consensus. He uses contrasts in personal pronouns to achieve an effective 'we're all in this together' stance:

Example 2b : partial repeat

15-20	Hal	you don't say:
		you don't do *tha:t*
		You say
		... an' *that's* what *we*'ve do:ne.

He uses these formulations to construct an imaginary dialogue in the finance department, engaging directly in an enactment of the 'reciprocity of perspectives' underlined by Schutz and later by Garfinkel. He constructs first the fiscal specialist's version (lines 15-20) and contrasts this with the approach used by his own team (lines 20-25). In a deft verbal dance, he makes them seem the same. This *contrastive* yet *cumulative* subtext of persuasion is what negotiation is all about. It is built into the sequential structure of talk *as* action.

Hal couples these conversational devices with another utterly routine procedure of eliciting concurrence by 'tagging' its solicitation at the end of utterances (e.g. "arright?" at lines 13, 29, 33) or by distinctly interrogative contours (e.g. line 26). His presentation of these ideas amounts to a very long spate of talk in conversational terms, although it is not untypical of what I have elsewhere termed 'position statements' in meetings (Boden 1994, cf. Schegloff 1982:77). The sort of close-fitted monitoring responses noted by conversation analysts in ordinary conversation are often suppressed in meetings. Here, however, given the small size of the meeting, Hal elicits quite routine responses from Paul (lines 3, 14, 19, 27, 30). When Paul finally responds to this persuasive flow, his protest is mild and mainly a clarification and amplification of other angles on the same problem.

These two interactants are largely consensual in their 'negotiation'. They work together regularly and know each other's practices (e.g. line 38), yet they must also align their quite different organizational agendas along shared tracks. Their verbal synchronicity embodies and enacts the accommodation necessary to get things done. Through their formulations and reformulations, they transform the abstract goals of the organization into quite practical local arrangements.

3. CONSTITUTING CONFLICT AND CONSENSUS

Viewed through the close-up lense of conversation analysis, interaction thus reveals the fine structure of everyday negotiation. Across the busy surface of a meeting, and more significantly, often across numerous meetings which themselves form sequential structures of interaction, organizational goals and agendas are surfaced, submerged and, occasionally, agreed and advanced. More often, they are side-tracked, subsumed, and transformed into a 'negotiated' compromise. If we now look at a more conflictual meeting, we can see just how several further sequential elements of conversational structure can serve instead to accomplish distance and dissent among interactants.

In the next extracts, sections of a TV station production meeting are presented. It is one of a series of meetings about commercial sponsorship of a local show. The producer of the show under discussion is Ken and Val is the station production manager;

other meeting participants are not involved in the short extracts used here. The meeting has barely begun and Val has just handed out copies of a budget breakdown to everyone present. Ken makes a provocative opening position statement:

Extract 3 : TV Station Production Meeting
(Simplified Transcript)

```
1    Ken      .h: Y'know Valerie I'm wo:rking at the slight disadva:ntage of having?
2             .h:: o:nly our la::st of twenny-nine diff'rent bu:dgets t' look a:t here,
3    Val      I::: had this one do::ne t'da::y?
4       →     (0.6)
5    Ken      Dated u:::h Ma:rch thuh (.) twenty:: (.) se::cond? ⌈This one i:::s-   ⌉
6    Val                                                        ⌊This one an'thee ⌋
7             other one that we ha:d? this one i:s si::mply (0.1) u:::h- a fully loa:ded
8             budget
9       →     (1.5)
10   Ken      Ye:s, that's the one I've no:t see:n ⌈before   ⌉
11   Val                                          ⌊h:::::  ⌋ We:ll, I jus' haddit
12            do:ne t'da:y?
13      →     (7.6)
14   Ken      O:kay thissiz ba:sic'lly the sa:me as the- as thuh Ma:rch (0.4)
15            twenty-second plu:::s? (.) some wi:ld numbers added at the bo::ttom,
16      →     (2.1)
17   Val      No:: edito::rial comment plea::se
```

We can immediately note a certain tension in this interaction. Framed by Ken with some sarcasm, Val's new budget breakdown provides a first staging post for the conflict to follow. Invoking combative personal pronouns (*I'm/I:::*, lines 1 and 3), Ken and Val align themselves on *opposite* sides of this first phase of negotiation. Through these different alignments, they both establish and embody their differing work identities and the discourse identities that will shape this meeting (cf. Maynard 1984:56). There is no attempt here, or later in the meeting, to merge "I" into "we" or to make "you" and "us" into a practical whole. More significantly, the pauses at lines 4, 9, 13, 16 underline a distinct sense of discord for member and analyst alike. Val responds to Ken's claim of being at a "slight disadvantage" with the offer that she has just had the budget done "today" (line 3), a claim that is not immediately taken up by Ken. Since pauses can mark the initiation of disagreement (Pomerantz 1984b, Sacks 1987), Ken's next turn is notable, as are the growing pauses in the next turns, and the pattern of inter-turn silences throughout much of the meeting (see Extract 4 below).

Val proposes that the current budget is the same as an earlier budget of March

22nd, but is simply fully loaded. This claim is met with a longer pause (line 9) and a recycled claim by Ken of not having seen it before, anticipated in overlap with Val's reiterated formulation of line 3 to the effect that this particular version had been done "today" (line 12). A considerable silence of 7.6 seconds ensues, after which Ken acknowledges the congruence of the two budgets which, he suggests, differ in that the current one has "some wi:ld numbers added at the bo::ttom". This contentious assessment produces another pause from Val (line 16), signalling incipient disagreement at the very least.

After the arrival of another meeting member (not shown here), Val attempts to restart the meeting on a different footing:

Example 4 : TV Station Production Meeting

```
20    Val    No:w? Didju thi::nk anymo:::re? (0.8) u:h Ke:nneth?, (0.4) o:n
21           thuh po:ssibility of redu:cing the (.) produ:ction hours,
22           (1.3)
23    Ken    Tch. I thou:ght?, that I should co::me to this mee:ting=and hea::r?
24           a::ll thuh good (.) idea::s that're gonna be discu::ssed and then
25           I'll go away an' thi::nk about a:ll so:rts? of thi:ngs
26           (0.3)
27           .h u::hm ((khn-khn)) Do I unnersta:n' that we're mee:ting here
28           ba::sically to fi:nd out if we've got a via:ble pro;ject? (.) that we
29           can se:ll?
30           (0.8)
31    Val    U:h we:'⌈ re  mee:ting he:re b a : : s? i c ⌉ ally becau::se
32    Ken          ⌊ Izzat thuh purpose'v this meeting? ⌋
33    Val    =you: had que:stions that I wanted to be sur:e you were
34           sa: ⌈ tisfied ⌉
35    Ken        ⌊ No: I h ⌋ ave no:: questions at a:ll? (0.2) U::hm- d- all- all my
36           questions are a:nswered (.) ri:ght he:re?
```

An apparently neutral enquiry, about whether Ken has considered reducing production hours, launches Val into another controversy. Far from encouraging the sort of collegial alignment we have seen in the hospital meetings above, Val's "Now + restart" produces another noteworthy pause from Ken. Selectively echoing only Val's initial formulation: "didju thi::nk anymo:::re?" (line 20), Ken says he "thought" he should come and listen and then go away and "think" about all sorts of things. Not a felicitous exchange, but consistent with the initial combative framing of the meeting. Ken then ignores Val's topic of production hours and offers his own formulation of the reason for this meeting. According to Ken the meeting is about the salesworthiness of his "viable" production.

After her own pause, Val now uses *Ken's* own phrasing as a verbal springboard. She builds off *his* phrase that "we're mee:ting here ba::sically ..." to offer *her* version, one limited simply to answering Ken's questions (lines 31-34). The reason for the meeting itself now becomes a matter of debate, as does a rather differential distribution of knowledge. Ken however counter-claims all his questions are answered by the budget he was just critiquing (lines 35-36), and after a brief side-sequence, he expands on this theme. Questions about different budgets become intertwined with questions about questions (and denials thereof):

Example 5 : TV Station Production Meeting continued

		((background talk))
43	Ken	U:::hm-
44		(3.2)
45		I- I don't pe:rson'lly have any grea:t questions cuz I thought
46		we'd pre::tty well reso::lved th'm with tha:t bu:dget dated March
47		the (.) twenty:: (0.2) se::cond? now you're sa:ying that we have a
48		ne::w ve:rsion he::re? (0.8) that I guess is dated toda:: ⌐ :y?⌐
49	Val	⌊ No⌋ ::
50		Ke::nneth it is no::t a new bu:dget, it is si::mply? (0.5) thuh
51		ve::ry sa:me bu:dget, with (.) those (.) fi:gures which should have
52		been appropriately a:dded (0.7) the o:verhead an'ma:nagement
53		(1.7)
54		Which i:z what e::nny (0.7) o:f ou:r bu:::dgets (0.6) should entai:l
55		(3.1)
56	Ken	We::ll I-
57		(1.0)
58		With respect it's the fi:rst time I've heard it but oka:::y?
59		(1.0)
60		U::hm
61		(1.7)
62	Val	Now the fa:ct that I had to::ld you tha:t- that I wou:ld nego:tiate
63		ou:t of those two factors,
64	Ken	Hm::hmm::?=
65	Val	=is something that you: and I had sha:::red?
66		(1.2)
67		That does not mean that the bu:dget (.) as it is to be: pre:se::nted
68		(0.8) would no:t ha:ve to ca::rry (0.1) those fa:ctors innit,
69		(0.7)
70		Now, ho:pefully ...

Notice again the long pauses between turns. Even the intra-turn pauses are potentially disruptive as they mark potential turn-transition options not taken up by the other speaker (e.g. lines 52 and 53). At line 56, Ken's "We::ll I- (1.0) With respect it's the fi:rst time I've *heard* it but oka:::y? (1.0) U::hm (1.7)" projects a marked disagreement. These interactants are operating in quite a different conversational environment than that invoked by Hal and Paul, above. The differences, for Val and Ken, are also located at the *sequential* and *structural* level of talk, which is to say that the 'infrastructure of interaction' provides the basis on which they construct their mutual hostilities (cf. Schegloff 1992:1338).

4. FRAMING NEGOTIATION

Negotiation is thus not simply an interactional matter, in some general sense, but is constituted in and through the structure of talk itself. By bracketing out assumptions about 'negotiation', we can begin to see the fine structural elements out of which it is constructed. We see, as noted at the outset, *how* social actors create talk-based environments of both consensus and conflict. We can see especially that the sequential flow of talk carries along with it all manner of interactional and organizational agendas which are, in their turn, shaped and reshaped through the talk itself.

A further example will explicate this point. We have seen that organizational agendas recur as matters of agreement and disagreement, consensus and conflict, in meetings. In the hospital meeting between Hal and Paul, views on costs versus revenue are seen to merge and creatively construct a shared view of the problem at hand. In the case of Val and Ken, the budget of March 22nd and questions about it become matters of considerable contention. These claims cannot fully be pursued here, of course, since the presentation and analysis of data of this kind is space-intensive. I wish simply to sketch the possibilities of tracking organizational agendas and accommodations as a means of tracing an alternative approach to understanding the basic organization of negotiation.

In another meeting, this one taken from a series of meetings in a university administration, budgets are also being debated. This meeting is part of a three-department attempt to solve a number of outstanding and pressing problems in the administration of graduate student funding. Present at the meeting are the representatives of the graduate school, the office of financial aids, and the Provost's office. In the segments presented here, we have the graduate dean (Dean) and the head of financial aids (Matt). My purpose here is not to analyze the meeting as a whole (see full discussion in Boden 1994), but to offer a more fine-grained consideration of the process of persuasion as a basic constitiuent of negotiation. The recurring theme of this particular meeting is the Dean's desire to change certain long-standing procedures in funding particular categories of graduate applicants. Throughout the meeting, he characterizes these complex activities as "shenanigans", as in this early formulation of the problem taken from several minutes into the meeting:

Extract 5 : Fellowship Meeting

```
31   Dean   ... An'- and 'A:Lways (.) fa:ced with thi:s:: (0.7) e:ndless (0.2)
32          problem .h:: a:n'- (0.6) try:- try:ing to look at o::ther wa:ys we
33          c'n achieve thee:- thuh thi:ng we're a::hfter which i:z (0.8) to:
34          ei:ther find a no:  ┌ ther so  ┐ urce'o mo:ney
35   (?)                       └ ((sniff)) ┘
36                 (1.1)
37   Dean   For ca:mpus fellowships? (0.8) so that we
38   →      do::n't ha:ve to engage in this shena:nigans
```

In framing a set of budgeting and accounting practices for graduate fellowships as "shenanigans", the Dean *typifies* what he calls an "endless problem" (lines 31-32), one he has been trying to solve in simpler ways. This framing, as in Maynard's (1984) study of plea-bargaining lawyers, consequentially shapes the unfolding interaction. Many minutes later, the Dean summarizes the position and reformulates the goal as one of removing barriers:

Extract 6 : Fellowship Meeting continued

```
167   Dean   In other words .h:: I'm sa::ying (0.5) what we do: is r'mo::ve
168          thuh barriers which create a S::Y:S:t'm (0.4) which has it's o::wn
169          inte:rnal inflexibilitie:s
170                 (0.6)
171   Matt   Y're ma:king uh ma::jor assumption. Lemme take you up on that
172          (          ) (It's my- it's my jo::b)
173                 (0.7)
174   Dean   No:, it's not your job, YOUR ┌ job is ┐ to
175   Matt                               └ U::hm  ┘
176   Dean   .h li:ssen
177   Dean   ┌ an' tuh   heh (h)  h e h (h) h e h ┐ an'(h)t'do
178   Matt   └ huh-huh ┌ HAH-HAH-HAH-hah-hah-hah  ┘
179   Jean            └ Heh-heh-heh-HEH-(h)-HEH-┘ heh
180   Dean   eggZA:CTly as I s ┌ :a:y      ┐
181   Matt                     └ WRO: ┘ NG! WRONG.
182   Dean   Heh-heh .h:
```

```
183   Matt   Le(h)'s- le- lemme make an assumption (0.5) that I::- I have uh
184          te::ndency t'do someti:mes is that the financial nee::d pro::cess
185          with a:ll it's wa::rts 'n- a::nd u::h
186          (1.2)
187          a::nd pro::blems ...
             ((continues))
```

Here the Dean suggests removing interdepartmental barriers to his own scheme (lines 167-168). After a brief pause, Matt takes him up on that. The mood is however congenial, the teasing and laughter collaborative. After several attempts to offer the view from the financial aids department, the Dean recycles his theme of the time-consuming and recursive nature of these "shenanigans":

Extract 6: Fellowship Meeting continued

```
356   Dean        An' le:t's crea:te some ge:nuine? merit ba:sed money (0.7) that
357               I don' hafta go:: (.) ca:p-in-ha::nd? .h: an' enga::ge in this::
358        →      she:na::nig'ns year a:hfter year ahfter year (ahfter year). Now
359               you'll get what I relea: ┌ se?        ┐
360   (?)                                  └ Khn ┘ khn=
361   Dean        =You'll get ev'ry pe:nny? of it becuz it's nee:d ba:sed what
362               I'm presently taking fro::m you? (0.5) is nee:d ba:sed mo:ney?
363               (1.2)
364               So 's: fa:r's you::r conce:rned it's uh wa:::sh, .h: now.h
365               getting addi:tional money is your o:th- iz your o:wn pro:blem
366               (0.2) ri::ght?
367               (1.6)
368               Getting addi:tional money is: something thet you're en ┌ ti:tled t- ┐
369   Matt                                                               └ Fr'm this- ┘
370               from this ne:w poo:l?=
371   Dean        =From the new poo::ls is- is something thet you: (0.2) ahre
372               enti:tled t'try: an'do::, o:ka::y? B'a:ll I'm saying i:z .h: le:t's
373               clear thuh wa:y so that I: get what I nee::d in thuh fi:::rst
374               instance b'cuz tha::t- look, let's put it thi:s way
375               (1.1)
376               E:nny? money that I get
377               (1.2)
378               relea:ses
379               (1.3)
380               Automa:tically what I'm pre::s'ntly 'm taking awa::y from you
381               (0.3) back to you so you gai:n somethi:ng
```

The meeting has been involved in an elaborate discussion of "pots" and "pools" of money which have been offered by the Dean as possible solutions to the problem he has identified. He now effectively offers some of the riches of these "new pools" (lines 371-372) to Matt, or, more accurately, he shows how by pursuing his own agenda he can accommodate the needs of the financial aids director. Having argued, in a highly sequential and iterative way toward this solution, the Dean now spells it out. He sums up his position in a routine reformulation. It will be useful to look at this *segmentally* constructed slice of persuasion in some detail (here with simplified transcription). To Matt's clarification request that he is talking about the "new pool", the Dean replies in the affirmative (lines 369-370):

clarification/ correction	From the new pools
self-retrieval	is- is something that <u>you</u> are entitled to try and do
agreement solicitation	Okay?
Reformulation 1	But all I'm saying is <u>let's</u> clear the way so that I <u>get</u> what I need in the <u>first</u> <u>in</u>stance because <u>that</u>
Reformulation 2	Look, let's put it this way
Pause	(1.1)
Proposal Stage 1	Any money that <u>I</u> get
Pause	(1.2)
Proposal Stage 2	releases
Pause	(1.3)
Proposal Stage 3a	automatically
Stage 3b	what I am presently taking away from you
Pause	(0.3)
Stage 3c	back to you
Stage 3d	so you <u>gain</u> something

(arrows labelled a, b, c)

Persuasion is a sequentially organized phenomenon. Here, our concern is with the *structure* of the sequence rather than on the semantic load it carries. First, the Dean responds to a clarification request, in the appropriate next slot for such a response and in a relevant turn shape, that is by 'echoing' the contours of Matt's turn. He also uses this first turn component to initiate his summary statement, by shifting stepwise from Matt's "this new pool" to "the new pools". He then retrieves his own overlapped and interrupted earlier turn, this time recycling it with greater emphasis (*you*), and tags an "okay?" on this claim of Matt's entitlement, soliciting agreement. The Dean then projects a reformulation yet again, breaks off, and recommences. Reformulation 2 is, however, distinctly different from its predecessor. That is, he is not just putting it another way in the sense of *any* other way, but is significantly shifting the interactional footing using a segmented series of steps. At the same time, he uses this measured announcement to move quite deftly from a self-serving stance of getting what he needs first to a version that converts benefits to him into considerable and trouble-free ("automatically") advantages to Matt's department. Slowing down his delivery to a deliberate rate, he spells out the deal in verbal increments. We are observing the structuring process of negotiation in action.

This turn is also structured by the Dean as a nested set of contrastive claims. The first (bracket [a]) is simple: I gain/you gain. The second (bracket [b]) is more detailed: any(thing) I get/you gain something. The third (bracket [c]) is directly and adjacently contrastive: away from you/back to you. In finely segmental units, negotiation is constituted as a practical and local matter.

'Negotiation' is thus rarely a singular event though there may, of course, be some cumulative moment. It is important however, I believe, to be attuned to both the sequential and recursive elements that cumulatively constitute a negotiated outcome. This recursivity is elemental in that each stage lays down conditions that *next* actors, in *next* interactions and under *next* contingencies must respond. The elements are constituted in and through the structured yet structuring properties of talk and these become the concrete conditions for successive *stages* of negotiation. The stages are, as has been frequently noted, here and elsewhere, sequential in ways that embed last actions and project next actions. This is the essence of what phenomenologists and ethnomethodologists call the retrospective/-prospective nature of action and accounts (Heritage 1984a).

5. CONCLUSION

This chapter has been about ordinary, everyday talk in organizations. Organizations are themselves often characterized as tense yet collaborative coalitions, circles, and groups within groups, with competing goals and multiple internal responses to a variety of external environments. These "circles of affiliation" (Jackall 1988) are played out critically in the blow-by-blow exchange of talk-based positions and plans. The force of one exchange, moreover, recursively lays down the conditions of the next. In fine ripples, the effects of many interactions occurring simultaneously and across time in any organization shape the flow and direction of action, creating structure that is, in turn, affected by later cross-currents, sometimes from distant disturbances. The conditions created in and through interaction thus have consequences far beyond the immediate interactional setting, embedding actors and activities in a very real world *of their own making*. Negotiation, in any general sense, is nested within and built through this shared world, sequentially and segmentally.

The fine tinkering and manoeuvring of actors dancing around agendas and arrangements, accommodating each other locally for a variety of personal, political, and organizational goals provides the very loose-coupling that allows the larger entity to be sustained as an entirely practical and effective operation. Out of quite practical contingencies, interactants create the fluid structures out of which negotiation is conjured, moment to moment.

When ethnomethodologists consider conversational data with recommended 'indifference' they may indeed discover negotiation, but it is a process that is, in Garfinkel's term, "in flight", namely dynamic and highly reflexive (Garfinkel 1967, Anderson, Hughes and Sharrock 1989). Social actors discover *from within* their shared activities the local logic of their collaborations. In so doing, they grant each other a kind of practical ethics or local rationality; they assume the other is being reasonable, is making reciprocal interpretations of the activities and will continue to do so in the interests of the shared work (Garfinkel 1967, Molotch and Boden 1985). In creating and recreating practical contexts of action, in other words, actors also and *reflexively* constitute those actions as reasonable or, more broadly, rational. Stretched too far, for instance, disagreements become conflict and working relations break down along with the shared assumptions that have guided them. But terms such as conflict or negotiation or even rationality are not usefully understood as *external* to local environments of action. Instead, they live in, flourish and grow through the local logic of everyday talk and, most especially, in the intensity and intimacy of face-to-face interaction. In this chapter, I have offered one way of considering negotiation-as-interaction.

CHAPTER 5

MAKING A BID FOR CHANGE: FORMULATIONS IN UNION/MANAGEMENT NEGOTIATIONS

ESTHER WALKER

1. INTRODUCTION

The process of making and seeking concessions is central to the negotiation of an agreement. However, at what moment to make an offer and how to orchestrate that activity are potentially problematic for negotiators. Firstly, a team may prefer to wait for the other side to make the first move, but if they are to make it themselves they want to be assured that it is in their interests to do so: once an offer has been made and accepted it cannot be retracted. Secondly, in order to minimize the risk of rejection the team needs to find a way of discovering whether the other side are also ready to make concessions.

The significance and problematic nature of concessionary activity is acknowledged within the literature, but its investigation is dominated by the traditional social psychological approach to negotiation. It tends to be studied either using Game Theoretical models through which the relationship between concessions and outcome can be explored,[1] or alongside other negotiation 'behaviours', with a view to identifying what constitutes effective negotiating practice (see Pruitt 1981, Hargie 1986). Both reflect a concern among researchers with the cognitive processes and individual

I would like to extend my thanks to Paul Drew for his helpful comments on an earlier draft of this chapter.

motivations which underlie concessionary activity, and a tendency not to be concerned with making empirical observations about how participants actually accomplish it in real-life negotiations.

One difficulty researchers have faced is engendered by the nature of concessionary activity itself. The participants' orientation to the consequentiality of making offers is demonstrated in the characteristically cautious way in which they are treated. But researchers have not had a sufficiently sensitive analytic tool for discerning and describing behaviour which is not overt and easily identifiable. As a result they have largely ignored implicitly made offers in their studies of official bids (Tutzauer 1992).

This represents a central lacuna in the research on concessionary behaviour. The problems surrounding the making of offers only emerge when negotiators *perform* them: that is, when they become goals for interactional accomplishment. Consequently, to find out how this activity is problematic for negotiators, and how they overcome these problems, one needs to attend to the sequential and linguistic details of the talk: a task which is possible using a Conversation Analytic perspective. Given the significance of concessionary activity to negotiations, it is insufficient for researchers to confine themselves to those instances where offers are being treated by negotiators as relatively unproblematic.

This chapter addresses these issues by reporting on a socially-organized practice through which negotiators accomplish concessionary activity implicitly and indirectly. The observations specifically relate to negotiating activity as it occurs in real-life union/ management meetings, and may therefore contrast with the way in which concessions are made in other kinds of negotiating activities.

The data comprise audio-recordings of face-to-face meetings held during the Spring of 1991 at a large engineering company in the north-east of England. These meetings vary in the degree of formality and in the nature of the problem which engendered them. Most of the excerpts reproduced here, however, are taken from a series of meetings in which the company's annual wage agreement was negotiated (they are identified as WGE:1, 2, 3 and 4). There were eight participants in these wage negotiations — four managers and four shop stewards; one of the members of the management team has the additional role of chairperson (identified as 'Andy' in the excerpts).

From detailed analyses of the talk it emerges that there are key moments when a bid is made to crystallize the issues into a basis upon which an agreement may subsequently be built. This bid is made by 'formulating' the sense of prior talk: that is, by one team saying-in-so-many-words-what-*we/you*-are-saying (see Garfinkel and Sacks 1970). In these negotiations, when a speaker proffers a formulation, they are heard to be identifying a concessionary modification to the recipient team's position which, if accepted, will establish an area of common ground. Formulations are therefore resolution-implicative: they are used as a device for initiating concessionary activity, thereby providing an opportunity for the two sides to reach agreement.

2. DEFINING FORMULATIONS WHICH INITIATE CONCESSIONARY ACTIVITY

In these negotiations, participants are formulating their own and one another's talk in various different ways. However, the focus of this chapter is a particular group of formulations which are specifically involved in the initiation of concessionary activity. This group comprises turns in which the speaker is formulating the *gist, upshot* or *resumé* of what the recipient team is saying, or of what *we* (i.e. *we all*) are saying, in the immediate prior talk. They are designed as demonstrations of understanding to which the appropriate response is confirmation or disconfirmation by the recipient team. Overwhelmingly, the occurrence of such formulations coincides with concessionary activity: that is, they occur during what may be called a 'concessionary phase'. Here, our interest is restricted to those formulations which occur at the onset, or near the beginning, of such phases; they are involved in locating and establishing an area of common ground, and are thus distinct, in the interactional work they are accomplishing, from those formulations which may subsequently occur to sort out the finer details of that common ground prior to resolution.

In talk-in-interaction generally, when a speaker formulates the gist, upshot or resumé of prior talk, what they are routinely doing is providing an explicit version of the sense of prior talk and treating that sense as self-evident (Heritage and Watson 1979, Garfinkel and Sacks 1970). The process of formulating entails making an interpretation of prior talk; but because there is no definitive version of "the sense of what we're saying" (see Garfinkel and Sacks 1970), any description is necessarily selective and designed for the task at hand. Consequently, when a speaker formulates the sense of prior talk they can usually be heard by the recipient to be doing more than demonstrating their understanding of it.

In institutional talk, formulations may acquire a particular implicativeness because they are used as a device for accomplishing interactive work which is made relevant by the institutional setting. Inherent in their design and analysis are the specialized inferential and participation frameworks which often characterize institutional talk (see Levinson 1992, Drew and Heritage 1992). As a result, the employment of formulations, and the interactive work they are used to accomplish, may be associated with a particular ascribed role. For example, in news interviews formulations are routinely used by the interviewer to prompt the interviewee to elaborate on their prior talk in some specific way (Heritage 1985).

In these negotiations, it is very rare that a team will formulate the recipient team's prior talk in order to demonstrate their understanding of it: to do such an activity implies that the speaker is accepting that version of the recipient team's position which they are presenting. Thus, when a formulation occurs, it is heard to be doing specialized negotiation work — the offering and seeking of concessions — and, as such, it is understood to have specific implications for the subsequent talk.

3. THE TRANSITIONAL ENVIRONMENT OF FORMULATIONS

3.1. Formulations are transitional in relation to prior talk

When a speaker provides a formulation of prior talk her/his activity is transitional in two respects: firstly, it constitutes a shift from the exchange of information and particulars about the issues under negotiation to a review of 'where we/you are'; and secondly, in formulating a *resumé* of prior talk the speaker may be discerning that a change has occurred in the negotiating situation which they are now 'revealing'.

3.1.1. *From the exchange of information to a review of the situation*
When an issue emerges, or is introduced for negotiation, the initial stage is characterized by the exchange of points of argument through which the teams discover and explore their different positions.[2] At each turn the recipient team's presentation of additional counter-material extends the discussion. If the recipient team chooses instead to recycle prior talk they are changing the nature of the activity which the participants are engaged in: a formulation postpones the phase in which further matters are raised for consideration and initiates a review of 'where we are'. This is illustrated in excerpts 1 and 2 (the relevant turns are indicated).

(1) [WGE:3:A:180]
(The management team are responding to a union complaint that the previous year's agreement on the issue of the shorter working week has been breached. Management: Bill (B); union: Pete (P).)

```
1   B   do you remember Pete those meetings. I mean your (.) when we
2       were talking about the (0.2) ec- economic state of the nation
3       (0.4) a- as it affected ((co. name)) then
4       (0.2)
```

```
 5   P     y:es=
 6   B     =you were asking an DARED (0.2) to ask (0.3) are we talking about
 7         (0.2) redundancies. (0.5) and in that situation that nobody round the
 8         table was going to say. (0.6) on either side. (0.7) and now let's discuss
 9         a shorter working week it just did not make sense to raise that (one)
10         (0.2)
11   P     mm=
12   B     =I mean (1.1) nobody (0.2) on on=er in in amongst (0.9) your
13         team (0.2) would've (1.8) wanted to: (.) or cared to have raised
14         it as a subject at that time,
15         (0.8)
16   P→    see what we've got here we've got two things. we've got an
17         agreement (0.7) (that we want). (1.2) and circumstances that you're
18         saying that we can't get it (0.3) (brought).
```

In this excerpt the participants have been disputing whether the lack of discussions on the shorter working week through the year constitutes a management breach of the previous year's agreement. Bill's initial turn in the excerpt (lines 1-14) extends this discussion by pointing out that the economic situation has been so bad that when they did meet to talk in the autumn *neither* side would have considered raising this matter. Instead of providing a counter-position the union side responds by formulating a resumé of "what we've got" (beginning line 16).

(2) [WGE:2:A:235]
(Management are responding to a union complaint that they are being prevented from discussing the issue of sick pay. Management: Kev (K); union: Pete (P).)

```
 1   K     and even if it was a favourable time what I'm saying is that we-
 2         (0.4) we would have to be talking (0.9) fairly toughly (0.3) about it
 3         and n- and (0.4) about this say we (0.8) that it was seen that we
 4         could well afford (0.7) a pro rata increase in sick payments. (0.8)
 5         then we would have to talk about .hhhhhhhh the interpretation
 6         of:=er:: (.) certain people's absences and so on and so forth and do
 7         and do and implementing the procedures I mean that's the sort of
 8         area I don't want to get in:to that (0.9) in these sort of negotiations.
 9         (0.6)
10   P     I se ⌐ e what you mean.
11   K        ⌊ where there's mon ⌐ ey on the ta:ble. (0.8) er:: (0.6)
12         there there is:: (.) there's quite (0.7) we're not talking about (0.4)
```

```
13          anybody genuine it's the- (.) it's the very small minority (1.1) er-
14          who (0.6) seem seem to be, (.) might be wrong. (0.8) I would never
15          ( ) if (they) hadn't seemed to be spoiling it for the majority.
16          (1.1)
17    P→    so what you would do is an in depth analys (.) analysing
18          ⌈ of it ⌉ (0.4) ⌈and you would like⌉ to do it away from=
19    K     ⌊ that's ⌋ what ⌊we w o u l d do ⌋
20    P     =a (0.3) wage negotiation.
```

In excerpt 2, as part of management's defence against a union allegation, Kev restates why he would be reluctant to discuss sick pay at these negotiations: it would involve dealing with the matter of a group of workers who are suspected of abusing the sick scheme (lines 1-15). Again, rather than presenting a counter-position, the union side recycles prior talk by formulating the upshot of the management's position (line 17).

3.1.2. 'Revealing' that a change has occurred in the negotiating situation

An explicit and collaborative assessment of 'where we are' by the negotiating teams becomes relevant at specific junctures in the talk: when the meeting is opened, or is re-opened following an adjournment, and when something has happened to change the negotiating situation (for example an issue has been resolved). Consequently, resumés of prior talk are associated with pivotal moments in the talk and this pivotal character can be used as a resource by participants. The prior talk can be treated as if it involves a change to the negotiating situation thus occasioning the relevance of a resumé. This discerned change is then 'revealed' by the speaker in their explicit formulation of 'where we are now'. This can be seen in excerpts 3 and 4.

(3) [WGE:2:A:314]

(Following an interjection, Pete returns to the issue of the shorter working week. Management: Andy (A), Kev (K) and Bill (B); union: Pete (P).)

```
1     P     thirty seven hour week. (.) can we get back to that then.
2           (1.5)
3     P     ⌈ yes.
4     (?)   ⌊ gkmm
5           (2.2)
6     P     on the thirty seven hour week if it's not viable to get the thirty seven
7           hour week at these negotiations
8           (1.7)
9     P     judging: (0.3) on the state of business in six month's time. (1.4) er:
10          maybe there (w)ould be some'at wrote in to agreement that we could
```

```
11        come back (0.3) and start negotiating on (0.6) shorter working week
12        then.
13        (1.9)
14   P    er::m
15        (1.8)
16   P    this'll be controversial: as regards and maybe you (know) (0.2) no
17        brief at all for this but=erm (1.0) to talk about (0.7) shorter working
18        week in six months time: judging: (0.6) how the bi- (0.3) business has
19        picked up. (0.9) you have a clearer idea of how you've done because
20        your next six months (0.7) should- (0.3) you expect should be: one of
21        your best (0.8) part of the year.
22        (1.1)
23        you've got May June July and it's (.) it's usually (1.2) is in our type of
24        work.
25        (0.3)
26   B    and we've usually got the orders in (0.3) by about now (0.2) to do that
27        Pete.
28        (0.5)
29   P    yeh I know we have (0.3) business b:::efore hand but we're just
30        gonna see how it's gonna look at (.) i:n the ⌐ next six months.
31  (B)                                             ⌊ ( )
32        (1.0)
33   P    because (0.9)⌐ you mu ⌐ st-
34   A              ⌊ h     ⌊ is that a suggestion that you're making
35        that we should (0.5) consider (0.8) that as part of
36        this agreement.
37        (0.3)
38   P    I thought it was you know when I asked him to put it ⌐ back on:=
39   K                                                      ⌊ mm
40   P    =to: (0.2) record.=
41   A    =that's what you're asking ⌐ okay just clarifying.
42   K                            ⌊ mm
43        (1.6)
44   A→   er:m (1.4) er so (1.0) you're (.) com- on the basis of feedback you're
45        getting from (0.3) from people. (0.3) you (0.7) started off giving me
46        the impression that we were (0.5) still hundreds of miles apart (0.9)
47        we now seem to have come down to a position where (0.3) in essence
48        what you're asking us to consider is the six percent on basic which
```

49   we've already offered you (0.5) but you would like in addition to that
50   for us to consider the possibility (0.9) of: (0.2) an increase (0.4) on
51   the (0.4) bonus rate? (0.7) and (.) to include (.) in (.) any agreement
52   we reach (0.5) a paragraph indicating the willingness to (0.9) have
53   dialogue on the subject of (a) thirty seven hour week (1.2) during the
54   period of this agreement.

Pete's initial turn in the extract (between lines 1-24) is understood by management to be a proposal: in his subsequent turn (lines 34-36) Andy describes the activity Pete is doing in terms of a proposal on which he requests Pete's clarification (*is that a suggestion that you're making that we should (0.5) consider (0.8) that as part of this agreement.*). Following Pete's confirmation of this description (lines 38 and 40) it is subsequently reconfirmed by Andy (line 41).

Andy explicitly identifies what he is doing as *just clarifying*. However, in the process of being reconfirmed, the activity the union are purported to be doing has been somewhat modified. Pete is initially asked to confirm a description which categorically identifies his action as a proposal (i.e. it is *a suggestion that you're making*). But in the reconfirmation it is described in terms of a request (*that's what you're asking*). This modification may be immaterial, but there is a significant difference in negotiations between 'proposing' (or 'suggesting') and 'requesting' (or 'asking'). If an activity is explicitly identified as a 'proposal', this precludes the interpretation that the turn constitutes a concession: 'proposals' certainly provide an opportunity for *an exchange* of concessions to be made, but they do not in themselves constitute a concession made by the speaker. On the other hand, such an interpretation is permissible if the activity is described as a 'request'.

Although there is no evidence that Andy's clarification request was strategically designed to set up his next action, it certainly facilitates it. Rather than beginning to consider the union 'proposal' (by, for example, identifying a drawback with it) Andy formulates a resumé of the union position which reveals that it has undergone some change (beginning line 44). He describes the union side as having *started off* giving the impression that the two sides were *still hundreds of miles apart* but *we now seem to have come down to a position where* the union side are asking for three things (lines 45-47). The implication is that this new union position is a move in the right direction. In doing this, Andy is treating the prior talk as constituting a concession and thus a change in the negotiating situation. Having recognized such a change, the appropriate next activity is for him to explicitly formulate it in a summary version of the union position.

As well as creating a transitional environment in which he can warrantably claim that the union side has made a concession, the activity of formulating prior talk enables Andy to describe that concession in a way that is acceptable to management. In his description management are under no obligation to make any concessions or to fulfil any commitments: these are issues which the union side are *asking* management *to consider*. In addition, the ramifications of the proposed paragraph which Pete details are constrained and weakened in Andy's version. Pete proposes that the paragraph would comprise an agreement to *start negotiating on (0.6) shorter working week* in six months time (line 11). However, this is formulated by Andy as *a paragraph indicating the willingness to (0.9) have dialogue on the subject of (a) thirty seven hour week (1.2) during the period of this agreement.* (lines 52-54). This description eliminates any of the implications which Pete's version has that such talks might precipitate the introduction of the shorter working week: it envisages *dialogue* on this issue and not *negotiations*; the talks would occur *during the period of this agreement.* and not in six months' time; and the paragraph will only be *indicating the willingness* to conduct such talks.

A similarly opportunistic resumé of prior talk occurs in excerpt 4:

(4) [WGE:3:A:240]
(During an ongoing discussion about the shorter working week, management identify the prohibitive problem of cost. Management: Bill (B), Andy (A) and Kev (K); union: Pete (P).)

```
    1   Bill  let's say it another way (1.7) if it costs a thousand pounds to build a
    2         (0.5) ((product name)) twenty five right now (0.7) then in a shorter
    3         working week it's no' (gotta) cost us any more. (0.4)
    4               (  )
    5   A      ⌊what we're con- that's the ⌐ concern ⌐
    6   B                                 ⌊or if we- ⌠ if we build (0.3) thirty
    7         ((product name)) twenty five...

          ((47 lines omitted))

    55  B      (0.2) you've got to know you can do that but even if you (1.2) even if
    56         you do that in thirty seven hour you've gotta realise that (1.2) there
    57         are other unit costs that don't go in you say we're gonna have: a er
    58         smaller wage bill (0.3) you could say (1.0) but there're other things
    59         which er (.) don't change (1.5) so (0.7) it's not a national thing it's
    60         gotta be a unit cost thing.
    61         (1.0)
```

62   P→ so what we're actually talking about now is that if we reduce working
63   week (it'll) put unit costs up (0.5) 'cos (the end of the week cost er)
64   (0.5) to work them two hours
65   (0.7)
66   P   ⌈ so we have to ⌉ find a way of <u>work</u>ing that into a cost
67   A   ⌊ I think wha- ⌋
68   (0.9)
69   P   ⌈ to get our shorter working week (.) cost the same
70   A   ⌊ (if)

In the first turn of the excerpt, Bill is resisting union pressure for a concession on the shorter working week by raising the matter of cost. This is pursued and contested in the ensuing (and omitted) spate of talk. In a subsequent union response (beginning line 62) Pete proffers a resumé of the prior talk, thereby claiming that something has happened to alter the trajectory of the discussion and to occasion a review of *what we're actually talking about now*.

As in the previous excerpt, by doing a resumé Pete is able to 'reveal' that a change has occurred in the negotiating situation. And furthermore, through recognizing and explicitly formulating this change the prior talk can be interpreted in a way which favours the union case. When management identify the problem of cost it is to oppose the reduction in the working week. Yet in Pete's interpretation, it becomes a direction in which they can move towards the eventual implementation of this union demand (lines 66-69).

3.2. Formulations are transitional in relation to subsequent talk

Formulations (i.e. gists, upshots and resumés), then, constitute a shift in the kind of negotiating activity in which the participants are engaged. Their transitional character is also evidenced by the talk which is subsequently generated. They are oriented to by the participants as resolution-implicative: the speaker is understood to be identifying a possible basis for agreement which, if taken up by the recipient team, can then be explored and defined. So they initiate a 'concessionary phase' in which the participants may achieve an agreement.

In excerpt 2 (cited again below), the incipient area of agreement identified in the initial formulation (lines 1-4) is subsequently shaped up by the participants and eventually leads to a resolution. This is a lengthy sequence, and consequently its mid-section has been omitted.

(2) [WGE:2:A:250] (continuation)
(Just prior to the extract, management have been defending themselves against the union criticism that they are obstructing talks on the sick pay. Management: Kev (K), Andy (A) and Bill (B); Union: Pete (P).)

```
1    P    so what you would do is an in depth analys (.) analysing
2         ┌ of it ┐ (0.4) ┌ and you would like ┐ to do it away from=
3    K    [ that's ] what  [ w e  w o u l d  do ]
4    P    =a (0.3) wage negotiation.
5         (0.5)
6    K    .t (.) e- ye- ye- but I will talk about it now but that's the sort of scene
7         I(w) I would like to set up for doing this and I think that would be
8         ┌ a good thing, ┐
9    A    [ and that's off ] the record is it?
10        (.)
11   K    Y:ES all this is off the record there's nothing being recorded. that's
12        (0.4) ·hh and I think it's fair that you know how we're thinking.
13        (0.5)
14   P    so you would like the shop stewards to take it on faith that (they)
15        would (.) be discussing this (0.8) a:t (a) different ti:me.
16        (1.1)
17   B    ( ┌ )
18   P    └ in dep ┌ th:
19   K              └ no- no- not this year.
20        (0.3)
21   B    no
22   P    no: ┌ I never said this year.
23   K        └ not thi-
24        (0.4)
25   K    but we WILL (0.3) YES definitely. (0.4) we will this is something we
26        could look at (0.3) and this is an area ·hhhhh
27        ┌ I c o u l d s a y ┐ in principle ┐ .hhh ┌ a-
28   P    [ (there's always) n ] ext y e a r. ]      [
29   A    └ (          )       ┘              └ but it is quite
30        possibly something which (0.4) could result in a:=er (1.4) fundamental
31        change? (0.3) which may not be:? (0.7) in your view (ve-) beneficial.
```

((60 lines omitted))

92 P   ⌊ <u>let</u> <u>sleeping</u> dogs lie for the time being.
93   (.)
94 A   <u>ab</u>solutely.
95   (0.3)
96 B   er but Andy <u>is</u> saying that there isn't (.) <u>money</u> (0.3) to talk about the
97   sick <u>pay</u> (0.6) <u>any</u>way.
98   (0.3)
99 P   I'm ⌈ (   ) that's what Andy is saying⌉
100 B   ⌊ I mean tha- that that's his <u>starting</u> ⌋ point and I was just
101   closing off to r:eiterate ⌈ that point. .hh
102 K   ⌊ mm?
103   (0.3)
104 K   mm.
105 B   tha-
106   (0.8)
107 B   ⌈ we've been round we've ⌉ <u>danced</u> all round the <u>trees</u> in that and=
108 P   ⌊ I know what he's saying ⌋
109 B   =you understand what the situation is but .hhh (0.6) it <u>mustn</u>'t leave
110   you with the flavour that there's any money (.) <u>left</u> (0.3) ⌈ <u>to</u> (0.4)
111 P   ⌊ (   )
112 B   ⌈ to have a ⌈ separate ⌈ nego<u>tia</u>tion on it.   ⌉
113 (?)   ⌊ yeh   ⌊   ⌊   ⌋
114 P   ⌊ no   ⌊ he never actually ⌠ <u>said</u> (0.3) that there was
115   any money there at <u>all</u>.
116   (0.3)
117 B   no
118   (0.6)
119 P   ⌈ he just (.) <u>gave</u> us ⌈ a reason   ⌉ why he wouldn't like to <u>talk</u> about it.
120 B   ⌊ that's right   ⌊ <u>that's</u> <u>right</u>. ⌋
121   (.)
122 B   mm
123   (0.5)
124 K   mm
125   (0.6)
126 A   okay

Through lines 1-31 of the excerpt, union and management negotiate an exchange of concessions which, in the ensuing talk, leads to agreement: the union side agree to concede the postponement of discussions and thus relinquish their demands for an increase in sick pay in exchange for a commitment from management that it will be discussed at a later date. Having established this common ground, the teams set about ensuring that they have a mutual understanding of what this agreement entails. Towards the end of the sequence that mutual understanding is demonstrated by Pete's idiomatic gloss of the management position (*let sleeping dogs lie for the time being.* line 92) and his subsequent formulation of what Andy is saying (lines 114-115 and 119).

However, the proposed basis for agreement which is presented by the formulation does not necessarily result in resolution. It may turn out to be inappropriate or unacceptable and the participants may then resume their exchange of points of argument. In excerpt 5, John's formulation of the gist of the prior management proposal (lines 1-2) generates a concessionary offer from them (lines 4-7). This offer is then explored in the subsequent talk.

(5) [WGE:3:A:300]
(Management have proposed that a paragraph be included in the agreement committing both sides to discussions on the shorter working week through the year. This mirrors the solution which was found to this problem in the previous year's negotiations. Management: Andy (A) and Bill (B); union: John (J) and Bob (Bo).)

```
 1  J   so what you're saying is we'll have the same (.) wording as what we
 2      had last year
 3      (0.4)
 4  A  ┌ no (0.2) ┌ I'm saying we could amend  ┌ the wording if you=
 5  B  └ no       └ (it's not)                  │
 6  (?)                                         └ (    )
 7  A  =┌ wish we would agree on some form of wording
 8  J   └ (amend)
 9      (0.4)
10  Bo  but (if) ┌ as we said (0.3) last┐ last week em (1.0) to be held in=
11  S            └ (              )     ┘
12  Bo  =the next six months
13      (.)
14  J   yeah
15      (2.3)
16  A   ( )
17      (3.4)
18  Bo  (plus) (.) (just) to be held in six months (0.2) no promises
19      (1.1)
20  B   (no) (.) well
```

```
21      (1.4)
22  Bo  ⌐( ) i- i- i- i t              ⌐ gives a- ( ⌐ ) line
23  A   ⌊ well okay at the end of the day ⌋          ⌊
24  (?)                                              ⌊ ( )
25      (0.3)
26  (?) yep
27      (.)
28  A   we can talk about what that paragraph says (0.3) that would then
29      become part of our discussions as to what that paragraph says. all I'm
30      asking is a basic question (0.6) would the inclusion of such a
31      statement help you (0.4) to recommend (0.2) and to get accepted (0.5)
32      a six percent increase on basic.
```

A basis upon which the union side might accept the management proposal is established through John's formulation and Andy's subsequent offer (lines 1-7). The union side then begins to shape this up by suggesting how the paragraph might be worded to make it acceptable to them (lines 10-22). However, this trajectory towards resolution is treated as premature by Andy who pursues a response to the general proposal he is making (lines 23 and then 28-32).

In sum, these excerpts illustrate the transitional character of formulations in these negotiations. The speaker creates a transitional environment by virtue of using a formulation wherein concessionary activity is initiated. In the formulation the speaker is revealing a possible way forward which can then be negotiated in the subsequent talk and perhaps lead to resolution. Consequently, formulations signal a shift from one kind of negotiating phase to another.[3]

4. FORMULATIONS AND THE ACCOMPLISHMENT OF IMPLICIT OFFERS

Through formulations, negotiators make implicit offers: they offer an exchange of concessions which may form the basis for agreement. In the design of formulations, in the recipient team's analysis of them, and in the speaker's subsequent turn, the participants display their mutual orientation to the resolution-implicativeness of formulations.

4.1. Formulations are designed to offer and seek concessions

Formulating prior talk entails making something of it, or making something out of it, which is then implicative for the subsequent talk. The interpretative process of selecting to excavate and focus on one or more inferrables whilst disattending to other possible aspects of the prior talk, enables a negotiator to attribute an intention to the recipient team and re-present it to them as the essence of what they are saying. Formulations are (nearly) always oriented to as making a tendentious interpretation of prior talk. The speaker may attribute an intention to the recipient team which is heard to be consonant with what the speaker can agree with: that is, an affiliative or 'optimistic formulation'. Alternatively, they may attribute an intention which is heard to be antithetical to what the speaker can agree with; such disaffiliative or 'pessimistic formulations' have a confrontational, accusatory character. Either way, formulations are concession-seeking and imply that if the recipient team 'makes' the concession by confirming or disconfirming the formulation the speaker will thereby accept it. How they are used as a device for promoting a change in the negotiating situation will be discussed with reference to the following two cases.

4.1.1. *Case 1*

We return again to excerpt 2. At the close of management's defence against the union allegation on sick pay, the union side formulate the upshot of their position (lines 22-25):

(2) [WGE:2:A:235]

(Management are defending themselves against a union complaint that they are being prevented from discussing the issue of sick pay. Management: Kev (K), Andy (A) and Bill (B); union: Pete (P).)

```
 1   A    I mean I think (0.9) that we have (0.6) quite accepted (0.5) a
 2            discussion on the subject but we have certainly (0.5) all we've said
 3            is that sorry we can't offer you anything on them. they have to stay as
 4            they are,
 5            (2.4)
 6   K    and even if it was a favourable time what I'm saying is that we- (0.4)
 7            we would have to be talking (0.9) fairly toughly (0.3) about it and n-
 8            and (0.4) about this say we (0.8) that it was seen that we could well
 9            afford (0.7) a pro rata increase in sick payments. (0.8) then we would
10            have to talk about .hhhhhhhh the interpretation of:=er:: (.) certain
11            people's absences and so on and so forth and do and do and
12            implementing the procedures I mean that's the sort of area I don't
13            want to get in:to that (0.9) in these sort of negotiations.
14            (0.6)
```

15 P   I <u>se</u> ⌐e what you mean. ⌐
16 K   ⌊<u>where</u> there's <u>mon</u>⌡ ey on the <u>ta:</u>ble. (0.8) er:: (0.6)
17   there there <u>is::</u> (.) there's <u>quite</u> (0.7) we're <u>not</u> talking about (0.4)
18   <u>any</u>body <u>gen</u>uine it's the- (.) it's the <u>very</u> <u>small</u> <u>minority</u> (1.1) er- who
19   (0.6) <u>seem</u> seem to be, (.) might be wrong. (0.8) I would
20   <u>never</u> ( ) if (they) hadn't seemed to be <u>spoil</u>ing it for the majority.
21   (1.1)
22 P →<u>so</u> what you would <u>do</u> is an in depth <u>analys</u> (.) analysing
23   ⌐ of it ⌐ (0.4) ⌐ and you would like⌐ to do it away from=
24 K   ⌊ <u>that's</u>⌡ what ⌊we w o u l d <u>do</u>⌡
25 P   =a (0.3) <u>wage</u> nego<u>tia</u>tion.
26   (0.5)
27 K   .t (.) e- ye- ye- but I <u>will</u> talk about it <u>now</u> but <u>that's</u> the <u>sort</u> of <u>scene</u>
28   I(w) I would <u>like</u> to set up for doing this and I think <u>that</u> would be
29   ⌐ a good <u>thing</u>,⌐
30 A   ⌊ and that's <u>off</u>⌡ the <u>record</u> is it?
31   (.)
32 K   <u>Y:ES</u> <u>all</u> this is off the record there's nothing being recorded. <u>that's</u>
33   (0.4) .hh and I think it's <u>fair</u> that you know how we're <u>think</u>ing.
34   (0.5)
35 Ṕ→ <u>so</u> you would <u>like</u> the shop stewards to take it on <u>faith</u> that (they)
36   would (.) be dis<u>cuss</u>ing this (0.8) a:t (a) <u>different</u> ti:me.
37   (1.1)
38 B   (⌐)
39 P   ⌊ in dep ⌐ th:
40 K   ⌊<u>no</u> <u>no</u> <u>not</u> this year.
41   (0.3)
42 B   <u>no</u>
43 P   no: ⌐ I never <u>said</u> this year.
44 K   ⌊ <u>not</u> thi-
45   (0.4)
46 K   but we <u>WILL</u> (0.3) <u>YES</u> <u>definitely</u>. (0.4) we will <u>this</u> is something we
47   <u>could</u> look at (0.3) and this is an area .hhhhh
48   ⌐ I c o u l d s a y ⌐ in principle⌐ .hhh ⌐ a-
49 P   ⌊ (there's always) n ⌊ext y e a r.⌡   ⌊
50 A   ⌊ (   )   ⌊ but it is quite
51   <u>poss</u>ibly something <u>which</u> (0.4) <u>could</u> <u>result</u> in <u>a:=er</u> (1.4) <u>fundamental</u>
52   <u>change</u>? (0.3) which may <u>not</u> be:? (0.7) in <u>your</u> view (ve-) bene<u>fi</u>cal.

In the first turn of this excerpt Andy makes the point that although they can discuss sick pay there is no money to concede any increase to it (lines 1-4). Kev's subsequent warning of the damage which such a discussion may effect to the negotiations (lines 6-20) is designed to accuse a group of workers implicitly of exploiting the sick scheme. This whole turn is designed very cautiously. He anticipates the potentially disruptive consequences of a discussion by saying that they would *have to be talking (0.9) fairly toughly* about it (line 7). But when, shortly afterwards, he explicates what it is they will have to talk about he is being demonstrably circumspect in his description. His circumlocutory phrase *the interpretation of:=er:: (.) certain people's absences* (lines 10-11) is carefully designed to invite the interpretation that he is being deliberately delicate and thus to induce the recipients to infer what the sensitive matter he is referring to might be. This display of 'doing delicate treatment' inheres in the perturbation occurring before the noun phrase (*of:=er:: (.)*) which implicates that he is describing something that requires cautious lexical selection. And his phrase *certain people's* (with the stress on *certain*) is loaded, displaying that he is being intentionally less specific than he could be. In other words, many of his descriptions throughout this turn are designed to be recognizable as glosses for more explicit and detailed versions which it is inappropriate to provide. Thus, having given a sufficient hint of the damaging matters they would have to talk about, he glosses over 'the rest of the story' (thereby hinting that there is more to it) with the generalized and all-encapsulating phrase *and so on and so forth* (line 11).

At a possible completion of Kev's turn, Pete indicates that he understands what is being implied (line 15). And when Kev continues (line 16) it is to talk further about this group of people who have been implicitly identified as transgressing. But again his talk is cautious and heavily mitigated — it is a *very small minority (1.1) er- who (0.6) seem seem to be, (.) might be wrong. (0.8) I would never ( ) if (they) hadn't seemed to be spoiling it for the majority* (lines 18-20).

So there is an implicit yet pointed meaning in Kev's turn which could be extracted and made explicit in a subsequent formulation (i.e. along the lines of *what you have just saying...is (0.5) that people are abusing sick scheme and you would like to see them stop* which Pete says shortly afterwards - see excerpt 10, section 5 below). However, Pete's formulation (lines 22-25) does not in any way focus on the management accusation against the workers. Instead, he formulates an upshot of the complaint: that management intend to conduct an in-depth analysis of the sick scheme. He therefore selects to shape up the prior talk in a way which presents an affiliative interpretation for development and in a way which curtails further talk on the divisive issue of the accusation. The design of this formulation suggests that he is intentionally selecting to re-present management's position in a way which fosters an incipient agreement. He is thereby indicating that he is prepared to engage in concessionary activity and that this version of management's position is one he could agree with.

Following management's qualified confirmation (lines 24 and 27-33), this direction towards agreement is pursued by Pete through a second formulation (lines 35-36). This subsequent formulation is overtly tendentious in that it attributes to management an intention which constitutes a concession. Management's prior talk is interpreted as implicating their wish that the shop stewards accept a promise from them that discussions will be held at some future time. Pete is making an offer which further defines the area of common ground: that is, the union side will accept the postponement of talks on sick pay if management promise to discuss it at a later date. If management confirm the formulation, they 'make' the concession and accept the bargain. In this way, rather than explicitly soliciting a concession through a self-generated and overt offer, Pete solicits it implicitly by treating the concession as if it arises naturally out of the sense of prior talk.

4.1.2. *Case 2*

This excerpt occurs just prior to excerpt 5. Management offer to concede the earlier union request (see excerpt 3) for a paragraph to be included in the agreement which refers to future discussions on the shorter working week. This is subsequently formulated by the union side to reveal what management are in fact saying:

(6) [WGE:3:A:265] (precedes excerpt 5)
(This follows a lengthy discussion of the shorter working week on which management are making no concessions. Management: Andy (A), Bill (B) and Sam (S); union: John (J).)

1	A	⌊ HAVing said that there is
2		no way we're gonna reduce the hours in these negotiations.
3		(1.1)
4	A	a- one <u>fully</u> appreciates as I've said so many times because I'm a very
5		understanding fellow all of us are
6		(1.3)
7	(?)	haha
8	A	would it (0.7) <u>assist</u> you to get the message over to you (0.4) the
9		people you represent. (1.2) and <u>would it</u> (0.9) <u>get</u> (0.4) <u>your support</u>
10		and recommendation (0.8) <u>if we were to</u> con<u>cede</u> (0.8) that with<u>in</u> this
11		agreement <u>we would</u> (0.6) re<u>iterate yet</u> again some paragraph with
12		regard to a thirty seven hour week.

```
13          (0.9)
14    A     now that's a FUNDAMENTAL CHANGE in our position.
15          (0.7)
16    B     (you said a thi ⌐ rty seven hour week) shor-
17    A               ∟ I'm just asking I'm not saying we're go ⌐ nna
18          do it
19    S     shorter work ⌐ ing ( )
20    B                ∟ shorter working not a thirty seven you said
21          thirty seven hour week (0.3) y ⌐ ou you
22    S                            ∟ shorter working ⌐ week.
23    A                                       ∟ shorter
24          working week okay (0.2) a shorter working week. (0.8) I mean tha- is
25          a fundamental ch- and I'm not saying we would do that I'm asking
26          your opin- your (1.3) I'm asking you whether (0.2) it would
27          (0.6)
28    B     help
29          (0.4)
30    A     help to get an agreement and whether you would be prepared to give
31          it your support (0.2) if such a thing would be (0.4) such a (0.8) s-
32          some sort of phraseology would be included in the (0.6) agreement
33          this year.
34          (1.0)
35    A     but I would argue. (0.5) that we included it last year and we did it
36          (0.5) and I know a lot of the people on the shop floor say we didn't do
37          it (1.0) I would argue that we included it and we did it (0.2) and the
38          result of it was that we agreed to make no change
39          (2.9)
40          and equally a- if we incorporate a paragraph this year (0.4) there is no
41          commitment to any change (.) but we would at least (0.5) discuss it
42          during the course of the year (0.5) and as we've seen i- (0.5) in the-
43          (0.7) ( ) here (0.4) there are a number of complexities which have to
44          be addressed anyway
45          (5.3)
46    A     comments
47          (0.9)
48   (?)    ( )
49          (5.3)
50    J →   so what you're saying is we'll have the same (0.2) wording as what
```

```
51        we had last year
52        (0.4)
53  A    ⎡ no (0.2) ⎡ I'm saying we could amend ⎡ the wording if you=
54  B    ⎣ no       ⎣ (it's not)               ⎢
55  (?)                                  (   ⎣ )
56  A    =⎡ wish we would agree on some form of wording
57  John: ⎣ (amend)
```

In two main respects Andy is designing the management position with caution. Firstly, he is circumspect about what activity he is performing here; he shifts between identifying it as an overt offer which constitutes a *FUNDAMENTAL CHANGE in our position* (line 14), and identifying it as an exploratory precursor to an offer -*I'm just asking I'm not saying we're gonna do it* (lines 17-18). Following the qualification by his co-team members of his reference to the 'thirty seven hour week' (lines 16-22), Andy again describes what activity he is doing. However, the ambivalence surrounding whether this counts as an 'offer' (or 'proposal') or not is manifest in the self-repairs occurring in this restatement — *I mean tha- is a fundamental ch- and I'm not saying we would do that I'm asking your opin- your (1.3) I'm asking you whether (0.2) it would* (lines 24-26).[4]

The second respect in which this turn is cautious is that Andy stipulates how restricted an 'offer' this is. In his presentation the paragraph does not commit management to implement any changes, it only constitutes an agreement to discuss the issue (lines 40-41); and the union side are dissuaded from harbouring any hope that these discussions might precipitate such changes by Andy's reminder that there are *a number of complexities which have to be addressed anyway* (lines 43-44).

The union side have alleged in the preceding talk that the previous year's paragraph did not in fact lead to discussions. Since Andy is now proposing the same solution his 'offer' may well attract a cynical interpretation from the shop stewards. He anticipates this by reasserting the management contention that last year's agreement was upheld (lines 35-38).

Andy thus makes it clear that he is offering to concede only that management will discuss the shorter working week, though there is little hope of such discussions leading to any changes. The implication is that the paragraph would provide only the smallest chance of effecting any change to the present situation, although management do not describe this in explicit terms. However, John confronts them with an explicit version of this implication in which the meagreness of the offer is intensified to depict the paragraph as 'empty' (lines 50-51); it is not simply that this 'proposal' offers no more guarantees than last year's, but that it offers *exactly* what they got last year.

Management are thereby attributed with the intention of presenting this as an 'offer' when they are not actually offering to give the union side anything.

By extracting and formulating an explicit version of an inauspicious implication of the recipient team's prior talk and designing it to be unacceptable, the speaker invites the recipient team to deny it. It implicates rejection of the proposal but, at the same time, it identifies a concessionary modification which the recipient team can make to their position. The speaker thereby creates a next 'slot' in which their version is disconfirmed and the recipient team's position is reformulated in a way which may offer the speaker its antithesis (lines 53 onwards). Such 'pessimistic formulations' can therefore be employed to highlight and subvert unfavourable implications of prior talk when a team is 'under pressure'. In other words, when a speaker discerns that the other side is giving little or no ground, they can present an explicit version of this interpretation which the recipient team will not find acceptable: the recipient team disconfirms the formulation and then reformulates their position to 'set the record straight', often in a way which is concessionary. Thus, a 'pessimistic formulation' can be used to generate a concession from the recipient team and thereby change the trajectory of the negotiation to make it more favourable to the speaker's team. Furthermore, it appears from these data, that this means of eliciting concessions is confined to the union side: i.e. it is used by the side that is seeking something through negotiations rather than by the side that is resisting giving ground.

So with a formulation the speaker is signalling that they are prepared to make an exchange of concessions; a possible way forward towards agreement is identified through a tendentious interpretation of prior talk. The negotiating work which formulations are involved in is oriented to by the recipient team.

4.2. The recipient team's response

When a speaker formulates a version of the sense of prior talk, the relevant next action is often a confirmation or disconfirmation from the recipient team (see Heritage and Watson 1979). However, in the design of this activity they display their understanding of the resolution-implicativeness of the formulation. Formulations make an implicit offer by identifying a concession which will make the recipient's position more acceptable to the speaker. The recipient team can then 'make' or reject that concession by confirming or disconfirming the formulation. Thus, formulations generate the negotiation of concessions and not the collaborative inspection of the sense of prior talk.

Although both 'optimistic' and 'pessimistic' formulations are routinely oriented to as presenting tendentious interpretations of prior talk which implicate the speaker's position, there is a difference in the kind of problems which they each present to the recipient team.

4.2.1. 'Pessimistic formulations'

The pejorative interpretation of the recipient's talk which 'pessimistic formulations' provide proposes that the two sides are in direct opposition; if the recipient team were to confirm it this confrontation would be established. They are built to be disconfirmed and always generate upfront and categorical disconfirmation. The recipient's denial is followed by a reformulation which 'sets the record straight' by showing what the recipient was 'actually saying' in their prior talk. The response is structured thus:

disconfirm [*no (that's not what we're saying/I said)*]

+ reformulation [*we are saying/I said...*]

The recipient team usually reformulates their position to ward off the potential confrontation by implementing a modification to bridge the gap between the teams exposed by the formulation. Such modifications usually demonstrate the unwarrantability of the speaker's interpretation by taking the form of compensatory offers. This is illustrated in excerpts 5 and 7:

(5) [WGE:3:A:300]
(Union formulate the gist of the prior management proposal. Management: Andy (A) and Bill (B); union: John (J).)

```
1   J        so what you're saying is we'll have the same (.) wording as what we
2            had last year
3            (0.4)
4   A→   ⌈ no (0.2) ⌈ I'm saying we could amend ⌈ the wording if you=
5   B →  ⌊ no        ⌊ (it's not)                 ⌊
6   (?)                                          ⌊ (    )
7   A    =⌈ wish we would agree on some form of wording
8   J     ⌊ (amend)
```

In excerpt 5, John's interpretation of the prior management proposal receives blunt disconfirmation from Andy and Bill (lines 4-5). In his subsequent restatement of what he *is saying*, Andy concedes that the wording could be amended *if you wish we would agree on some form of wording* (lines 4 and 7). Management are treating the formulation as resolution-implicative: that is, the union side are heard to be indicating how the management position can be modified to make it more acceptable.

(7) [LWK:185]
(The participants are discussing the union's contention that the increased amount of el

work (i.e. one-off jobs) is having a detrimental effect on their wage packets for which they want remedying action from management. Management are not conceding to take action. Management: Sam (S); union: Brian (B).)

```
1   B   so (.) what you're actually saying (that) you're gonna get
2       no movement on this el work.
3       (0.6)
4   S   that's not what I said,
5       (0.6)
6   B   ( )=
7   S   =all I'm saying is at the moment I can't see any justification for
8       it (0.8) based on the evidence I've got in front of me just now.
9       (0.9) .h one hand is saying YEH they've got a little bit on that
10      (0.8) but that's saying that when you're working (0.6) and if
11      we'd full volume you'd be earning more money than you've
12      ever done before
```

In excerpt 7, management's unwillingness to take action on the issue under negotiation is interpreted by the union side as constituting a final and unreasonable decision on the matter (lines 1-2). Sam denies this and then reformulates his position to reveal that his decision is temporary — the reason he is taking no action is because he wants to do some investigating first to discover whether it is justified (lines 7-12). Thus, he 'offers' the union side the possibility that the investigation will work in their favour and action will be taken.

So a 'pessimistic formulation' provides a straightforward option to the recipient team; it is in both parties' interests that it gets disconfirmed in order to avert further confrontation. It may be that in their subsequent reformulation the recipient's position remains unchanged, but nevertheless they display no doubt over whether the formulation should be disconfirmed or not (as co-team responses evidence, as in excerpt 5). 'Optimistic formulations' on the other hand warrant a more complex and cautious treatment.

4.2.2. 'Optimistic formulations'

'Optimistic formulations' are transparently being used as a strategic device to seek a concession and they are designed to maximize the recipient team's acceptance of it. It is in the speaker's interests to furnish a low-key description of the concession initially and to disclose the hidden 'extras' once it has been accepted by the recipient team as a way forward. The recipient team orients to the strategical and consequential character of the formulation's lexical design. In particular, they are alive to the potential 'gloss' character of the lexical forms (see Jefferson 1985). In other words, they orient to the possibility that the speaker is selecting this form to gloss over details which they will subsequently reveal. The recipient team infers what details lie implicit in a suspected gloss and the first thing they do in their response is to address them. This is illustrated in the management's responses to the two formulations encountered earlier:

(2a) [WGE:2:A:235] (detail)
(Management: Kev (K) and Andy (A); union: Pete (P))

```
  1   P    so what you would do is an in depth analys (.) analysing
  2         ⌈ of it ⌉ (0.4) ⌈ and you would like ⌉ to do it away from=
  3   K     ⌊ that's ⌋ what ⌊ w e   w o u l d   do ⌋
  4   P    =a (0.3) wage negotiation.
  5         (0.5)
  6   K    .t (.) e- ye- ye- but I will talk about it now but that's the sort of scene
  7         I(w) I would like to set up for doing this and I think that would be
  8         ⌈ a good thing, ⌉
  9   A    ⌊ and that's off ⌋ the record is it?
 10         (.)
 11   K    Y:ES all this is off the record there's nothing being recorded. that's
           (0.4) .hh and I think it's fair that you know how we're thinking.
```

Although Pete's initial formulation (lines 1-4 above) appears to furnish an innocuous interpretation of prior talk, it is not treated as such by management. Kev's response is cautious and this care displays his understanding that the formulation is resolution-implicative, and thus how he responds will have significant consequences for the subsequent talk.

His initial categorical confirmation of Pete's claim that management intend to look at the matter in depth (line 3), is qualified following Pete's continuation. Kev hesitates to confirm this additional component of Pete's formulation; his inchoate confirmation (*e- ye- ye-* line 6) is curtailed with a qualificatory self-repair in which he emphatically asserts that *but I will talk about it now* (line 6). In making this qualification he is recognizing a way in which his confirmation may be misinterpreted. This possibility connects with an earlier union allegation that management are preventing them from discussing sick pay. If he confirms Pete's formulation as it stands he may unwittingly find himself accused of revealing that management do not want to discuss sick pay after all. So before making any confirmation, Kev disambiguates Pete's *you would like to...* (line 2) to make it clear that he is saying what he *would prefer* to do and not what he *is only willing* to do. Having made this qualification he then confirms the intention which the formulation is attributing to his team (lines 6-8).

He does not, however, confirm that intention as it is presented to him; rather his confirmation is realized by a reformulation. This means that the concession he 'makes' is one which is formulated by himself and consequently one which he defines. His version is nonspecific: he describes Pete's formulation as the *sort of scene I(w) I would like to set up* (line 6-7). A co-team member (Andy) then makes an additional qualification (line 9) to ensure that they are all aware that this concession is unofficial (and consequently management cannot be held to it).

So in their response management orient to the resolution-implicativeness of the formulation. They understand Pete to be tendentiously interpreting prior talk to promote a way forward which favours his (i.e. the union's) side. In sanctioning this as an area of common ground, management cautiously delimit it to obviate any unwanted consequences which such an action might bring and to make it acceptable to them.

Management's cautiousness continues in their response to Pete's subsequent formulation (lines 1-2 in the following extract):

(2) [WGE:2:A:235] (detail)

```
1    P    so you would like the shop stewards to take it on faith that (they)
2         would (.) be discussing this (0.8) a:t (a) different ti:me.
3         (1.1)
4    B    ( r )
5    P       Lin dep r th:
6    K              L no no not this year.
7         (0.3)
8    B    no
9    P    no: r I never said this year.
10   K       L not thi-
11        (0.4)
12   K    but we WILL (0.3) YES definitely. (0.4) we will this is something we
13        could look at (0.3) and this is an area .hhhhh
14        r I  c o u l d  s a y  r in principle r .hhh r a-
15   P    [ (there's always) n ] ext y e a r.  ]      [
16   A    L (            )                            L but it is quite
17        possibly something which (0.4) could result in a:=er (1.4) fundamental
18        change? (0.3) which may not be:? (0.7) in your view (ve-) beneficial.
```

Management understand this formulation to be concession-seeking. Again, the first thing they do is to discern the nature of the concession being sought and to address any unacceptable elements they identify. Kev's *no no not this year.* (line 6) refutes a recognized implication of Pete's formulation; Kev is treating the phrase *a:t (a) different ti:me.* (line 2) as a gloss, strategically designed to conceal a more specific time scale which Pete has in mind. By anticipating it here, Kev ensures that it will not emerge later as a condition of the agreement being formed.

When the time limit has been excluded Kev confirms the formulation, thus accepting the concession (lines 12-14). However, as in the previous excerpt, that confirmation is accomplished through a reformulation. The concession he 'makes' is a qualified version of the one which Pete describes. His confirmation that management will discuss it at a later date may be initially emphatic (*but we WILL (0.3) YES definitely* line 12) but in the reformulation he qualifies it to *something we could look at* (line 12-13).

Again, management collaborate in responding to the union formulation. In his caveat, Andy (lines 16-18) is addressing a possible motive for the union side's promotion and acceptance of this 'bargain' by ensuring that they are not under the impression that such discussions would necessarily give them anything. He is therefore orienting to the concessionary work being done here.

The recipient team, then, discerns in an 'optimistic formulation' a concession which could form the basis for agreement. If it is acceptable to them they qualify and reformulate it so that the foundation being laid is carefully delimited. In doing this they orient to the strategic character of the formulation and to the fact that in its design there may be unfavourable consequences for them. The recipient's analysis of formulations is endorsed by what the speaker does in their next turn.

4.3. The speaker's subsequent turn

If a formulation is intended as a display of the speaker's understanding of the prior talk, and that formulation is subsequently qualified or disconfirmed, then it is revealed that the speaker has misunderstood. In some forms of talk, for example in ordinary conversation, such a realization is routinely displayed by the token *oh* (see Heritage 1984b). However, in these negotiations, qualifications and disconfirmations do not generate the management of misunderstanding — activities like apologies or displays of change-of-state do not occur. Instead, the speaker analyses the recipient's qualifications and disconfirmations as doing concessionary activity and specifically as accepting or rejecting an offer. This is cogently illustrated in the following excerpt:

(8) [WGE:3:A:180] (continuation of excerpt 1)
(Just prior to this excerpt, management defensively point out that the economic situation

at the time of the autumn talks was such that *neither* side would have dared to raise the issue of the shorter working week. Management: Andy (A) and Bill (B); union: Pete (P).)

```
 1   P    you're not actually saying that you DON'T want a shorter working
 2        week if I'm right. (0.6) ┌ you're just saying that you can't afford=
 3   (?)                           └ ((cough))
 4   P    =one at this: (0.6) particular time.
 5        (0.3)
 6   B    .t .hh ┌ can I- ┐
 7   A          └ we are ┘ realistic enough to appreciate (0.3) that (0.7) factors
 8        (0.3) impinging on us from outside (0.8) MAY WELL ONE day result
 9        in us having to: (0.5) to e- oo- (0.6) ach ┌ ieve a thirty seven=
10   B                                              └ bu-
11   A    =hour working week. but the ┌ circumstances withIN must be (0.6)
12   B                                └ bu-
13   A    suitable (0.7) to enable us to do it.
14        (0.8)
15   P    can I put that into a (0.8) bit more straightforward manner ( ) (0.9)
16        you're saying that 'til it's agreed nationally ((co. name))
17        ┌ won't have it=
18   A    └ no
19   A    =no ┌ we're not saying that at all ┐
20   B        └ no we're not saying that     ┘
21   P    ( )
22        (0.2)
23   B    let's say it another way
24        (1.7)
25        if it costs a thousand pounds to build a (0.5) ((product name)) twenty
26        five right now (0.7) then in a shorter working week it's not (gotta)
27        cost us any more. (0.4)
28        ( ┌ )
29   A      └ what we're con- that's the ┌ concern ┐
```

In this excerpt, Pete's initial formulation (lines 1-4) tentatively proposes that the lack of concessions on the shorter working week through these negotiations is a result of the economic situation and not a result of management's opposition to its implementation. The implication is that as soon as the economic situation is favourable management will be prepared to make concessions in this direction. The formulation highlights two possible explanations for management's position on the shorter working week: either they are adverse to it, or they are constrained by the economic situation. These alternatives have very different consequences for management. It may be that they are indeed opposed to a reduction in the working week, but to go on record saying this is likely to have serious repercussions for the negotiations. In order to avoid this management are in the position of having to confirm that the lack of movement is due to the economic situation. Pete's formulation is designed to elicit a confirmation that the obstruction is entirely an economic matter, thereby securing an official disavowal from management that the obstruction is caused by their own disinclination.

However, management indirectly and delicately disconfirm the formulation by reformulating their position to distance themselves from the intention it attributes to them (lines 7-13). This action is analyzed by Pete as a rejection of his offer and not as disconfirmation of his understanding of the management position. By declining the opportunity to confirm the formulation, management are heard to be saying that they are against the shorter working week. They are confronted with an explicit and intensified version of this implication in Pete's subsequent turn (lines 15-17). Pete re-presents this circumspect disconfirmation as equivalent to saying that they intend to hold out until the bitter end — the company *won't have it* until it is agreed nationally. So whilst in his initial formulation Pete tendentiously interprets management's position optimistically to propose an area of common ground, when that is disconfirmed, he interprets their position in the contrary direction to expose its oppositional character. By formulating an explicit version of the implication of their prior turn, Pete can elicit a denial that this is what management meant and a reformulation in which they may make a conciliatory offer.

A disconfirmation, then, generates a pursuit of the concession which is being sought through the 'optimistic formulation'. If the recipient team qualifies such a formulation, they are understood to be identifying an unacceptable element of the concession being sought. The speaker may be prompted to facilitate the recipient's acceptance by disclaiming the intention which the qualification imputes to them. To return to excerpt 5, Kev's rejection of a suspected time limit attributes an intention to Pete which he subsequently disclaims — *no: I never said this year.* (at the line indicated):

(2) [WGE:2:A:235] (detail)

       Pete <u>so</u> you would <u>like</u> the shop stewards to take it on <u>faith</u> that (they)
             would (.) be dis<u>cuss</u>ing this (0.8) a:t (a) <u>different</u> ti:me.
             (1.1)
       Bill (⌈)
       Pete ⌊ in dep ⌈ th:
       Kev   ⌊ <u>no</u> <u>no</u> <u>not</u> this year.

(0.3)
Bill no
→ Pete no: ⌜ I never said this year.
Kev   ⌞ not thi-
(0.4)
Kev but we WILL (0.3) YES definitely. (0.4) we will this is something we
could look at (0.3) and this is an area .hhhhh
⌜ I c o u l d s a y ⌜ in principle .hhh ⌜ a-

Alternatively, a qualification may be challenged by the speaker. In excerpt 9 (below), Pete qualifies management's formulation on the grounds that it omits the mention of six months (line 1). In response, Andy does not treat this as an omission which he now 'realizes' he made and which needs to be rectified; he is therefore not treating his prior formulation as an attempt to impartially represent the union position. Instead, he requests confirmation that this is something which the union side want (line 4):

(9) [WGE:2:A:314] (continuation of excerpt 3)

(Management have just formulated a resumé of the union position following a union proposal. Management: Andy (A); union: Pete (P).)

```
1   P    n:o (0.3) that's not what I said.
2        (1.0)
3   P    I says in six months time to have a look at it (.) again
4   A→   you want to be specific and say six months do you
5        (1.3)
6   P    I think you have to ( ) but I mean if you: (.) talked about it for six
7        months as well (1.2) it would take you up to next m- pay negotiations.
8        (1.0)
9   (?)  ⌜ mm hm
10  P    ⌞ because I'm not (.) stabbing you down onto one (.) exact spot
11       (.) because I know it might be a (.) bit controversial on: (.) your side.
12       (1.1)
13  P    .hh but ⌜ you  ⌜ must get ⌝ some discussion ⌜ going.
14  A           ⌞ but  ⌞ I mean- ⌟               ⌞ okay s-
```

By questioning the union qualification, Andy is heard to be indicating management's unwillingness to concede this point. The union side do not simply confirm that they want to be specific about the six months, but they provide a supportive argument for its inclusion which is designed to persuade management to accept: they reveal that such an inclusion does not commit management to implementing any changes (lines 6-13).

What these two excerpts illustrate is that, just as a speaker is heard to be proposing a 'way forward' when they provide a formulation of prior talk, so the recipient (or the speaker in a subsequent turn) is heard to be negotiating that 'way forward' through doing qualifications or understanding checks. In the organization of their talk during these formulation sequences, the participants are mutually orienting to doing concessionary activity, and specifically, to the negotiating work being accomplished through a formulation.

5. DESIGN PROPERTIES OF FORMULATIONS

The formulations under discussion are designed as demonstrations/checks of understanding. The speaker is formulating the gist, upshot or a resumé of prior talk and is presenting it as the sense of that talk. In this way, the speaker is effectively putting words into the recipient's mouth. This is very evident in the design of *gists* wherein the speaker identifies their action as saying-in-so-many-words-what-you-are-saying; thus, they are presenting a version of what the recipient team *is (actually) saying* as illustrated in the following excerpts:

(5) [WGE:3:A:300] (detail)

John   so what you're saying is we'll have the <u>same</u> (.) <u>word</u>ing as what we had
last year

(8) [WGE:3:A:180] (detail)

Pete   you're not actually saying that you <u>DON'T</u> want a shorter working
week <u>if I'm right</u>. (0.6) ⌈ you're just saying that you can't afford=
(?)   ⌊ ((cough))
Pete   =one at this: (0.6) particular <u>time</u>.

(8) [WGE:3:A:180] (detail)

Pete   can I put that into a (0.8) bit more straightforward manner ( ) (0.9)
you're saying that '<u>til</u> it's agreed <u>nation</u>ally ((co. name))
⌈ won't have it=

(7) [LWK:185] (detail)

John   you can jump in anytime you <u>like</u> here Brian?
(1.9)

Brian so (.) <u>what</u> you're actually <u>saying</u> (that) you're gonna get
       <u>no</u> movement on this el work.

(10) [WGE:3:A:180]

Pete   I'm just tryin'a thi ⌈ nk what <u>you're:</u> actually saying I mean
Kev   ⌊ yeh

Pete   (0.4) <u>what</u> you have just saying off reco ⌈ rd is (0.5) that=
Kev   ⌊ hmm <u>mm</u>

Pete   =people are a<u>busing</u> <u>sick</u> scheme and you would like ⌈ to see=
(Sam)   ⌊ phhh

Pete   =them <u>stop,</u>

(11) [WGE:1:A:269]

Pete   do I (0.2) <u>IF</u> <u>I</u> understand this right <u>we</u> <u>are</u> <u>not</u> in the position to make a
       claim. (1.0) the firm is saying that they are in a position
       (.)
       ⌈t o <u>o f f</u> ⌉ <u>er</u> us (0.2) <u>just</u> a six percent rise.
Kev   ⌊no (<u>that's</u>) ⌋

5.1. You're saying vs. you mean

In the design of *gists* the speaker purports to be reflecting the recipient's words back to them, rather than making an interpretation of what those words mean. This reflects a significant characteristic of these formulation sequences and, it appears, of these industrial relations negotiations in general. In formulations the speaker makes an implicit offer by interpreting prior talk, and that offer is then negotiated through ostensibly assessing whether that interpretation is acceptable or not. However, in doing this the participants maintain the sense of working on the level of literal representation rather than on the level of interpretation. The disconfirmation of 'pessimistic formulations' and the qualification or disavowal of an intention which is being attributed to a speaker, are accomplished through the speaker's reinvocation of what they did or did not say. This is shown in excerpts 8 and 9 which are reproduced again below:

(8) [WGE:3:A:180] (detail)

P   can I put that into a (0.8) bit more straightforward manner ( ) (0.9)
       you're saying that '<u>til</u> it's agreed <u>nation</u>ally ((co. name))

```
                  ┌ won't have it=
    A             └ no
    A →     =no ┌ we're not saying that at all ┐
    B →         └ no we're not saying that     ┘
    P       ( )
            (0.2)
    B →     let's say it another way (1.7) if it costs a thousand pounds to build a
            (0.5) ((product name)) twenty five right now (0.7) then in a shorter
            working week it's not (gotta) cost us any more. (0.4)
```

(9) [WGE:2:A:314] (detail)

```
    P →     n:o (0.3) that's not what I said.
            (1.0)
    P →     I says in six months time to have a look at it (.) again
    A       you want to be specific and say six months do you
```

The participants make and contest interpretations of one another's talk without explicitly marking that they are referring to *meaning*. The implication of this practice is that negotiators treat their talk as a literal representation of meaning (i.e. what-you-say-is-what-you-mean). Thus, when participants are working on the sense of their prior talk in the accomplishment of concessionary activity, they are collaboratively sustaining the literality of their talk and avoiding overt references to meaning.

A possible reason for this may lie in the characteristic circumspection of the negotiation talk which is represented in these data. Through cautious lexical and phrasal selection, the participants design their talk so that they will be heard to be saying what they want to be heard to be saying. However, this does not mean that speakers are being careful to spell out exactly what their position is. On the contrary, a principle purpose of this circumspection seems to be to create ambiguity. What can be read between the 'lines' is just as critical as the 'lines' themselves, and talk is crafted so as to invite the recipient to make specific inferences. So while a speaker is being observably precise and decisive about the design of their talk, and thus ostensibly spelling-out-exactly-what-our-position-is, they are implicitly conveying other things about what their position might be. Negotiators are alive to this possible paradox; they are aware of the multiplicity and ambiguity of their talk and of the way in which it is used for strategic purposes, but they do not explicitly refer to this kind of strategic work. There appears to be a consensual commitment to maintaining the 'literalness of our talk', manifest in the ways in which negotiators work on the strategic, inferential level under the guise of treating the talk as if it were literal. Perhaps the covert strategic behaviour of negotations makes it somehow problematic to make overt interpretations of one another's talk.

5.2. The circumspection of 'optimistic formulations' vs. the bluntness of 'pessimistic formulations'

Although 'optimistic' and 'pessimistic' formulations are both involved in seeking concessions, they accomplish it in different ways. 'Pessimistic formulations' provide a device for discounting inauspicious implications of prior talk and generating concessions, whilst 'optimistic formulations' provide a device for creating an opportunity out of prior talk for making concessions. This difference inheres in three distinguishing characteristics, two of which have already been discussed. Firstly, their sequential environment: 'pessimistic formulations' occur where the speaker discerns in prior talk an unwillingness on the behalf of the recipient team to make any concessions; in other words, where the speaker may consider their team to be 'under pressure'. 'Optimistic formulations', on the other hand, seem to occur opportunistically at any point where the speaker locates a way of shaping up prior talk in order to 'reveal' a way forward. Secondly, their sequential consequences: 'pessimistic formulations' receive upfront and categorical disconfirmation, whereas if the recipient team disconfirms an 'optimistic formulation', they do so indirectly and with mitigation. This leads to the third characteristic. In their different responses to 'optimistic' and 'pessimistic' formulations, the recipient team is orienting to the non-equivalence of these two kinds of formulations and this non-equivalence is built into their design by the speaker. 'Optimistic' and 'pessimistic formulations' are contrastively designed.

In line with the work they are used to accomplish, 'pessimistic formulations' are built to be disconfirmed. The unpropitiousness of the prior talk's implication is exacerbated in the formulation to maximize its unacceptance. It proffers a confrontational version of the recipient's talk and this inheres in its characteristic unequivocal and unmitigated design:

(5) [WGE:3:A:300] (detail)

> John   so what you're saying is we'll have the <u>same</u> (.) <u>word</u>ing as what we
>   had last year

(7) [LWK:185] (detail)
>   Brian   so (.) <u>wha</u>t you're actually <u>say</u>ing (that) you're gonna get <u>no</u> movement

on this el work.

(8) [WGE:3:A:180] (detail)
        Pete   can I put that into a (0.8) bit more straightforward manner ( ) (0.9)
                    you're saying that 'til it's agreed nationally ((co. name)) won't
                    have it=

Conversely, formulations which are built to be confirmed are characteristically circumspect and mitigated, and are thus designed to promote the concession being sought:

(8) [WGE:3:A:180] (detail)
        Pete   you're not actually saying that you DON'T want a shorter working
                    week if I'm right. (0.6)⌈ you're just saying that you can't=
        (?)   ⌊ ((cough))
        Pete   =afford one at this: (0.6) particular time.

In this extract, Pete's circumlocutory design minimizes and obscures the concession he is seeking. He does not explicitly claim that management are in favour of the shorter working week, but he implies it with his cautious phrase *you're not actually saying that you DON'T want a shorter working week*. Its tentative design promotes management's confirmation — for example, by displaying uncertainty through the hedge *if I'm right*. The affiliative and persuasive character of this activity is constituted in these mitigating design features.

        In the negotiation literature, these kind of mitigating design features have been associated with factors which are exogenous to the negotiating activity itself (e.g. politeness, relative power) and are therefore treated as superfluous to it (see, e.g., Brown 1977, Putnam and Roloff 1992, O'Donnell 1990, Neu 1988, also Bell this volume). However, as these formulations testify, the mitigated design of an activity is consonant with the interactive work it is being used to accomplish, and specifically, with the *negotiation work* it is accomplishing.

6. FORMULATIONS AND STRATEGIC BEHAVIOUR

Within the literature the strategical nature of negotiation has been treated as a primary, if not the superordinate, characteristic. Social psychologists tend to conceptualize negotiation as a game of strategy (Hosking and Morley 1991) in which the central research concern is to find a way of tracking and modelling the cognitive processes which underlie participants' strategic behaviour. The decision-making process is investigated to see how it affects the negotiation outcome, and, through this process, researchers seek to identify what constitutes 'good' negotiating practice. This theoretically-driven research leads to a specific notion about how strategic behaviour is relevant to the negotiating activity, and in turn, about how it should be explored.

Strategic behaviour is conceptualized as the consciously motivated action of individuals. It is instantiated not in the performance of those actions but in the cognitive states which triggered them. Consequently its investigation depends on the analyst being able to recover the speaker's cognitive state from their linguistic utterance. Both social psychological and linguistic research have focused on the negotiation 'behaviours' or 'strategies' which *underlie* the talk, identifying generalized patterns of strategic behaviour through taxonomic and quantitative research methods (see, e.g., Angelmar and Stern 1978, Donohue et al. 1984). This approach is problematic both in relation to the empirical character of talk-in-interaction, and in relation to what is relevant to the negotiating process.

Firstly, talk-in-interaction is not a straightforward product of, and therefore a reflection of, individuals' intentions. Interactants ascribe intentions to one another through their talk and thus treat the talk as under their voluntary control. But there is a gap between individuals' inclinations and the socially-organized practices to which they necessarily orient in order that their actions are understood in the way intended (Drew forthcoming, Wootton 1989). Interactants cannot do what they want, where they want, how they want, because they need to organize their behaviour in accordance with the sequential procedures and design principles through which orderly talk is constructed. The recipient's analysis of a turn-at-talk does not depend on their ability to access what is *actually* in the speaker's mind, rather it is derived from their orientation to these shared practices. The intention which the recipient attributes to the speaker *is that which the speaker presents to them*; the speaker's cognitive state is unavailable to the recipient as it is unavailable to the observer. So the perception of 'negotiation talk' as a window into the step-by-step strategic action of individuals is erroneous because it fails to regard talk-in-interaction in general, and negotiation talk in particular, as socially-organized activities.

Secondly, from the social psychological perspective *all* strategic behaviour is equivalent not only in its role in the negotiation process, but also in its relevance for the negotiators themselves. However, a distinction should at least be made between strategic behaviour which is designed to be concealed from the recipient team, and that which is designed to be available to them.[5] It is the former kind of behaviour which researchers have concerned themselves with, and it is related to practices like manipulation and deception. But as well as being dependent on the analyst's discovery of the speaker's intention, such strategic behaviour is perhaps not of central interest to the negotiation process. After all, if a team strategically misrepresents their position and the recipient team is unaware of the deception and responds accordingly, then it is immaterial to the negotiation process whether the speaker was behaving strategically or not. Strategic behaviour becomes interesting and analysable when it inheres in the organization of the talk, and thus, when it is *demonstrably relevant* to the negotiators themselves (see Schegloff 1992). This is evident in the interactional work of formulations and in the participants' mutual orientation to that work.

The ability of 'optimistic formulations' to function as strategic devices for the accomplishment of implicit offers depends on their strategical character being discernable by the recipient team. They are transparent by virtue of the fact that they have become conventionally associated with this work so that they form part of a recognizable sequential procedure. This kind of strategic behaviour has nothing to do with the speaker as an individual — it is not engendered by them. Rather the speaker is orienting to a socially-organized practice for accomplishing implicit offers in negotiations. On the occurrence of a formulation the speaker is inviting the attribution of a specific intention. They are immediately understood to be laying the foundations for a possible agreement. The inextricable association between formulations and concessionary activity is evidenced by the observation that (on the few occasions) when a formulation is intended as a demonstration or check of understanding, the speaker explicitly identifies that this is the activity they are doing. An example appears in excerpt 12 (the lines in which the formulation (F) and the response (R) begin are indicated):

(12) [SSN:4:2A:450]
(Union have just suggested that if management refuse to recognize qualification by experience, maybe they would make a commitment to the training of Clerical Assistants. Management: Brian (B); union: Neil (N).)

```
1   F → B    s::o:: (.) er let me just try and replay that back to you (until)
2             understand what you just said
3             (0.3)
4      N      (mm)
5      B      so you're saying (0.2) that er::: (1.4) er::m (1.1) for those people
6             who are (0.3) on on the substantial clerical assistants that we
7             would provide (.) training or qualification experiences so that if
8             they wanted to (0.8) extend their (0.7) their career aspirations
```

```
9              then they (0.3) would be able to do so
10             (0.6)
11  R → N      .t (.) yeh what we- (0.3) what we're not saying we're not seeking
12             to change our arg- our argument is we feel you should be
13             recognizing qualification by experience (0.3) to a greater extent
14             than you have done
15             (0.5)
16      B    ⌈ (er:)
17      N    ⌊ .hh the county council is very clearly coming down and
18             drawing a line ⌈ between spinal column points twenty one an'=
19             =twenty two      ⌊
20      B                        ⌊ yes
21      B    yeh
22             (0.5)
23      N    there's always been the opportunity for clerical assistants if they
24             choose (0.4) to seek training (0.6) we are conscious from our side
25             that (.) it's (0.3) been more difficult (0.7) in recent times for them
26             to get (0.4) those secondments and that training
27             (1.9)
28      N    on behalf of a group of very experienced and committed ⌈ staff=
29      B                                                              ⌊ mm
30             (0.6)
31      N    =we're asking for you to put back that level of commitment .hh to
32             try and provide them with the opportunity (0.3) to enter the main
33             stream clerical officer grades (0.9) if they want to do so
```

In lines 5-9 Brian formulates the gist of the prior union position, but he prefaces his formulation with a metacomment (lines 1-2) which explicitly identifies the projected action as a demonstration of understanding. By treating this metacomment as necessary, he is orienting to the likelihood that without it his formulation would not be understood in this way. A significant byproduct of doing this metacomment is that it indicates to the recipient team what the speaker is *not* doing (i.e. a resolution-implicative formulation). However, despite this explicit identification, the union side respond to the activity as if it is (or could be) resolution implicative. Neil begins by making it clear that the union side's prior talk does *not* constitute a concession (lines 11-14). Only then does he confirm Brian's understanding, but he does so by reformulating his position (lines 17-32). So formulations are recognized to be strategic and are treated cautiously even if the speaker claims not to be using them in this way.

The consciously strategical nature of 'pessimistic formulations' is less discernable. Whereas with 'optimistic formulations' the recipient team orients to the intentionality of their strategic deployment in the design of their response, with 'pessimistic formulations' such an orientation is not evident. In their categorical denial and reformulation the recipient team are treating the formulation as concession-seeking and as specifying what that concession comprises. But they are not demonstrably treating it as intentionally strategic.

The point is that 'pessimistic formulations' occur in a particular sequential environment, and so they may be occasioned by the sequential environment itself rather than being a result of the speaker's strategic intention. In other words, it may be just the kind of activity which it is appropriate to do at this point to get the team out of a 'tight spot'. However, there is a pattern to the design and implicativeness of these formulations; they constitute a sequential procedure in which they are functioning as a device to generate concessions. Such procedures may be sufficiently available to the participants for their conscious deployment (Drew forthcoming). One instance where a 'pessimistic formulation' is evidently being strategically employed is in excerpt 8 (cited below):

(8)   [WGE:3:A:180]

```
 1    P    you're not actually saying that you DON'T want a shorter working
 2         week if I'm right. (0.6) ⌈ you're just saying that you can't afford=
 3   (?)                            ⌊ ((cough))
 4    P    =one at this: (0.6) particular time.
 5         (0.3)
 6    B    .t .hh ⌈ can I-      ⌉
 7    A           ⌊ we are ⌋ realistic enough to appreciate (0.3) that (0.7) factors
 8         (0.3) impinging on us from outside (0.8) MAY WELL ONE day result
 9         in us having to: (0.5) to e- oo- (0.6) ach ⌈ ieve a thirty seven=
10    B                                               ⌊ bu-
11    A    =hour working week. but the ⌈ circumstances withIN must be (0.6)
12    B                                 ⌊ bu-
13    A    suitable (0.7) to enable us to do it.
14         (0.8)
15    P    can I put that into a (0.8) bit more straightforward manner ( ) (0.9)
16         you're saying that 'til it's agreed nationally ((co. name)) won't
17         have it=
```

In this excerpt, having failed to elicit a concession through affiliative action (lines 1-

4), Pete pursues it through disaffiliative action (lines 15-17). A 'pessimistic formulation' may thus afford a way of escalating concession seeking activity through subsequent tries.

A final point is that strategic behaviour seems to have been associated with being clandestine. Certainly, it is associated with competitiveness, the negotiating teams working against one another in their selection of strategies to ensure that they get the most favourable outcome. However, as formulations illustrate, behaving in an observably strategic manner does not provoke indignation, but is treated as acceptable and reasonable. Also, this strategic behaviour enables a potentially troublesome activity to be accomplished indirectly and the speaker's ability to do this relies on the recipient team's collaboration; formulations are not strategic devices which serve one team's purpose to the detriment of the other, rather they are means through which both teams can manage a task which they face as negotiators.

7. CONCLUSION

In these institutional negotiations, formulations provide one way in which negotiators can signal that they are prepared to engage in concessionary activity. Consequently, employing formulations enables the participants to overcome a central difficulty associated with making offers: namely, how to 'test the water' in order to reduce the chances of having their offer rejected. Formulations are able to accomplish this work because they form part of a routine sequential procedure which is oriented to by the participants as resolution-implicative. In providing a formulation, the speaker is selecting to extract and focus on a particular implication of prior talk, and this interpretative process is understood by the recipient to be tendentiously designed to indicate what the speaker can agree to.

So although formulations occur infrequently in these data, they constitute key moments in the talk when a bid is made to change the negotiating situation, providing an opportunity for the two teams to establish a basis upon which agreement may be built. Through confirming (or disconfirming) the formulation the recipient team 'makes' the concessionary modification which the speaker is promoting, thereby approving this as a potential direction towards resolution which can then be developed in the subsequent talk.

In this way, formulations enable negotiators to move towards resolution cautiously: negotiators are able to lay the foundations upon which an agreement may be built without overtly engaging in concessionary activity. Thus, it is not only the offer itself which is accomplished implicitly, but also the negotiation or rejection of that offer: through qualifications, reformulations and disconfirmations, the recipient team is heard to be accepting or rejecting the offer. In these formulation sequences, the participants are negotiating offers through ostensibly working on the sense of prior talk which enables them to avoid the divisiveness and awkwardness which is likely to accompany explicit rejections of overt offers.

NOTES

1. See Putnam and Jones 1982 for a review of this literature.

2. Phase models of the negotiation process incorporate some 'initiation' phase in which the teams discover the extent and nature of their conflicting goals. See Holmes (1992) for a review of this work.

3. Ethnographic phase models of the negotiation process (as it occurs in the negotiation meeting) (e.g. Douglas 1962, Gulliver 1979) have been criticized by conversation analysts for failing to construct empirical descriptions for the identification of these phases in the talk (see Firth 1991, Francis 1982). The observations being made here about formulations suggest how one might build an empirical account of negotiation 'phases' which is demonstrably relevant to the participants themselves. This endeavour is concomitant with the wider objectives of conversation analysis (see Schegloff 1992).

4. As this and a previous excerpt (excerpt 3) demonstrate there is sometimes an ambivalence among participants over what kind of activity a turn is doing, both in relation to its design and in relation to the way it is analyzed by the recipient. This is an area which needs exploring, but it appears that there are a number of highly consequential activities in (formal) negotiations which can pass as less consequential activities (e.g. an overt 'offer' may pass as a 'suggestion' or an implicit 'offer' may pass as an 'understanding check' and vice versa); the activity may therefore need to be categorically identified for subsequent talk, but, in turn, its ambivalence can be used as a resource to, for example, keep the speaker's options open. How an activity might be described then, is a relevant interactional issue for negotiators and is part of their orientation to the negotiating activity. This highlights the inappropriateness of a prevailing approach to negotiation in which categorical labels are assigned to the 'function' or 'behaviour' proposedly instantiated by a turn at talk (e.g. Donohue 1981, Angelmar and Stern 1978).

5. A speaker's ability to design their talk so that its strategical character is transparent to the recipient rests on the distinction between what a speaker may be doing on an official level vs. the implicit endeavours which that official action may be involved in accomplishing. Various sequential phenomena in which such strategical practices are instantiated have been identified in both ordinary conversation and institutional talk (see, e.g., Pomerantz 1980, Drew 1984, Bergmann 1992).

CHAPTER 6

MASKED NEGOTIATION IN A JAPANESE WORK SETTING

KIMBERLY JONES

1. INTRODUCTION

In his study of a mediation that took place in Northern Thailand, Bilmes stresses that any general knowledge of human activities must be rooted in a knowledge of how people from specific cultures carry out those activities on specific occasions (1992:570). Despite a vast body of work on the topic of negotiation, however, there has been relatively little detailed analysis of the language used in actual negotiations. This is especially true in the case of negotiations in non-European languages, with a few notable exceptions (e.g. Bilmes 1992a, Kulik 1992, Lindstrom 1992).

This chapter is an attempt to add to our knowledge of the general phenomenon of negotiation by considering a specific instance of negotiation activity: a Japanese discussion of job-related rights and responsibilities that took place between two co-workers, a female instructor of Japanese and the slightly older male teaching assistant who was working for her. At first glance, calling their conversation a "negotiation"

I am grateful to the participants in the Negotiations in the Workplace symposium who commented on a previous version of this chapter, and especially to Jack Bilmes, who was the discussant for the paper, to Alan Firth, and to Doug Maynard. Phil Gabriel, Keiko Hirokawa, Scott Jacobson, Shoji Takano, and Malcah Yaeger-Dror also offered helpful comments at a later stage of writing. Most of all I thank "Sakurai-san" and "Kimura-san", the participants in the conversation I describe in this chapter, for their cooperation and patience.

141

seems problematic. Certainly it was not a formal labor negotiation such as might occur at a meeting between company managers and union representatives. Francis (1986), in distinguishing between negotiation talk and ordinary conversation, suggests (among other criteria) that the former takes place at events which participants would recognize as negotiations. However, the participants in the conversation I analyze would almost certainly not have said that they were involved in a negotiation. In fact, it is likely that they would have denied emphatically that they were doing any such thing.[1]

Nonetheless, a careful analysis of the conversation, combined with a knowledge of the cultural context in which it occurred, makes it clear that negotiation was indeed taking place. The participants, who held very different positions on the issues discussed, tried to achieve a joint stance on which they could agree — a stance that would then have committed them to specific actions. However, I argue that because the issues being discussed would generally not be considered open to negotiation in Japanese culture and because of cultural beliefs about the importance of interpersonal harmony,[2] the two participants tried to mask the nature of the activity in which they were involved, presenting it both to themselves and to onlookers as something other than a negotiation. The effectiveness of this masking activity and the fact that the instructor and the teaching assistant ultimately failed to come to any agreement combine to obscure the negotiation activity in which they were engaged. The conversation shows how the cultural ideals of harmony and hierarchy constrain and shape some informal negotiations in Japan.

2. CULTURAL BACKGROUND

Negotiation, involving as it does the presentation and management of diverse viewpoints and goals, is a potentially difficult activity in any society. Because even amicable negotiations tend to draw attention to the differences between the parties involved, negotiation is especially difficult in a culture such as that of Japan, in which cultural values emphasize the importance of avoiding confrontation and maintaining harmony. The Japanese preference for avoiding overt discussion of conflict is well documented in the anthropological and sociological literature. Commonly cited ways of dealing with conflicts involve displacing or ignoring them and employing indirect third-party mediation, which allows the main parties to avoid meeting until after a compromise has been reached.[3]

Even in Japan, certain types of negotiations are considered acceptable, and even expected. This is most true in institutional settings, as with labor or business negotiations. Nevertheless, the popularity of books offering frustrated English-speaking business people advice on how to negotiate with their Japanese counterparts is ample evidence that negotiation is inevitably embedded in a specific language and a specific culture. Such books typically emphasize the ways in which the Japanese dislike of confrontation colors business negotiations. Formal negotiations are said to be mere rituals rather than occasions for reaching decisions together, for negotiation sessions tend to confirm outcomes that are predetermined by societal expectations, by previous third-party negotiation, or by consensus garnered through earlier discussions between the various parties to a decision (see, e.g., Graham and Sano 1984, March 1988).

The negotiation of problems that arise between co-workers is particularly difficult. Because maintaining a good relationship is felt to be an important part of being able to work together comfortably and effectively, the workplace is a setting in which overt confrontation is seen as inappropriate and as a threat to the smooth functioning of the organization.[4]

2.1. Background to the Conversation[5]

The conversation I will consider occurred one morning in the mid-1980s in a small office at a university in the United States. The office was shared by a group of four teachers who were teaching a Japanese language class together. All four were present that morning: Sakurai-san, a 30-year-old female instructor; Kimura-san, a 31-year-old male teaching assistant; and two American teaching assistants in their late 20s, of whom I was one. The primary participants in the conversation, Sakurai and Kimura, had known each other for only a few weeks. I had previously obtained permission to record in our office at any time, and my colleagues were not aware that I was taping that day.

Analyzing a conversation between people I knew well, and in which I was in fact a participant, gives me an intimate knowledge of the participants and the setting. It also made possible quite candid follow-up interviews with Sakurai and Kimura. While it is necessarily to be skeptical about participants' after-the-fact claims about conversations, I would argue, following Moerman (1988) and Bilmes (1992a), that ignoring sources of information that lie outside the immediate conversation is likely to lead to a less complete understanding of what occurred. This is especially true when the culture within which the talk took place is foreign to the analyst. Therefore, in looking for evidence of ways in which Japanese speakers engage in informal negotiations, I used not only the considerable amount of linguistic evidence within the conversation, but also my general knowledge of Japanese culture and my particular knowledge of these participants and their relationship, of events that took place before this conversation, and of what the participants themselves later said about their conversation.

The presence of two Americans raises the question of whether the talk was a natural Japanese interaction. The other American was not involved in the conversation at all, and both Sakurai and Kimura stopped speaking to me as they became caught up in their talk. Japanese speakers who helped with transcription noticed no sign of any "foreigner talk". Three somewhat uncommon English borrowings do show it to be typical of conversations between Japanese living in the United States, which often contain a higher than usual number of loan-words. While the talk does not seem to be stilted or unnatural, the presence of an audience was certainly a very important part of the speech context. Japanese with whom I have discussed this suggest that the presence of others who are not directly involved in a negotiation typically results in a more subdued and indirect interaction.

The talk leading up to the conversation in question involved the contents of a memo from our supervisor, an American woman only a few years older than Sakurai and Kimura. In the memo, which was addressed to me, she had explained how a number of routine tasks were to be carried out and had asked that I convey her directions to my co-workers. Previous instructions to us evidently had not been carried out adequately, for the memo primarily reiterated directions she had given before. Among the instructions that I was to pass on to Kimura was her request that he put three copies of any course materials he made in an envelope and leave it in her mailbox.

Kimura was obviously displeased on hearing the instructions. In the conversation that followed, he complained about the fact that our supervisor had made unilateral decisions about the requirements of our jobs. There are two reasons he may have felt this was a problem. First, a preferred decision-making strategy in a Japanese work context is to achieve consensus at all levels before formally reaching a conclusion. The process of developing a consensus is known as *nemawashi*, a metaphorical extension of a gardening term (*ne* [root] plus *mawashi* [going around]) which refers to cutting around the roots of a tree a year or two ahead of time to facilitate transplanting. In this case, there had been no *nemawashi*, and our supervisor had simply decided what was to be done without consulting with us.

A second potential source of friction was the fact that our supervisor was an American woman not much older than Kimura. While it is true that Kimura expressed a desire for prior consultation, *nemawashi* is typically thought of as a technique for making relatively major decisions. Certainly it is not uncommon for Japanese managers to make decisions about when their employees should complete tasks or about how those tasks should be carried out. Had these events taken place in Japan and had the supervisor involved been more 'typical' — that is, older, male, and Japanese — Kimura might have been less sensitive about following instructions. As it was, however, the fact that our supervisor was a woman, the lack of a substantial age difference, the fact that his status as a native speaker of Japanese gave him a certain authority in her eyes, and even, perhaps, his belief that America was a relatively egalitarian society — any or all of these factors may have rendered their relationship ambiguous to him.

Given Kimura's discontent with the instructions and with the lack of prior consultation, he had at least three potential courses of action for attempting to change the situation. One possibility would be to negotiate directly with our supervisor to try to persuade her to change her instructions and perhaps to consult with him ahead of time in the future. Another would be to try to manipulate our supervisor into opening negotiations with him. Still a third option would be to enlist the support of his immediate superior, Sakurai, and to have her, or the two of them together, approach our supervisor.

None of these options is ideal. A Japanese worker is expected to fulfill job obligations as requested rather than to counter a superior by trying to negotiate the conditions of the job. In a discussion of protests by Japanese status inferiors attempting to remedy perceived injustices, Pharr (1990) points out the difficulty of effective protest. She argues that in the absence of a tradition which values publicly expressing one's feelings (especially negative feelings) and struggling to obtain individual rights, would-be protesters must convince not only others, but also themselves, that they have a right to protest. Doing so is difficult for a number of reasons, including the high values placed on deferring to authority, fitting into one's place in the social hierarchy, exhibiting self-sacrifice and endurance, avoiding overt confrontation, and achieving consensus and compromise (Pharr 1990). Perhaps because of these cultural constraints against protest and confrontation, Kimura chose the least direct of the various options available to him and opened negotiations with Sakurai rather than dealing directly with our supervisor.

3. THE CONVERSATION[6]

Oishi (1985) comments that the general rule for any type of discussion in Japanese calls for a long tensionless introduction. However, as soon as Kimura understands the message from our supervisor, he immediately begins to complain forcefully about the instructions, threatening not to obey the directions he has just received (appendix, lines 1 and 3). He uses dramatization and strategic style-shifting to paint a picture of himself as a rebel, unafraid of disobeying what he claims are inappropriate orders. At the same time, he introduces some humorous elements into the talk, leaving open the possibility that his words can be taken as joking. Sakurai cooperates by laughing after each of the two points where he uses the final particle *ne*, which speakers use to appeal to listeners for agreement.

Kimura speaks very rapidly in line 1, saying that hearing instructions like this makes him feel like disobeying: *Soo iu no o kiku to boku sakaraitaku naru no ne¿* Sakurai gives a quick laugh and says something unintelligible. Kimura then emphasizes what he has said by repeating his utterance in similar words in line 3. His initial statement there is even stronger than line 1 because he omits the final particle *ne*, thus turning his sentence into a flat declaration. He then expresses his intention to refuse to do as requested. However, the force of his threat is softened by the petty nature of the proposed disobedience — he will turn in materials on time as requested, but without putting them in envelopes — and by his somewhat humorous portrayal of a scene in which he turns in the materials without first putting them in envelopes, our supervisor complains, and he defiantly asks her the reasons behind the requirement that we use envelopes. Line 3 is also softened slightly by the use of *kedo* before the final particle *nee*. A speaker who ends a sentence with a final trailing *kedo* leaves the floor open for possible objections from other participants.

Here and throughout the conversation, Kimura switches rapidly between predicates in direct-style (an informal or intimate register) and distal-style (a more distant or formal register).[7] He begins line 3 in direct style, which makes his complaint more forceful and the envisioned scene more vivid. He then switches to distal style when quoting what he plans to ask our supervisor. Paradoxically, this use of distal style also adds vividness. Direct quotation is less frequent in Japanese than in English, and putting the quote in the distal style that he would use were he actually to say this to our supervisor makes the scene seem more immediate. The last sentence of line 3, directed at Sakurai and at me, is also in distal style.

Sakurai outranks Kimura, and they had not known each other for long at the time of this conversation. This suggests that he might tend to use distal forms when speaking to her. However, he is slightly older than she, and he had also been teaching in this language program for longer. When I interviewed her, she said that from early in their acquaintance they had ordinarily used direct style with each other. She interpreted his use of distal forms in this conversation as an indication of anger. She also pointed out that partway through the conversation he switched from the less formal first-person pronoun *boku* to the more formal *watasi*. Listening to this section of the tape again, she promptly said: *Monku o yutte ru. Watasi to yutte ru kara.* ("He's complaining. Because he's saying *watasi*".)

In addition to his strategic use of distal-style quotation, Kimura also mimics the belligerent tone of voice that he proposes using when he talks to our supervisor. Given the usual rules of interaction between superiors and subordinates in Japanese society, and given Kimura's usual behavior with our supervisor, it is unlikely that he would really take this tone. The belligerent intonation dramatizes his proposed rebellion. At the same time, however, it seems slightly outrageous and thus at least potentially humorous, reminiscent of the fantasized claims of physical prowess which Maynard (1985) found used to frame a children's dispute as a playful one.

Sakurai's laugh in response to his initial complaint in line 1 also suggests that it might be possible to treat the situation as somewhat of a joke. Had she instead made a stern pronouncement about disobedience being an inappropriate response, a quite different conversation would have resulted. In response to line 3, Sakurai laughs again. In fact, there is a high frequency of laughter throughout the talk despite the fact that it is not a particularly amusing conversation. Most of the laughter comes from Sakurai, who takes a relatively conciliatory approach to Kimura's complaints. Yamada notes the occurrence of "nervous laughter" (which she contrasts with "funny laughter") from Japanese involved in confrontational talk (1989:377-380). Certainly, Sakurai's laughter has a nervous edge to it and is one way she indicates that she is uncomfortable with the talk. However, elsewhere I have proposed that we need to recognize laughter that falls somewhere between Yamada's two poles — laughter produced by nervous participants that is nonetheless "funny laughter", occurring in response to participants who deliberately try to lighten the atmosphere (Jones 1990:300). If a complaint or a statement of rebellion can be laughed at, it can be treated as less serious and less threatening than might otherwise be true.

Regardless of whether Kimura really intended to follow through on his threats, his humorous way of speaking and his exaggeration of his own audacity to the point where it becomes slightly ridiculous provide Sakurai with a reason for acting amused. Conversely, Sakurai's laughter gives Kimura the opportunity to adopt a joking tone. The two of them cooperate to make their confrontation less threatening than it might otherwise have been and to mask the fact that they are dealing with serious concerns.

While Kimura's threat seems trivial, refusing to fulfill one's job responsibilities is a standard technique in Japanese culture for protesting perceived inequity (Pharr 1990:111). When I interviewed her later, Sakurai commented that Kimura might well have intended to disobey the envelope order. He evidently did not feel he could complain directly to our supervisor. At any rate, he never did so. However, had he disobeyed one or more of her instructions, she might have been provoked into asking him why he was not doing as she had requested. He could then have taken the opportunity to discuss his dissatisfaction with her.

During the next section of the conversation (omitted from the transcript), Kimura tried to get me to clarify our supervisor's instructions. He then began to develop the theme of rebellion, expressing in quite forceful terms his belief that authority, particularly arbitrary authority, should be resisted. In line 19, Kimura uses the verb *sakarau* again.

This time, however, it is in the perfective aspect, treating his rebellion as an accomplished fact: "It's that I *disobeyed*". After a pause of approximately one second, he says authoritatively that one must maintain some resistance (line 19; *rezisutansu o nokosu*; more literally, to keep some resistance in reserve). Through his use of the word *rezisutansu*, a loan-word from English "resistance" that is used especially of wartime resistance movements, Kimura invokes a battle metaphor. To this statement Sakurai simply replies *soo desu ka* with sentence-final falling intonation ("Is that right".), and she and I both laugh. Kimura continues in line 21, saying that we must teach our supervisor a lesson (*omoi sirasu*) — the lesson being that we will not always meekly say "yes, yes" and do as we are told (*hai hai to yuu koto o kiku*).

After his initial, somewhat softer, statements and his depiction of a hypothetical rebellion, Kimura has moved to stronger, but still fairly general statements concerning the necessity of resistance when faced with unreasonable demands. Sakurai continues to laugh or make minimal responses without taking the floor. Then at the end of line 23, after a pause of two seconds, Kimura makes his strongest statement of resistance, saying resolutely: *Da kara dyuu wa mamoranai* ("And so, I won't meet the deadlines".).[8] This threat to refuse to meet the deadlines for turning in work clearly poses a more serious threat to the team-teaching effort than did the threat to turn in his materials sans envelope. Sakurai, who as the instructor in charge of the course is responsible for making sure that job responsibilities are met, begins to protest.

Kimura's announcement that he will not meet the deadlines is followed by a one-second pause and laughter from Sakurai before she responds in line 24. Up to this point in the conversation, Kimura has been stating his position in ever stronger terms, and Sakurai has not objected or tried to defend our supervisor. Even when Kimura says that our supervisor must be taught a lesson, hardly a respectful phrase to use about a superior, Sakurai does not oppose him explicitly; she merely echoes the verb *omoi sirasu* laughingly in a questioning, incredulous tone. Kimura simply says *soo soo* ("right, right"), and continues. This shows one potential risk of deciding not to express opposition explicitly — such a strategy is off-record, and thus deniable and less face-threatening (Brown and Levinson 1987), but it is also easier to ignore than is more overt opposition.

It is only after Kimura announces that he will not meet the deadlines that Sakurai finally begins to attempt to dissuade him from his proposed rebellion, saying *tyotto, sore wa de mo mazui n zya nai desu ka?* ("Isn't it that that's a bit of a bad idea?" Or, less literally, "That's not a good idea, is it?"). Although Sakurai opposes Kimura quite bluntly here, she softens her utterance in three ways: she laughs as she speaks; she uses a hedge, *tyotto*, ("a bit"); and she phrases her sentence as a negative question (rather than, for example, a declarative, which would have sounded stronger). She also uses distal style, softening the impact of her blunt opposition by establishing a bit of distance between Kimura and herself. This style-shifting is particularly significant because it is one of only two times in the conversation that she uses a distal form.[9] However mitigated the utterance, however, it signals the point where Sakurai begins an attempt to persuade Kimura that he should agree to follow orders.

In answer to Sakurai's opposition, Kimura laughs, but he also elaborates on his position, saying in line 25 that he too has *tugoo* ("circumstances"). (The phrase *watasi ni mo tugoo ga aru* ["I, too, have circumstances".] is used to remind others that they should not be selfish and think only of their own convenience.)

Sakurai next resorts to two canonical strategies for disagreeing in Japanese — canonical in that Japanese speakers often suggest them as appropriate ways to disagree if disagreement cannot be avoided. One strategy is to acknowledge or even agree with the opposed position before expressing one's disagreement. The other is to disparage oneself somehow before disagreeing.[10] Both of these strategies serve to mitigate disagreement. However, because of their canonical status as good ways to handle bad situations, they also make it clear that the speaker is engaging in disagreement (Jones 1990, 1992).

Sakurai tries the first of these two strategies in line 26, beginning by acknowledging what Kimura has just said. Kimura interrupts with a further protest before she can finish her utterance. Line 27 is the closest he comes to openly mentioning what he would no doubt like to see as the outcome of their talk — for Sakurai to take his side and talk to our supervisor. He does not directly request that she do so, however. Rather, his utterance is framed as a question about Sakurai's feelings: "Don't you want to say, 'Please don't decide without at least consulting us?'". This is followed by 2.5 seconds of silence, the longest pause in the conversation, after which Kimura adds an emphatic "nee", again seeking agreement.

Sakurai begins to speak once more in line 28, only to be interrupted by Kimura yet again. She then resorts to ordering him to wait a minute (line 30). When he agrees to do so, she next tries the second strategy mentioned above, disparaging herself by implying that the problem is at least partially her fault because she has failed to post a chart listing the deadlines so that everyone will know when they are (lines 32 and 34). With this utterance, she also attempts to redefine Kimura's complaint, suggesting that the real obstacle to his compliance is that he may not know when the deadlines are. (This is unlikely, since upcoming tasks and the relevant deadlines were typically discussed in staff meetings.)

Kimura makes a minimal response in line 35, and Sakurai then concludes her argument by stating that the existence of deadlines is an inevitable part of any job. Her statement, *tumari, dyuu wa zettai* ("in short, deadlines are absolutes"), is remarkably parallel to Kimura's threat to disregard the deadlines in line 23. Each begins with a conjunction relating the statement to the preceding talk, followed by the topic *dyuu* ("deadlines") and a predicate commenting on the topic. Kimura's comment is *mamoranai* ("I won't meet [them]); Sakurai's is *zettai* (literally, "absolute"). She continues, explaining what she means by saying that deadlines are absolutes, and again her choice of words neatly parallels Kimura's: while he speaks of the necessity of *rezisutansu* (resistance), she uses the word *eguzisutansu* (from English "existence"). *Eguzisutansu* is not a commonly used loan-word in Japanese, and it seems likely that Sakurai uses it because of Kimura's use of *rezisutansu*, whether to minimize the differences between them by using similar language (Hasegawa 1985) or to try to top his use of an English loan-word.[11] Her use of words and constructions that parallel his also adds a game-like quality to the talk.

In line 37 Kimura first acknowledges what Sakurai has said and then begins to object again. However, this time he is interrupted by Sakurai, who suggests that the real problem is not the existence of deadlines but rather, whether those deadlines are appropriate. In making this suggestion, she takes a stance somewhat closer to Kimura's, since he has been complaining that he has not been consulted about when deadlines should be.

Kimura agrees emphatically with her assessment, and his stance too begins to shift slightly. Although pronouns are less frequently used in Japanese than in English, they are used with greater frequency in conversations involving conflict (Jones 1990). At this point in the conversation, Kimura has already referred to himself with a first-person pronoun (either *boku* or *watasi*) several times, always in forceful statements of his position (lines 1, 3, 19, and 25). Now, however, he switches to the first-person plural *watasi-tati* and states that our supervisor is making decisions without consulting *us* (line 39), thus putting Sakurai and himself on one side of the conflict and our supervisor on the other.

At this point, Sakurai and Kimura have at least managed to agree that whether or not the deadlines are appropriate is an important issue. Their basic difference of opinion, however, remains unresolved: Kimura has shown no signs of changing his position that inappropriate deadlines should be ignored, and Sakurai has shown no sign of believing rebellion is either desirable or necessary. Kimura gets in the last word in lines 39 and 41, when he comments that it is true that our supervisor makes decisions without talking with us, and then, turning back to his own desk, mutters something partially inaudible under his breath in a dissatisfied tone of voice. Sakurai makes no further response, and she and I also return to our desks to settle down to work again. A small degree of superficial agreement has been reached, but the overall impression one is left with at the end of this talk is of the participants having hastily dropped a topic that became too hot to handle.

4. MASKING NEGOTIATION

An hour after this conversation ended, Sakurai and I were alone in the office working quietly at our desks when she suddenly sighed and said: *Ningen kankee wa muzukasii* ("Human relationships are difficult"). A few weeks later, I mentioned to both Sakurai and Kimura that I had the "envelope conversation" on tape. Both recognized immediately the conversation to which I was referring, and both seemed somewhat embarrassed. Their embarrassment was still obvious when I listened to the tape with them in individual follow-up interviews later.

It is clear that the conversation was a significant one for both Sakurai and Kimura. From a non-Japanese perspective, however, it is less easy to recognize the negotiation of job issues that takes place. Firth (personal communication) has said that a critical aspect of negotiation is that some outcome or decision is dependent on the collaborative work of the parties involved, but these co-workers do not seem to reach a decision together. Part of the difficulty is that they fail to achieve a mutually acceptable outcome. Unable to agree on a joint stance and a course of action, they abruptly break off their conversation, turn their backs on each other, and walk back to their desks. Had they reached a compromise, or had Sakurai offered to talk to our supervisor on Kimura's behalf, the negotiation that took place would be more transparent.

An even more important factor in obscuring what is going on in the conversation is that Sakurai and Kimura actively work to mask the fact that they are negotiating. Kimura never asks Sakurai to intervene for him. He threatens and postures, then attempts to get her to agree that we should be consulted before our supervisor makes decisions. Sakurai first tries to avoid the issue by laughing and refraining from protesting as Kimura complains. Once she begins to argue for her position, she uses hedges, style-shifting, and canonical strategies to mitigate her utterances. Both participants cooperate in an attempt to construct an alternative, playful, reading of their conversation. Kimura contributes to the attempt at lightness by his dramatic portrayal of himself as a rebel and by his excessively forceful language. Sakurai helps by laughing at Kimura's words and by using words and constructions which parallel his. Neither could have hoped to achieve a lighter tone without the work of the other. Unfortunately, even working together they are ultimately unsuccessful: the tension grows, and they break off their conversation abruptly.

Sakurai and Kimura work to mask their negotiation because admitting that a negotiation was underway would have entailed violating at least two cultural ideals—the ideal of harmony and the ideal of hierarchy. Given the value placed on harmony and the threat that a lack of accord poses to a relationship, Japanese co-workers try not to end up on different sides of an issue. Overt negotiations may be aimed at achieving an agreement between the parties involved, but they also make painfully obvious the existence of differing opinions and goals. To engage in open negotiation is to admit to a lack of harmony. In addition, because of the value placed on social hierarchy in Japanese culture, subordinates are not expected to negotiate over whether they will obey a superior's orders. Because overt negotiation would have called attention to the fact that Kimura was attempting to negotiate orders from a superior, the participants keep their negotiation off-record, and thus deniable.

This does not mean that they are unaware of the negotiation in which they are involved. Kimura has no other options he finds acceptable for dealing with what he perceives as unfair job requirements. Sakurai knows this, for she later commented that he would not have felt comfortable bringing up these issues with our supervisor. She understands the Japanese custom of employing third-party mediation, and, as a Japanese in a position of authority, albeit limited authority, she expects to have to take care of her subordinates. In fact, she often passed on Kimura's complaints to our supervisor. Sakurai must recognize at least the possibility that she is being urged to take action on his behalf in this case as well. As for Kimura, because of the cultural background they share, he knows he need not take the risk of explicitly asking her to intercede for him. He can count on her to at least consider doing so if he can make his feelings known to her, especially if he can persuade her to share his view of the situation.

The work of masking the negotiation is made somewhat easier because it is very common in Japan for people with grievances to complain to uninvolved third parties as a way of venting their feelings.[12] If challenged, Kimura could always claim that he was simply letting off steam rather than seriously attempting to change the conditions of his job. In fact, when I interviewed him later, he did say at one point that he had been speaking partially in jest. Complaints give aggrieved parties opportunities to express their feelings without confronting the people who have offended them. More direct expressions of negative emotion are generally felt to be childish and inappropriate. People who complain do not necessarily harbor any expectation that the person complained to will intercede, or even has the power to intercede, on their behalf. A sympathetic listener may be all that they are looking for. The advantage of Kimura's negotiating strategy is that his talk can be taken as complaining for the sake of complaining. If necessary, he could safely deny any serious intent to enlist Sakurai's assistance in dealing with our supervisor.

Nevertheless, both Sakurai and Kimura treat the issue as one that needs resolution, and both work to find common ground between their positions. For each, the desired outcome seems to be a joint stance on which they can agree. Agreement, had they reached it, would have entailed certain actions. Had Sakurai prevailed, she would have committed herself to posting a list of deadlines, expecting in return that Kimura would comply with those deadlines. Had Kimura convinced Sakurai that he was being treated unfairly, he could have expected her to intervene with our supervisor for him, ideally leading to a situation where deadlines were set only after discussion with all of the teachers.

The actual outcome fell somewhere in the middle. Sakurai did not consult with our supervisor about this issue. Our supervisor continued to set the deadlines, and Sakurai posted them in our office. Kimura sometimes complied with them. At other times he turned in his work late enough to inconvenience our supervisor, although never so late that the students did not have materials by the time they needed them. It is unclear whether he did this because he was genuinely too busy to get his work done on time or whether it was a form of covert protest.

5. CONCLUSION

A knowledge of Japanese culture proved to be crucial to understanding how the participants in this talk were engaging in negotiation, showing the necessity of analyzing negotiations (and other types of talk) in terms of the cultural context in which they are rooted. On the surface, Sakurai's and Kimura's conversation seems to be interpretable as a simple gripe session in which he complains about the conditions of his job and she tries to smooth things over.

Despite the superficial resemblance to a gripe session, however, Sakurai and Kimura are clearly trying to achieve a joint stance on the issue of job rights and responsibilities. Had they been able to do so, the agreed-upon stance would have had consequences for their future actions. Given the cultural context in which this conversation takes place, Kimura must have expected to initiate a negotiation when he broached his complaint with Sakurai. The tradition of indirect mediation in Japanese culture gives him every reason to hope she might intercede with our supervisor for him if he can persuade her of the validity of his complaints. On the other hand, he can not expect her simply to listen sympathetically and approvingly, given her responsibility for the course and her position as his supervisor (despite the fact that their relative status was complicated by issues of age, gender, and the fact that he had been at the university for longer than she). And indeed, her response to his complaints, while not entirely unsympathetic, was to try to persuade him to agree to her point of view and to accept her offer to post a list of deadlines as a compromise that would make it possible for him to comply with the requirements of his job.

This conversation also shows that not only is negotiation activity not limited to formal negotiations, but that participants engaged in informal negotiation may at times deny that that is what they are doing and may even actively work to mask the negotiation work in which they are involved. This is especially likely to happen when there are cultural constraints against negotiating in specific settings or over specific issues. In a Japanese context, the high values placed on interpersonal harmony and on fitting into one's appropriate place in a social hierarchy are powerful constraints on negotiations.

Looking at how Sakurai and Kimura managed to mask the negotiation they were conducting makes clear that it is essential that researchers studying negotiation not assume that it is easily recognized. When participants work to mask their negotiations as Sakurai and Kimura did, there may be relatively little to distinguish the resulting talk from 'ordinary conversation'. A masked negotiation is no less a negotiation, however, and an understanding of such cases is important if we are to have a well-rounded view of the more general phenomenon of negotiation.

NOTES

1. Note that it is only these participants, not other Japanese, who would likely deny the negotiation that is going on in the conversation.

2. I do not wish to imply that Japanese interactions are more "harmonious" than those in other cultures. I have previously argued that the "myth of harmony", the idea that Japanese interactions should be and are harmonious, is an inadequate reflection of what actually happens in Japanese interactions. Nonetheless, the myth remains a powerful constraint on how conflicts are managed in Japanese talk (Jones 1990, 1992).

3. See, for example, Beardsley, Hall, and Ward (1959), Dore (1978), Moeran (1989:chap.2), Smith (1978), and Smith and Wiswell (1982). Only recently has there been some study of more overt mechanisms for managing conflicts that arise in Japan. Recent work on the language used in interpersonal conflicts in Japanese includes Jones (1990, 1992), Nakata (1992), Noda (1990, 1992), Szatrowski (1992), and Watanabe (1992). There has been somewhat more exploration of conflicts in institutional settings. See, for example, Pharr (1990) and most of the studies in Krauss, Rohlen, and Steinhoff (1984).

4. There are exceptions, of course. In some workplaces overt confrontation seems to have become accepted as the normal way of doing business. Shoji Takano (personal communication) has commented that staff meetings in a high school where he once taught were routinely occasions for quite acrimonious debate.

5. The discussion in this section and the following one is adapted from a more general study of conflict in Japanese conversation (Jones 1990) which was supported by a Fulbright-Hays Dissertation Fellowship and a University of Michigan Rackham Graduate School Predoctoral Fellowship. I am grateful to Polly Szatrowski, Pete Becker, and John Swales for their support and criticism throughout that study.

6. The transcript of this conversation (in the appendix) gives the transliterated Japanese conversation above and an English translation below. I have adapted transcription conventions suggested by Jefferson (Sacks, Schegloff, and Jefferson 1974:731-733) and Jorden (1987):

(1.5)	pauses greater than 1 second given in number of seconds, to the nearest half-second
/	encompasses talk which overlaps with that of another speaker
=	latching; no perceptible gap between the end of one speaker's talk and the beginning of another's
(?)	unclear speech
[]	clarifying comments about paralinguistic features such as intonation, gestures, and laughter-part of a word followed by a hyphen indicates a false start, with the word broken off at that point
ne!	the particle *ne* pronounced with higher pitch at the beginning and falling slightly in pitch at the end; emphatic in tone
ne¿	the particle *ne* pronounced with a higher pitch than the preceding words, sometimes with a slight rise in pitch from beginning to end of the particle; a request for confirmation

7. The terms are those of Jorden (1987). Direct style is used in close interpersonal relationships in informal settings. It can also be used to impart a more sincere or vivid tone to an utterance. Distal (*desu-masu*) forms are used between people who are not close and in more formal or public settings. Ikuta (1980, 1983) discusses style shifts within a single conversation and shows that a shift to direct style may be used to show empathy or a shift to distal style used to show deference when broaching a personal topic. Selting (1985) documents a similar strategic use of style shifts in German. The moderator of the radio talk show from which her data comes shifted towards an interlocutor's style when he wanted to gain cooperation and shifted in the opposite direction during a dispute, thus establishing greater interpersonal distance.

8. *Dyuu,* a Japanese pronunciation of the English word "due", was used by teachers in this language program to refer to a deadline when work was due.

9. With the exception of *desyoo,* the distal tentative form of the copula. The corresponding direct form, *daroo,* is generally considered very blunt or masculine when used by women in mixed company. The other use of distal style is line 20.

10. These strategies are not unique to Japanese, of course (see, for example, Pomerantz 1984b). However, the degree to which they are considered canonical, and the degree to which the first, mitigating, utterance is often elaborated are both quite high in Japanese.

11. *Eguzisutansu* is sufficiently uncommon that two native speakers helping me transcribe the conversation had a very difficult time understanding what Sakurai had said. They at first thought that she had

made a mistake, repeating the word *rezisutansu* in a context where it made no sense, and it was only after listening to the tape repeatedly that they realized what the word was.

12. Polly Szatrowski first brought this to my attention.

APPENDIX

1 Kimura: Soo iu no o kiku to boku sakaraitaku naru no ne¿

2 Sakurai: [laughs] (?)

3 Kimura: Soo iu no o kiku to sakaraitaku naru no. Iya, boku huutoo tukawanai de iyoo to omou. Soide, monku o iwareru ka mo sirenai kedo, "Doo site desu ka?" to kiite mitai yoo ni omou n desu kedo nee! [S. laughs.]

1 Kimura: It's that when I hear things like that, I get so I want to disobey, you know?

2 Sakurai: [laughs] (?)

3 Kimura: It's that when I hear things like that, I get so I want to disobey. No, I think I won't use envelopes. And so, I'll probably get a complaint, but it's that I think I'd like to try asking "Why is it?" you know?

[S. laughs]

(intervening talk omitted)

19 Kimura: Watasi ga sakaratta n da. (1.0) Soo iu huu ni, dokka no tokoro de, tyotto nee, koo rezisutansu o nokosit-okanai to dame na n desu yo.

20 Sakurai: Soo desu ka.= [S. and I laugh.]

21 Kimura: =Nee. Nan to yuu ka. (1.0) Dokka de koo, zenbu o, hai hai to yuu koto o kiku wake zya nai to yuu koto o tyotto omoi sirasite okanai to=

22 Sakurai: [laughing, but with incredulous, disapproving tone] =Omoi sirasuu?

19 Kimura: It's that I disobeyed. (1.0) It's that you have to maintain a little, you know, resistance in that way at some point.

20 Sakurai: Is that right.= [S. and I laugh.]

21 Kimura: =Right? How to say this. (1.0) If you don't at some point teach her a lesson a bit — that you won't just say "Yes, yes" and do as you're told in everything=

22 Sakurai: [laughing, but with incredulous, disapproving tone] =Teach her a lesson?

23 Kimura: Soo soo. (1.5) Itumo soo. Mae kara soo da kedo. (1.5) Daitai wakatte ru n desu kedo ne¿ (2.0) Da kara dyuu wa mamoranai.

(1.0)

24 Sakurai: [laughing] (Da kara?) tyotto, sore wa de mo mazui n zya nai desu ka? [K. laughs]
Sonna.
25 Kimura: Datte, watasi ni mo tugoo ga arimasu kara.
26 Sakurai: Nn. Soo da /kedo (?)/
27 Kimura: /Soodan/ mo sinai de kimenai de kudasai tte iitai zya nai. (2.5) /Nee!/
28 Sakurai: /Da ka/raa, [laughing] da kara watasi ga /ne?/
29 Kimura: /Zen/bu, kanozyo no uiru dattara=
30 Sakurai: =Iya, tyotto matte!= [laughs]
31 Kimura: =Hai.=
32 Sakurai: =Da karaa,=
33 Kimura: =Hai hai.=

23 Kimura: *Right, right. (1.5) It's always like that. It's been that way, but... (1.5) I understand for*
the most part, but, you know? (2.0) And so, I won't meet the deadlines.
(1.0)
24 Sakurai: *[laughing] (That's why?) Isn't it that that's a bit of a bad idea? [K. laughs] Something*
like that.
25 Kimura: *After all, I have my own circumstances to consider too.*
26 Sakurai: *Mm, that's true, /but (?)/*
27 Kimura: *Don't you want to say, "Please don't decide without at least /consult/ing us?" (2.5) /*
Really!/
28 Sakurai: */That's wh/yy, [laughing] that's why I, /you know?/*
29 Kimura: *If /every/thing is up to her=*
30 Sakurai: *=No, wait a minute!= [laughs]*
31 Kimura: *=Yes.=*
32 Sakurai: *=That's why,=*
33 Kimura: *=Yes, yes.=*

34 Sakurai: =watasi ga sensy-, eeto, syuumatu ni, koko ni minna ni sengen o site, nanka ga doko
made to ka haru to yutta no o hatte inai n da kedo, [K. laughs] sore ga areba ii wake
desyoo?=
35 Kimura: =Nn.=
36 Sakurai: =Tumari, dyuu wa zettai. (1.0) Eguzisutansu desyoo? Datte, dyuu no nai sigoto nanka
nai zya nai.=
37 Kimura: =Nn. Sorya soo da kedo,
(1.0)
/(?) dyuu wa,/
38 Sakurai: /Da kara sono dyuu/ ga seetoo ka doo ka to /yuu koto ga mondai na/ wake desyoo?=
39 Kimura: /Soo soo. Soo./ =Watasi-tati to, da kara hanasi o sinai de kimete iru to yuu koto wa

zizitu da si ne¿=
40 Sakurai: =Nn.
               (1.5)
41 Kimura: ( ) na n da yo ne¿

34 Sakurai: =I, last w-, um, last weekend, I said I'd post something here for everyone saying what
*   lesson was until when — I haven't posted that yet, but, [K. laughs] if we had that it'd*
*   be OK, right?=*
35 Kimura: =Mm.=
36 Sakurai: =In short, deadlines are absolutes. (1.0) They exist, right? After all, there's no such
*   thing as a job without deadlines, now is there.=*
37 Kimura: =Mm. That's true, but
*   (1.0)*
*   /(?) deadlines,/*
38 Sakurai: /And so it's whether those dead-lines/ are justified or not /that's the problem,/ isn't it?
39 Kimura: /Right, right. Right/ So, it's a fact that she's deciding without talking with us, right?=
40 Sakurai: =Mm.
*   (1.5)*
41 Kimura: It's that it's ( ).

(At this point the conversation ended abruptly as Kimura and Sakurai turned away from each other to return to their desks.)

CHAPTER 7

PRACTICES IN THE WORK OF ORDERING SOFTWARE DEVELOPMENT

GRAHAM BUTTON

WES SHARROCK

1. INTRODUCTION

This chapter examines the relationship between the formal representations of software development that are portrayed in development methodologies, and the actual work of software development as that was negotiated in the unfolding, contingent, and situated activities and interactions of a group of software engineers engaged in the development of embedded software for a photo-copier. It is part of a series of ethnomethodological studies of the work of computer programmers and software engineers[1], and is concerned with the idea of negotiated, or achieved, *order* of work within organizational settings rather than face to face negotiations.

The concept of 'negotiated order' was originally introduced by sociologists associated with the symbolic interactionist perspective to address some problems with the way in which social order had been classically understood (in particular, see Strauss

This research was supported by the Economic and Social Research Council, grant no. G00230092. We would like to thank Bob Anderson and Alan Firth for their comments on previous drafts.

159

et al. 1964). From the interactionist point of view social order can be understood as something produced *within, through and over* the course of the day to day affairs of society rather than, as classically understood, something external to and ordering of those same affairs. The initial site of application for this conception was the division of labour within a psychiatric hospital (Strauss et al. 1964), and it focused upon the way in which the specific, day to day working arrangements of the wards within the hospital were arrived at, and the relation of this to the official, 'formal' distribution of authority and division of labour obtaining within the hospital. The actual division of labour within the hospital was something which was continually being 'worked at' by those who were party to it, and relative to the official, formal schemes which exhibited a standard, unvarying pattern of work, the actual, working division of labour was very commonly a matter of varying short term arrangements, subject to frequent revision. The working out of that division of labour was substantially a localized matter, completed in accordance with the specific circumstances of (for example) the individual ward, embedded in the continuing history of relationships to be found there. The concept of 'negotiation' is employed in a metaphoric sense to capture the extent to which the production of order is done *interactionally,* arrived at in transactions between the participants which sometimes involved actual negotiations, in the sense of explicit bargaining, but which more often involved the give-and-take of reciprocally adjusted responses.

Ethnomethodology certainly shares with the idea of 'negotiated order' a sense of the way the organization of social affairs is being constantly worked at, 'on the spot', and in and through the transactions of the locally involved participants. However, the concept of 'negotiated order' owes much to its heritage to the (loosely) symbolic interactionist approach and whilst, again, there is some kinship with ethnomethodology, nevertheless there are significant differences between them. A fully adequate summary of the differences between ethnomethodology and symbolic interactionist approaches is not possible within the confines of this brief introduction, and the most simple and succinct way in which we can delineate the demarcation of direction, here, is to say that ethnomethodology pursues the notion that the 'order' it seeks to describe is endogenous to the activities under investigation. It insists, in a very strong way, that the order which it seeks to identify is the order that those under study give to and find in their activities, and thus if, as in the study we are about to report, those activities are work activities, then ethnomethodological studies seek to locate the kind of orderliness that those doing such work seek for in that work. In summarily describing the activities of a Suicide Prevention Centre, Harold Garfinkel neatly summarizes many of the features which those working in that organization saw as prominent features of the organization of their work. Thus, he says of them that:

"The work by SPC [Suicide Prevention Centre] members of conducting their inquiries was part and parcel of the day's work. Recognized by staff members as constituent features of the day's work, their inquiries were thereby intimately connected to the terms of employment, to various internal and external chains of reportage, supervision, and review, and to similar organizationally supplied "priorities of relevances" for assessments of what "realistically", "practically", or "reasonably" needed to be done and could be done, how quickly, with what resources, seeing whom, talking about what, for how long, and so on. Such considerations furnished "We did what we could, and for all reasonable interests here is what we came out with" its features of organizationally appropriate sense, fact, impersonality, anonymity of authorship, purpose, reproducibility — i.e. of a properly and visibly rational account of the inquiry". (Garfinkel 1967: 13).

We will be reporting on the work of software engineers, not suicide investigators, but the features of the latter's work which Garfinkel emphasizes are ones which are not distinctive to their tasks but are characteristic of all kinds of persons working in organizations. As will be seen, the relevance of terms of employment, chains of reportage, supervision and review, assessments of what 'realistically', 'practically' or 'reasonably' needed to be done and other considerations that Garfinkel adduces also loom large in our report. This report aims to sketch out some of the ways in which those engaged in software development seek, in doing their work, to provide it with orderly organization.

We are particularly concerned here with the way in which the implementation of changes in the working methods of a group of software engineers involved in the production of the embedded software for a photocopier was 'negotiated'. For a variety of reasons, which we detail below, it was considered necessary to organize the software development for a new engineering project around a 'development methodology',[2] a programming language, and a set of CASE (Computer Assisted Software Engineering) tools, which would be largely unfamiliar to those in the newly created project team, those who would be managing the development and those who would be carrying it out.

The details of the case depict the way in which the engineers 'negotiate' their work arrangements, the emphasis being upon the ways in which they *negotiated a set of working practices* which facilitated getting the design job done. As has been noted (in studies of deviance, for example) the people who bring in new rules and procedures are often not the same people who have to apply those rules and procedures, with the consequence that the problems involved in implementing the rules and procedures are often different from those their implementation is envisaged as solving. This was certainly true in this case, where the introduction of the new procedures was substantially motivated by the necessity to assemble a sufficiently skilled project team, but where the problems for those doing the project's work were those of making effective use of relatively unfamiliar procedures, even as they were learning them. The problems were not confronted individually, for the purpose of a 'development methodology' is to structure and co-ordinate the work of a team, and the programming language is, of course, to be used in the writing of segments of a unified piece of code. It could not, therefore, be a matter of team members each finding an independent solution to their own problems of ignorance and inexperience with these new ways, but required they make a collective response, innovating locally shared and standardized practices for the deployment of the prescribed development procedures. As the details of the case will show, a significant aspect of the 'negotiation' within the project team was involved in enabling them, on the one hand, to bridge the gap between the conditions required for the genuine and effective operation of the prescribed procedures, and on the other the actions necessitated by the comparably unfavourable actual circumstances that the project was encumbered with.

2. ORDERING SOFTWARE DEVELOPMENT

A problem faced by software development teams is one of *organizing an orderly development*. An example of what this means in and for the work of development that is relevant for this present study is one of interfacing code that has been written within a multi-engineering environment. A multi-engineering environment is a working environment in which different engineering tasks have been assigned to different personnel within the development team or to sub-groups within the team. Thus one person may have responsibility for the operating system, and another for the faults system. Within this division of labour a number of organizational problems having to do with the co-ordination of the development work have to be addressed. For example, ensuring that different parts of a development are ready on time, and that they fit together, or interface correctly with one another. Thus, as part of their development work software engineers have to work at methodically ordering the smooth and efficient unfolding of the development.

One of these problems, that of ensuring that the different parts of a development fit one another, is particularly acute in a multi-engineering environment because of a feature of computer code which is that it is *authored*. We mean by this that computer code displays the hall-mark of the person who has written it. In this respect computer code is not anonymous and engineers, and other programmers use literary categories that embody characteristics of writers to describe code; they refer to *the style* of the code, *the structure* of the programme, and *its elegance* and *sophistication*. Computer code embodies stylistic characteristics because there is no *one* way of solving a programming problem and thus different engineers or programmers will solve a problem in their *own way*. Although different solutions may work and the code run, nevertheless one way may be more elegant than another. Code written by one person may thus display their style of solution. Consequently, the style and the structure of code may be dependent upon its author and thus code may, in part, be a very individualistic product.

The fact that code is *authored* presents a problem in multi-engineering environments because different parts of the software that have been built by different individuals have to be fitted together into a seamless product. This can cause problems within a development *team* because the way in which one person may organize their development can have consequences for the way in which another person may organize theirs, and in the light of one person's work, another may have to change or make adjustments to their work. The orderly production of software must then address the problems that authorship can occasion within multi-engineering environments. Thus code that may bear the hall-marks of different styles and different structures has to be integrated, and that integration is ongoingly worked at and negotiated over the course of a development, as one feature of the work of development. In this respect attending to the organization of an orderly development means that *part of the work of engineering software is to work to impose and negotiate an overall structure on the fluidity of the development.*

There are a number of standard practices that computer scientists and software engineers engage in, in an attempt to address development problems such as the one we have been describing. One of these is to *document* the development. Documenting the development consists of the production of a written rationale for the development processes. This rationale builds into the development a life-history of the development which in turn reveals the logic of the development. Thus, in the course of development, the ongoing documentation of the development provides an unfolding logic which software engineers can use as a guide to their development activities. By referring to the logic they are able to shape or tailor their own work to fit into that logic. Documenting the development is, then, *good engineering practice*[3] because it allows different engineers to standardize their work by referring to the unfolding logic of the development.

A further practice is to properly *define* the specifications for the development. Properly defined specifications act as another touchstone in the engineering of the software. The specifications are an instrument used to organize the writing of the code, for code has to be written to the specifications; the code has to build in the specifications. In this way the specifications act as a constraint over the writing of the code and, in as much as all of the engineers on a development are working to the same constraint, writing to specifications becomes another *good engineering practice* through which development is standardized.

With the documentation in hand and knowing the specifications, software engineers are able to organize the proper interfacing of their multiple developments. This is because adhering to good engineering practice can standardize their development work which means that the different parts of a development will have a better fit with one another. In this respect a proper analysis of the requirements for a development, the proper definition of specifications for the development based upon the requirements analysis and the proper documentation of the development are seen by development managers as essential for organizing the ordering of development work.

However, good engineering practice not withstanding, when faced with the organizational and working realities of a development, engineers cut corners, attempt quick solutions and fixes and engage in *bad practices*.[4] For example, one of the realities of software development is working to 'schedule'. "Deliverables" must be ready at specified times, if they are not the project is subject to time-slippage which threatens its continuation. Thus as audit dates loom, engineers organize their work so as to provide the deliverables as scheduled. The schedule is thus a constraint under which the engineers have to organize their work.

Engineers can be observed to work under a variety of such constraints. For example, the good engineering practices mentioned above are another constraint on their work. Thus developing software is to be working under the auspices of numerous constraints and the ones we have encountered so far are: engage in good engineering practice; document the development; write to specifications; provide a proper definition of interfaces; and provide the deliverable on time.

Not unsurprisingly, these constraints can conflict with one another. For example, properly documenting the code takes time, but time is a precious commodity as an audit date approaches. In the face of conflicting constraints, engineers engage in a number of 'common' — as opposed to formally specified — working activities. For example, they play one constrain off against another, juggle constraints, and relax constraints. Thus, faced with having to juggle conflicting constraints, engineers may relax one constraint in favour of another. However, not all constraints are equally weighted and time is a constraint that is preferentially oriented to. This can be seen in the way in which they organize their work to relax other constraints in preference to the time constraint. Thus in the face of threats to the production of the deliverable to the audit team on time, other constraints are progressively relaxed. Despite the best intentions and the professional standing of working to good practice, engineers will cut corners and engage in improvised bad practices to hit an audit target, for quite simply time-slippage overshadows development, threatening to curtail it.[5]

Although these 'common' practices may result in providing the deliverable on time, they may, nevertheless, cause problems in the future. For example, if the documentation is partial or patchy for one part of the development it becomes more difficult to seamlessly integrate further parts of the development. This is because documentation is a part of the solution to organizing the overall structure of a development. Without that solution the problem it was devised to attend to can run rampant within a development. In this respect relying upon engineers to engage in "good practice" to organize the structure of a software development may be problematic, for they may abandon good practice in favour of getting the job done on time, whatever they have to do to achieve this.

Faced with this problem, software engineers and computer scientists have attempted to provide ways to support software development to ensure both orderly development and good practice. That is, they have attempted to devise ways of structuring software development that *enforce* good practice. To this end they have constructed *development methodologies* and *development environments*. Both may be used to structure a software development in such a way that it requires engineers to, for example, engage in a rigorous analysis of requirements from out of which specifications for development can be defined, and requires that engineers write to those specifications and document their development.

Development methodologies are used to provide for a *structured approach* to development.[6] An example of a methodology that is pertinent for this study is "Yourdon methodology".[7] Yourdon is a tool that is intended to achieve disciplined requirements analysis. A principal feature is the use of diagrams known as 'data flow diagrams' which depict the structure of the proposed system as a flow of data between its constituent parts. It is associated with the idea of structured design and provides a means by which engineers can proceed from using data flow diagrams to understand what is required from a system, to the actual design of that system. It does so by basically separating design from implementation through a process of modelling. The Yourdon Structured Method involves distinct phases of modelling: a feasibility modelling, essential (the essence of a system) modelling, and implementation modelling. Thus, in short, the Yourdon Structured method introduces a structure of formally ordered sequential steps into software development by requiring software engineers to build representations of data and process and to engage in successive, and distinct, phases of modelling.

In addition to development methodologies, software engineers and computer scientists have also devised development environments, *Computer Aided Software Engineering* (CASE). Computer software packages have been built that furnish software engineers with tools that they can use in developing new software. In CASE the development is substantially 'mechanised', i.e. is extensively computerized, ideally imposing the necessity to follow the standard procedures that are built into the software upon the development engineers. Thus in the same way in which a word processor makes someone who is using it engage in particular and fixed procedures for executing a processing task, so too does CASE force the engineers who are using it to execute development tasks in a particular way. That way purportedly instantiates good engineering practice, and thus engineers who are using CASE in their developments have to follow the good practices built into the working of the software. For example, CASE enforces standards by making engineers use the same definitions, and it also facilitates documentation by semi-automating the documentation process. It is frequently used with a graphical based methodology such as Yourdon to produce engineering drawings.

We just want to briefly mention another development device which is important for this study but is often overlooked as a way of supporting development because it is such an integral feature of any development, and this is a programming language. Although there are a wide variety of programming languages there are a number of criteria that divide them up into different categories. Thus some are purpose built for particular programming tasks, others are general purpose programming languages. Some languages are structured, others are not. Some are "high level" and some are "low level" which refers to the degree of involvement the language has with the actual machine circuitry. Some languages can support the particular demands of modern engineering, the best known in this regard being ADA, PLC and C. C, the language that is important for this study has caused controversy because it does not easily fit into the standard categories. Thus it displays some high level and some low level characteristics; it is structured but breaks important rules of structured programming; it is a special purpose language but is used for general purpose programming. It is, however, frequently used in commercial development because it *can* provide for a structured approach to programming whilst at the same time allowing engineers a high degree of flexibility because of its "low level" character.

We mentioned that part of the work of software development is to ongoingly work at imposing an overall structure on development as it unfolds and to methodically organize its unfolding. Software engineers use methodologies such as Yourdon and environments such as CASE, as tools through which to shape that structure and to enforce "good practice" within the development. It may appear, and this is often the impression that is given by those who manufacture and sell CASE that "all" software engineers have to do is to follow the processes provided by the CASE software. It is also sometimes put that "all" engineers have to do is to follow the methodology and adhere to its principles. That is, within the literature, engineers are exhorted to follow the development methodology and use the program. However, such exhortations are often found disappointing in practice, optimistic overestimations of what the package can actually do and there is much cynicism about such packages and their associated claims, with some of the managers of development projects regarding CASE tools as things that come in almost "over my dead body" and even gleefully expect that they will not work well, if at all. Although the engineers may regard the methodologies and CASE tools as "a good thing" in principle, they nonetheless are not surprised to find that they are either not using these tools in practice, nor using them in the ways they are officially intended to be, or adding to their burdens by having to make the tools work. Such tools typically make no provision for the existence of the practical work of implementing the methodologies and using the environments in actual working circumstances. Following a development methodology and using a development environment is not, then, simply a matter of cranking a handle. What following the methodology consists of needs to be determined from out of the particulars of a development. Crafting the software using the development tools of a methodology and an environment involves figuring out how to make the tools work in the circumstances of development; developing a 'know how' in their application. This 'know how' is absent in the literature on development methodologies and environments. It is to this 'know how' that this chapter is directed. In order to describe some aspects of what knowing consists of as displayed in the detailed practices of the work of development, some ethnographically generated data taken from the work of a software development team will be discussed.[8]

3. THE PROBLEMS OF A SOFTWARE ENGINEERING GROUP

This project, which we will call 'Archer', encountered a problem with conforming to its schedule which was largely a result of the way in which the project was initiated.

The project's task was to 're-engineer' a photocopying machine which had been originally produced by the Japanese arm of the multinational company in whose UK development and manufacturing site the project team was based. The company had developed a stop-gap strategy of re-engineering successful machines to adapt them to the needs of wider markets that would enable them to introduce new models into markets without having to invest in the full development of new models whilst they awaited the development of machines which would embody a whole new technology — digital processing. One reason for choosing this model for adaptation was that it was a very fast copier. Indeed, the fastest copier in its class. The possession of this distinguishing feature was considered important for advertising and promotion purposes though it would mean severe engineering difficulties would have to be overcome in order to maintain the feature which provided, after all, only a marginal difference over rival machines.

One problem which the project immediately faced was that of recruiting a team which would have the quality and skills necessary to carry through the job. Amongst the company's engineers, re-engineering work was not well regarded, for they did not see it as calling for their design skills and therefore as work which could have much interest for them. Signing up for this project would be joining a 'mickey mouse' enterprise. The management had set the project up so that it would attract dedicated, skilled and experienced photocopier engineers who were, furthermore, in short supply within the company.[9] The attraction was to set up the project so that it would supply career opportunities for engineers who worked on it, allowing them to acquire valued software skills which were not usually available within the company. These included the adoption of a reputed 'software development methodology', the *Yourdon method*, the purchase of a CASE development environment, and the selection of 'C' as the programming language for the project.

Software development methodologies are controversial systems for the organization of project teamwork. They are often condemned as attempts to impose 'Tayloristic' conceptions of the organization of work, seeking to break down the operations involved in software design to the very smallest components and to order them according to a strict sequential formula. These methodologies are often ones which are commercially available and can be bought as packages, and amongst these Yourdon is very prominent and perhaps the best regarded. We should emphasize that the engineers we were studying did not subscribe to such criticisms of methodologies, but looked upon them with favour and were particularly impressed with the idea of working with the Yourdon method.

The idea behind CASE is that the various aspects of work on a complex software development project can be integrated through the computer system, to the extent that the complexities of such work can be unified within a single, closely knit framework, such that one can talk of a particular form of CASE as providing an 'environment' for the project's work. The integration of the work requires that it be unified by a common approach to work, and this is one of the features which attracted managers to CASE, for the operation of the system was only possible if it was done in conjunction with a development methodology of the sort that Yourdon comprises. From the managers' point of view, the incorporation of the methodology into the very technology the team are using is likely to be a more effective way of enforcing the consistent use of that method. One general problem of software development is that of documentation. It is an acknowledged problem to get software engineers to keep detailed and careful records of what they have been doing to the software system, though this documentation is often vital to subsequent work on and maintenance of the software. The CASE technology is an attempt to automate the production of documentation and thus remove reliance upon the willingness of engineers.

The company's own programming language — Sequel — is largely unknown outside its world, it being specifically developed for use with photocopying equipment. C, however, is a generally used, widely known programming language which allows for real-time processing[10] and a flexible approach to programming problems. In that respect, it could be argued that it has a technical superiority to Sequel.

The justification given to the organization for the adoption of these unusual and costly software development supports was on technical grounds. It was argued that because the development would be technically complicated due to the requirement that the machine be 'superfast' it would not be adequate to rely entirely upon the engineers' grasp of 'good practice'. This would need supplementing by supports which would systematically enforce good practice. So, for example, Yourdon methodology would impose a disciplined rigour in the initial definition of the requirements that the machine was to satisfy. Also, Yourdon would ensure that the work on the development was 'structured' and thus provided with detailed and thorough orderliness. It was argued that the CASE technology would ensure that the engineers would write to requirements and produce full documentation. C would allow the engineers effectively to write the software for the real time processing that a modern photocopier requires.

There was, then, a technical justification for the organization of the project around these supports, but there was, in addition, a justification in terms of organizational considerations, particularly with respect to the recruitment of a technically proficient team. The first justification addressed *the engineering of the software* and the second was oriented to *engineering the development team*. Working on the project would enable engineers to learn to use the Yourdon methodology, the CASE technology and the language C, thus acquiring skills which were not otherwise available in the company and which were in considerable demand outside it. The technical supports were used by the project manager to lure highly experienced engineers onto his project. In practice, the two rationales came into conflict with one another, and we will now examine the way in which that conflict manifested itself and was managed.

4. TROUBLES ON THE PROJECT

The ways in which the project was organized generated troubles. The decision to re-engineer a Japanese machine created unanticipated problems in obtaining the detailed technical documentation. This was in Japanese, and no one had made provision for the translation of this data. The assumption had been that the technical experience of the Japanese development team which had worked on this model would also be available, but the fact that the working engineers had no English had not been appreciated. The difficulties in communication created considerable delays, and the project's work was rescheduled. Once work was underway, the project began to experience slippage even on the renegotiated schedule, falling behind on its target and audit dates.

These troubles were troubles enough, but the project was also beset with problems in the development work which were largely due to the very decisions which management had made to bring in the supporting Yourdon method, CASE technology and the programming language C. Using these was exacerbating the time slippage that was being experienced because of the other problems in the following ways.

First, following the Yourdon method requires strict adherence to a sequence of steps. The first and necessary step is a thorough analysis of the requirements that the machine is to meet. Part of the point is to integrate decisions about hardware and software by ensuring that the requirements for both are worked out systematically in conjunction with one another. However, the re-engineering exercise was not intended to involve the thorough reworking of the machine's hardware, and the character of this was already determined before the software engineers got to work. In fact, the hardware was developed and waiting, and the hardware engineers were eager to get their machines into test, which they could not do without relatively developed software. The proper pursuit of the Yourdon methodology of requirement definition and analysis would take much longer than hardware were prepared to countenance. The software engineers could normally have developed some test software — what they would call a 'quick and dirty' solution — for they were used to pressure from hardware to deliver quickly, if not early. However, if they were to adhere to Yourdon, then they could not do this.

The engineers were, of course, learning to use these technologies *on the project*. The whole point of adopting the technologies was that they were unfamiliar, and their attractive power was precisely to draw those who not had experience of them. However, no realistic allowance had been made for time to teach the engineers to use these technologies. The management team was aware of this difficulty with the CASE technology, and in response to it they hired in a expert consultant in the proprietary CASE technology employed. His function was disseminate his knowledge amongst the engineers through, effectively, sitting with them at their work, and working through the CASE procedures in the project's real time environment. However, the CASE consultant did not operate in this way, but instead took on the work of dealing with the CASE system, becoming in effect one more member of the team, doing some of the software development work himself rather than teaching the members of the team. As a result, the other engineers were not so proficient in CASE as they might have been and so their semi-skilled efforts to use it meant that their work went more slowly than it would have without CASE.

C is acknowledged within industry and the programming community to be a very powerful programming language, but it is not uncontroversial and it does not share one feature which is prized in many other rival languages, namely, a highly structured character. As we have explained elsewhere (Button and Sharrock forthcoming), the writing of code to a 'professional' standard is not just a matter of designing it to be proficient in operating the system in which it is installed. There is a major concern with the intelligibility of code to others than those who have written it. Some languages — such as LISP — provide a good deal of built-in structure to code, which greatly facilitates its understanding by those who might have to read it. C does not provide such automatic structuring, and this is often regarded as a serious deficiency where the reciprocal reading of different engineer's code is important, as on Project Archer, for it was a 'modular' development requiring that engineers write separate sub-units of code and that these then be interfaced with each other in the full system. The capacity of one engineer to adapt his code to that of another depended upon his being able to make sense of it, but this was something that C made difficult.

Thus, the managerial decisions concerning the engineering of the project team had been successful, but they were proving less so with respect to the engineering of the software system. These resources would ideally have ensured a very well worked out software system *if they were applied systematically* but in fact they were not being.[11] We cannot emphasize strongly enough the importance that scheduling had for those projects we studied. There were many objectives to be achieved, but sticking to schedule would, in practice, become the predominant one. Minimizing the risk of slippage was a omnirelevant preoccupation, and at times where project reviews and audits were imminent it would become the overriding concern. Thus, the tension on Archer was between using the technologies *properly* and getting the work done *in time* .

5. SOLVING THE PROBLEMS IN PRACTICE

The imperative of keeping as close to schedule as possible meant that the software engineers on Archer had to *renegotiate* the official procedures of the project amongst themselves in order to achieve practicable ways of carrying out the project's work. They developed situated practices which enabled them to preserve the technical justification for the project's technology, whilst deviating from it. Their work is, after all, organizationally accountable and should their deviations from the method become public knowledge then it might call into question the character and quality of that work. If, for example, the very purpose of Yourdon is to provide a systematic and disciplined working out of the software, then failure to adhere to Yourdon might be perceived as resorting to disorderly and undisciplined practices, posing questions as to the quality of the resulting software. Keeping the confidence of others in the soundness and standards of the software development was important to the group. In order to illustrate this we will describe some of the ways in which they negotiated shared practices for the management of their predicament.

(a) The situated use of Yourdon:
As we have noted, one of the strong pressures on the software team was coming from the hardware engineers, who needed test software to meet their own schedules. The software engineers knew that if they stuck to Yourdon they could not meet those demands, and they certainly could not provide early and incompletely developed releases to the hardware team. However, they recognized the urgency and legitimacy of the hardware team's demands and, further, of the overall shared interest in the project reaching its deadlines. Therefore, they decided to provide the software releases requested. They had no doubts about their capacity to produce good work whilst departing from Yourdon. These were, remember, experienced, skilled, high quality software engineers who would indeed pride themselves on being able to write good software without benefit of methodology. The problem in setting Yourdon aside whilst getting the software written was not its effect on the software, but upon their own credibility (and associatedly of the software) within the setting. Methods like Yourdon are not primarily addressed to the problem of getting workable quality software written, but of organizing development work in bureaucratically accountable and manageable ways.

In order to ensure that the deviation between practice and precept did not rebound upon them, the engineers developed the distinction between *'following Yourdon'* and *'saying they were following Yourdon'* .

They did not altogether *abandon* Yourdon. The phrase 'saying they were following Yourdon' acknowledged that though they were indeed using Yourdon, it was only in the sense of taking advantage of some of the techniques included within the total methodology's package, and which meant that they were not, in practice, using these techniques in the ways they were intended to be used. Thus, the remark that they were 'saying they were following Yourdon' was a rueful recognition that the method was as often honoured in the breach as the observance. The extent to which they were 'shortcutting' on or improvizing around the methodology was not something they felt that they could publicly admit to without organizationally jeopardizing the project's very being. Further, to make public their difficulties with the method would have risked what they saw as misinterpretation, that the fault lay with the methods and not with the conditions under which they had to be used.

Under the cover of 'saying they were following Yourdon' they negotiated between themselves a 'quick and dirty' method that consisted in the provision of a series of software releases. These releases would not have been possible under the Yourdon method, which requires that software be debugged, tested and operational before it is released. Therefore, the versions were well short of that standard, and the software engineers knew that they had innumerable bugs. The role of the releases was to let the hardware engineers get on with their work and ease the pressure on the software group. The software was released with the engineers knowing it was full of bugs and that they would have to return to it, but their objective was to get the software *right in the end*. Adherence to Yourdon would have been one way of achieving this objective, but it was not one which was compatible with their organizational position, for they did not want to be the ones who were found to be holding up the whole project. Their own locally negotiated practices would also achieve the objective of getting the software right *in the end* but would do so in a way which would solve the immediate problems of placating hardware. Once they had handed over a software release, they could then continue their work on it, solving the problems they had not had time to fix so far.

(b) Working C:
We have mentioned how decisions in setting up the project generated subsequent problems. This was the case with the decision to purchase a particular (low cost) processing chip for the machine which had consequences for the use of the programming language C.

The processing chip was cheaper than others because it had a lower capacity, and when it came to the programming of it to enable real time operations it proved technically impossible to do this in C. The number of lines of code required to express the real time operations in C was greater than the chip could handle. The engineers had a problem as to how to achieve the real time requirements. Their solution was to move (in programming this chip) from coding in C to using assembler programming language.[12]

This shift from C to assembler was a temporary measure. They would continue to code in C for most tasks, but would programme this chip in assembler language. The technical argument necessary to justify the management's decision to use C had been in terms of the acknowledged technical qualities of that language. These justifications had had to be given to a departmental manager who was notable for his scepticism about new technologies, and who was also notable for expressing his views very forcibly, especially when events proved him right. Bringing in C and CASE had been done very much against his inclinations. The fact that C was unsuitable to the programming of this important chip would, the engineers expected, have been seized upon by this manager as evidence of the project manager's mistakes, and it was a mistake they were not prepared have exposed, perhaps putting their project at risk. They were pleased to be working in C for the professional, career reasons we have mentioned, but they were not especially pleased with C. In fact, in most respects, they would have been happier to be working in assembler language, one with which they were already familiar and which they regarded as superior in engineering (as opposed to programming) terms. Assembler allowed them to organize more efficient software use of the machine's hardware potential.

The departure from C was not, however, explained in terms of the failure of C. In some aspects of its operation, C is similar to assembler language. The two languages differ in respect of being 'higher' and 'lower' level language. A computer runs in machine code. Programming in machine code is very difficult and programming languages such as C were developed to make programming easier. However, a programme written in a high level language such as C has to be turned into machine code (by the machine) in order for it to work. The more removed from machine code a programming language is, the higher the level of its expressions. Assembler is a language that is used to convert high level languages into machine code, and is thus closer to machine code than those languages such as C. However, whilst a high level language, and unlike other high level languages, C embodies some features of assembler. This is because C, in its development has been very much associated with 'hackers' who have traditionally hacked in machine code and in assembler.

Whilst they abandoned C, the engineers did so by reference to the virtues of C that were shared with assembler. Thus they presented their reasons for abandoning C as attempting to maximize some qualities of C. They argued that using assembler was not a proof of the unsoundness of the decision to use C, but a testimony to the fact that the decision was a good one. Within the context of the organization they preserved the rationale for its use, in their rhetoric for abandoning it. Thus ironically, abandoning C was done in the name of using C.

The engineers continue to work in C in most of their other programming tasks. However, they had to develop a whole series of shared practices to make C *workable* for the purposes of the project. The interfacing of code modules would be critical to the project's success and one of the rationales for using C was that this was a modern, up to date, proficient engineering language. The danger with C, though, is that because it is a high level language which also retains some characteristic of 'low level' languages, it is easy for programmers to slip into writing what is called 'esoteric code'. By this is meant code which no one but its writer can easily understand. Because of the multi-engineering nature of this project (which was broken down into a series of modules, as we have noted) esoteric code would create serious problems in interfacing code written for the various modules. Indeed, if the engineers had followed the manuals for writing in C, they would have had no way of solving the interfacing problem because C, as presented in the text books does not address this problem. In other words, within the context of this development text book C would not provide them with workable code, for their purposes.

In order to work around this problem the engineers negotiated a set of agreed, and written down, standard guidelines, which provided a set of conventions that would determine the meaning of their code. The production of 'working C' out of 'textbook C' required the pooling of the various techniques individual engineers had contrived to get their code writing done, and the guidelines provided a codification of informal practice. The engineers were writing C in the same way, but these guidelines were intimately anchored in the tasks and problems of the working group and could not necessarily be used in any other community. The guidelines became an instrument through which they could use the language within their community. The guidelines were thus a situatedly negotiated method for transforming 'textbook C' into 'working C', and without which they could not have avoided severe problems in unifying the software system. The compilation of the guidelines made their technical work organizationally accountable, for its assembly ensured the useability of C which reinforced the technical decision to use it in the first place.[13]

(c) Reworking CASE:

The idea behind CASE is that it creates a systematic environment comprised of powerful software development tools, combined in such ways as to enhance the individual designer's efficiency, whilst closely integrating the efforts of the diverse individuals making up a team. Many of the devices which CASE provides are of a graphical nature, providing purportedly powerful ways of analyzing design problems, working out designs etc. CASE tools must embody assumptions about the way the working group is organized. One way of organizing a software development team is around its most skilled member — a project 'guru' as they are sometimes called. This skilled member is conventionally given considerable design freedom and "the goal (of CASE environments) is to provide freedom for the lone designer or the most skilled team member, allowing this person to concentrate fully on developing the requirements and design specifications" (Fisher 1991:33).

Project Archer did not conform to such assumptions. We have described how it was organized as a modular development, involving multi-engineering. There was not the degree of interdependence envisaged in the 'guru' assumption, and each of the different designers had a good deal of latitude in their design decisions. This meant that there had to be a strong degree of co-ordination and collaboration amongst them to maintain cohesiveness of purpose and design, but their CASE system, inasmuch as it was based upon assumptions of a team that was centrally led, did not conveniently support their kind of collaboration. Thus, the engineers were (a) delayed by their attempts to use an unfamiliar CASE system and (b) further delayed taking time from their tightly scheduled work to ensure co-ordination which should have been provided by the CASE environment.

Indeed, as the project developed, the engineers abandoned the use of the CASE environment for most purposes, and particularly for those tasks the environment was supposed to enhance. As we have indicated, they surrendered much of the work that used CASE to the hired-in consultant, who had mutated from an adviser into an engineer. Even that work which was done in CASE, however, was hardly ever work which actually required the CASE environment. The consultant judged that they were using very little of the system's potential — he estimated that it was about 10% of its technical capacity.

Again, and for reasons akin to those given above about the defensiveness over the selection of these expensive and problematic tools, the fact that CASE was of little actual use was not one to be noised abroad. Again, the impression was given that the technology was proving effective, this time as an effect of its actual use. As we have said, CASE technology consists in part of graphical representations and the only devices that were used from this environment were the devices which generated graphical representations. This powerful technology, notionally capable of a multiplicity of functions within the design process, was being used virtually as a drawing instrument. It did provide very impressive looking diagrams and documents. These diagrams and documents were use as *documentary evidence* that the CASE technology was in use, conveying the impression that the diagrams and documents were the end product of the environment's systematic use. Patently, they were products of the CASE technology's devices, and the assumption which anyone outside the software team might be expected to make was that they have been generated out of the CASE system, and not solely through its use as a presentational device. In the conduct of their work, the engineers distinguished between *the processes of development* and *the presentation of the development processes.*

6. CONCLUSION

We have been describing the work of a software development team within an engineering project. These engineers were engaged in work which was intricately interdependent and which involved them in working together to create a joint product. The successful conduct of the project required the co-ordination of their work activities and the integration of the different outputs of their work into a single, working software system which must interdigitate with the electro-mechanical operations of the photocopier. The co-ordination and integration of the work often required very specific shared understandings within the group, and toward this end the engineers were provided with a quite elaborate apparatus involving the corporation's planning and scheduling procedures as well as the Yourdon methodology and CASE technology. The engineers found (and not necessarily to their surprise) that the level of agreement they required could not be achieved through reliance upon this apparatus alone. Indeed, in many ways, it became a necessary feature of their work to establish common understandings of the ways in which this apparatus was in practice to be applied. In other words, they had to continually negotiate many of the terms of their work between themselves.

We describe them as *negotiating* these understandings because arriving at them was a matter of having to work them out together in the face of the problems with which they had to contend and as part of their work. This working out consisted of the development of *ad hoc* ways of making the formal apparatuses with which they were provided workable within the details of their development. Our interest has been in the way the engineers had to contrive a set of shared practices for software development, ways of doing the work around, or even despite, the organizing apparatus they were provided with. We have, then, been describing how they made their work manageable and resolved some of the conflicts and tensions they were confronted with, detailing, thus, the practices by which they 'said they were using Yourdon' to sustain others' confidence in their product, the way they alternated between C and assembler to get round the memory problem, the elaboration of a set of local conventions for the use of C in search of sufficient standardization in code writing practice to minimize conflicts between the code interfaces of the software modules, the way they made use of CASE tools as drawing devices to enhance the quality of their presentations.

It was through the working out of these practices as part of their day to day work that the engineers were, in part, able to achieve an orderliness to their development activities. This orderliness was not a given feature of merely working to the schemes they were provided with but of improvising ways of making those schemes work within the practicalities of working within an organization. It is in this sense that we understand the idea of "negotiated order" to involve the examination of the way in which people attempt to order the work they are doing. This chapter has described some of these ways.

NOTES

1. For other related studies see Button, Sharrock and Anderson (1990), Sharrock and Button (1991), Sharrock, Button and Anderson, (forthcoming), Button and Sharrock, forthcoming a and b.

2. Development methodologies are schemes — often available as commercial products, as was the 'Yourdon methodology' introduced in this case — which seek to provide an explicit and methodic order to the work of software development, specifying a set of procedures which should regulate the sequencing of the work activities on the project.

3. This is not our judgement but an engineering description of quality processes. See for example the British Standards Institute Total Quality Processes Directive 5770 for engineers.

4. Again, this is not our judgement; within the engineering community 'bad practices' are understood as cutting across or violating laid-down procedures. It is important to stress that we are not criticizing the engineers here, nor suggesting that they were bad at their job. As we will see, such activities can be skilful responses to the organizational exigencies surrounding their development work and actually testify to the high calibre of the engineering that was going on.

5. Many engineers have their own experiences of working on projects that were curtailed because the time-slippage became unacceptable to the company.

6. See Ableson, Susman and Susman (1985) for an introduction to structured programming.

7. See Yourdon and Constantine (1979).

8. The material on which this study is based was collected using the usual array of field-work techniques. One of the authors (Graham Button) worked with the development team, recording their conversations and meetings where possible; making notes about what could be seen; talking with members of the team; asking them questions about what they were doing; receiving lectures and directions from them as to what software engineering was *really* about; reading the manuals they read; collecting and trying to make sense of the documents they produced; homing in on one of the engineers and keeping him company over the course of numerous working days; eating meals and engaging in company gossip with them; being taken around the site and being introduced to other groups and individuals they had to deal with; keeping a daily field-work diary; transcribing the conversations that were recorded; and the like.

9. Within the company that figures in this report, project managers and task leaders assemble project teams in part by persuading engineers currently employed on other projects to request reassignment to the one they are forming. For example, one of the most experience engineers on Archer was previously working on a project at the conpany's development site in Holland. He was approached by

Archer's task leader with whom he had previously worked to request transfer from his current project. He was so highly valued for his familiarity with photocopying software that Archer's budget was stretched to provide him with hotel accommodation during the week and to fly him back and forth to Holland at weekends.

10. Real-time processing refers to computer processing activities that coincide with clock-time. So, for example, to put up the time on a digital watch requires that the processing chip process information in real-time.

11. We should note that the engineers did not attribute their difficulties to Yourdon. Indeed, they were admiring of the method, and longed to have the opportunity to use it as it is intended to be used. Their complaints were levelled at the project managers who they accused of failing to realise the extent to which the method would require supporting. In particular, for underestimating the time it would take to follow Yourdon's principles. It should also be borne in mind that project scheduling is something of a 'black art', very often involving guesswork and being most successful where one can estimate on the basis of how long things have taken before. For a classic discussion of the fateful character of scheduling, see Brooks (1982).

12. Assembler programming language is closer to machine code than 'high-level languages' such as C, and therefore requires less processing to turn its procedures into machine code.

13. Brian Torode (personal communication) has made the point that the engineers would then have to implement the guidelines, and that this implementation would also be susceptible to local contingencies and require *ad hoc* judgements of which the issuing of another set of guidelines may have been a solution. His point is that this would be endless and thus our description of the way in which the engineers used the set of guidelines they constructed does not capture the full extent of their practices. Unfortunately, the engineers asked us not to reproduce the guidelines and we respect their wishes. However, if we had given examples taken from them it would be possible to see that the guidelines were developed to standardize, *for all practical purposes*, some engineering activities. Because we cannot refer to the guidelines themselves we will have to take an example from another field of work with which we are familiar in order to illustrate what we mean here. Within carpentry there may be guidelines in the form of specifications issued for the construction of an artefact such as a chest of drawers. The guidelines will state that dovetail joints and countersunk screws should be used. Now, of course, making a dove-tail joint will be susceptible to local conditions such as the sharpness of the saw, the quality of the wood, and the ease with which the screw may go in. Also, the quality of the joint may vary from one carpenter to another. However, if a group of carpenters are collaborating in building the chest of drawers, the guideline can be used as an instrument to standardize its construction in important ways so that it does not, for example, emerge as a chest with some drawers dovetailed and others mitred. The guidelines for using C were of this order, they ensured that the equivalents of the screws and joints were constructed and used in standardized ways. The question of how to cut a joint, and how to screw in a screw and the variations in the build of one dovetail joint over another is another

issue entirely and not one that would be answered in issuing another set of guidelines but in other ways having to do with other aspects of working practice. Torode's point seems to raise the issue of an infinite regress, but, if it does, then it does not seem cogent, for it perhaps carries the suggestion that the software engineers are judgemental dopes (Garfinkel 1967), or that we view them as such. Patently, the local guidelines for C were recipient designed, worked out to the level of detail that the engineers regarded as sufficient for their practical purposes, relative to (at least) the time they had available, the problems they faced and the things they knew about each other. Torode's question seems to ask: how much is enough? A question which, of course, can never be answered in the abstract. Torode's question also seems to forget Garfinkel's (1967) observation that matters of applying standardizing schemes such as guidelines are done *for all practical purposes*; it is they (members) not us (observer-analysts) that draw a line on the matter: for the engineer's practical purposes and to the engineers' satifaction (attested by their being able to interface their different modules), the guidelines they negotiated between themselves solved, as a practical matter of their work, the practical problems of working in C to a sufficent standard for their purposes.

SECTION III

NEGOTIATION IN COMMODITY TRADING

CHAPTER 8

TALKING FOR A CHANGE:
COMMODITY NEGOTIATING BY TELEPHONE

ALAN FIRTH

1. INTRODUCTION

When people negotiate, they frequently do so in attempts to *change* existing circumstances in mutually acceptable ways. In this chapter I examine the discourse-based work undertaken by commodity traders in their attempts to negotiate mutually acceptable changes to terms and conditions of sale. Attention is focused on the way negotiations are undertaken by telephone. The telephone is one of the technological icons of the twentieth century, yet it is only recently that research has begun uncovering how it is used communicatively for work-related ends. Surprisingly little empirical research has been carried out into how people at work actually communicate by telephone, how the uses of communication technologies (such as telephones) impact upon work practices, and how work activities (such as negotiations) undertaken by telephone are discursively structured and organized. This chapter attempts to make a contribution to knowledge in these areas. More centrally for the purposes of this volume,

---

This chapter is based on Firth (1991:chap. 5), and is a revised and enlarged version of a paper presented at the 'Negotiations in the Workplace' symposium, Aalborg University, May, 1992, and at the 'Linguistics Seminar', Gothenburg University, October, 1993. The present version has benefited from discussions with colleagues at both venues and, in particular, from the suggestions and comments of Dennis Day and Jack Bilmes.

the chapter seeks to contribute to our general understanding of negotiation as both a context-shaped and context-shaping *discourse phenomenon.*

The materials examined are transcripts of five audio-recorded international telephone negotiations, undertaken within the export section of 'Melko Dairies', a large Danish-based conglomerate. Each of the five telephone negotiations is conducted in 'lingua franca' English — i.e. English used between nonnative speakers — (see Firth 1990), and involves a Danish Export Manager and Middle East-based wholesalers.

In an attempt to detail the 'local', emergent character of the calls, as well as the calls' *participant relevant* features, I deploy the micro-analytic methodology of (ethnomethodological) conversation analysis, and supplement this with ethnographic observations of the Melko work setting.[1] The chapter thus endeavours to describe the *locally-produced* and *interactionally-achieved* discourse structure of the telephone negotiations, and to show how this structure is reflexively tied to the particular work context. That is to say, while the import of the negotiations obtains through their perceived work-related function (in this case to resolve difficulties surrounding the exchange of scarce resources), and while they are carried out under the auspices of the implicated trading companies, actual engagement in the negotiations both makes visible and 'reproduces' the institutional frameworks within which the negotiations are embedded (cf. Heritage 1984a:290).[2] In this sense, the negotiations are linguistic and interactional instantiations of '(trading) organizations in action' (see Boden 1994).

Analyses demonstrate that the telephone negotiations exhibit stable patterns of discourse structure. The calls are compact, 'to-the-point', and overwhelmingly 'single-topic' encounters. In early sections of the calls, parties 'get to work' in methodic ways by locating the 'problem' at hand; an 'account' — in the form of an 'excuse' or 'justification' (see Scott and Lyman 1968) — then follows the 'problem', whereupon the 'account' is subsequently 'probed' and incrementally 'unpacked'. Such sequences of talk inform and precede the exchange of substantive offers and proposals. It is in these sequences that the parties display a mutual desire to resolve the 'problem' *during the call itself.* This can be seen most clearly in the way argumentative talk is minimized, and in the way 'offers' and 'counteroffers' are exchanged in attempts to reach mutual agreement.

In both the opening and closing segments of each call, the negotiating parties demonstrate that the call is an *embedded part of a series* of interrelated and ongoing work tasks. This allows us to observe that, for the participants, the telephone negotiations are not separated from the work context — a feature that is frequently overlooked in much existing negotiation research. Rather, the negotiations are shown to be simultaneously contingent upon, constitutive of, and consequential for work practices in those contexts.

2. THE MELKO CALLS: AN OVERVIEW

2.1. Adjacency relations

Although some research has been carried out into the role and effects of communication media in the negotiation process (for a review, see Poole, Shannon, and DeSanctis 1992), I am not aware of studies that have attempted to describe the way negotiations undertaken via electronic media — telephone included — are discursively organized and structured. As we shall discover, although the telephone negotiations evince features observed in face-to-face negotiation encounters, many features of the telephone negotiations can be traced to the participants' orientations to the constraints imposed by the telephone medium itself.

The most detailed descriptive studies of telephone *talk* have undoubtedly been undertaken within the field of conversation analysis. However, while telephone talk has figured prominently in conversation analysis (hereafter, CA), relatively little CA-based work has detailed the *overall* structural organization of individual telephone calls. Most commonly, attention has been focused on particular 'sections' of calls, predominantly 'openings' (Schegloff 1972a, 1979) and 'closings' (Schegloff and Sacks 1973, Button 1991). One notable exception is the work of J. Whalen, M. Whalen and Zimmerman [e.g., Zimmerman (1984), J. Whalen, Zimmerman and Whalen (1988), and Zimmerman (1992)]. Analyzing the overall structures of calls for emergency assistance, it was discovered that, as distinct from 'mundane', conversational calls, the emergency calls "reveal a *definite underlying organization* with distinct segments, each of which performs specific functions" (Zimmerman 1984:211, emphasis added).[3] Whalen and Zimmerman (1990:469) tabulated the 'achieved organization' of the emergency calls as follows:

> Opening/identification/acknowledgment
> Request
> Interrogative series
> Response
> Closing[4]

The authors point out that the observed structural configuration of the calls is not a 'plan of action' or a rigid 'template' prescribing what parties to emergency calls must do; rather it is the participants' interpretative *resource* that is oriented to and contingently modified, augmented, "used repetitively or not at all because the contingencies to which these components are responsive are altered, unusual, recurrent, or absent" (Zimmerman

1992:461).

In the 'opening/identification/acknowledgment' sequence of the emergency calls the parties align their identities and project the nature of the call. The 'request' segment may be formulated by the caller in one of three possible formats. First as a 'request' for the emergency service (fire, police, ambulance), second as a 'report' naming a perceivedly policeable trouble (e.g., 'accident' or 'break in'), and third as a 'description' of a problem. The request for assistance is a 'first pair part' of an 'adjacency pair'.[5] However, the projected 'second pair part' (namely the 'response') does not normarily occur in the next sequential position. Rather, it is routinely preceded by an 'interrogative series'. This is an elaborate 'insertion sequence' (Schegloff 1972a) within which the call-taker both elicits requisite information (e.g. details of the problem, location, name of caller) and assesses the veridicality and hence the 'policeable nature' of the complaint/ emergency (see Whalen and Zimmerman 1990:470). As the authors put it: "We suggest that the interrogative series functions as an insertion sequence that provides a canonical procedure for dealing with matters that are preliminary to (and conditional for) an emergency response" (ibid.). The 'response' segment of the call is the call-taker's promise of assistance (prototypically formatted as 'Okay, we'll get somebody over there'). Such utterances initiate the 'pre-closing' section of the call, enabling both parties to produce a 'terminal exchange' sequence (i.e., 'bye-bye'), thereby 'closing' the call down.

The structure described by Whalen and Zimmerman sheds light on both the contextual embeddedness and the displayed structure of the Melko negotiation calls. The structures of both types of calls may be accounted for in terms of adjacency relations. However, whereas Whalen and Zimmerman suggested that the internal structures of their calls were organized around a dominant 'request-response' adjacency pair, in the Melko materials the telephone call itself occurs *following* the production of an adjacent 'offer-nonacceptance' or 'offer-counteroffer' sequence. That is, preceding each telephone call, Melko have made an 'offer' — in writing — to sell specific commodities at specified prices; this offer has been responded to — also in writing — either with the customer's (1) nonacceptance and request for a 'new' offer, or (2) a counteroffer (i.e. a lower price). The talk-based 'work' during the subsequent call is demonstrably contingent upon, and sensitive to, this preceding sequence. Specifically, telephone talk is concerned with negotiating the mutual acceptability of the offer. The oriented-to result, it appears, is definitive 'acceptance' or 'rejection' of the offer, with 'acceptance' quite clearly being the 'preferred' action. Hence either of these two actions is effectively held in abeyance pending negotiational 'work' carried out in both written and telephonic modes.

A crucial feature of that 'negotiational work' is the sequentially-ordered production, during the call itself, of a 'revised' or 'renegotiated' offer, which is in turn either accepted or rejected. This (sometimes recursive) adjacency sequence, we shall observe forthwith, is overwhelmingly preceded by talk that jointly addresses the perceived causes of or reasons for the non-acceptability of the initial offer (i.e., the offer made in writing). Such talk both assessses the justifiability and informs the production of a 'revised' offer.

Now, when definitive 'acceptance' is reached in telephone talk, this occasions a further 'offer-acceptance' adjacency sequence produced in writing (See Table 1, below; for reasons of space, the written sequences cannot be examined here). This sequence is a response to the organizational and legal exigencies of the trading companies.

So the negotiation calls are sequentially 'placed' after the original offer and its nonacceptance or counteroffer, yet prior to (and demonstrably in pursuit of) the offer's *institutionally preferred* reply, namely acceptance. That is, on the basis of the parties' joint actions, it appears that both seller and buyer orient to 'acceptance' of the 'offer' as the 'preferred' reply. Thus, although 'acceptance' of the offer is by no means an inevitability, the telephone negotiations are clearly the locus of a joint, talk-based effort to secure acceptance. So when the customer responds to the original offer by producing (in writing) a 'counteroffer', in those cases where the customer's 'counteroffer' is not acceptable, a Melko representative engages the other party in telephone talk.

2.2. The calls' gross structure

A further important similarity in the two data types is the parties' joint orientation to the 'negotiability' of the relevant details underlying the initial action ('request' for assistance in the emergency calls, 'offer' in the Melko calls). For what appears to be the case in both the emergency calls and the Melko calls is that participants are oriented to contingently augmenting and questioning the details of the initial action in order to produce a situationally appropriate reply to the request/offer.

The most conspicuous differences between the emergency calls and the Melko calls are to be found in (a) the way that the commodity traders routinely utilize and orient to a variety of communicative media in order to undertake their joint work tasks, and (b) in the content and structure of the interactional patterns produced. The differences emanating from the former mean that the interconnected actions are effectively 'stretched' temporally by virtue of the utilization of both written (telex or telefax) and telephonic modes. The differences in interactional patterns, while influenced by the utilization of different modes of communication, also reflect the differences in (standing) social relationships and work tasks facing the parties concerned. For example, as distinct from the emergency calls, the initial sections of the Melko calls are frequently occupied with talk centring on 'casual' topics such as the weather or vacations. 'Work talk', i.e. talk that addresses a specific work-related 'problem', routinely follows 'casual talk', and is oriented to as being initiated through the accomplished sequential placement of a reference to a written message wherein misalignment was communicated.[6] Such a reference is important for a number of reasons, one being that the reference 'connects', or 'ties', the current call to a specific, preceding activity. By so doing, this *retrospective tying reference* underscores (and thus accomplishes) the fact that, though the parties' joint work activities are separated spatio-temporally, the activities are nevertheless systematically organized, coherent, and thus a meaningful part of the demonstrably encompassing task of commodity trading.

Following the 'tying' reference, two interactionally distinct and relatively ordered types of 'work talk' ensue. In the first type, the parties are concerned with jointly *defining* the cause and nature of the 'problem' giving rise to the misalignment. Indirectly, such talk allows the parties to display the extent to which their stances vis-à-vis prices are negotiable. In this sense the talk here is not only 'problem-defining', but, ultimately, problem-solving in orientation. Talk of this nature is overwhelmingly followed by the solicitation or volunteering of an explicit 'offer'. The recipient is then faced with the decision of whether or not to align with the 'offer', a decision that has consequences for the content and trajectory of subsequent discourse. In these *bargaining sequences* (following Maynard 1984), while the parties are still engaged in 'defining' the problem confronting them, different interactional patterns prevail, as substantive offers and counteroffers are exchanged until agreement has been reached, deferred, or, as the case may be, abandoned. Parties routinely display acceptance of an offer and thus orient to the termination of such sequences in their locally- and sequentially-accomplished placement of references to, or requests for, a *prospective* communication (e.g. a telex or telefax 'confirming' the details of the oral agreement). From this juncture either the call's 'closing' is initiated, or the topic is shifted to other work-related matters. But in cases where other work-related topics are broached following 'bargaining sequences', both the topic and the calls themselves are commonly 'closed down' by a reference to the agreed 'arrangement' to send written confirmation of the negotiated offer.

The gross organizational structure of the Melko 'negotiation' calls examined here, and the calls' relationship to other communicative modes, is tabulated (see Table 1) (the items in brackets are interactionally optional).

The sections that follow describe the structure of the calls in some detail, though main emphasis will be afforded the calls' 'problem-defining series' and 'bargaining sequences'.

TABLE 1: GROSS ORGANIZATIONAL STRUCTURE OF THE MELKO 'NEGOTIATION' CALLS

(a) Melko's 'initial' offer	*WRITTEN MODE (1)*
(b) Customer's counteroffer/request for 'new' offer	

(c) Telephone call	*TELEPHONE MODE (2)*
opening	
(switchboard request)	
modified 'core' sequence	
(casual talk)	
retrospective 'tying' reference	
problem-defining series	
bargaining sequence	
prospective 'tying' reference	
closing	

(d) Melko's revised offer	*WRITTEN MODE (3)*
(e) Customer's acceptance ($\rightarrow$ COMMODITIES DISPATCHED)	

3. ANALYZING THE CALLS

3.1. Call Openings[7]

The openings of telephone calls may appear analytically trivial, interactionally vacuous, and merely routine. However, the 'routine' appearance itself, as Schegloff (1972a, 1979, 1986) has demonstrated, must properly be seen as a finely-coordinated 'achievement' of the parties involved. Despite appearances, telephone openings are 'interactionally dense', being the product of a delicately ordered monitoring process. Analytically and interactionally, openings are important in that they are the locus of a multiplicity of functions associated with the initiation of encounters — telephone negotiations included. A function of central importance in openings is establishing 'what kind of call this is'. As Schegloff (1979:25) puts it,

> "The opening is a place where the type of conversation being opened can be proferred, displayed, accepted, rejected, modified — in short, incipiently constituted by the parties to it".

Due to the lack of visual information, the telephone provides a set of contingencies for the parties to deal with in initiating each encounter. These minimally include the requirement for confirmation that the channel is open, followed by the need for recognition and/or identification. In his analyses of conversational calls, Schegloff (1986) identified what he termed a 'canonical core opening sequence' which accounted for his (North American) materials. This canonical sequence comprises four adjacency sequences, those being (a) 'summons-answer' (the 'summons' being the ringing of the telephone, the 'answer' the first 'hello', or equivalent), (b) an 'identification/recognition' sequence that establishes the identities of the caller and answerer (the caller, identifying/ recognizing the answerer's first 'hello', shows this recognition, which the answerer, in next turn, confirms), (c) a 'greeting' sequence, in which 'hi's' (etc.) are exchanged, and finally (d) an 'initial inquiry-response' (e.g., 'howareyou-okay') sequence.[8]

In the Melko calls, there are two types of 'openings', one of which is analogous to, though not identical with, Schegloff's 'core opening sequence'. The difference in type appears to be dependent upon who answers the ringing telephone within the called organization. The two types of openings are (1) the 'switchboard request' (Schegloff 1979) and (2) a 'modified core sequence'. It is this latter sequence that is analogous to Schegloff's 'canonical core sequence'. Let us briefly examine each opening type.

3.1.1. *The 'Switchboard Request'*

Somewhat surprisingly — perhaps to Western observers at least — in a number of calls in the corpus, the person *answering* the ringing telephone does not disclose the identity of the called organization in first-turn position. This applies particularly to calls made to companies in the Middle East region. The decision not to 'categorically self-identify' has interactional consequences. To see this, consider the following call opening; here Michael Hansen (H) calls a Saudi Arabian company:

(1)   ((ring))

1	A	ello?
2	H	mpt yes hell<u>o</u> uh <u>sau</u>di royal <u>im</u>port <u>ex</u>port c<u>o</u>mpany,
3	A	ye:s
4	H	it's uh m<u>i</u>chael <u>han</u>sen uh melko <u>dai</u>ries sp<u>eak</u>↓ing.
5		(0.8)
6		could I speak to mister <u>gup</u>ta please?
7	A	°<u>mo</u>ment°
8		(16.1) ((electronic tune))
9	B	all<u>o</u>:?
10	H	yes hell<u>o</u> uh m<u>i</u>chael <u>han</u>sen melko dairies ↓<u>spea</u>king
11	B	u-<u>one</u> m'nute.
12		(4.0)

13 G hall<u>o</u>?
14 H hello mister g<u>u</u>pta (.) how are <u>you</u>?
15 G fi:ne (.) how're <u>you:</u>

As distinct from Whalen and Zimmerman's (op. cit.) emergency calls, where the call-taker routinely categorically self-identifies in first turn position (e.g. 'Mid-City police and fire'), in the current corpus the ringing telephone is most frequently answered with a single 'hello' — analogous to Schegloff's (op. cit.) conversational calls. This may suggest that the answerer is not oriented to the 'institutional' setting when answering the ringing telephone.[9] That the *caller* orients to the 'institutional' setting, however, is clear from his first turn at talk, which offers a 'candidate recognition' of the called organization (line 2). The '[h]ello' answer (line 1), then, has interactional consequences that are *informed by and articulate with the work-related nature of the call*, for in cases where the caller is unable to recognize the first 'hello', confirmation is required that the desired *organization* (and not, e.g., a private individual) has been reached. In order for this to be done, caller, in second turn, names the desired organization, thus projecting confirmation (or otherwise) in next turn. Upon confirmation of this (line 3), caller then identifies himself as an *organizational member* (line 4) and, following a 0.8 second 'gap', produces what Schegloff (1979:33) has termed a 'switchboard request' for a particular other ('mister gupta') within the called organization (line 6). Thus, in the opening seconds of the call, as a result of the emergent order and formulations of things said (e.g. organizational names and affiliations), the call being dealt with is rendered visible as work-related; it is, thusfar, little more than one organizational member calling to speak to another. What that member is calling about is disclosed subsequently, in accordance with the unfolding contingencies of the call itself.

A subsequent unidentified voice-token ('allo', line 9) occasions the caller's repetition of 'self-identification' as an organizational member (line 10); this alone is sufficient for the answerer to deduce that the matter is to be dealt with by someone else. It is first when G comes to the telephone — in line 13 — that the remaining section of the opening approximates Schegloff's (1986) 'canonical core sequence', though in a modified form. (The modification being that the opening is more 'compact'. This is so since the 'identification/recognition' and 'greeting' components are collapsed into one, rather than three, turns). The caller, in producing a greeting+address term and in initiating a 'howareyou' sequence in a single turn (line 14), displays his recognition of G from the preceding 'hello' (line 13). The 'howareyou' is reciprocated in next turn (line 15), thus displaying G's recognition of the caller's identity.

3.1.2. *The 'Modified Core Sequence'*

'Modified core sequence' types are analogous to the openings of (North American) conversational calls. As Schegloff (op. cit.) noted, there can be several variants of the canonical 'core' sequence, and this is substantiated in the present corpus. The basic requirements informing the sequence are that the channel is opened, relevant identities are disclosed and/or recognized, greetings and 'howareyou's' exchanged. It is particularly these latter two sequences — invariably produced when caller and answerer are acquainted — that furnish the openings with 'conversational' characteristics. But in the Melko corpus, when caller recognizes the identity of the answerer through a first turn 'hello', a modified, more compact version of Schegloff's (op. cit.) 'canonical core sequences' is routinely produced. Completion of the opening sequence — reached after the second 'howareyou' (or equivalent) — presents the parties with the call's *anchor position* (Schegloff op. cit.:116); that is, the position from which the 'first topic' may legitimately be introduced. Consider the following extract:

```
(2)   ((ring))
      1   Y   ello:
      2   A   yes hello youseff it's anna from melko?
      3   Y   yes hi↓how're you anna
      4   A   fine, an' you?
```

In this extract, the caller is able to identify the answerer on the basis of the first-turn 'hello'. This is displayed by the caller — in line 2 — producing a greeting ('hello') and then naming the answerer, in addition to categorically self-identifying ('Anna from Melko'). The answerer responds first by returning the greeting ('hi') and then by initiating a 'howareyou' sequence. The caller, A, reciprocates the 'howareyou', after which point the parties have reached the so-called 'anchor position' in the call.

The following section addresses the way the parties 'move off' this 'anchor position' provided by the opening sequence, and 'move into' one of two types of talk: 'casual talk' or 'work talk'.

3.2. Casual Talk

3.2.1. *'Casual Talk' or 'Work Talk'?*

Once the 'howareyou' has been reciprocated, the 'anchor position' has been reached, and there appears to be at least two options available to the person whose turn it is to talk. The options are whether to engage in talk on 'casual' topics such as the weather or vacation plans, or to 'get down to business', so to speak, and thus circumvent 'casual' talk. Both options have relevance, inasmuch as the parties are acquainted with one another, have a history of previous mutual dealings, and would, we may presume, have vested interests in maintaining cordial, personable relations — interests that may be directly attended to in 'casual' talk. To this extent the relevance and import of casual talk is clearly apparent. On the other hand, the call is recognizably being made from and to a workplace, during working hours, and in response to a work-defined matter. (Calls are not made for purely 'social' ends.) Furthermore, the called party, perhaps being unprepared for the call received, may be engaged in other pressing matters, which may potentially counterbalance the advantages of casual talk. How is this 'dilemma' — to do, or not to do casual talk — resolved?

To begin with it is important to see it as an *interactional* dilemma, resolved *locally* on a turn-by-turn, collaborative basis. And there are, it appears, methodic ways of managing the transition from 'anchor position' to either 'casual talk' or 'work talk'. It is these methodic ways I shall briefly attempt to describe in this section.

Consider, first, a call where the parties engage in casual talk. The following segment is a continuation of extract (1):

(3)

```
16   H    fine than' you (.) you know now the summer time had-
17        t-come to d'nmark as well (.) ((laugh)) hh:uh=
18   G    =((laughing)) huh hh:eh heh heh heh :.hh
19   H    so for:: the:- us here in denmark it's hot
20        (.) it's uh twenty five degree, (.) .hh but for y ⌜ou it will be-
21   G                                                      ⌞ya:h,
22   H    it would be cold (.) I think
23   G    no, here in this pwu:h forty- forty two
24   H    yes?
25        (1.0)
26   H    ⌜⌜well
27   G    ⌞⌞yes
28        (1.0)
29   H    well I prefer twendy five. (.) it's better to me
30        (0.9)
31   G    yeah
32        (1.1)
33   H    GOOD↓ uh I ↑got a telex for uh- from you
34        (1.3)
35   H    yo⌜u don'-
36   G      ⌞yeah
```

What seems to be of crucial importance initially is how the recipient of the second (i.e. reciprocated) 'howareyou' responds. For example, in the extract above, the caller, H, first responds to the 'howareyou' inquiry with 'fine than[k] you' (line 16) and, with barely a perceptible pause, produces a *topicalizer*: 'you know now the summer time has come to Denmark as well' (lines 16-17). The turn is completed with H's single laugh token (line 17), onto which G 'latches' a longer spate of laugh tokens (line 18). G's laugh tokens have been viewed by H as a '*positive' response* to the topicalizer, and clearly have interactional consequences, since H, in next turn, now *elaborates* on the topic (lines 19-22) by comparing current weather conditions in Denmark with those in Saudi Arabia.[10] This occasions an on-topic response from G (line 23). However, rather than producing extended topical talk in subsequent turns, the parties proceed to implicitly 'negotiate' curtailment of such talk.

To see this, note that G's turn at line 23 is met with H's 'yes?' (line 24). A one-second 'gap' then arises (line 25), after which H and G briefly overlap each other. Then a further one-second 'gap' arises (line 28). This is followed by H's 'well I prefer twendy five, it's better to me' (line 29). This utterance, rather than being topicalized and elaborated by G in next turn, is followed by a one-second 'gap', which precedes G's 'yeah' (line 31). Yet another one-second 'gap' occurs at line 32, the cumulative result of which appears to be an indication of both parties' desire to curtail further 'casual' talk. As a result of both parties' actions, then, 'casual' talk can be seen to have 'petered out'. This at least appears to be H's interpretation, for he now shifts topic, and marks the shift with 'good' (line 33), enunciated with falling intonation and heavily stressed. H then makes a *retrospective tying reference* to a telex ('I got a telex from you', line 33). The transition is thus made — or at least proposed at this juncture — from casual talk to talk centring directly on work-related matters. G's 'yeah' (line 36) would seem to display both acceptance and recognition of the topic shift.

What we see in this short segment is how the parties, on a joint basis, through 'topicalizers', 'elicitors', 'elaborations' and through their sensitivity to 'gaps' between turns, 'move off' the 'anchor position' in the call, and by so doing 'negotiate' the appropriacy, content, tenor, trajectory and duration of the 'casual' talk.

In the two following calls, unlike the case above, 'casual' talk is not engaged in. Here, the outstanding 'business-at-hand', namely the nonacceptance of the offer, is afforded 'first topic'[11] status:

(4)

```
8    H    I'm fine thank you
9         (2.2)
10   G    ye:s (.) sir:↓
11        (0.5)
```

```
12  H    we::ll y- you told me that uh (.) czechoslovakian are selli::ng (.) feta
13       very chea:ply.
14       (0.3)
15  G    yeah (.) we are- we are receiving
16       (2.2)
17  H    ye:s
```

Note that, following H's response to the second 'howareyou', a relatively long (two-second) 'gap' arises (line 9). As we saw in extract (3), the slot following the 'howareyou' is a legitimate sequential position for 'topicalizers' to be produced, yet in this case H refrains from adding a topicalizer to his response. Following the two seconds of silence, G produces the utterance 'yes sir', enunciated with falling intonation (line 10). This utterance appears to be prospectively oriented: it demonstrably has the characteristics of an elicitor. This is so inasmuch as (a) it is preceded by a relatively long (2.2 second) 'gap' (line 9), and (b) does not initiate 'casual' talk in a sequential position where it visibly may have done so. Certainly this is H's interpretation of what the 'yes sir' does, for in his next turn he makes reference to an antecedent communication wherein G had informed him that 'Czechoslovakian are selling feta very cheaply' (lines 12-13). And G, in his next turn (line 15), both accepts and displays recognition of the work-related topic by addressing his talk to the matter now raised. Hence, in this segment, it is not so much G that unilaterally acts to circumvent 'casual' talk and elicit 'work' talk; rather, both parties, through the multilateral coordination of actions, appear to be 'steering' the talk directly from the 'anchor position' into the direction of a (or *the*) work-relevant topic. The following extract displays close similarities to extract (4):

(5)
```
5   H    well I- I'm fine
6        (2.0)
7   H    [[erm
8   G    [[ye:s
9        (0.9)
10  H    I have (.) just (.) received telex (.) from uh ma- from you or from
11       mahib.
12  G    this er: (.) four 'undred fifty gram is three five seven five. (.) and big
13       block (.) is impossible this uh:
14       (1.5)
15  H    ye⌈s
```

Once again, H's response to the 'howareyou' is brief: it does not 'topicalize'. Also, the response is not followed by the other party's topicalizer, but by a two-second 'gap' (line 6). In overlap, G produces a 'yes', which H (in line 10) interprets as a work-topic elicitor. Observe again how the work topic is actually initiated by H: by referring back — i.e. retrospectively — to a particular 'telex'. G's response is to produce a 'formulation' or summary of the telex, and to impart his reactions to the 'impossibility' of the situation (line 13).

3.3. The Problem-Defining Series

The segments ((3)-(5)) above provide insight into how the parties methodically coordinate their actions in ways that allow them to move from conversation-like openings and initiate talk that is visibly work-related. The work-related talk is here equated with the parties' engagement in activity that directly addresses a specific 'problem' communicated in an earlier written correspondence. As I shall endeavour to reveal in this section, such talk initially involves attempting to *define* — on a joint basis — the nature and cause of the 'problem' that has led to misalignment. It is upon the basis of the 'definition' of the problem that the parties decide not only *how* to pursue agreement, but also *whether* agreement is economically feasible and thus an institutionally defensible possibility.

3.3.1. *Retrospective 'Tying' Reference*
In the first part of this section, attention will be given to retrospective 'tying' references. In functional terms, the references carry a heavy interactional load. 'Tying' references imbue the current interaction with 'linking' properties that mark this call as one-in-a-series of interrelated activities. Additionally, the references are oriented to as (a) signalling either a closing down or circumvention of 'casual' talk, (b) proposing commencement of a specific topic that is demonstrably work relevant, (c) formulating the rudiments of the 'problem' facing both parties, and by so doing (d) establishing a 'working agenda' for subsequent talk. In this way, the reference marks the initiation and informs the focus of subsequent 'problem-defining' talk. Consider first the following extract:

(6)

```
33   H    GOOD↓uh I ↑got a telex for uh- from you
34        (1.3)
35   H    yo ⌈u don'-
36   G       ⌊yeah
37   H    you don' u:h (.) accept our pri↓ces.
```

```
38        (1.2)
39   G    for this uh chedd↓ar.
40   H    yes (0.7)⌐u:h
                  ⌊
```

Analyses suggest that the reference to a preceding written correspondence consists of two relatively ordered components. The first component contains a reference to the *mode* (telex, telefax) and/or the *sender* of the message (exemplified in H's 'I got a telex from you', line 33). The second component is a résumé, or *formulation*, of the contents or action-status of the preceding written correspondence (exemplified in H's 'you don't accept our prices', line 37). While the caller routinely provides the first component, either the caller or the called party may provide the formulation component. Furthermore, on some occasions, as in extract (6) above, the actual wording of the formulation component is not produced unilaterally but multilaterally — on a collaborative basis.

Note that H's reference to a preceding telex (line 33) is followed by a 1.3 second 'gap'. The 'gap' is oriented to by H as G's (momentary) inability to recollect the specific telex, for at line 37 (and in an aborted attempt at line 35) H increases the recognizability of the telex by offering a *formulation* of the message's perceived action status ('you don't accept our prices').[12] After a one-second 'gap', G responds by adding a syntactically-felicitous continuer ('for this uh cheddar', line 39), thereby (a) displaying his recognition of the telex, (b) confirming the accuracy of the H's characterization of the telex ('you don't accept our prices'), and (c) providing the formulation with additional relevant detail.

The same three functions — indication of recognition, confirmation of accuracy, and provision of additional detail — can also be observed in G's response (line 15) to H's reference in the following extract:

(7)

```
12   H     we::ll y- you told me that uh (.) czechoslovakian are selli::ng (.) feta
13         very chea:ply↓
14         (0.3)
15   G→    yeah (.) we are- we are receiving
16         (2.2)
17   H     ye:s
18         (0.7)
19   G     we received this (.) three container?
20   H     I see
```

H's reference to a preceding communication contains information about the sender and a 'formulation' of the message: 'well you told me that Czechoslovakian are selling feta very cheaply', lines 12-13). As Heritage and Watson (1979) observed, formulations are oriented to as 'confirmation-elicitors', as evidenced by G's next turn 'yeah' (line 15). Note, however, that following this confirmation, G reveals information not previously disclosed, yet perceivedly relevant to the current interaction; he adds: 'we are receiving' (line 15). A subsequent two-second 'gap' (line 16), H's 'yes' (line 17) and a further 0.7 second 'gap' appears to elicit yet additional detail from G, for it is now revealed that G's company are currently in the process of receiving 'three containers' of feta from Czechoslovakian producers (line 19).

Formulations of the written communications may also be provided by the called party, as the following extract shows. In this extract, H has called G:

(8)

```
10   H   I have (.) just (.) received telex. (.) from uh ma- from you or from
11       mahib.
12   G   this u:h (.) four 'undred fifty gram is three five seven five. (.) and
13       big block (.) is impossible this u:h
14       (1.5)
15   H   ye ⌈ s
16   G      ⌊ three three seven five (.) there
17       is only two 'undred dollar diff'rence.
```

There is a great deal of compactness in these turns, and this extract is again a good example of how the parties methodically and systematically initiate and develop work-relevant talk. In this case, the formulation component of the reference is provided by G in lines 12-13 and 16-17. The formulation not only summarizes the information disclosed in the preceding message (e.g. '450 gram is three five seven five and big block ... three three seven five'), it also *problematizes* the information ('[it] is impossible this', line 13) and accounts for the selfsame problematization ('there is only two 'undred dollar difference', lines 16-17).

3.3.2. 'Defining' the Problem

A large number of negotiation scholars have claimed that a pervasive feature of the negotiation process is that parties proceed from a 'problem-defining' or 'problem-clarifying' phase to a 'resolution' phase; that is, a phase of interaction wherein substantive proposals are exchanged (see, e.g., Douglas 1962, Morley and Stephenson 1977, Gulliver 1979, Bacharach and Lawler 1981, Maynard 1984, Holmes 1992 for a review). The feature appears to obtain across the wide range of negotiations. For example, Bacharach and Lawler (1981:164) contend that, regardless of the matter being negotiated, substantive proposals are first dealt with once the negotiating parties establish a "*consensual definition of an issue*". As Maynard (1984:88) puts it: "The general maxim seems to be that bargaining ... must be preceeded [sic] by relevant discussion, or by solicits or announcements that allow such discussion to happen". There is, however, a striking paucity of work undertaken on the way such 'defining' phases are accomplished through discourse. Maynard's work on plea bargaining (see Maynard 1984, 1990) is one of the few studies that attempts to detail the discursive and interactional character of 'problem-', or 'issue-defining' phases. Maynard observed that, in his materials, "the real business of bargaining" (op. cit.:90) — which he defined as the exchange of substantive proposals and/or offers — most often occurred after the Public Defender or District Attorney (or both) had 'settled the facts' of the case by narrating 'what happened' in the events leading to the defendant's arrest, or had provided a 'person-description' of the defendant (see Maynard 1984:chap. 6). Such tellings were constructed neither in a neutral, 'check-list' fashion nor in an ad hoc manner; rather they were strategically motivated, "carefully selected and used contextually to justify negotiators' positions" (op. cit.:145). Apart from justifying the attorney's position in subsequent bargaining sequences, narratives of 'what happened', as well as 'person-descriptions', ultimately made public (and thus made negotiable) professional and lay theories about how and why crimes are committed, and how defendants should be appropriately treated.

Similar to Maynard's (op. cit.) findings, in the Melko calls an exchange of substantive proposals is routinely preceded by talk that explicitly addresses itself to the cause and nature of a 'problem' perceived to be the reason for the parties' misaligned positions (i.e. the customer's nonacceptance of an offer). As noted above, invariably, prior to the telephone interaction, the 'problem' has been broached in writing, as the customer communicates nonacceptance of prices through the provision of an account for the nonacceptance. Accounts not only explicate the perceived cause of the problem, they also provide insight into the parties' reasoning about 'normal' and 'rational' trading behaviour. It is these causes, perceptions and reasonings that are subjected to various 'probings' in subsequent telephone interaction.

As we have observed, in telephonic mode the 'problem' communicated initially in writing is typically 'recycled' in the 'formulation' component of the 'tying' reference. This formulation invariably occasions an *account* for the perceived 'problem'. Following this, almost as a matter of routine, in subsequent talk the account is systematically and incrementally 'unpacked' of its perceived componential layerings. Thus, by furnishing the discourse with accounts, and in the responses those accounts occasion, the parties engage *jointly* in the task of *defining* the problem-at-hand. It appears to be the case that only when the 'problem' has been 'defined' adequately — i.e. adequate 'for-all-practical-purposes', rather than definitively — do the parties engage in the exchange of substantive proposals.

Importantly, then, the formulation of the 'problem' is oriented to as providing a rudimentary, working definition of the problem-at-hand. The rudimentary character of the formulation is made evident in the parties' subsequent joint actions, wherein the 'problem' is accounted for and then 'probed' and elaborated in various ways. In the following case, for example, the 'formulation' is jointly produced in lines 37-39; in the next turn, following H's 'yes' (line 40), G accounts for the formulated problem:

(9)

```
33  H   GOOD↓uh I ↑got a telex for uh- from you
34      (1.3)
35  H   yo┌u don'-
36  G     └yeah
37  H   you don' u:h (.) accept our pri↓ces.
38      (1.2)
39  G   for this uh chedd↓ar.
40  H   yes (0.7) ┌ u:h
41  G→            └ because all uh this- in riyadh I don' know
42      how they are selling this uh (.) less than our cost uh
43      which you have quoted.
44      (0.6)
45  H   u:h but (.) are they selling uh ↑danish cheddar cheese?
```

G's 'account' is initiated at line 41 (arrowed). As a linguistic device that justifies (or excuses) an untoward or unexpected action (following Austin 1961; see also Semin and Manstead 1983, Buttny 1993), G's account is prototypically formatted, beginning with the word 'because'. The design of the account is clearly predicated on the basis of a preceding message, as indicated in G's use of the pro-term 'they' (line 42), the referent of which is not recoverable from preceding talk. The 'they' refers, however, to the wording contained in G's preceding telex (the referent being 'other local importers'; see Firth in press (a)), the identification of which both H and G have already jointly established (in lines 33-40).

H's response to the account is neither to 'honour' it (cf. e.g. Read 1992) nor orient to it as 'incontestable' (cf. Heritage 1984a:272). Rather H *probes* the account by questioning it ('but are they selling uh Danish cheddar cheese?' line 45). This sequential configuration — account followed by other party's 'probing' action — is pervasive in the telephone calls, and is important in the sense that it begins the process of both 'opening' and 'contesting' the account. An account, we may thus observe, is oriented to as containing certain 'vulnerabilities' (cf. Whalen and Zimmerman 1990). That is, in these calls an account is seen to be partial and selective; it demonstrably cannot 'tell the whole story' of why, for example, an offer has been deemed unacceptable. Therefore its detail, veracity, and implied prudence is routinely 'probed' by the recipient. Incrementally, through the emergent discourse, accounts are 'expanded' or 'unpacked' (Jefferson 1986). And both parties are clearly oriented to the 'probeability', 'contestability' and 'expandability' of accounts, as the following extract also reveals:

(10)

```
19  G    we received this (.) three container?
20  H    I see
21  G    beca- because you:r price is very hi::gh
22  H    yes?
23       (0.8)
24  G    that's why we are taking now this from u::h (0.6) .hh now this three
25       container we brought
26  H    yes? (0.5) but uh tell me uh y- you a:re receiving that in uh dubai
27       I think
28       (0.8)
29  G    yeah (.) we'll take in dubai
```

G's account is located at line 21; it is followed by H's elicitor ('yes', line 22) and G's supplementary detail (lines 24-25). H's 'probing' of the account occurs at lines 22 and 26-27. The sequence that follows (see extract (11) below) reveals that the probing of the account is not oriented to as being motivated by a need for propositional information alone: questions following accounts are often recognized as being potentially tendentious and strategically motivated. That is, questions following accounts appear to have a *challenge trajectory* inasmuch as the question can be treated as the initiation of an attempt to challenge the legitimacy and prudence of the account offered; thus:

(11)

```
30  H    an' then you have the oncarriage from dubai
31       (0.5)
32  G    on our own truck
33  H    yes? (1.5) I ⌈ see
34  G            ⌊ now this u::h (.) .hh from dubai (.) also this uh truck
35       charges uh fuh cheaper than uh (.) before
36  H    I see (.) o:kay=
```

In line 29 (extract (10)) G responds to H's inquiry into the port of entry of the competitors' goods. H (line 30, extract (11)) then seeks information on delivery procedures following arrival of the goods at port. This statement ('then you have the on-carriage from Dubai',

line 30) is what Labov and Fanshel (1977:100) have labelled a 'B-event' which, in that
it makes a claim about the interlocutor's current state of knowledge, projects G's
confirmation of the accuracy of the claim. At this point, however, G orients to a perceived
tendentiousness and 'challenge trajectory' inherent in his projected answer, and responds
'on our *own* truck' (line 32). This response pre-empts H's potential challenge to the
legitimacy of G's account (the challenge being that others' prices are not in fact cheaper
once additional transportation costs are taken into consideration). H's subsequent 'I
see' utterances (lines 33 and 36) appear to concede that the premise behind the
questioning is false.

Although accounts are routinely 'unpacked', the 'unpacking' is not invariably
accomplished via the other party's questioning. Producing an account for an untoward
state of affairs can be accomplished multilaterally. As well as justifying or excusing
unwanted or unpropitious actions, accounts may be oriented to as 'blaming' the account
recipient for the current state of affairs (In so doing, the account-giver is also implicitly
attempting to establish the cause and thus proposing a 'definition' of the problem).
When this interpretation is given to an account the recipient may respond to the perceived
blaming action with an account ('excuse') for the current state of affairs. This second
account attempts to deflect 'blame' to another source. The result is that the 'problem' is
defined jointly, and thus accomplished in more detailed and subtle ways than may
otherwise have been possible. In the following case, G's account (lines 12-13, 16-17)
is followed by H's account:

(12)

```
10   H    I have (.) just (.) received telex. (.) from uh ma- from you or from
11        mahib.
12   G →this u:h (.) four 'undred fifty gram is three five seven five. (.) and big
13      →block (.) is impossible this u:h
14        (1.5)
15   H    ye⌈s
16   G →    ⌊three three seven five. (.) there
17      →     is only two 'undred dollar diff'rence.
18   H    u:h that's right (.) an' the reason is uh that when I quoted you the four
19        'undred fifty gram (.) ⌈ the you ess ((U.S.)) dollar was
20   G                          ⌊ yes
21   H    u:h (.) higher (.) than it is today
22        (0.9)
23   G    mm hmm
24        (1.3)
25   H    erm (.) because u:h (.) uh three thousand three hundred, it's uh two
```

26		hundred dollar below my <u>cost</u> price
27		(1.1)
28	G	oh ↓no::
29	H	that's <u>right</u>?
30	G	no no no
31		(3.4)
32	H	I-=
33	G	=no this <u>big</u> block <u>must</u> be cheaper this uh
34	H	norm'ly <u>should</u> be: (.) <u>cheap</u>er. (.)

In the turns arrowed, G formulates the contents of his preceding telex by remarking that H's offer of 3575 US dollars for 450 gram and 3375 for 'big block' packagings is 'impossible'. He notes that 'there is only two hundred dollar difference' (lines 16-17) (where 'normal' price differentials are greater: see H's turn at line 34). While G's turn accounts for his nonacceptance of the offer, it is treated by H as a 'complaint' about the current situation. H's turn at line 18 first confirms there is indeed 'only two hundred dollar difference' (with the words 'that's right'), and then accounts for the state of affairs by observing that the US dollar rate was higher when the original offer had been made: 'the reason is that when I quoted you ... the US dollar was higher than it is today' (lines 18-21). (Preceding the call, G had made a telexed counteroffer of 3300 for the 'big block' packagings). H's account here acknowledges that the current state of affairs is problematic, yet places responsibility for the problem elsewhere — namely fluctuating currency rates. To H, then, the 'impossible' is justifiably possible.

The account for the 'impossible' state of affairs now allows H to indirectly reject G's counteroffer *and* account for the rejection, since the (counter)offered 3300 is, H reveals, 'two hundred dollars below my cost price' (lines 25-26). H's revelation that his 'cost price' is 3500 elicits a token of disappointment from G: 'oh no::' — enunciated with heavy falling intonation (line 28). Doubtless aware that 'cost price' is H's 'break even' margin, and therefore likely to be below H's actual selling price, G now displays incredulity towards H's disclosure: 'no, no, no' (line 30), adding 'big block must be cheaper' (line 33), which H reformulates as 'normally should be cheaper' (line 34). In the emergent course of the discourse, both parties are thus engaged in defining and redefining the 'problem' confronting them.

Where accounts are questioned, however, the questioning may occasion actions that appear to override the sequential constraints that questions normally impose, as in the following case (this extract is a continuation of (9)):

(13)

45	H	u:h but (.) are they selling uh ↑<u>da</u>nish cheddar cheese?=

```
46  G   =but uh we have also received uh prices from other party
47  H   yes?
48  G   less than your- ((laughing)) less: than your
49      pr(h)i:c(h)es::? hh::
50  H   I see (.) I think our ┌ prob-
51  G                         └ becuz you know that uh all cheese
52      item, we are taking only from you
53  H   °yes° (.) I think the ┌ problem
54  G                         └ and always we believe on your u:h
55      pri↓ces.
56  H   I think the problem is u::h y'know the: (0.8) ee:ee
57      s::ee ((EEC)) subsidy for the cheddar cheese, and the
58      o ┌ ther cheeses was reduced
59  G     └ but uh why did uh other party they are giving u:h
60      (.) one undred fifty to two undred dollars less than
61      yours?
62  H   oh SO much? (0.8) becau ┌ se
63  G                           └ ↑ye:s
64      (1.3)
65  H   °it's strange°
66      (1.6)
```

H's question ('are they selling uh Danish cheddar cheese?', line 45) is followed by G's disclosure that 'we have also received prices from other party' (line 46). On the surface, this response appears incoherent in relation to the preceding turn. Yet to the recipient this is visibly not the case, since H neither repeats the question nor initiates a 'repair' in his next turn 'slot' (line 47). Instead, H's 'yes?' appears to prompt G to reveal additional detail in the subsequent turn. G then discloses that competitors are offering to sell cheese to G's company at prices below Melko's (lines 48-49). It may be that the (work-related) 'gravity' of G's disclosure at line 46 legitimates it overriding the sequential constraints established by H's question at line 45. An additional factor may be that, as a result of H's questioning (and potential challenging) of G's account, G now recognizes the necessity to lay his 'best (negotiating) card' on the table, so to speak. And that 'best card' is the disclosure that G's company have actually received a cheaper offer from H's competitors.

H then glosses the current state of affairs as 'our prob[lem]' (line 50), and makes two (aborted) attempts to reveal the cause of the 'problem' (at lines 50 and 53) before stating that 'the problem is the EEC subsidy' (lines 56-57). G's response is to ask a rhetorical question that both displays his awareness of the EEC subsidy reduction and challenges the veridicality of Hansen's perception of the cause of the problem. G asks: 'but why did other party they are giving one hundred and fifty to two hundred dollars less than yours?' (lines 59-61). In the next turn, H intimates surprise at this disclosure ('oh SO much?', line 62), thereby implicitly acknowledging that his 'definition' of the 'problem' is erroneous. Once again, then, in this extract we see how the parties, by jointly attempting to delineate the problem confronting them, incrementally 'tease out' and make public situationally-relevant information, thereby serving the purposes of joint 'problem-defining'.

The incremental disclosure of relevant information can also be observed in the following extract. Here H questions G about the competitor's offer/quotation:

(14)

```
86   H    yes (.) u:h the quotation you have received, is that
87        with fixed weight? (0.5) becau:se u:h .hh we can get it with
88        uh (0.4) u::h different weights (.) on (.) each unit,
89        but an average around four undred an' fifty, but they
90        can be from four hundred to five hundred gram. (0.4) but
91        we have decided to=
92   G    =NO, NO (.) one uh fix uh this
93        four hundred fifty grams.
94   H    it's a fixed uh ┌ weight? ┐
95   G                   └ fixed.  ┘ (.) yes
96   H    yes (0.4) uhuh
97   G    four hundred fifty gram fixed
98        (1.3)
99        this price. (.) a hundred dollar- hundred an' five dollar difference
100       (0.9)
101       then u:h in u:h yellow colour also 'bout hundred dollar difference
102       then white u:h two hundred twenty five gram, .hh you
103       'ave quoted three four zero five, they have quoted three
104       two nine zero.
105       (1.0)
106  H    °three two, nine zero.°
```

H's repetition of the question of whether the competing quotation concerns 'fixed weight' commodities (i.e. 'the quotation you've received, is that with fixed weight?', lines 86-87 is repeated — though in modified form — at line 94) occasions G's *detailed* disclosure relating to the competitor's offer. Thus, in his turn beginning at line 97, G first incorporates the information sought previously by H (whether the goods were packaged in 'fixed weights'), and then calculates that there is a 'hundred and five dollar difference' (line 99) in price between the 450 gram packagings in the two competing offers. Additional detailed information is next disclosed relating to 'yellow' and 'white' cheddar, and the differences between the two offers (lines 101-104). So whereas the 'problem' in the initial stages of this particular telephone negotiation was formulated as 'you don't accept our prices' (extract (9), line 37), through a series of turns wherein the 'problem' is incrementally probed and 'expanded', the nature of 'problem' is here shown to be considerably more detailed and complex. For not only does G reject H's prices for cheddar, it is subsequently revealed that he (G) has received an improved offer from H's competitor, that H's explanation for the 'problem' is unacceptable, and that the competitor is offering cheese at $150-$200 below H's price. Further revelations apprise H of the specific price differences between the two offers.

To conclude this section, let us briefly recap the discursive and interactional purposes served by accounts and their responses. The series of account-question-response is a pervasive feature of these calls. Moreover it is one methodic way in which both parties (a) display an orientation to nonacceptance as a temporary 'hindrance' rather than a de facto refusal to purchase, (b) disclose and negotiate situationally-relevant information pertaining to a definition of the current 'problem', and (c) assess the feasibility of either soliciting or volunteering substantive proposals to resolve the 'problem'. Hence, talk arising out of this 'problem-defining' series allows us to observe how both parties' actions lead to disclosures that *incrementally* reveal the perceived market-related factors underlying the current misalignment. So it is not that one party simply discloses information in an ad hoc or incidental fashion. Rather, information is exchanged and managed contingently by the two parties, in accordance with the emergent courses of action and the unfolding patterns of discourse — both of which are reflexively underpinned by and explicate the parties' perceptions of 'normal', 'rational' and 'fair' trading behaviour.

3.4. The Bargaining Sequence

Following a series of turns that collectively addresses the nature and cause of the 'problem' confronting the trading parties, a shift in interactional emphasis becomes apparent: one of the parties solicits or makes a substantive proposal or offer. The proposal/offer is invariably a revision of the offer made previously in writing. The recipient is then in a position of either aligning with the action and thus accepting the offer, or not aligning, in which case either a rejection or a counteroffer is made. And it is in this way, generally speaking, that the parties proceed until an offer is accepted, or until one or both of the parties decide that agreement is not feasible.

In these sections of the Melko calls, the interactional patterns are similar to the 'bargaining sequence' described by Maynard (1984) in his study of plea bargaining discourse. Maynard (op. cit.) proposed that his plea bargaining materials could be accounted for in terms of the participants' orientations to and production of a two-part 'bargaining sequence', consisting of (1) a turn in which speaker exhibits a position, and (2) a next turn where the recipient displays alignment or nonalignment with the initially exhibited position (op. cit.:78). It was observed that

> "Bargaining sequences regularly consist of two parts ... that are relatively ordered ... and discriminatively related ... [T]hese sequences are often elaborated in systematic ways so that their parts are not necessarily adjacently positioned and produced by different speakers".

Maynard noted that "two principal devices are used to initiate most bargaining sequences: the proposal, and the position-report" (ibid.). 'Proposal' is the collective term for actions such as 'offers', 'suggestions', 'asking-fors', and 'proposals'. Two 'proposal' actions and their responses are exemplified in the following exchanges between the District Attorney (DA) and the Public Defender (PD):

(15)

| DA3: | How 'bout three months |
| PD1: | Naw, that's too much |

(16)

| DA3: | Let's put this down for a go |
| PD2: | Arright go it is |

'Proposals' make acceptance or rejection relevant in the next turn. Thus, whereas the proposal is rejected in (15), it is accepted in (16). A second principal way of initiating a 'bargaining sequence' in Maynard's materials was the production of a 'position-report'; these were utterances that displayed personal preferences or desires, typically formatted as 'I'd like', 'I think', or 'I want'. For example:

(17)

| DA1: | I think she should be placed on probation and do jail time |

Maynard (op. cit.:81-83) suggested that 'position-reports' may be ways of performing a 'mitigated' or 'downgraded' version of the proposal, and that they may be resources that provide a method of presenting a different focus on the case-at-hand. It was also shown that the first turn in the 'bargaining sequence' was regularly preceded by the other party's 'solicit' (request for an offer), or by an 'announcement' that an offer is about to be made. Such items, while allowing systematic movement into the bargaining sequence, also provide the opportunity for discussion of other relevant items before the sequence is started (op. cit.:87). The bargaining sequence is minimally produced across two turns, where the position-report or the proposal is met by an occasioned *reply*, namely either acceptance or rejection. But the sequence can be elaborated internally, in that a *response*, rather than a 'reply', follows the proposal or position-report. A 'response' "speaks to other aspects of the prior move instead of addressing what it directly implicates" (op. cit.:92-93). A characteristic 'response' is a counterproposal, noted Maynard; such actions make visible "a contrasting position of the one who speaks it and simultaneously suggests what trouble exists with respect to the opposed position" (op. cit.:93).

As we shall observe, Maynard's conceptual apparatus and findings will prove useful in the analysis of 'bargaining sequences' evident in the Melko calls. The examination here will concentrate briefly on three features of the 'bargaining sequences' in the calls: first the opening of the 'bargaining sequence' (i.e. the placement of 'suggestions', 'proposals' or 'offers'); second the way proposals are formatted, and third the sequential implications of a proposal.

At the outset, it can be noted that the Melko calls' 'bargaining sequence' is commonly initiated by the seller's unsolicited 'proposal'; on some occasions, the prospective buyer solicits a 'proposal', and in one call it is the buyer who initiates the sequence with his own (unsolicited) 'proposal'. In the current data corpus there are no instances of either 'announcements' or 'position reports'.

The following extract exemplifies a 'proposal-nonalignment' sequence; H's 'proposal' occurs at lines 75-76 (arrowed):

(18)

```
69  G    y'know this very small quantity this
70       (0.4)
71  H    yes, ahah (.) because uh y'know the ee ee see ((EEC))
72       subsidy was reduced with sixty dollar per tonne
73       (1.0)
74  G    yeah
75  H→   an' u:h (.) that sixty dolla:r (0.7) u:h I will uh accept
76   →   to:- to cover myself
77       (0.8)
78  G    NO this uh cheese is cheddar cheese, four hundred fifty
79       gram. (.) you 'ave quoted three two four five (0·8) but
80       we received price three one four zero.
```

G's turn at line 69 is part of an attempt to 'define' the nature and cause of the specific problem at hand; note that, in so doing, G appeals to apparently shared knowledge: 'y'know this very small quantity this'. The information disclosed by G is accepted by H in next turn ('yes, ahah', line 71). In the same turn H performs an action that both justifies and projects a revised proposal; he first elicits from his interlocutor acknowledgement of awareness of the recent EEC subsidy by formulating his turn in a two-part 'cause-effect' format; the 'cause' component also appeals to apparently shared knowledge: 'because y'know the EEC subsidy was reduced with sixty dollars per tonne' (lines 71-72). H awaits G's confirmatory 'yeah' (line 74) before producing the 'effect' component: a proposal to reduce his offer by $60 per tonne (lines 75-76). Observe that the proposal is framed as a mitigated concession: H will 'accept to cover' the difference (i.e. the reduction of $60) himself. However, the proposal occasions an emphatic rejection ('NO', line 78), from which point G proceeds to disclose additional situationally-relevant information that *accounts for* his rejection. Although produced on the basis of a rejection, G's disclosure here should properly be seen as a collaborative action, in that, by specifying the differences in the two competing offers, he is furnishing the talk with resources that aid the interlocutor's efforts to compete. That is, in apprising H of the details of the competitor's offer, G is providing information relevant for H's subsequent and potentially 'improved' offer.

The following extract — which is a continuation of extract (11) — is rather more complex than the previous case, though again the 'bargaining sequence' of 'proposal-nonalignment' obtains; H's 'proposal' occurs at lines 50-51:

(19)

```
37  G    =yeah
38  H    but listen the:- the ⌈ very best-  ⌉
39  G                          ⌊ but uh    ⌋ these uh- these u:h shipping per-
40       uh company they are charging I think same
41       (1.2)
42       same as before
43       (0.7)
44  H    it's probably the same (.) let's see a:h: (1.0) ah-ah- wha:t I can do now
45       for the:: shipment from uh dubai to uh dohah is around (.) u:h forty
46       dollar per:: per tonne.
47       (1.0)
48  G    uh hu(hh:)h:
49       (3.5)
50  H→   .hh but listen, the- the very best I can do for the sixteen kilo feta now
51    →  is one thousand six hundred an' sixty
```

```
52        (3.8)
53   G    dubai? (0.3) or dohah?
54   H    dohah
55        (2.0)
56   G    no we will take dubai one thousand six hundred
57        (1.0)
58   H    u:h that's (.) you know uh that's- that's not imposs- eller not possible
59        for me because you know there .hhh is the problem with thee u:h (.)
60        minimum prices (.) I had to uh follow the minimums prices. (0.7) .hh
61        an' that i:s (.) one thousand six hundred an' fifty (.) see en eff ((CNF:
62        Cost and Freight)) uh (.) dubai
```

In the segment immediately preceding this extract (see (11)), H had unsuccessfully challenged G's account which stated that competitors' prices were cheaper than Melko's. And once again, following such 'problem-defining' talk, at line 38 (above), H appears to be in the process of formulating a proposal ('but listen, the very best-') when his turn is interrupted by G (line 39). G provides additional information pertaining to his preceding account of competitors' (shipping) prices. This occasions H's on-topic disclosure of Melko's shipping price (lines 44-46). H then produces a proposal to effect the resolution of the 'problem' of the feta cheese. He says: 'but listen, the very *best* I can do ... now is 1660', lines 50-51). The formulation 'the very *best* I can do' is interesting inasmuch as it suggests this offer is H's *resistance point* (see Tedeschi and Rosenfeld 1980:227); i.e., H's minimum selling price. Clearly though, judging from the subsequent response, G does not see things this way. First he *responds* to H's proposal by initiating an 'insertion sequence' (see Sacks 1992b:528 [Lecture 1, 1972], Schegloff 1972a). G's utterance 'Dubai or Dohah?' (line 53) operates to obtain information both relevant to and in pursuit of the proposal's reply — acceptance or rejection. The sought-after information — 'Dohah' — is provided by H at line 54, from which point G is able to respond to H's proposal. This he does by producing a turn-initial rejection marker 'no' (line 56) and a *counterproposal*: 'we will take in Dubai 1600' (line 56). While the counterproposal displays nonalignment with the preceding proposal, it also reestablishes the opening of the bargaining sequence, since H is now in a position of aligning or nonaligning with the (counter)offer. But in next turn (beginning at line 58) H — once again appealing to shared knowledge — rejects G's counterproposal and accounts for the rejection, remarking 'you know that's not ... possible for me because you know there is a problem with the minimum prices' (lines 58-60).

In the following extract the prospective buyer (G) solicits a proposal from the seller (H) following H's comments on the current exchange rate:

(20)

89	H	but- but I- I <u>hope</u> it will increase again because it makes uh
90		business very difficult
91		(1.6)
92	G→	mm huh (1.4) okay, how <u>much</u> you can give us?
93	H	well I- if I give ⌜ you
94	G	⌊ WE CAN GIVE YOU THREE THREE SEVEN
95		(.) this u:h three: (1.5) <u>three</u> three (.) seven <u>five</u>↓
96	H	no but (.) I- it's imp<u>oss</u>ible (.) because my <u>cost</u> price is <u>three</u>
97		<u>thou</u>sand <u>five</u> <u>hun</u>dred
98		(1.0)
99	G	no::=
100	H	=that's what- that's what I have to <u>pay</u> er to the dairy, an' to pay (.)
101		for the freight
102	G	then I think <u>leave</u> this uh
103		(1.8)
104	H	uh but I- I- I'm ready to sell at <u>cost</u> price which is <u>three</u> thousand
105		five <u>hun</u>dred
106		(0.5)
107	G	no: (.) this er: (1.5) because we cannot uh- you know this uh our
108		margin is very small margin, then we cannot uh this uh (.) sell with
109		uh uh (.) they wi- they also:: ob<u>jec</u>tion (.) because uh four- four
110		'undred fifty gram and uh with big block is too much <u>diff</u>rence.

Although the buyer, G, solicits a proposal (line 92), he actually interrupts H's subsequent turn at talk, thus preventing H from producing a proposal. One reason for the interruption may be that G, noticing H's apparent reticence in making the requested proposal (H says: 'well I- if I give' before being interrupted at line 93), elects to foreclose a potential discussion on the feasibility of a proposal by putting an offer 'on the table' himself, perhaps in the hope of precipitating a solution to the current problem. Another possibility may be that G, suddenly recalling that 3500 is H's 'cost price' (this had been revealed by H previously in the call — see extract 12, lines 25-26), offers a lower price in an attempt to draw H into a compromise. This would be predicated on the assumption that H's (selling price) proposal would have been above 3500 (i.e., the 'cost price' is normarily *below* the selling price). So in the way G has made public his proposal of 3375, the 'outer limits' of the putative *bargaining range* have been established. It is now H — as the producer of next-turn — who is given the opportunity to make an offer *within* the 'boundaries' of the bargaining range: a move that would be to G's advantage. This suggests that, in cases where one party is able to deduce the magnitude of the other party's proposal prior to that proposal actually being made, getting a proposal 'in first' may have important strategic advantages.

Yet in next turn (beginning at line 96) H's 'no' rejects G's proposal, accounting for the rejection with a reiteration that his 'cost price' is 3500. Following a one-second 'gap' (line 98), G's response — 'no' — is ambiguous, in that it could feasibly be a response to (a) H's rejection of G's offer, or (b) the perceived validity and reasonableness of H's account, or even (c) the implied proposal to sell at a price above 3500. Judging by the next-turn response, it would appear that H hears the 'no' as nonacceptance of the validity and reasonableness of his account (i.e. alternative (b)), for H remarks that it is this amount — 3500 — that he is compelled to 'pay the dairy and the freight' (lines 100-101). H's account, then, which is 'expanded' as a result of both parties' actions, is furnished with a 'no-fault' quality. G's response is to propose that the current order be cancelled; he says: 'then I think *leave* this' (line 102). This action occasions H's proposal, which emphasizes that he is 'ready to sell at *cost* price' (line 104). Such a proposal, while perhaps ordinarily viewed as a significant concession, is nevertheless rejected by G in next turn. And the rejection — marked by turn-initial 'no' (line 107) — is accounted for in terms of the unsaleability of commodities at the offered price.

When either party displays an unwillingness to adjust their buying or selling price proposals, rather than reaching a 'deadlock' situation, other negotiating tactics are instigated. One particularly common tactic is that known as *logrolling*. This involves combining otherwise separate issues and negotiating them simultaneously. Importantly, though, 'logrolling' is oriented to as 'second option', in that the parties evince a preference to treat issues on an individual basis. It appears to be the case that only when treatment of the single issue has reached an apparent interactional impasse that 'logrolling' is instigated. In the talk preceding the following extract, for example, H's "very best" proposal — to sell at 1660 — had been rejected by G. H's next action, reproduced below, is to retain the selling price yet propose that the prospective buyer accepts a specific number of 'free cartons':

(21)

```
98   H     .hh but u::h li- (1.5) listen uh I- I told you the best I c'n do was one
99         thousand six hundred an' sixty: .hh tell me (.) i- if I: (.) I owe you
100        uh fifty cartons (0.9) or forty nine car ⌈ tons↓ ⌉ I owe you fifty
101  G                                             ⌊ yes   ⌋
102  H     cartons of feta cheese
103  G     ye:s
104        (1.1)
105  H→   if we say a::h I charge you one thousand six hundred an' sixty an'
```

```
106          uh
107   →      include uh sixty five cartons
108          (1.5)
109   →      free of charge
110          (3.2)
111   →      could that help you?
112          (1.7)
113   G      .hh uh just a minute
114          (19.2) ((Arabic-speaking voices can be heard faintly in background))
115          uh this one- uh one six five zero dubai or dohah?
116   H      .hh uh one six six zero (.) uh dohah
```

H's 'logrolling' proposal occurs at lines 107-111. Observe first how H formulates his proposal: 'if we say [X] could that help you?'. By formulating his proposal in this way, emphasis is placed on H's willingness to *help* the other party out of his current 'predicament'. Rather than produce an occasioned 'reply' to the proposal, however, G responds by asking H to wait 'just a minute' (line 113), thereby holding his 'reply' in abeyance. Arabic-speaking voices can then be heard faintly in the background. By virtue of the 'conditional relevance' of H's 'logrolling' proposal, both the request to wait 'just a minute', and the background voices, may be seen to foreshadow and be concerned with the contingencies of the impending reply. After nineteen seconds of third-party discussion, G speaks to H again. He does so by making an erroneous reference to the price offered ('one six *five* zero') and asks for information about the port of entry (line 115). In next turn, H first 'corrects' G's error by repeating the actual proposed price (stressing the fallacious digit: 'one six *six* zero'), and then discloses that the port of entry is Dohah (line 116). The next extract, from the same telephone negotiation, follows an additional 'insertion sequence' (not reproduced here), and occurs moments later:

(22)

```
130   G      ah: make it seventy five an' we're finished
131          (2.0)
132   H      I: (.) no no that's too much
133          (0.7)
134   G      NO (.) make it u:h
135          (1.1)
136   H      we- we split it (.) let's say ⌐ uh
137   G                                    ⌊ ah?
138   H      seventy
139          (0.8)
```

140 G   no seventy <u>five</u> (.) make it seventy <u>five</u> finished
141   (4.5)
142   ((voice in background calls out))
143 S   the best regards to hansen
144 G   ((laughing)) he he ⌈he huh mister shami's
145 H   ⌊I ca- I can
146 G   also giving regards to <u>you</u>
147 H   yes uh thank you gi- give him uh my best regard uh a:s well (.) .hh
148   but uh (.) no <u>listen</u> I- I c'n only give you uh <u>seventy</u>:.
149   (1.1)
150 G   okay (.) up to <u>you</u> this.
151   (2.5)
152 H   an' uh then I have w- one other <u>prob</u>lem uh regarding the retail
153   <u>pack</u> cheese.
154   (1.2)
155 G   yes

G's 'proposal' that H 'make[s] it seventy five an' we're finished' (line 130) is a response to H's preceding proposal of sixty five 'free cartons' (see extract (21), line 107). G's *counterproposal* at line 130 above reinstates the first move in the 'bargaining sequence'. The remark 'an' we're finished' serves to add an incentive for H to align with the proposal since G appears to suggest that alignment would result in the closing of the deal as well as termination of this particular exchange. But in next turn H rejects the proposal, and accounts for the rejection by noting that seventy five cartons is 'too much' (line 132). G's response — 'no, *make* it' (line 134) — has a kind of 'backward loop' effect on the progression of the discourse. It simultaneously rejects H's rejection and reinstates the conditional relevance of his (G's) own preceding proposal. And it transpires that G's action is not without effect, for H's response now is to produce a revised proposal which is a *compromise* between the two preceding proposals; H says: 'we split it, let's say seventy' (lines 136 and 138). G also refuses to align with this proposal, however, and once again — for the third time — reinstates his own proposal that seventy five cartons be given away free. A relatively long interturn 'gap' of 4.5 seconds ensues (line 141). In the way that a reply is relevant, the silence may be seen to be H's. At this point, a hitherto unidentified voice in the background can be heard distinctly, calling out "the best regards to hansen" (line 143). The voice, it transpires, is that of 'mister shami' (line 144), G's supervisor. This 'greeting', which is reciprocated by H in line 147, serves to 'break the frame' (Goffman 1974) of the current activity by an engagement in what Goffman (1981:9) has called *crossplay* (i.e., "communication between ratified participants and bystanders", ibid.).

The placement of a 'greeting' here is demonstrably marked (linguistic) behaviour, and this suggests that the 'greeting' is so placed and designed as to be interpreted as a playful cajole amidst the 'serious' work of price bargaining. Additionally, of course, the exchange displays an air of amicability, reminding H that the parties enjoy cordial relations. However, inasmuch as such cordial relations are based upon a history of successful transactions, the interjection might also be seen to serve a more calculated purpose, namely to attempt — albeit indirectly — to unblock the current impasse, so to speak, and thus to secure H's acceptance of G's proposal. But in reengaging the bargaining sequence in line 148, H once again rejects the proposal and repeats his own proposal of seventy cartons (line 148). On this occasion, G, doubtless realising H's determination not to compromise any further, conveys 'acceptance' in his 'okay, up to you this' (line 150).

Rather than dwelling on the acceptance, or seeking a more explicit confirmation of G's acceptance of the proposal, in the subsequent turn H shifts topic to 'one other problem regarding the retail pack' (line 152-153). This action is of analytical interest in that it underscores the matter-of-fact, perfunctory way in which agreement has been communicated; as such it accomplishes and makes visible the 'routine' character of the trading work being done.

3.5. Closing the Call: Prospective 'Tying' Reference

The participants' 'prospective tying references' — i.e., invocations of upcoming, future communications — operate in similar ways to the operations afforded references to preceding communications; that is, as 'activity-unifying', 'text-linking', and interpretative, resources. There are also differences, however, not least in the way that references to upcoming communications may be hearable as 'acceptance' of an 'offer' and thus as the resolution of the current misalignment. Hence, with the proviso that sequential placement considerations are accounted for, the references simultaneously signal 'agreement', 'finalization' and 'acceptance' of the offered (usually revised) prices. In this way, the reference to a prospective communication is often 'closing implicative' for both the current topic of discussion and the call itself. In the following extract, reference to a prospective communication is oriented to as being indicative of alignment and as topic closing implicative, though in this case the reference does not initiate the call's 'closing section' (see below). Here (23) H and G have each been proposing and in various ways producing nonaligned responses to suggested price revisions. At this particular juncture, H states that he will reduce his original price for feta cheese by

$20; note how G responds (at lines 130 and 132) to the revised 'offer':
(23)
```
     127  H     uh:: th:e maximum I c'n give on the feta cheese (0.6)
     128         is twenty dollar less than uh your first off↓er
     129         (1.0)
     130  G→    huh ↓hmm
     131         (2.1)
     132  G→    then- can you- can you send us a: telex an' we will confirm this °↓uh°
     133  H     yes (.) I will send you a telex. ⌐ uh just
     134  G                                       ⌊ okay
     135  H     one other question ⌐ uh
     136  G                         ⌊ yes
```

G's response to H's 'offer' is 'huh hmm', followed by a request that the offer be put in writing (arrowed in the above extract). The interesting feature to note here is the way that G's request for H to 'send a telex' — i.e. put his offer in writing — is hearable as acceptance of H's revised 'offer' (the revised offer can be seen in a subsequent written document sent by H to G; see Firth in press). Additionally, this particular reference to an upcoming communication is hearable as topic-closing implicative. In other words, G's agreement on the conditions of sale allows H to change topic, hence H's "just one other question" (lines 133-135) and G's implicit acknowledgement of the appropriacy of the topic change ("yes") in the following turn (line 136).

Schegloff and Sacks (1973) demonstrate how the orderly accomplishment of 'closings' in conversation (i.e. the arrival at a 'terminal exchange', e.g., 'goodbye-goodbye') is dependent upon the participants' mutual "reference to a properly initiated closing *section*" (op. cit.:300, original emphasis). That is, 'terminal exchanges' do not simply happen at incidental moments, but are socially accomplished, being arrived at once the parties have passed through a sequentially-organized 'closing section'. This closing section, Schegloff and Sacks (op. cit.) observe, is prototypically initiated by a 'possible pre-closing' token (e.g. 'okay', 'well', 'allright', etc., enunciated stressed and with falling intonation contour). The 'possible pre-closing' token does not automatically initiate a 'closing section', but rather *invites* the coparticipant to 'move into' it. This is so since the 'possible pre-closing' is an indication that the utterer has nothing more to add on the preceding topic; the interlocutor may then treat the utterance in a number of ways: either (a) produce more talk on (the immediately preceding) topic, (b) initiate a new topic (thereby producing what Schegloff and Sacks (op. cit.) call an 'unmentioned mentionable'), or (c) 'move into' the closing section already (tentatively) initiated by the 'possible pre-closing' token.

A common characteristic of the calls in the corpus is the way in which the negotiated 'new offer' and the reference to a prospective communication containing the new offer is 'recycled' later in the call — particularly as a method of initiating the call's 'pre-closing'. The following extract provides a good example of the reference's accomplished nature and its interactional effects. At the opening of this segment, Mohammed (M) is in the process of answering H's question about a storage problem; previously in the same call the two parties had agreed on new terms of sale:

(24)

```
256  M    [...] ↑so we cleared that up u:h while he was with us (.) last week=
257  H    =I:: see, fine.
258       (0.6)
259  M→   but uh (.) michael yu- you will uh send us a new telex (.) yes?
260  H    I will send you a new offer, yes (.) ⌐I can send it this afternoon
261  M                                        ⌐excellent
262  H    okay?
263  M    o::kay, have a nice day michael
264  H    same to you, ba-↓bye
265  M    ↑goodbye ((end of call))
```

M's utterance on line 259 is clearly formatted (beginning with the stressed disjunct marker 'but') so as to be hearable as being dislocated from the immediately preceding topic; it thus reintroduces, or recycles, an 'arrangement' made earlier in the call (on 'arrangements', see Schegloff and Sacks op. cit.; Button 1991). By so doing, the prospective reference directs the talk towards the closing section of the call, as subsequent turns confirm. But such references also have an additional role to play in these calls: they demonstrate the fact that the work being done is organized with regard to the serial and sequential arrangement of actions, and as such highlight the current call as 'one-in-a-series' of interrelated work tasks connected with commodity trading. The 'negotiation' call is thus made visible as one of those tasks.

4. CONCLUSION

This chapter has attempted to provide a detailed, transcript-based description of the ways in which 'negotiation' telephone calls are discursively structured and organized, while also attempting to show how that structure was relevant to and constitutive of the encompassing work activity being undertaken. It was argued that, though locally and contingently managed, the calls are structured in stable, iterative ways. Calls were seen to be 'opened' in methodic ways, as the parties moved into or circumvented 'casual' talk before initiating talk that directly addressed the work-related 'problem' that constituted the reason for the call. By so doing, the parties were seen to orient to an orderly and locally-accomplished 'point of entry' into the negotiation calls. This 'point of entry' was reached most visibly in the way the current call was 'tied' to a preceding communication, and thus shown to be an embedded part of a series of interrelated work tasks. The so-called 'retrospective tying reference', and its accompanying 'formulation' of the contents of the preceding message, served to establish a rudimentary 'working agenda' for subsequent talk. This talk centred on the parties' attempts to define — on a joint, collaborative basis — the nature of the problem confronting them. Such activity was most commonly undertaken in the way the parties offered and responded to 'accounts'. By systematically 'probing' and 'unpacking' the perceived componential layers of the accounts offered, the problem could be 'defined' in incremental, situationally-relevant ways, in accordance with both the unfolding discourse and the perceived stance of the other party (cf. Bilmes this volume). Once the trading-related problem was defined adequately for the purposes-at-hand, the parties routinely exchanged substantive proposals and counterproposals in order to effect the problem's resolution. The sequentially-accomplished placement of a reference to an upcoming, prospective communication was seen to be a method of communicating 'acceptance' of a proposal, as well as a routine way of initiating the call's 'closing section'. As with the 'retrospective tying reference', such utterances are important in that they link the current activity to relevant 'work tasks' within the work setting.

A characteristic feature of the calls examined is their compactness, caused in large part by the parties' displayed preference for resolving the work-related conflict *during the call itself*. For this reason, 'casual' talk components in the calls are evanescent or omitted entirely. Similarly, though the parties question and probe each other's accounts and explanations as a matter of routine, the questioning, reason-giving and the occasioned responses evidence a willingness to give credence to the bulk of details provided, as well as a desire to minimize 'argumentative' talk in order to make possible the exchange of substantive proposals. Such a willingness increases the likelihood of resolving the conflict during the actual call.

An important element in the way the parties orient to and undertake their work tasks is related to the telephone medium. Rather than being a mere conduit of communication, the medium itself carries important symbolic meaning for the implicated parties, implicitly signalling such things as the perceived momentary status of the parties' inter-organizational relations, the perceived seriousness of the problem confronting them, and a preference not only to 'talk things over', but to do so with the intention of resolving the 'problem' promptly, amicably, and in institutionally-sanctioned ways. And, as we have seen, both parties are clearly oriented to the necessity of 'talking things over' prior to exchanging substantive offers and proposals. Thus, in order that improved, revised offers may be made and accepted, a certain amount of interactional 'work' has to be seen to have taken place. Commodities are to be bought and sold, but not at any price, not 'for nothing' but for *something*, namely a mutually agreeable price arrived at through an exchange of recognizably 'good organizational reasons', formulated in ways sensitive to the trading context and the unfolding discourse. The stable and 'routine' ways in which the negotiation calls are undertaken is thus a contingent achievement, part and parcel of the normal, everyday work of international commodity trading. This chapter has been an initial attempt to describe the locally-accomplished nature of that discourse-based work.

NOTES

1. The practice of combining ethnographic observations with conversation analytic methodology follows work by scholars such as Maynard (1984, 1989), Moerman (1988), Goodwin (1990), and Bilmes (1992a). Conversation analysis (CA) is concerned with detailing the interactional and sequentially-based character of naturally-occurring interactive talk. A central task for the conversation analyst is to make analyses isomorphic with participants' own ongoing 'analyses'. This is possible because, since talk is produced and understood on a turn-by-turn basis, conversationalists organize their conduct so as to have it identifiable by coparticipants. Participants are obliged to continually 'analyse' others' (re)actions, and to make their 'analyses' public in the actions (e.g. turns at talk) performed. This turn-by-turn-structuring feature of talk is a resource that is exploited by the professional conversation analyst. Limitations of space preclude a description of conversation analytic methodology. The interested reader may consult a continually growing CA literature, the origins of which are contained in Harvey Sacks' lectures (see Sacks 1992a,b). Seminal papers include Schegloff and Sacks (1973) and Sacks, Schegloff and Jefferson (1974). See also the collected studies in Atkinson and Heritage (1984), Boden and Zimmerman (1991) and Drew and Heritage (1992). Useful methodological overviews are provided by Levinson (1983:chap. 6), Heritage (1984a:chap. 8) and Zimmerman (1988).

2. This view of context — as a locally-produced phenomenon activated through social action — has been articulated throughout the work of ethnomethodologists and conversation analysts. Garfinkel (1967:33), for example, wrote that "Any setting organizes its activities to make its properties as an organized environment of practical activities detectable, countable, recordable, tell-a-story-aboutable, analyzable — in short, *accountable*". Similarly, Heritage (1984a:290), in his description of conversation analytic methods, writes:

> It is ... through the specific, detailed and local design of turns and sequences that 'institutional' contexts are observably and reportably — i.e. accountably — brought into being. [...] This observation suggests that, notwithstanding the panoply and power of place and role, *it is within these local sequences of talk, and only there, that these*

institutions are ultimately and accountably talked into being. (emphasis in original)
For a recent and useful overview of the 'language-context' relationship, see Goodwin and Duranti (1992).

3. For a recent and useful discussion of 'institutional' as distinct from 'mundane' types of interaction, see Drew and Heritage (1992:3-65).

4. The following call displays the sequential configuration described in the model: Whalen and Zimmerman (1990:468)

1	CT	Mid-city police and fire
2	C	Yes kin ya get uh kin ya get somebody over here right away we've got uh gal that's just .hh ready tuh pass out. She's hh oh: (1.0) she's passed out, okay
3	CT	Okay what address?
4	C	Okay thirty thirteen Sixteenth Avenue an hurry, she's passed right out, she's forty five years ol:d an=
5	CT	=(thirty) what?
6	C	Okay, <u>three</u> <u>zero</u> one <u>three</u> Sixteenth Avenue South
7	CT	Sixteenth Avenue South, iz that uh single famil ⌈ y home?
8	C	⌊ Yes yes yes. We'll be watchin for um.
9	CT	You don't know what's wrong with her though=
10	C	=I have no idea, she just got dizzy, an gotup tuh get air an passed right out.
11	CT	Okay we'll get somebody over there=
12	C	=Hurry
13	CT	Mnhm ((click))

The OPENING/IDENTIFICATION/ACKNOWLEDGEMENT sequence occurs at turn 1 and the initial component of turn 2 (caller's 'yes' is the acknowledgement token). The REQUEST segment (turn 2: 'kin ya get ...') occurs next, while the INTERROGATIVE SERIES occupies turns 3 to 10. The RESPONSE move occurs at turn 11, followed by the call's CLOSING sequence.

5. 'Adjacency pairs' have been extensively discussed in the literature and cannot, for reasons of space, be given detailed attention here [see, though, Schegloff and Sacks (1973); Sacks et al. (1974); Heritage (1984a:245-264); Levinson (1983:303-308)]. Briefly, the notion originated with Sacks' observation that the basic orderliness in discourse sequencing may be in part accounted for in terms of the way some utterance types commonly appear adjacent to certain other types (see, e.g., Sacks 1992a:671[Lecture 6, Fall 1967]). Related to this is the notion of 'sequential implicativeness' (Schegloff and Sacks op. cit.:296). This notion holds that "an utterance projects for the sequentially following

turn(s) the relevance of a determinate range of occurrences (be they utterance types, activities, speaker selections, etc.)" (ibid). Schegloff and Sacks (op. cit.) were to observe that sequential implicativeness is readily apparent in tightly-organized two-part sequences of utterances. These sequences they called 'adjacency pairs'. Such pairs consist of sequences which exhibit the following five features: (1) two utterances in length, (2) adjacently positioned, (3) with different speakers producing each utterance in a (4) relatively ordered sequence, where (5) the first pair part 'expects' or is 'discriminatively related' to the second (op. cit.: 295-296). To these five features, the following rule of adjacency pair operation was added: "given the recognizable production of a first pair part, on its first possible completion its speaker should stop and a next speaker should start and produce a second pair part from the pair type of which the first is recognizably a member" (op. cit.:296).

6. For an analysis of such written messages, and the sequential organization underpinning them, see Firth (in press).

7. Due to limitations of space, my treatment of openings, 'casual' talk, 'tying' references and closings will be brief. Rather than giving a detailed account of these aspects of the calls, my intention here is to give the reader a reasonably firm 'overall' sense of how the negotiation calls are initiated and developed. More detailed treatment of these aspects of the calls is presently underway.

8. This sequence can be observed in the following segment, where Carla (C) calls Ida (I): Schegloff (1986:115):

1	(a) →		((RING))
2		I	Hello
3	(b) →	C	Hello Ida?
4		I	Yeah
5	(c) →	C	Hi,=This is Carla
6		I	Hi Carla.
7	(d) →	C	How are you.
8		I	Okay:.
9		C	Good.=
10		I	=How about you.
11		C	Fine. Don wants to know ...

9. Paradoxically perhaps, the decision to answer with a single 'hello' may well be seen as displaying sensitivity to the institutional, and not least *international,* setting. This is so inasmuch as the answerer's 'hello' is, to a large extent, language-neutral; i.e., the 'answer' is not formulated in the local vernacular, thus displaying sensitivity to the possibility of the caller being (in this case) a non-Arabic speaker. Similarly, by formulating the answer in a minimal way as observed (i.e., with a bi-syllabic 'hello' token), the answerer also orients to the possibility of caller being a non-English speaker.

10. There would appear to be an unnoticed or at least unattended misunderstanding in the sequence

beginning at line 19 and ending at line 24, where it appears that G hears H's 'in Denmark it's ... twenty five degree but for you it will be- it would be cold, I think' not as a *comparative* (i.e. 'but that temperature would be cold by your standards') but as an *estimation* of the current climatic conditions in Saudi Arabia (i.e. 'it must be cold in Saudi Arabia now'). Subsequent turns (H's 'yes?' at line 24, and G's 'yes' at line 27) show that neither party draws attention to the apparent misunderstanding. In this sense it is interactionally irrelevant.

11. For a discussion on the significance of 'first topic' in telephone calls, see Schegloff and Sacks (1973:300-301).

12. Garfinkel and Sacks (1970:350) wrote on 'formulations':
> "A member may treat some part of the conversation as an occasion to describe that conversation, to explain it, or characterize it, or explicate, or translate, or summarize, or furnish the gist of it ... That is to say, a member may use some part of the conversation as an occasion to *formulate* the conversation ..." (original emphasis)

Heritage and Watson (1979:138) proposed that "the primary business of formulations is to demonstrate understanding and, presumptively, to have that understanding attended to and, as a first preference, endorsed". See also Walker (this volume).

CHAPTER 9

'NEGOTIATING ACTIVITY' IN TECHNICAL PROBLEM SOLVING

JOHANNES WAGNER

1. INTRODUCTION

Negotiation is a key concept in several fields of study. In what has been called 'mainstream social science', in anthropology, social psychology, and economics a huge literature on negotiation has been produced (for a review, see, e.g., Gulliver 1979). The role of *communication* in negotiations has been investigated in a number of studies (for a recent overview see Putnam and Roloff 1992). In most cases, 'negotiation' is understood as a formal, face-to-face, problem-solving encounter. However, in ethnomethodology and conversation analysis (hereafter CA), the term 'negotiation' has been used in a different, more encompassing, sense. 'Negotiation of meaning', for example, is understood by conversation analysts as the *process* of interactively *making sense* by means of conversational resources. Within the framework of CA, meaning is accomplished locally, jointly and collaboratively by participants in conversation (cf. Bilmes 1986:133). This interactive conception of meaning has exerted significant influence on linguistic pragmatics and the study of discourse in general (Levinson 1983, Mey 1993). It challenges the tendency in linguistics to operate with pre-defined semantic concepts and situation-independent definitions of linguistic entities.

Recent CA-informed work has led to a new understanding of negotiation — an understanding predicated on the realization that the negotiation process is organized locally and *sequentially*. A sequential model of bargaining interaction was introduced by Maynard (1984). In his investigations of plea bargaining, Maynard demonstrated that *bargaining sequences* can evolve as elaborations of what he terms 'proposal-alignment' sequences. Maynard's conception of negotiation was applied to the analysis of international buyer-seller interaction by Firth (1991). Firth distinguished between negotiation *encounters* and negotiating *activity*, thereby dissolving an overall concept of negotiation:

> "'Negotiation Encounter' is characterised as a single-location encounter, formally- and physically-defined, involving parties with potentially conflicting wants and needs, while 'negotiating activity' is interactionally-defined, being contingent on the parties' mutual discourse actions" (Firth 1991:8).

While Douglas (1962) and others attempted to develop a sequential, *phase-based* format on the macro level of analysis, Maynard and Firth describe a sequential structure on the micro analytic level. Firth defines 'negotiating activity' as being

> "initiated by one party's display of misalignment with a substantive proposal, offer, request, or suggestion of the opposing party, and terminated when definitive agreement on one or more substantive issues is reached. The demonstrable end-goal orientation for the parties involved in negotiating activity is thus mutual alignment". (1991:145)

The two concepts are not necessarily associated. 'Negotiation Encounters' may take place without 'negotiating activity' occurring, and vice versa (Firth 1991:9). In a recent study, Francis (in press) discusses methodological problems when employing CA in analyses of institutional (i.e. 'work') settings. He claims that "one has to show closely and in detail how the *conversational and institutional levels* are connected in a systematic fashion at an utterance-by-utterance level. [...] It is this kind of close and detailed demonstration which is absent in Maynard's discussion" (emphasis added). Francis' main point is that Maynard's analysis does not show a formally defined discourse system where "the sequential organization of talk provides the analytic key", but is an *ad hoc* analysis heavily dependent on unstated assumptions pertaining to the institutional context. He argues his case through an analysis of a meeting in a British advertising agency.

In this chapter I investigate whether the concept of 'negotiating activity' is useful for the description of technical problem solving. In the first part of the chapter I sketch a procedure for solving technical problems. The second part describes how two technical problems are handled during several telephone and telefax communications. In the final section the chapter's findings are discussed.

2. CASE 1: A PROCEDURE FOR SOLVING TECHNICAL PROBLEMS

As my point of departure I sketch a model of technical problem solving exemplified by a transcript of a telephone call between production engineers from a Danish and a British company. The call analyzed here follows the Danish company's purchase of a large machine from the British producer. During the process of assembling, installing and testing the machine, several technical problems become apparent. To solve them, 'FM' (the head of the Danish production staff) calls the British company several times on the telephone. In one of these conversations he talks to several employees successively. Among them is 'RG', the engineer who actually designed the part of the machine with which the Danes, for the time being, are having problems.
Example 1:[1]

```
1    TT    tell RG coz he designed ┌ it
2    FM                            └ yes, okay
            (3.0)
3    RG    hello
4    FM    hello
5    RG    good afternoon ┌ h:
6    FM                   └ yes good afternoon
            (2.0)
7    RG    right, I believe you have a little problem ((clears throat))
8    FM    I think so, yes
9    RG    .h as I understand it eh you cannot close the box (1.0) is that correct?
10   FM    yes (.) that is correct
11   RG    right (.) .h now am I correct in saying that you cannot close the box
            because the brushes are coming down on (.) the top of the
            feed rod (1.0)
12   FM    .h hu- yes but- a moment I can- (0.5) I can't (.) close the box
            because the: thread ba:rs
            (1.5)
            e::::h (.) h. keep the: thi: e::h (.) the motors
            (2.5)
13   RG    right .h ┌ ((**))
14   FM             └ that is (.) problem one (0.5) if I changed (0.5) the ba:r
            (.) the treadba:r (.)
15   RG    hu ┌ hu
16   FM       └ to eh to adjusting the- the motors
```

17 RG yeah (1.0)

18 FM then I cannot get the f<u>ee</u>d stock (.) in the brush unit (0.5)

19 RG right (.) .h now wh- what I'd like to suggest (.) is that (0.5) in: the
         pneumatic control panel (.)

20 FM h:

21 RG yeah which ⌈ is

22 FM   ⌊ yes

23 RG situated just underneath the platform (.)

24 FM yes

25 RG .h top left hand corner (0.5)

26 FM ye ⌈ s

27 RG   ⌊ in the pneumatic control panel where there are two: solid eyed
         (..) valves (.)

28 FM yes

29 RG .h one is marked (.) number (.) oh two four (1.0) .h and one is
         marked number (.) oh two three

30 FM yes

31 RG right?

32 FM yes

33 RG .h now oh two four (.) is a stop (.) and reset (.)

34 FM ye::es (.)

35 RG now if there- if you look at that solid eyed valve there is a small
         button a small white button on it

36 FM yes

37 RG if you press that button (.) .h all the (.) cylinders and the motors
         should go back to the reset position .h which should be retr<u>a</u>cted
         (1.5)

38 FM .h yes but I m not sure (.) that (.) th<u>a</u>t is the problem
         (3.0)
         .h when I got the- the motors placed now as (.) Bill (.) showed me
         on a fax

39 RG yeah h:

40 FM the brush (.) motors (.) hit each other (.) in the box (1.0)

41 RG yeah .h that- that I think is because (1.0) they are all (.) in this fully
         forward position (.) all at the <u>o</u>ne t<u>i</u>me (0.5) <u>no</u>rmally (.) when the
         machine is running (0.5) the motors (.) are: oscillating backwards
         and forwards=

42 FM =yes it could be

```
43  RG  do ⌈ you
44  FM     ⌊ yes
45  RG  understand me .h
46  FM  I can ⌈ under-
47  RG        ⌊ but-
48  FM  stand you now (.) exactly, yes
49  RG  yeah (1.0) so ⌈ ((**))
50  FM                ⌊ if I press (.) these two buttons=
51  RG  =no don't- just the- the one button (.) on soloid-e solonide number
        (.) zero (.) two (.) ⌈ four
52  FM                       ⌊ four yes
53  RG  .h that should bring ((**)) all the motors back to the retracted
        position (.) .h then the box should be closed (.) and then (.) the
        brushing should be started (.) then the motors will oscillate back
        and forwards (.) but they- they shouldn't hit each other when they
        are actually oscillating (1.0)
54  FM  exactly I think I can eh follow you (0.5) its only (.) eh when I eh:
        reset this button (.) the motors will eh go into place (.) where they
        can close the box
55  RG  that- that is correct yeah=
56  FM  yes and when the box is closed they don't hi:t each other
57  RG  that' s correct (.)
58  FM  I think - yes (.) I will absolutely try that
59  RG  yeah (1.0) now obviously if it- if that doesnt work .h please come
        back to us and we'll have a look at it again
```

The problem-solving activity in the data moves through several (sub)topics, each related to a 'problem' with the operation of a particular machine. Initially, the parties ascertain that there is a *problem* (see turn 7) and then attempt to discover what the problem pertains to. This has been partly achieved before the transcript begins (involving a different call-taker), though the acknowledged 'problematic' state of affairs is 'rerun' in turns (9) and (10).

In turn (11) RG indicates — by his use of 'right' and 'now' — that he is developing the topic; he then produces an *explanation* for the problem which has the form 'X because Y', and is formulated as a question to his interlocutor. FM answers the question ('yes', turn 12) and follows up with a different explanation: 'X because Z' (turns 12-18). At this moment two alternative explanations compete, but instead of trying to reach an agreement, RG moves to the next topic. In turns (19) to (37) he proposes his solution.

At first FM objects ('but I'm not sure *that* is the problem', turn 38), but a little later later, in turn 42, he indicates his acceptance of FM's proposal ('yes it could be'). The topic is gradually closed down in turns (46) to (49).

In (50), FM begins summarizing RG's proposal, but, making a mistake relating to the proposed solution, is interrupted by RG who repeats the proposal (turn 51). Finally, in (54), FM produces a very brief summary and connects it in turn (56) explicitly to the previously-defined problem. In (58) FM states his intention to implement the proposed solution ('yes I will absolutely try that').

On the basis of Example 1, two observations can be made. The first is related to the way the participants proceed in the problem solving process, the second to the formulation of the solution.

The participants proceed by moving through different (sub)topics during their talk: the definition of the problem, explanations of why the problem arose, proposals for a solution, and agreement about the solution to be implemented. The succession of (sub)topics will now provisionally be interpreted as a sequence of steps in solving technical problems. I will refer to it as 'Sequence A':

1. One party (FM) proposes that a technical problem exists; other party (RG) accepts the existence of the problem (9).
2. One party proposes a solution (RG in turn 19 onwards); other party accepts that the proposal is valid (FM in 42).
3. Both parties accept the proposal as a solution (56-57).
4. The solution is implemented. (This is not covered in the transcript, but in turn (58) FM announces his intention to implement the proposed solution).

In turn (38), FM displays *misalignment* with respect to RG's proposal for a solution, but he aligns cautiously in (42). According to work by Maynard (1984) and Firth (1991), this may be understood as a *misalignment-alignment sequence* and, according to Firth's definition quoted above, as initiating 'negotiating activity'. The misalignment is marked in (12), a first alignment is reached in (42) and a final one in (58). Between (12) and (58), the explanation for and solution of the problem is negotiated.

In the institutional framework in which the Danish and the British engineers are operating, definitive alignment has to be reached — as a work-related 'mandate', so to speak. Both parties have to attempt to find a technical solution to the problem. If this is not achieved, both companies would experience difficulties of different sorts. The British company would have sold a machine which does not function, while the Danes would lose production capacity for an indefinite period of time.

If problem solving in technical interactions proceeds as in Sequence A, it may be expected that *negotiating activities* may occur in relation to step 1, i.e. in connection with the proposal of a problem, and in step 2, i.e. in connection with the proposal of solutions.

At this point, it is apposite to comment on the theoretical status of Sequence A. Different approaches to discourse and conversation have endeavoured to describe sequences of actions or topics. Arguably the most compelling findings have been made within CA. One of the main interests of CA is to describe the formal, sequential organization of interactive talk (Heritage 1984a). One of the most powerful concepts in this respect is that of *adjacency pair* (see Schegloff and Sacks 1973). It is the adjacency pair concept that provides the underlying model for the notion of 'negotiating activity'.

While adjacency pairs are generalizable elements of conversation in a purely formal, sequential perspective, 'Sequence A' is here forwarded as nothing more than a possible, tentative model for carrying out technical problem solving. It is certainly theoretically much weaker than sequences described by conversation analysts (e.g. Maynard's 'bargaining sequence'). Sequence A does not reflect the sequential organization of talk-in-interaction. Rather it describes a pattern for carrying out a certain type of activity. Sequence A has, perhaps, more the status of a *language game* (Wittgenstein 1958), or a *language activity* (Levinson 1979), or a 'Handlungsmuster' [action pattern] (Rehbein 1977, Ehlich and Rehbein 1986, Rehbein in press). These terms refer to socially shared procedures with certain describable features which have to be *locally and contingently* realized in relation to the resources in talk. In this respect, concepts from CA merge with models for 'language games'. The following sections of this chapter investigate such cases.

The second observation is concerned with linguistic aspects of example 1, i.e. how the explanation is verbally formed and related to the solution. In turn (11) (above) RG produces an 'X because explanation Y', where he lexically focuses on *movement* (i.e., 'the brushes are coming down'). Movement is again formulated in (37), which is the proposed solution to the problem: the motors should go back; they have to be retracted to close the box. And again in (47), movement is verbalized: 'forward position, oscillating backwards and forwards'. In RG's formulation, the defined problem has to do with the movements of the motors and from there, a proper solution is developed.

In (12), FM explains the problem in a different way. He talks about *assembling* the machine: 'adjust' (16), 'get... into' (18), 'got ... placed' (38). But when FM in (54) finally summarizes what RG has proposed as a solution, he adopts RG's semantic focus on movement: 'the motors will go into place'. It can thus be said that FM aligns in two different ways. He accepts RG's solution and he adopts RG's *formulation* of the solution (on 'formulations' in negotiations, see Walker, this volume).

At this point I can conclude that the data investigated in this section show a sequence of topics which can be preliminarily understood as a sequence of actions to solve technical problems. 'Negotiating activity' has been shown to occur during this process and to be closely related to linguistic activities. In the next section I will show how 'negotiation activity' is used to initiate problem solving activities which are variations of Sequence A.

3. 'UNFOLDING' PROBLEM SOLVING THROUGH NEGOTIATING ACTIVI-TIES

3.1. Background

The following data involve two cooperating companies, one located in Denmark, the other in Belgium. In this study, they will be called 'DanTech' and 'BelgiTech'. DanTech produces ventilator systems with special features for open fireplaces. The company has several product lines with different specifications, performances and sizes.

In 1990, the Belgian Gas Board gave new directions concerning the installation of open, gas-fuelled fireplaces, effective from February 1, 1991. According to these guidelines, ventilators with special features have to be installed in new buildings and as parts of refurbishings. By introducing such directives, the Board creates a market for ventilators that can function as required.

In late 1990, BelgiTech (who has been retailing DanTechs products for a couple of years) suggests that DanTech and BelgiTech should cooperate in developing a ventilator system specially designed for the new specifications in Belgium. In October 1990, BelgiTech's managing director, pseudonymously referred to as 'van den Bosch', visits DanTech for preliminary discussion of the plans to cooperate.

On May 2 and 3, 1991, a second meeting is held in Denmark. van den Bosch and DanTech's leading managers participate in the meeting. During the meeting, van den Bosch specifies how a particular ventilator from DanTech's program has to be modified to meet the new Belgian directives. Both companies decide to take on the job. They agree to a division of labour in such a way that DanTech modifies the ventilator, while BelgiTech develops a new electronic control system for the whole unit. BelgiTech states explicitly that they want DanTech to deliver a complete ventilator unit, since they themselves are basically a retail company. Both companies agree on the price level (the whole unit is not supposed to cost more than twice the unmodified ventilator) and on development costs which are to be shared equally between the two companies. In the summer of 1991, the first prototype (prototype I) is tested and accepted by the Belgium Gas Board. Despite the Boards's approval, BelgiTech finds several technical faults which are corrected in connection with the test of prototype II, which has a different motor. Prototype II is tested for the first time in September 1991 with poor results. However, by November 1991, the first units are produced and shipped.

For both companies, several employees are involved during 1990 and 1991, though most communication is channelled through van den Bosch (BelgiTech's manager) and 'Clausen', an engineer who works in DanTech's export department. Both men communicate with each other in German. While Clausen is virtually bilingual in Danish and German (he was raised near the Danish-German border), German is a foreign language for all other employees involved in the case at both companies (including van den Bosch). The data show some minor, mostly lexical, language problems on behalf of van den Bosch, but they play no major role in the interactants' problem solving activity. Since the focus of this study is on the problem solving activity, aspects of foreign language use are neglected in this chapter.

During the case, three modes of communication are used: face-to-face meetings between van den Bosch and DanTech's engineers and managers ('Hansen', 'Madsen', 'Clausen' and 'Svenssen'), telephone calls and telefax communications between employees of the two companies. My data therefore consist of:

— written materials. These are telefax communications and minutes of the May 2 and 3 meeting. The meeting — i.e., the 'negotiation encounter' itself — has not been recorded.

— spoken data, i.e. telephone calls between van den Bosch and Clausen, which were audio-taped and subsequently transcribed.

Additionally, I was given access to internal economic data about DanTech, for example the strategy plan for the company, their export plans, and several key-employees' evaluations of the company's economic policy.

The written and spoken communications occur on the following dates:

June 24	Fax from BelgiTech
July 1	Phone call
July 5	Fax from DanTech
August 28	Fax from DanTech
August 29	Phone call
September 13	Phone call
	Fax from DanTech
September 20	Fax from BelgiTech
September 25	Fax from BelgiTech
September 27	Fax from DanTech
November 12	Fax from DanTech

The interaction in both media (telefax and telephone) is organized topically. Each topic is a technical problem. This 'problem' is the reason for the interaction (i.e. in one or several telephone calls or telefaxes). In each interaction the 'problem' is defined, discussed, and resolved in one way or the other. During a single (written or spoken) interaction, several topics are opened, dealt with, and closed. As a rule, topics are not 'reopened' during the same conversation (or in the same telefax). The same topic, though, may be handled in different communications, many of them over several months.

I will discuss two minor topics which are both related to the electrical installation of the ventilator unit:
— the type of cable,
— the connection between the ventilator and the pressostate.[2]

3.2. Case 2: The ground wire

On June 24, shortly before the first prototype is tested, BelgiTech telefaxes 10 "remarks" concerning this prototype. It is the first time the electrical connections are mentioned at all. Referring to the "Belgian Gas Board", van den Bosch states: "Der electronische Anschluss soll nicht ausgeführt werden mit einem Erde-Anschluss. In der Anschlusskabel sind also nur 5 Faden". [The electronic connection must not include a ground wire. As a consequence, the connection cable should only include 5 wires.]

van den Bosch here requests 'X', as a result of Board's directive. He strengthens his request by referring to a higher authority, since the Board has the power to accept or reject the final product. However, due to the passive grammatical construction, it is not shown whether the request is made by the Board itself or by BelgiTech on behalf of the Board. As a matter of fact it later turns out that this request was made by BelgiTech in anticipation of the Board's decision.

By requesting 'X' because of the Board's directives, van den Bosch not only defines a technical problem to be solved, but formulates an obligation to implement a certain technical feature. Interestingly, though, he talks about a *solution* when he continues with the matter in a telephone call a few days later. Here he asks how far the implementation has proceeded. Putting his question syntactically as a statement (see turn 3, below), van den Bosch appears to presuppose that his 'solution' cannot be negotiated.

Example 2[3]

Telephone call, approximately July 1

1	vdB	the other cable (.) and a plug (1.0)
2	C	yes (.)
3→	vdB	you found a solution
4	C	no
5	vdB	.h and you won't
6	C	er (2.0) er no it (0.5) er (1.0) well the cable (.) we haven't found anything or well haven't found yet (.) that can be used as it is (1.5) er (.)
7	vdB	if the producers of your cable the- being ready five cable or (0.5) without (.) er (1.5)
8	C	er (1.0) well I asked er (1.0) well I asked the (0.5) R and D department to (.) er (.) find one but they say that (0.5) er (1.0) there are only a few of them
9	vdB	but I only need one
10	C	ye(h)(h)s:: ((chuckles)) .h right (1.0) er (3.0) but (1.0) well that er (.) in any case we are aware (0.5) that we have to find something (.) ⌈ but
11	vdB	⌊ yeah
12	C	er (1.0) you (.) for the test or (1.0) er we surely won't find any solution neither for the cable nor the plug (1.5)
13	vdB	no (0.5)
14	C	er no

Clausen tells van den Bosch in (6) that for the time being the specified technical solution cannot be implemented. So far Clausen accepts van den Bosch's remark as it stands. The interaction has not yet moved into problem solving activity comparable to sequence A.

In (12) Clausen talks about 'any solution', which implies that there might be 'other' solutions. He hereby announces that van den Bosch's 'obligation' has the status of a negotiable *proposal,* and that it might not be a valid one. By explicitly talking about 'solutions', both participants indicate that somewhere there is a 'problem' to be solved. So both participants appear to orient to the interaction as 'problem-solving activity', without at this point defining the actual technical problem. In relation to Sequence A, it could be said that both participants enter the sequence at step 2: van den Bosch has proposed what he now calls a 'solution', but so far Clausen has not accepted it as valid, though he has accepted it as being *a* solution.

Some days later, on July 5, Clausen summarizes the status of 'Project ABZ' in a telefax. Since the DanTech company begins a holiday that day, and BelgiTech will be on holiday when DanTech's personnel return, nothing is expected to happen during the next 4-6 weeks. Concerning the ground wire, Clausen remarks "Vorläufig müssen wir das Kabel beibehalten und evtl. den Erdleiter abschneiden. Es wird schwierig sein, ein ande–res geeignetes Kabel zu finden". [For the time being we have to keep the cable as it is and possibly cut off the ground wire. It will be difficult to find another cable which can be used].

Clausen here does several things at the same time. He proposes — in a guarded way ("Vorläufig" [for the time being], "evtl." [possibly]) — a different solution: Y. He hereby once again treats van den Bosch's initial remark in the telefax of June 24 as being a *proposal* for a solution and not an *obligation*. But more importantly, in cautiously introducing a new proposal he indicates that van den Bosch's proposal may not be valid. Now there are two competing proposals, and none of them has been agreed upon as being valid.

So, by introducing his own proposal, Clausen displays 'misalignment' with van den Bosch's proposal. Following Firth (1991), he initiates *negotiating activity*. With regard to Sequence A, the interaction remains at step 2, but still, the technical problem to be solved has not yet been defined.

In the next call of August 29, Clausen describes the current state of the cable business: DanTech is able to buy a cable with five wires if the order is at least ten thousand metres. This is far beyond any quantity DanTech could use in the production of the ventilator unit, and Clausen argues that the solution proposed by van den Bosch is not economically feasible. van den Bosch reacts sympathetically, expressing his understanding for the fact that the purchase of ten kilometers of cable would not be a viable alternative. With regard to Sequence A, Clausen and van den Bosch are still performing negotiating activity in step 2. Later in the call, however, Clausen enters step 1 and tries to solve the problem himself:

Example 3

Telephone call of August 29

```
1     C      well we- we will natur- will naturally be eager to find such a
             cable (.) .h but anyway we think (.) it is (.) a bit unusual that
             (0.5) er (.) that you so er (1.0) strongly insist that there must not
             be a ground wire (.) cause we think it is (.) it is (.) very common
             (.) to use a cable with  ⌈ a
2     vdB                             ⌊ yes
3     C      surplus conductors
             (3.0)
```

		but I don't know it is er: (1.0) a demand of the board ⌈ isn't it
4	vdB	⌊ yes they
		they say plainly if there is a ground wire in it (0.5) then (0.5) eh
		you give people the id<u>ea</u> that it has to be connected
5	C	yes
6	vdB	but that is not that that that you don't n<u>ee</u>d
7	C	no (.) but er well nothing would- er happen if you would (.) the (2.0)
8	vdB	yes but (.) the electrical gentlemen from the board they are very er (0.5) yes how do you say it (0.5) narrow- narrow in it er (3.0) they don't have a big margin
9	C	no
10	vdB	if it is a question of regulations (2.0)
11	C	yes (0.5) er (3.0) that you mean er (.) that it is a (1.0) .h a crucial problem how do you call it a (.) it is essential (.) er for the (.) er test (1.0)
12	vdB	yes I (.) we have not 0.5 no we did (.) from the protoype we returned (.) to you
13	C	yes
14	vdB	we had removed the ground wire
15	C	yes (.)
16	vdB	you did see that didn't you
17	C	yes (1.0)
18	vdB	and that way it went to the test
19	C	yes
20	vdB	that means if we later (0.5) deliver (.) the MZ (0.5) with a ground wire which has been cut off (.) then it is not in accordance (.) with what we sent to the test (.) with what is tested (.) and we are in (0.5) how do you say (1.0) we make a mistake
21	C	yes yes (1.5) ⌈ ehm
22	vdB	⌊ well I make notes (.) make notes h: there are still problems to be solved
23	C	yes
24	vdB	the ground wire (.) would have to be removed
25	C	yes

Clausen argues in turn (1) that there is no real technical problem at all, since technically speaking, a surplus conductor would not do any harm and is common technical practice.

Again he states his point cautiously. He formulates 'Y because of normal practice'. Clausen here not only enters step 1 of Sequence A, but initiates 'negotiating activity' pertaining to the definition of the problem.

Again van den Bosch refers to the Gas Board (4). According to van den Bosch, he and Clausen are not able to decide on technical grounds, but have to act with respect to van den Bosch's expectations of the Board's future actions. In this way, van den Bosch 'reestablishes' his proposal of 'X because of the Board'. In (22) and (23) the topic is closed by both participants agreeing that a 'problem' remains to be solved. As Clausen puts it in turn (11), it is 'essential for the test' of the whole unit.

At this point, both participants have reached a point where they are doing negotiating activity pertaining to the *definition of the problem* (cf. Firth, this volume), and about possible solutions. The final solution comes, surprisingly perhaps, in a call made on September 13, where van den Bosch informs Clausen that the Board has accepted that the ground wire be cut off.

The first technical problem has now been solved. Interactionally the topic is closed in a telefax of the same day, where Clausen states: "Das Gasinstitut hat akzeptiert, dass der nicht notwendige Erdleiter einfach abgeschnitten wird". [The national Board did accept that the ground wire can be cut off].

In this interaction we find the following sequence (B):

June 24	vdB requests 'X', due to the Board's directives.
July 1	C accepts 'X', hereby redefining vdB's request as a proposal.
	C mentions difficulties in implementing 'X'.
July 5	C proposes a provisional solution 'Y'.
August 29	C rejects proposal 'X'.
	C defines the technical problem 'Y' as a result of 'normal practice'.
	vdB again claims 'X' due to the Board's directives.
	vdB and C agree that there is a 'problem' to be solved.
Sept. 13	vdB states that the Board accepts 'Y'.
Sept. 13	C acknowledges that 'Y' is accepted.

It can be concluded that the problem concerning the ground wire is solved in an entirely different sequence to the way the problem is solved in section 2. Compared to Sequence A, the topic 'ground wire' is initiated as a 'request', which is subsequently redefined as a 'proposal'. A second 'proposal' is introduced and it is not until then that the problem itself is defined. 'Negotiating activity' has a key role in making the problem-solving process explicitly recognizable for the interactants.

3.3. Case 3: The plug and socket connection

As mentioned above, in the telefax of June 24 van den Bosch produces a remark on another topic: "Der Ventilator und Pressostat mussen mit 5 polige Stecker und Kontaktdoze angeschlossen werden" [The ventilator and the pressostate have to be connected with a five-poled plug and socket]. Again, van den Bosch formulates the request as an *obligation*. In the call of July 1 (see example 2), Clausen accepts van den Bosch's remark as valid and implementable. But at the same time he refers to it as a 'solution'. Hereby he defines — interactively — van den Bosch's request as the problem to be solved. The solution is any appropriate plug connection.

In a telefax of July 5, Clausen asks BelgiTech to look for a plug connection in Belgium, since DanTech is unable to find a suitable product in Denmark: "Eine vernünftige Steckerlösung haben wir noch nicht finden können, und bitten Sie eventuell in Belgien eine Lösung zu finden". [We haven't found a good solution for the plugs, and ask you kindly to look for a solution in Belgium]. For the time being, both participants agree on the problem. Furthermore, they agree about a 'solution' which therefore is valid, and they are currently searching for a way to implement the solution.

Two months later, on August 28, DanTech informs BelgiTech by telefax about several changes in the faulty prototype I. Concerning the topic in question, Clausen mentions: "hiermit eine Prinzipskizze mit den Änderungen zu Prototyp I". [herewith a drawing with the changes of prototype I] "1. Kabel- und Panserschlauch = 2 mm" [Cable and armed tube = 2 mm].

Without refering to the earlier conversation on this topic, Clausen now proposes an alternative to the plug solution. Accordingly, ventilator and pressostate should be connected by a long cable and not by a plug connection at all. By introducing this proposal, Clausen redefines van den Bosch's earlier request as being a proposal and as being no longer valid. In a call one day later (August 29), Clausen explains why:

Example 4

Telephone call of August 29

1	vdB	er first point (.) cable and armed tube is two millimetres is written there .h but it isn't
2	C	er two metres
3	vdB	two mEters (.) that's what I thought
4	C	yes
5	vdB	why (1.0)
6	C	er (1.0) 'cause er (0.5) er then you have the possibility of lifting off the ventilator (.) er and the sound absorber (1.0)
7	vdB	yes yes -
8	C	er
9	vdB	so (.) it hasn't become a plug and socket connection

10 C   no er we couldn't find a (1.0) plug and socket (0.5) connection
           (0.5)
11 vdB   you couldn't find it
12 C   no

Clausen defines the technical problem no longer as the kind of plug and socket to be
installed, but as the possibility of removing the ventilator from the installation. This
may be necessary for maintaining and serving the unit. To connect both parts of the
unit by a long cable instead of a removable plug connection is certainly not a very
elegant solution as van den Bosch points out later, but it solves the problem technically.
So at this point, van den Bosch's request has been redefined by Clausen as a technical
problem which is now redefined as being a possible solution to a different technical
problem.

   Both participants have entered a problem solving process. They seem to agree
on the problem. In any case, Clausen's latest definition of the problem is not challenged
by van den Bosch. But they have not agreed about the solution. In the same call van
den Bosch announces that his company is still working on the plug and socket solution
and concludes that both companies have to decide upon it later. At this point in the
problem solving process, both companies work independently on their own proposal.

   In a call on September 13, van den Bosch announces that BelgiTech now has
found an effective, attractive and cheap plug and socket set in Belgium. van den Bosch
advises DanTech to purchase the set in Denmark.

Example 5
Telephone call of September 13
   1   vdB and then we have still one eh (1.0) open question (.) that is the
             plug connection
   2   C   yes
   3   vdB you haven't found (0.5)
   4   C   no eh
   5   vdB a solution (0.5)
   6   C   no no ⌈ ne
   7   vdB   ⌊ we did
   8   C   did you
   9   vdB we found one
  10   C   yes
  11   vdB and it looks (.) very (.) good and doesn't cost so much money either
  12   C   uh huh
  13   vdB so the question is er how how can we best (.) organize it (.) 'cause
             I wouldn't like it that way that we buy the plug (.) and send it to
             you (.) I would prefer to get the set as complete (.) as possible

14 C   yes

Later in the same call, Clausen admits that the two metres of cable is not a good solution, and both agree that the cable should measure only one meter. This is also stated in a telefax from the same day: "BelgiTech hat einen geeigneten Stecker gefunden und schickt uns Daten + evt. Prototyp. Preis für kompletten Stecker etwa 70 DCr. Erwünscht ist nur 1 m Kabel/Panserschlauch" [BelgiTech did find an appropriate plug and sent us the data + eventually a prototype. Price of the complete plug about 70 Danish kroner. The cable/armed tube should only be 1m].

On September 20, DanTech informs BelgiTech: "Mit Rücksicht auf die Steckerverbindung finden wir kein geeignetes Produkt, dass der Rauchsauger weniger als DKK 400,- netto verteuren würde" [Concerning the plug, we can find no suitable product which would not increase the price of the ventilator by at least 400 Danish kroner]. The text continues:

"Die Lösung mit dem verlängerten Kabel ist unseres Erachtens vorzuzioehen. Alternativ müssen RS und Schalldämpfer zu teilen sein — wie Prototyp 1" [The solution with the prolonged cable is in our opinion preferable. As an alternative, ventilator and sound absorber have to be detachable — as prototype I] (Telefax of September 27).

The temporary agreement on the plug solution is now cancelled again. Clausen does not accept BelgiTech's proposal due to the price being higher than BelgiTech had originally given. The reason can be found in the minutes of the May 2 and 3 meeting, where price limits for the whole unit were defined.

The modification marks the statement as a proposal still open for negotiation. Both companies have not reached definitive alignment on the matter. But in a telefax of November 12, DanTech simply decides: "Dazu haben wir noch einen Punkt, den wir gerne sofort abgeklärt haben möchten, und zwar: KABEL: — Nach den vielen hin und her betr. mit/ohne Stecker und langes/kurzes Kabel wurdenm die ersten 10 Stück mit 2 m langem Kabel geliefert" [And then we have another item on the list which we would like to have clarified immediately, this concerns the cable: — after all this toing and froing concerning with/without plug and long/short cable we'll send the first 10 products with a 2 meter cable]. The text continues:

"Wir gehen davon aus, dass die nächsten 25 Stück mit 1 m Kabel geliefert werden sollen, und dass Ihr auch hier für die Steckerverbindung sorgt" [We proceed on the assumption that the next 25 items will be delivered with a 1 meter cable and that you will provide the plug connection as well].

In a way, this is a decision, but not a *solution* to the problem. 'Negotiating activity' does not lead to alignment but to a decision on the part of one of the participants, namely that DanTech implements its own solution — the two parts are to be connected via a cable, and BelgiTech install a plug. This decision is made on the basis of DanTech knowing that van den Bosch had remarked that he would prefer to receive the set as complete as possible.

During the series of interactions, the topic proceeds through the following stages:

June 24	vdB requests 'X'.
July 1	C accepts 'X', hereby redefining vdB's request as a proposal; C mentions difficulties in implementing 'X'.
July 5	C asks vdB to find a way of implementing 'X'.
August 28	C proposes 'Y'.
August 29	C defines the technical problem.
	Both companies agree on the problem. They work independently on their solutions and agree that a final solution still has to be decided upon.
Sept. 13	vdB announces that 'X' can be implemented.
Sept. 13	C confirms vdB's announcement.
Sept. 27	C rejects the implementation of 'X'.
Nov. 12	C decides that solution 'Y' be implemented.

4. CONCLUSION

In this chapter I have analyzed three different cases of problem solving by employing two different concepts of 'sequence'. The first was the problem solving sequence (Sequence A) which was modelled on the interaction observed in the first Case. The second was the concept of 'negotiating activity' which was adopted from Firth (1991). As mentioned previously, the two sequences have a different theoretical status. I will now briefly discuss the consequences of my analysis for both concepts.

In Case 1, the interaction proceeds nicely from the 'definition of the problem' through a negotiation of different solutions towards the consensus regarding which solution to implement. In the two other cases examined, one participant begins with a request. The definition of the problem and its possible solutions are unfolded in the interaction by the participants' movements towards the definitive solution. Apparently, what I had referred to as Sequence A is not a sequence which can be generalized to any other case of problem solving. However, since Case 1 is a problem solving interaction and an instruction, the form of the sequence might have to do with this second function of the interaction.

It still can be said that participants have to perform certain actions to solve a problem: They have to agree that there *is* a problem, they have to *find* a solution, and to *implement* it. Taking all three cases into account, it can be said that participants have to interact on certain topics; but they do not have to do this in a particularized sequence. The interaction may proceed from 'definition of the problem' towards its 'solution' (as in Case 1), or from a 'solution' towards a 'definition of the problem' (as in Case 3).

Apparently, and perhaps most crucially, the participants do not even have to agree on the problem. On a superficial level it could be said that the problem concerning Case 1 is to close the box, concerning Case 2 to find a suitable cable-connection, and concerning Case 3 the possibility of removing the ventilator from the pressostate. But only in Case 3 do the participants apparently agree on the problem; in the other two cases both participants formulate the problem in different ways.

In Case 1, the British technician defines the problem as 'the box cannot be closed because the motors are not retracted', while his Danish counterpart defines the problem as 'the box cannot be closed because there is something wrong with the way the machine is assembled'. In Case 2 van den Bosch defines the problem as: 'the connection cable must not have a surplus cable because as a result of the Board's directives', while Clausen argues that a surplus connector is 'standard practice'. In both cases, the definition of the problem and the proposed solution are very closely related, most evidently in Case 1, where the relationship is also visible linguistically.

The close relationship between problem and solution may be problematic for established theories of the 'language game' type. Action models — for example Rehbein's 'Handlungsmuster' [action patterns] (Rehbein 1977, Rehbein in press) — employ clearly defined entities (for example 'stages' or 'positions') in their models of interactions, which have to be approached before other entities can be approached. The theory describes a logical sequence which must not be confused with a temporal sequence: a logical model may allow for very different temporal sequences. The problem is, though, whether entities are as clearly defined as logical models would like them to be. As shown in my data, 'problem definition' and 'proposals for solution' cannot always be clearly distinguished. They are not 'stages' to be entered or 'positions' to be reached and left, but topics where boundaries are hard to define. The agreement about a problem may at the same time indicate agreement about the solution. One consequence of these tight relations between elements of the problem solving process is that 'language game' models must be closer related to ongoing interaction than they are at present.

This brings us to 'negotiating activity' as the second type of sequence employed in my analysis. 'Negotiating activity' is found in all three cases. As expected (cf. section 2), it is found in talk concerning both the problem and its solution.

Negotiating activity, though, is used differently from that in Firth's study. Regarding his data corpus, Firth concludes: "The demonstrable end-goal orientation for the parties involved in negotiating activity is ... mutual alignment" (Firth 1991:145). This is not the case in technical problem solving. The 'demonstrable end-goal' here is to *solve* the problem, not to reach alignment on some particular issue. This is most clearly demonstrated in Case 3, where the parties disagree openly. Expressing misalignment and inducing 'negotiating activity' is a component in the problem-solving process. Since the end-goal of the ongoing interaction is not the parties' mutual alignment but the solution of a technical problem, 'negotiating activity' stops when any final solution is reached. 'Negotiating activity', therefore, is a weaker concept in my data than in the interactions described by Firth (1991).

This may have to do with the context. In the DanTech data, the problems to be solved are part of Product Development. Both companies work under severe time constraints. As mentioned in section 3, the market for the new product was already established by February 1, 1991, while the development process started in May 1991. This may lead to the consequence that both companies are more focused on solutions than on problems. The status of the technical problem itself may reinforce this focus: The electrical connections are minor problems, they simply have to be solved in one way or the other. In this way, DanTech's decision to leave the instalment of a plug to BelgiTech is perfectly understandable. DanTech quite simply does not care very much which solution is chosen for this specific problem.

While Maynard (1984) and Firth (1991) describe what appear to be more or less stable and routinized interactions where 'negotiating activity' serves an "institutional mandate" (cf. Maynard 1984:12) to process cases or agree on details underlying the exchange of resources, *technical* problem solving appears to be a much more *ad hoc*, incidental activity — at least for van den Bosch and Clausen. Normally, as part of their work responsibilities, neither party is engaged in product development.

This makes the institutional context and the interactants' work tasks and work profiles crucial variables for the sequential nature of 'negotiating activity'. If 'negotiating activity' is as dependent on the institutional context as it seems to be, it is not a particularly powerful concept for describing the sequencing of a particular type of talk-in-interaction. Instead of being formally-defined and formally-oriented-to sequences of talk, 'negotiation activity' in my data works as an *ad hoc* concept to be employed in different ways in different institutional settings. Consequently, further empirical and micro-analytic work on 'negotiation activities' in different contexts is required.

Finally, some observations can be made about the role of linguistic elements. It has been shown in Case 1 that the action-based alignment vis-à-vis proposals is simultaneously a linguistic alignment. The role of linguistic formulations was central in the two other cases where van den Bosch opens with a request that develops into problem-solving activity. The data used in this study are not sufficient to further an integration of sequential aspects of discourse and their verbal formulation, but this is also an area where further research is needed.

NOTES

1. All names have been changed. For 'BelgiTech', even the name of the country has been changed.

2. A pressostate is a device that regulates air pressure or air flow (cf. thermostat).

3. The data used here are translated from German. Concerning spoken data, a translation is very diffi-cult due to false starts, hesitation, and other talk-phenomena which are different in German and Eng-lish. To ease understanding, a content-oriented translation rather than an interlinear translation has been chosen. The original data are found in an appendix to this chapter.

APPENDIX

Example 2
Telephone call approximately July 1

1	vdB	ehm (3.0) die andere kabel (.) und ein stecker (1.0)
2	C	ja (.)
3	vdB	dafür haben sie ein lösung gefunden
4	C	nein
5	vdB	.h kommt auch nicht
6	C	ehm (2.0) eh nein das s- (0.5) e.h (1.0) n- (0.5) aså den kabel (.) e haben wir (.) nichts gefunden oder ja noch nichts gefunden (6) was unmittelbar gebraucht werden könnte (1.5) ehm (.)
7	vdB	wenn die hersteller von ihre kabel die- die fertig sein .h fünf ((***)) kabel oder (0.5) ohne (.) eh elle (1.5)
8	C	ehm (1.0) na ich hab eh (1.0) ich hab aso eh (0.5) konstruktionsabteilung gebeten daß (.) eh (.) eins zu finden aber die sagen daß (0.5) eh (1.0) s gibt nur wenige ausführungen (.)
9	vdB	aber ich brauch nür eine
10	C	ja (lacht) .h richtich (1.0) ehm (3.0) aber (1.0) gut das i eh (.) wir ham auf jeden fall (0.5) sin wir darauf aufmerksam dass wir da e- etwas finden müssen (.) ⌐ aber
11	vdB	⌊ ja
12	C	ehm (1.0) ihr e- (.) e vor de- für die prüfung oder (1.0) eh da werden wir sicher da keine lösung finden weder mit dem kabel noch mit dem stecker (1.5)
13	vdB	nei (0.5)
14	C	eh nein

Example 3

Telephone call of August 29

1	C	ehm (1.0) und ehm (1.0) aso (.) man ehm (1.0) also w wir habn natü- wollten natürich gern versuchen so ein kabel zu finden (.) .h aber immer noch eh finden wir (.) es ist (.) etwas (.) ungewöhnlich daß (0.5) e:h (.) daß ihr so eh (1.0) eh hart drauf besteht daß keine erdkabel da sein(.) darf (.) denn wir meinen das ist ja (.) das ist ja (.) recht gewöhnlich (.) daß man eh kabel braucht mit (1.0) ⌈ einer
2	vdB	⌊ ja
3	C	extra leitern (3.0) aber ich weiß nich ist es e:h (1.0) ein verlangen von eh dem- eh gasinstitut ⌈ oder
4	vdB	⌊ ja die die sagt ganz einfach wann ein erdleitung da rin ist (0.5) dann (0.5) eh gibt man das idee dass man auch erden muss
5	C	ja
6	vdB	aber das is nicht- das das das (.) das brauch man nicht (1.5)
7	C	nein (.) aber: aso es würde auch nichts (1.0) eh passieren wenn mans tun würde (.) das (2.0)
8	vdB	ja: aber (.) die elektrischen he- herren vom gasinstitüt .h die sind ganz eh (0.5) ja wie heisst das (0.5) eng- eng dadrin eh (3.0) die haben nich so viele spielraum (.)
9	C	nein
10	B	wenn es um vorschriften geht (2.0)
11	C	ja (0.5) ehm (3.0) das du meinst aso eh (.) das ist also eine (1.0) .h eine kardinalfrage wie nennt man das eine (.) das ist entscheidend (.) eh für die (.) eh prüfung (1.0)
12	vdB	ja i- ich wi- (.) wir haben jetz (0.5) nein wir haben (.) das prototyp was sie zu ihn (.) zurück (.)geschickt ist
13	C	ja (0.5)
14	vdB	davon habn wir die- (.) erd (0.5) leitung (0.5) herausgezogen
15	C	ja (.)
16	vdB	das haben sie gesehn nich
17	C	ja (1.0)
18	vdB	und damit ist er zum (.) prüfung geweisen (0.5)
19	C	ja
20	vdB	das bedeutet wenn wir na- l letzendlich später (0.5) die (.) eh (.) em set (.) liefern (0.5) mit ein abgeschnttene erdleitung (.) dann is es nicht in übereinstimmung (.) mit das was wir geprüft haben (.) wofür wir die prüfung haben (.) und sind wir in über (0.5) in eh wie heißt das (1.0) dann machen wir fehler
21	C	ja ja (1.5) ⌈ ehm
22	vdB	⌊ also ich ich schreiben auf we- (.) schreiben sie mal mit h: da sin noch zu lösen problemen

23	C	ja (1.5)
24	vdB	die erdleitung (.) muss eigentlich heraus (1.5)
25	C	ja

Example 4

Telephone call of August 29

1	vdB	eh erster punkt (.) kabel und panzerschlauch ist zwei millimeter steht dort .h is es aber nich=
2	C	eh zwei meter
3	vdB	zwei meter (.) das dachte ich schon
4	C	ja
5	vdB	warum (1.0)
6	C	ehm (1.0) weil eh (0.5) ehm (.) dann hat man die möglichkeit den eh rauchsauger (.) eh und mIt schalldämpfer abzuheben (1.0)
7	vdB	jaja (1.0)
8	C	e:hm
9	vdB	also ein (.) steckerverbindung is es nicht geworden
10	C	nein eh wir ham keine (1.0) keine stecker (0.5) verbindung finden können (0.5)
11	B	das haben sie nicht finden können
12	C	nein

Example 5

Telephone call of September 13

1	vdB	ehm dann ham wir noch eines (1.0) eh (.) fragn ganz offenstehn (.) das is die steckerverbindung (0.5)
2	C	ja
3	vdB	da ham sie noch kein (0.5)
4	C	nein eh
5	vdB	lösung gefunden (0.5)
6	C	nein kei ⌈ ne
7	vdB	⌊ wir aber
8	C	haben sie auch a- (.)
9	vdB	wir haben eine gefunden
10	C	ja
11	vdB	und das sieht (.) ja (.) sehr gut aus und des kostet auch nich so viel geld
12	C	aha
13	vdB	nur is der frag von eh wie wie können wir das am besten (.) organisieren denn (.) ich möchte es nich so haben daß wir die stecker (.) kaufen das dann an ihnen zuschicke (.) ich möchte am am liebsten die das ganze gerät so viel wie möglich (.) eh komplet DanTech bekommen
14	C	ja

CHAPTER 10

'DEVIATIONS' IN AN INTERCULTURAL BUSINESS NEGOTIATION

HELEN E. MARRIOTT

1. INTRODUCTION

International business negotiations often involve participants from different linguistic and cultural communities where at least one of the parties communicates in a non-native language (cf. e.g., Firth this volume, Wagner this volume). Abundant evidence points to communication problems on the linguistic and sociolinguistic levels and to differences in cultural norms or rules of behaviour (e.g., Ferraro 1990, Marriott 1991b, Mulholland 1991, Ulijn and Gorter 1989). In negotiations between Australian and Japanese business personnel, (Australian) English regularly serves as the base language, especially when the setting is an Australian one. The level of English competence of Japanese interactants who are either temporarily assigned to Australia or who visit on short-term business assignments varies enormously, ranging from those with high competence to others with minimal or negligible competence. Given the distance between the English and the Japanese communicative systems, it is not surprising that communication problems are found in many business, including negotiation, situations. Although these communication problems have been studied for a variety of situations, and although different methodological procedures have been adopted (cf. Asaoka 1987,

My thanks to Alan Firth for his detailed comments on a draft of this chapter.

Murie 1976, Neustupny 1985a), there has been relatively little study to date of negotiation interaction in naturally-occurring situations.

This chapter examines one negotiation *encounter*. This type of situation is contrasted with negotiation *activity*, where the latter can take place in a wide variety of contexts (cf. Firth's Introduction, and Wagner this volume). Here, the 'encounter' category is a business negotiation. Alongside other categories like industrial, political and diplomatic negotiations, this encounter represents a common type of negotiation encounter. Negotiation encounters may be free-standing, independent encounters, or part of a series of related encounters. The encounter to be examined here is an initial negotiation which represents the first step in a series of encounters involving one Australian seller and one Japanese buyer. The chapter examines the nature of the communication problems which arise and the ways in which these problems are resolved, or left unresolved.

A corporate institutional seller-buyer negotiation of the type reported here may usefully be said to stand at one end of a continuum of sales interaction. At the other end are sales transactions involving individuals at retail venues. In the description to follow, a tentative distinction is made between sales (or seller-buyer, buyer-seller) negotiations and sales transactions. Various distinctions can be made between these two types of interaction. Firstly, in a sales negotiation individuals — often more than one — act as representatives of their corporate institutions, whereas in a sales transaction the buyer prototypically makes a purchase as a private individual (cf. Ventola 1987). Secondly, although variations are possible (for example, hire purchase arrangements), sales transactions are often concluded on a single occasion. On the other hand, *negotiations* generally occur over a series of encounters and often through a variety of communicative channels, such as face-to-face meetings, telephone, telefax or other forms (cf. Firth 1991). Similarly, the time taken to conclude a negotiation and a sales transaction varies. Thirdly, the types of goods involved in negotiations and transactions may be vastly different. Either can involve the sale of goods or services, but in the case of a negotiation, some other form may occur, such as a proposal to establish a joint venture or other cooperative arrangements. Furthermore, even where goods and services are involved, the cost and size of the purchase is generally different.

This study uses as its framework Neustupny's taxonomy of deviations. Basic to this taxonomy is the concept of *norm*. Although there are some problematic issues relating to use of this concept, including the problems of variation and 'base' category, Neustupny (1985b) argues that it is a powerful concept to use in explicating some of the processes found in interactive situations — whether these be internal situations involving native participants, or intercultural contact situations where native and non-native participants interact. He claims that one of the most conspicuous features of intercultural situations is, in fact, the presence of *deviations from the norm of the base language*. Neustupny (1985a) proposes five major types of deviance: propositional deviance, presentational deviance, performance deviance, correction deviance and discord deviance. These terms are used in the following manner:

1. Propositional deviance refers to "the inability to formulate or comprehend a proposition. In other words, what was to be said was not said (in whole or in part) and what was to be understood remained uncomprehended".

2. Presentational deviance relates to "the inability to send or receive information other than the bare proposition: to communicate about the speaker's attitudes, intention or personality".

3. Performance deviance concerns the "inability of speakers and/or hearers to perform a message according to norms prevalent in internal (native) situations".

4. Correction deviance refers to "the inability to correct" (in other words, 'repair') (cf. Schegloff, Jefferson and Sacks 1977).

5. *Discord deviance or dissonance* arises when *"participants feel that a foreign feature of the situation does not match with a native means of communicating about it or vice-versa"*. For example, features of the addressee or the content might give rise to discord deviance (Neustupny 1985: 50-52).

Although in the above taxonomy 'discord deviance' is one of the five types of deviations, it is given special attention in this chapter since this category has been neglected in previous research (cf. Marriott 1990).

Neustupny's work on deviance differs from much of the earlier work falling under the rubric of 'Error Analysis'. Rather than focusing on the linguistic (phonological, syntactic, semantic) level (cf. Corder 1967, 1981), Neustupny has emphasized the importance of deviations of a non-linguistic nature, including those which occur at the discourse (i.e. extra-sentential) level. In this regard he has also emphasized the importance of studying the interpretative or evaluative behaviour of participants in contact situations, in other words, their decoding activity, in addition to their productive or encoding behaviour.

Some studies have already been undertaken on decoding in relation to the way in which the deviations of a non-native speaker are evaluated. Criteria which have been used to rate the seriousness of errors include intelligibility, acceptability and irritation (Eisentein 1983, Khalil 1985). Needless to say, most previous research has concentrated on the syntactic level, and experimental studies have been utilized as the main methodological procedure (cf. e.g., Chastain 1980, Johansson 1975, 1978, Piazza 1980). Piazza (1980), for instance, concluded that the less comprehensible a grammatical error was, the higher the irritation for the listener, and Chastain (1980) found that although most sentence errors did not effect the intelligibility of messages, certain errors were regarded as unacceptable by native speakers. In his study on 'error gravity', Johansson (1975, 1978) concluded that the degree of listener misunderstanding was greater with phonological deviations, but he also discovered that mispronounced sounds in isolated words were rated as more significant than those in sentences. Other researchers have looked at the tolerance levels of different types of raters. For example, Hadden compared teachers' and non-teachers' perceptions of the discourse of second language learners and concluded that non-teachers were more tolerant of students' linguistic performance than were teachers of English as a second language (Hadden 1991). A similar finding was made by Barbaux (1990), who examined the way in which different types of native speakers judged the acceptability of the verbal and non-verbal conduct of foreign learners of French.

Utilization of Neustupny's framework enables us to identify a much broader range of deviations in discourse than has been the case in previous studies. Existing work concentrates almost solely on propositional deviance. In relation to the categories listed above, reference will also be made to Neustupny's *language management model* which contains four stages. These stages can apply to either the speaker, the addressee or to both. Here, (1) deviations from the norm of the base language of the encounter are either noticed or remain unnoticed by participants; (2) a deviation may be evaluated either positively or negatively (and thus, in the latter case, becomes an inadequacy); (3) there may be a decision to make an adjustment of the inadequacy (the negatively-evaluated feature), or alternatively, a decision to take no action; and, finally (4) implementation of an adjustment strategy (Neustupny 1988: 3-4). In this chapter the main concern is with the first two stages.

2. DATA AND METHODOLOGY

An initial dyadic negotiation interaction of forty minutes' duration between an Australian seller and a Japanese buyer was recorded onto video tape. This was an authentic, naturally-occurring situation and was the first meeting of the two business interactants.

The initial contact occurred when the Japanese visited an exhibition and saw the cheese products of a particular Australian company on display. He left his business card there, and subsequently received a telephone call from the Australian owner who arranged the face-to-face meeting. The interaction was thus initiated by the Australian who arranged the meeting in order to sell his company's product in Japan. The meeting took place in the office of the Japanese businessman in Melbourne, Australia. After the appointment had been arranged and in response to an earlier request, the Japanese businessman invited me to video record the interaction.

Both participants were male with only a minimal age difference (41 years for the Australian and 43 years for the Japanese). However, other work-related differences were considerable. The Australian businessman was the owner of a small cheese manufacturing company which was just beginning to expand into overseas markets. On the other hand, the potential buyer of the cheese was a Japanese representative of a large Japanese manufacturing and importation company which specialized in dairy products and which was supported by a network of overseas offices. Consequently, the companies' positions in their respective communities were quite unequal.

The educational backgrounds of the two participants were also dissimilar. As regards general education levels, the Japanese businessman was a university graduate. This contrasted with the Australian who had not completed secondary education. The Japanese businessman had studied English during his period of formal education and he had also taken an intensive six months training course in English and courses in international business techniques.

The experiential backgrounds of the two were also different. The Japanese participant had travelled overseas on business on four occasions, and even though this was his first period of residence overseas, he had experienced prolonged contact with foreign business personnel in Japan. The Australian did not possess much experience in international business negotiations, only once having had contact with a Japanese company.

Subsequent to the negotiation, individual follow-up interviews were conducted with both participants in order to gain insight into their *evaluative* behaviour — i.e. their perceptions of the negotiation. The interviews sought to discover the participants' perceptions of their own actions and the actions of the other interactant. During these follow-up interviews the video recording was replayed, and general as well as specific questions were asked. These interviews were also video recorded. The follow-up interview provides insight into the processes which occur at the time of the original interaction. It also permits us to clarify certain communication problems (including avoidance of communication), and also to verify the participants' perceptions of 'discord' in communication. This kind of *retrospective* method does, of course, have its limitations in that participants may either consciously or unconsciously report inaccurate information about their behaviour and the reasons for it, or they may remain unaware of some aspects of their actions. Nevertheless, I argue that the follow-up interview is a valuable method for investigating the participants' perceptions and evaluations which are not encoded on the surface of the discourse produced during the actual negotiation.

3. THE NEGOTIATION

In the particular negotiation under examination, the seller visited the office of the buyer with some product samples. A previous paper (Marriott forthcoming) analyzed the content of the discourse according to the structural elements found within the negotiation. Use of the term *structural element* follows Ventola (1987), who employs the term to identify the speech functions performed by linguistic realizations in interaction. The following structural elements were identified in the negotiation: Greeting, Seating Allocation, Display-Inspect Goods, Seek Information, Proposal, Support Case, Clarify Prior Information, Summarize Prior Information, Specify Limited Need, Offer Goods, Agreement, Self-Evaluation, Maintain Contact and Closing (Marriott forthcoming). These elements appear in the order given in Table 1. This table also displays the initiator of the activity.

As mentioned above, there are different categories of deviations on the *global* level of the interaction. The following analysis examines propositional deviance, correction deviance, performance deviance and discord deviance. Instances of presentational deviance, as defined by Neustupny, were not identified in the data. It will be argued that although propositional deviance and correction deviance are the most frequently occurring types of deviance, participants tend to evaluate discord deviance more seriously than they do the other types of deviance.

3.1. Propositional deviance

The Japanese interactant's grammatical competence in English is somewhat low, and, as a result, there are a large number of propositional deviations on his part. However, generally, the conversation continues to flow, with or without self-correction or other correction which is implemented by the Australian. Deviations occur in both the productive and receptive competence of the Japanese businessman, and these are found not only on the phonological, lexical and syntactic levels but also on the level of discourse. To a large extent, the repetitive topics found in the discourse are due to

TABLE 1

STRUCTURAL ELEMENTS IN THE NEGOTIATION

AUSTRALIAN SELLER		*JAPANESE BUYER*
1. GREETING		GREETING
	2.	SEATING ALLOCATION
	3.	INTRODUCTION
4. DISPLAY GOODS		INSPECT
	5.	SEEK INFORMATION
6. PROPOSAL		
	7.	SEEK INFORMATION
8. SUPPORT CASE		
	9.	SEEK INFORMATION
	10.	CLARIFY PRIOR INFORMATION
	11.	SEEK INFORMATION
	12.	CLARIFY PRIOR INFORMATION
	13.	SEEK INFORMATION
	14.	CLARIFY PRIOR INFORMATION
	15.	SUMMARIZE PRIOR INFORMATION
16. SUPPORT CASE		
	17.	SPECIFY LIMITED NEED
18. SUPPORT CASE		
	19.	CLARIFY PRIOR INFORMATION
	20.	SEEK INFORMATION
	21.	SEEK INFORMATION
22. PRESENT GOODS		
	23.	SUMMARIZE PRIOR INFORMATION
24. SUPPORT CASE		
25. RE-PRESENT GOODS		
	26.	AGREEMENT
	27.	CLARIFY PRIOR INFORMATION
	28.	SEEK INFORMATION
	29.	SEEK INFORMATION
	30.	SELF-EVALUATION
	31.	MAINTAIN CONTACT
	32.	CLARIFY PRIOR INFORMATION
	33.	SEEK INFORMATION
	34.	CLOSING

corrective activity on the part of the Japanese to clarify the messages transmitted by the Australian.

The Japanese businessman employs two types of strategies as correction mechanisms: clarifying prior information and summarizing prior information. In all, the negotiation contains six Clarify Prior Information elements, all initiated by the Japanese, who re-introduces topics already covered. Similarly, in another two elements the Japanese businessman summarizes information which was presented earlier in the negotiation. In seeking correction of important matters through these moves, he is clearly being selective during the negotiation. The clarifying issues cover relationships of corporations mentioned by the seller, previous arrangements with another Japanese company, unit size, arrangements overseas, source of know-how and use of the samples; the two cases of summarizing information cover the patent/know-how issue and the profit-sharing arrangement. Invariably, the Clarifying Prior Information elements are elicitations, whereas the Summarizing elements assume the form of statements. The two Summarize Prior Information components reveal his accurate comprehension of the previous talk, as in the example found in fragment (1), lines 2-4:

(1) (After clarifying details relating to the size of the product, the Japanese businessman writes a note in his notebook)

1	J	Right. ((lays his pen down)) ((10 second pause))
2		And eh ah so you you don't have any propriety of eh the license of
3		the- or another patent, but you have ah know-how how to make this
4		((glances at first page of his notes))
5	A	Yeah, yeah, there's many people who have tried to make it
6		((continues))

(element 15)

In like manner, two of the clarifying elements also indicate the Japanese businessman's comprehension of previous talk. Nevertheless, on four occasions, prior information is either misunderstood (elements 10, 12 and 27) or not understood or recalled (element 14). Fragments (2) to (5) contain these instances:

(2) (Following the provision of detailed information by the Australian on the details of Australian sales, there is a long (15 sec.) pause.)

1	J	((J places his pen down and gazes at his notes. Then, while holding
2		a package of cheese in his hand, says the following))
3		Ah, oh I- I cannot clear and eh ((company name)) and eh your product
4		You also use- you also use this brand name ((company name))?
5	A	No no we sell to ((company name)) and they do the distribution and
6		((continues))

(element 10)

(3) (The Australian outlines his business intentions, suggesting that samples be sent to test the market, after which the product could be made in Japan.)

1	A	If it's good
2	J	huh huh
3	A	we could then make it in Japan with a joint venture.
4	J	huh huh (.) ah if eh you- you contact, no contact- no if you deliver to the
5		((name of Japanese company)) directly from
6	A	We haven't done.
7	J	You haven't done?

(element 12)

(4) (After agreeing to introduce the product to his head office, the Japanese businessman requests some samples)

1	J	... and eh maybe one month later they- they give us ah comments from
2		our head office, right?
3	A	all right mm
4	J	And eh also you have eh you got the knowledge of how to make this
5		cheese from the New Zealand Dairy Board?
6	A	No no ⌈ that's our knowledge.
7	J	⌊ no

(element 27)

(5) (In providing information requested by his interactant, the Australian lists details of size and price. Following this, the Japanese clarifies the size of the item.)

1	J	It eh what the container eh quan- quantity of each block? ((J
2		outstretches his two arms to indicate a block))
3	A	Two kilos.

(element 14)

Use of these types of verbal activity as corrective devices show that the Japanese businessman is aware of inadequacies or potential inadequacies in his own decoding behaviour and seeks to compensate for them. When asked during the follow-up interview to comment on his (perceived) frequent tendency to *clarify* information, he responded saying it was a strategy he used to compensate for his inadequate English. In this regard, the management of the interaction by the Japanese is well handled, and he draws upon these strategies frequently as a means of checking and confirming.

The Australian businessman admitted that he experienced some difficulties in decoding the discourse of the Japanese, stating, "there were times when I didn't understand one hundred per cent". Also, upon reviewing the video-tape, the Australian stated in one instance that he may have originally interpreted the discourse of the Japanese incorrectly. Interestingly, the Australian believed that if the Japanese made notes it signalled that the latter comprehends what was being said to him. For instance, the Australian claimed: "if they <u>do</u> write in English it's a big help to see if you think they're comprehending", and "It makes it easier for <u>me</u> to think that he's understanding if I can watch what he's writing". The Australian made these claims in relation to one of the sequences where there was a communication breakdown over his explanation of the distribution of profits. On the basis of what we can deduce about the Japanese businessman's actual comprehension in this and other contexts, the Australian's equation of writing activity on the part of the Japanese businessman with understanding is not necessarily accurate. This claim by the Australian is stereotypical but may contribute — unjustifiably — to his own confidence in gauging whether or not his foreign interactant understands the content of the conversation. Other interviews with Australian business personnel who participate in contact situations with the Japanese (cf. Marriott 1993) confirm the existence of problems for them in sometimes being able to ascertain whether or not their interactive partners are understanding what is being said and/or done. In this regard we can claim that an even more serious problem exists when the participant of a contact situation remains unaware of the fact that the foreign interactant may be experiencing problems in comprehension.

Despite these problems in communication concerning the transmission of propositional content, instances where communicative breakdown visibly occurs is limited to a small number of cases. Nevertheless, there is some evidence that the flow of conversation masks other instances of decoding difficulty for the Japanese. The Japanese businessman did not seem to understand all the lexical items used by the Australian, and when several items were checked in the follow-up interview, this was confirmed. However, we can claim that the Japanese did manage to identify the situationally important issues and sought correction of these, as discussed above.

3.2. Correction deviance

As a means of remedying his inadequate English and by so doing clarifying the message transmitted by the Australian, the Japanese businessman engages in corrective activity, as noted above. The Australian is also compelled to resort to other-correction on a number of occasions. For example:

(6) (The Japanese businessman comments on having previously eaten the cheese, and the Australian responds by enumerating possible variations to the ingredients. His partner

then changes the topic.)

1	J	Ah really. And can <u>you</u> eh visit your plant or not? Can <u>I</u>?
2	A	Sorry?
3	J	Can I eh visit your plant or not?
4	A	Sure ((nods head vertically))
5	J	Is it OK?
6	A	Yeah. It's on the card, there.

(element 31)

Even though the Japanese self-corrects his deviation (line 1), his addressee seeks clarification (line 2), whereupon the subsequent correct rephrasing (line 3) of the question enables the Australian to decode the message as intended and 'answer' the question (lines 4 and 6). In most instances the attempts at correction are executed successfully, as in fragment (6) above. However, on other occasions correction is not successful and sometimes the corrective adjustment itself contains new deviations, as in the following illustration. In this instance the Japanese begins by summarizing prior information about the profit-sharing arrangements, but then seeks more details:

(7) (The Japanese is presented with some samples of the cheese by the Australian. The Japanese then returns to a topic which had previously been discussed.)

1	J	The condition of the eh you- you share the share if you will
2		share ah profit eh one-third, one-third, one-third, for instance if
3		it's only dividend, the profit is divided to=
4	A	=That's the way we've been working so far
5	J	mm mm
6	A	right
7	J	mm mm
8	A	We could have another arrangement but in Ireland
9	J	yes
10	A	they make one thousand pounds per ton profit (.) ⌐ a
11	J	⌊ uh huh
12	A	thousand pounds sterling
13		((The Japanese commences to write))
14	J	Yeah eh per <u>year</u>
15	A	profit <u>per ton</u>
16	J	one thousand <u>per ton</u>
17	A	one dollar- one <u>pound</u> per kilo profit
18	J	Pardon? What? One heh?
19		((The Japanese gazes at the Australian))

20	A	One pound <u>sterling</u>
21	J	one pound st- <u>steel</u> (.) ah ah
22	A	<u>English</u> pounds
23	J	Huh hmm one pound steel steeling
24	A	yes LSD you know
25	J	Uh huh (.) one pounds steeling (.) steeling gold yeah.
26	A	Yeah neh pound per <u>pound</u> no oh sorry <u>one</u> <u>thou</u>sand pounds
27	J	thousand ((begins to write))
28	A	sterling=
29	J	=yes
30	A	is the profit for one ton. All right. Now we share that. They give
31		me three hundred dollars.

(element 24)

In the sequence above, the Japanese begins writing once he is apprised of the extent of the company's profit (line 13); during the writing activity the Japanese seeks confirmation of his understanding of the preceding turn (line 14: 'yeah eh per *year*'). The Australian corrects this to *per ton* in his next turn (15). In the Australian's attempt to clarify further (line 17), a 'self-repair' arises in mid-turn; this appears to cause a problem in understanding for the Japanese, who in the next turn initiates an 'other repair' (see Schegloff, Jefferson and Sacks 1977). The subsequent problem, it appears, arises as a result of the open-endedness of the Japanese businessman's *pardon? what?* (line 18), for in the next turn the Australian interprets the 'what?' as indicative of a problem in understanding the type of *currency* being talked about. The Australian's response to the 'what?', then, is to stress 'one pound *sterling* (line 20). However, the next-turn response shows the Japanese to be either unfamiliar with the word 'sterling', unable to hear the word clearly (hearing it instead as 'steel'), or unable to pronounce it in a recognizable way (i.e. recognizable to his interlocutor) — see line 21. The Australian interprets the deviant pronunciation of "sterling" by the Japanese as indicative of lack of understanding (as shown by his *'English* pounds' — line 22). However, his interpretation of a lexical problem on the part of the Japanese appears to be incorrect, for in line 25 the Japanese suggests a knowledge of 'sterling' as being equated with precious metals, hence 'gold'.

3.3. Performance deviance

In this intercultural negotiation the Australian businessman varies his normal linguistic behaviour by speaking more slowly, a feature of which he himself was aware, as disclosed in the post-negotiation interview: "I try to speak slower than normal". The Japanese interactant concurred, claiming: "Today because I am Japanese hehheh (laughing) he reduce the speed". The slowing of speech by the Australian was not negatively evaluated by either party; in fact, it is a form of 'foreigner talk' which receives positive evaluation. As such, the feature does not attract categorization as an inadequacy because there is no negative evaluation by either participant.

3.4. Discord deviance

Despite the existence of considerable propositional deviance and also a fair amount of correction deviance in the present data, it is proposed that the most serious category of deviance is *discord deviance*, also referred to as *dissonance*. In this section, dissonance is discussed in relation to three factors of communicative behaviour: content, form and medium (cf. Hymes 1972, Neustupny 1973, 1991).

3.4.1. *Content*
The Australian's perception of dissonance is particularly strong in relation to the content of the discourse. Of the structural elements found in the negotiation, the Proposal contains the Australian seller's offer and the response of the Japanese addressee. The interaction is contained in the following fragment:

(8) (Preceding talk has focused on the Australian's previous contacts with other Japanese companies about the potential for business.)

1	A	And that's the only dealings I've had with Japan.
2	J	Uh huh huh ah right. ((J picks up a package of cheese and examines it
3		again))
4		(8.0)
5	A	So there's nothing ah that's been finalized. If you're interested in
6		doing something we can make it here or we can show you how
7	J	mm
8	A	how to make it in Japan.
9	J	Mm (2.0) so for a moment eh yeah I'm- I also am interested in this ah
10		those kind of product but not eh familiar in Japan for the Japanese ah
11		palate.
12	A	yeah
13	J	Ah so that for my introduction eh for my job ah to introduce to those
14		products to my our company

```
15  A   yeah
16  J   in Japan so that first I'd- we'll have- I'd like to have this eh those kind
17      of sample and eh send to my head office ┌and if you have any. We
18  A                                            └right
19  J   also as you know we also produce such- such kind of not such kind of
20      ((laughing)) hehheh this cheese but processed cheese we produce a lot
21      of che- cheese
22  A   yeah, yeah
23  J   maybe ah yeah about six, sixty thousand tons in Japan we deliver to
24      throughout Japan so that and additionally we eh now ah making ah
25      another items in our products line.
```

(element 6)

In examining the development of the offer and the response found in this Proposal, it is notable that although the Japanese encodes a mildly cooperative response, stating his interest in the kinds of products being offered by the Australian businessman (line 9), he then modifies his position by stating the unfamiliarity of the Japanese with such speciality cheese (lines 10-11). In elaborating his response, he then refers to his role in Australia (lines 13-17) and outlines his company's participation in cheese marketing in Japan (lines 19-25). Despite the declaration of interest by the Japanese contained in the above sequence, a major source of frustration for the Australian (reported in the subsequent interview) was uncertainty regarding the Japanese businessman's commitment to actually purchase.

The Australian seller repeats his proposal later in the negotiation, an action which is triggered by the Japanese businessman who directly inquires about the objective of the Australian's visit (lines 1-2, below). The sequence of talk containing the repetition of the proposal is reproduced in fragment (9):

(9) (Following clarification of his local distributor, the Australian refers to three Asian countries where his company is trying to establish new business.)

```
1  J   And eh what your object to eh visit to me, is that eh introduce
2      for eh this
3  A   We'd like to sell to Japan
4  J   sell to Japan
5  A   yeh
6  J   uh huh
7  A   or make it in Japan.
8  J   mm ah here yes
9  A   Either way, whichever is the best.
```

10 J   mm
11 A   Maybe make it here for um six months and eh if it's acceptable
12 J   ah six, six months
13 A   well we could send some samples from ⌐ Australia
14 J   ⌊ in Melbourne uh huh
15 A   and just test the market (.) if it's good we could then make it in Japan
16 J   uh huh (.) uh huh
17 A   with a joint venture.

(element 11)

Here the seller repeats his alternative proposal (lines 3 and 7) and then expands upon the option of selling products to Japan (lines 11, 13 and 15). Throughout, the Japanese buyer only produces minimal-response acknowledgment signals like 'uh huh' or 'mm' (e.g. lines 6, 8, 10 and 14). At a much later stage in the negotiation, the Japanese buyer encodes an Agreement, found in fragment (10), where he elaborates upon the message he actually generated in fragment (8) above:

(10) (After a long sequence of talk where the Australian stresses the high profitability of his product, he refers again to the samples, mentioning that he will also send some new ones together with brochures.)

1 J   Yes okay (1.0) ah as a first stage I'd like to ah introduce to our
2   head office and ((***)) so that and eh I sound is it possible to
3   market or or produce in Japan so that eh at the first stage I would
4   like to have some sample and I will deliver to our head office
5 A   all right
6 J   and eh maybe one month later they- they give us ah comments
7   from our head office, right?
8 A   All right mm

(element 26)

Despite the statements of the Japanese participant's positive responses found in fragments (8) and (10) above, and to a lesser extent in (9), during the follow-up interview the Australian subsequently revealed his uncertainty regarding the conclusion of the interaction. At first this dissatisfaction was not strongly verbalized:

(11)

INT As a result then what did you expect from today's meeting? The
     results, were they as expected?
A   Ah yes, there's nothing positive. I'm introducing our product.

However, the Australian's dissatisfaction with the response of the Japanese was later made explicit:

(12)

> A   Well basically there's no trouble spot except that I don't really
>   know what he's going to do. It finished a little bit
>   unconcluded.

Then, in the closing segment of the interview, the Australian intensified his disclosure of dissatisfaction:

(13)

> INT   Is there anything else you'd like to bring out, either
>   specifically or in general?
> A   No not really nothing we haven't discussed, just that there
>   wasn't any clear conclusion to the meeting. I have to ring him
>   up. Sure he wants to have a look at the factory, so it's not
>   'we'll ring you'. So I think it's open to proceed.

In summary, with regard to the content of the negotiation, specifically those elements relating to the generation of the Proposal, responses to it, its repetition, and the final response of the buyer in the form of an Agreement, *dissonance* clearly exists on the side of the Australian seller who wanted the Japanese buyer to produce a more explicit personal demonstration of interest.

Within their respective business spheres the two interactants belong to rather different subgroups or subcultures which, in turn, are likely to be characterized by a number of dissimilarities (cf. Knapp and Knapp-Potthoff 1987:5). Whereas the Japanese businessman belongs to the commonly labelled 'large industry' category, the Australian's company is representative of 'small industry'. One outcome of this difference is that as owner and superordinate of a tiny Australian manufacturing company, the seller can independently make decisions, whereas the Japanese representative is continually required to seek advice from the Tokyo head office. His main role in Australia is one of information gathering. This exerts an important socio-structural influence on the communicative behaviour — and concomitant communicative expectations — of the two businessmen.

In contrast to the considerable amount of communicative dissonance felt by the Australian seller, the Japanese buyer had no perception of discord expressed by the Australian. The interaction provided the setting for him to discover the seller's intentions and to begin to gather information, as revealed in the follow-up interview, quoted in the following fragment:

(14)

> J   ... but I eh, today's meeting was first meeting so that I had- I'd like to have <u>just</u> information what the company is and what sort of company and what what they intended to ...

The feeling of dissonance, then, is not a feature characterizing both interactants; in this context only the Australian experiences dissonance with respect to the *outcome* of the interaction. This instance thus shows that when 'dissonance' is experienced, one party may remain unaware of the feeling of discord experienced by the other party. And there was no evidence to show that the Japanese was cognizant of the Australian's perceived dissonance.

3.4.2. *Message form*

Dissonance is also found in relation to the message form or order in which content is presented. An analysis of the structural elements shows that much of the business information supporting the Australian seller's Proposal is encoded as a result of the elicitations from the Japanese interactant (Marriott forthcoming). In total, there are ten Seek Information elements, all of which are opened by the Japanese businessman. These include topics on export details, patent, production quantity, pricing policy, equipment requirements, use of chemicals, details on cheese varieties, use of cheese and variation in packaging. The Australian, on the other hand, supplies information through four Support Case elements covering a comparison with rival firms, his company's market position and profitability. Nevertheless, the Japanese was responsible for the development of most of the discourse topics.

       In the follow-up interview, the Japanese reveals his dissatisfaction with having to elicit so many business details from the Australian. This is shown in fragment (15):

(15)

> INT   Did you ask a lot of questions today?
>
> J   huh huh.
>
> INT   or did you expect that he would give you more information?
>
> J   I expect to get ah I ask him his because eh not ah his explanation not enough for me.
>
> INT   Is it normal that you have to ask many questions?
>
> J   ...in Japan maybe the salesman speak more more, more explanation about the eh his companys and the condition of the trading.

By observing in fragment (15) that sellers in Japanese situations would tend to initiate the supply of information and provide more background details, the speaker seeks to account for the performance of the Australian in terms of cultural differences, an explanation which is often advanced in intercultural situations to account for perceived differences (cf. Gudykunst and Kim 1984:25). However, I would argue that the actual reason for dissonance in this case is that the deviation experienced on the part of the Australian is a result of a conflict over role relationships; simply put, the Australian expects different things from the Japanese than he actually got. Needless to say, there is no guarantee that the generalized claim made by the Japanese about sellers in native situations is accurate.

Surprisingly, the Australian takes a contrary stance, maintaining that the Japanese buyer does not ask many questions, a fact which cannot be verified on the basis of data given — namely that all the ten Seek Information elements were initiated by the Japanese, and that only a limited amount of information was supplied by the Australian through his four Support Case elements. The pertinent section of the follow-up interview which reveals the perception of the Japanese is provided in fragment (16):

(16)

A	He didn't ask me many questions.
INT	He <u>didn't</u> ask many questions? you could have expected more?
A	I volunteered the price. I didn't think he was going to ask.
INT	Why might you have felt that?
A	That's one of the first things any buyer asks, 'how much?'.
INT	And he didn't?
A	No I told him half-way through. As a rule it's price first quality second. 'Is it saleable within the price range that I can operate on?'
INT	So he took a different approach then?
A	Yeah no, he didn't ask a lot of questions. He didn't ask about the packaging, how many in a container, how we ship them and fly or ship it. A lot of things that you'd normally expect, perhaps in the second meeting.
INT	That comes up in the second meeting?
A	Well maybe with him, but with normal people, well say at a normal meeting introducing a line there's virtually a check list of things they need to know. We can pack a hundred to a carton. If that's not good for supermarkets, it can be sixties or twelves.

In the case of the message factor in the communication, then, dissonance is felt on both sides, but the two participants advance different explanations for this phenomenon. The Australian's account suggests that he has a different manner of organizing the information for transmission, where price is considered to be the most important one. The Japanese buyer gives no indication that he shares this viewpoint. Actually, it emerges in the follow-up interview, and is partially transparent in the negotiation interaction itself, that, for the buyer, the most important element is whether or not the seller possesses a patent.

Another problem relates to the total amount of verbal activity on each side, including initiation of topics. An examination of the Australian's actual verbal activity reveals that his perception of his own behaviour is inaccurate. Candlin has argued that participants' perceptions of what happens in discourse may be contrary to actual language use due to disparate 'discoursal sets' (Candlin, Coleman and Burton 1983).

3.4.3. *Medium*

Medium, otherwise known as channel, refers to the medium of transmission and is another source of dissonance in this data, though to a milder degree in comparison with the dissonance in relation to content and message form. The negotiation is primarily effected through a face-to-face meeting, which is a communicative norm consistently shared by both the Australian and the Japanese.

There is some dissonance, however, with regard to the utilization of the written channel in the interaction. Although the Japanese produces a brochure of his own company during the opening segment, immediately after the greetings, it is only towards the end of the encounter that the Australian admits he has not brought with him a company brochure because his supply is exhausted. The omission by the seller on this occasion is perhaps indicative of the lesser importance placed upon the written language channel in business negotiations by members of the Australian cultural community (Marriott 1990:55). Although it can be argued that many small Japanese companies did not have written documentation in the 1960s, thus paralleling the situation in Australia today, events suggest that small Australian companies are now negotiating with large Japanese companies and that dissonance arises due to different communicative norms. The Australian's lack of priority attention to the presentation of written information at the first meeting seems to stand in contrast to the importance afforded the written channel by the Japanese businessman. In the follow-up interview the Japanese twice refers to his future action of sending a report to his head office together with brochures of the Australian company. Since this topic was not directly raised in the follow-up interview it is not possible to confirm the extent of the feeling of dissonance on the side of the Japanese. However, any feeling of dissonance may have been somewhat modified as a result of the Australian's promise of a presentation of brochures in the near future.

4. CONCLUSION

We could expect that the interactants of this negotiation, especially the native speaker of English, would negatively evaluate the amount of communicative problems — especially those of a propositional and corrective nature — made manifest in the interaction. However, this is not the case, a finding which lends support to the claim that in intercultural contact situations, participants often somehow *suspend* their (native-speaker) norms by taking a 'relaxed' attitude towards the amount of communicative deviations which occur in the discourse (Neustupny 1985b). For example, one form of performative deviation — the slowing of speech — was evaluated positively rather than negatively by both participants.

On the other hand, it has been argued that *discord deviance* emerged as a serious form of deviance in the intercultural negotiation examined here. It was found in its strongest form in the Australian seller's dissatisfaction with the Japanese businessman's failure to encode a response to the Australian's proposal in the form and manner normatively expected. It was this feature in the interaction which the Australian evaluated most negatively. However, on the basis of one case study it is clearly not possible to account conclusively for the dissatisfaction on the part of the Australian. Nevertheless, the suggestion has been made that membership of different socio-structural groups effects the actions, expectations and attitudes of the two participants. We saw that the Japanese businessman was an overseas representative whose major work task is to transmit information to his Tokyo Head Office. In contrast, the Australian is the owner of a very small company, and therefore capable of making decisions which would not be possible for his Japanese negotiator. It seems, however, that the Australian was not fully aware of this difference. The differences in decision-making *power* between the Japanese buyer and the Australian seller thus appeared to exert an influence on the way the parties carried out and perceived the negotiation.

The perception of dissonance also characterized both interactants with regard to *medium*. It was suggested that differences in the utilization of written documentation was another form of dissonance for the Japanese interactant, though perhaps of a milder variety in comparison with the dissonance relating to content and message form.

One of the findings of this chapter pertains to the way in which correction of discourse content is managed. The Japanese businessman frequently sought clarification of prior information and also, on occasions, summarized prior messages in order to confirm his interpretation. Such *corrective activity* on his part increased his ability to communicate in a foreign language. In contrast, the Australian took little initiative with regard to correction strategies. He did not engage in repetitive strategies unless correction was explicitly requested by the Japanese, nor did he employ verbal strategies to check his interactant's comprehension. Moreover, his perception of the Japanese businessman's note writing as an indicator of understanding was not shown to be accurate.

The concept of *deviance* is admittedly a difficult one, and difficult to specify with precision. However, on the basis of analyses of the data transcripts, and based on post-negotiation interviews, this chapter has attempted to show that the concept is *one* useful tool for understanding how international negotiations succeed or fail to do so. The concept of 'deviance' thus has relevance for work in negotiation discourse and negotiation interaction especially when the data is extracted from situations where the participants originate in different communicative and cultural communities. In such contexts, there may be occasions when numerous communication problems occur, due to one or both participants' inadequate socio-linguistic competence. As a result, a diversity of 'unseen' culturally-based norms of communication (cf. Hymes 1974) may negatively impinge upon the negotiation process. On the basis of the data examined in this chapter, it seems that while participants in business negotiations tend to be tolerant of certain types of communicative deviations, especially propositional and correction deviance, other 'deviations' surface in the discourse, giving rise to undesirable consequences. Parties may thus be lenient towards the presentational and performance deviance of their negotiation partners, though critical of what I have called *discord deviance*. This category is all the more serious because it is little understood by the participants themselves, yet appears to be a cause of several misunderstandings during the negotiation.

The negligible amount of work of a micro-analytical type which focuses on communication problems in naturally-occurring negotiations is the major reason why so little is known in this area. In order to advance this type of research, more in-depth work is needed on native speaker negotiation encounters which, in turn, will allow contrastive patterns to be identified in international negotiations, though contrastive analyses cannot — and cannot claim to — give a full picture of what actually occurs in an intercultural contact situation. While caution is needed in generalizing about communicative and socio-cultural patterns, it is only on the basis of empirical data that we can develop a detailed understanding of the phenomena involved. For this reason, more detailed, micro-analytic studies are needed, covering individuals with different backgrounds, including different languages, and working in a variety of institutional settings.

Finally, this chapter has also attempted to stress the importance of investigating evaluative behaviour. As shown in the analysis, interactants may evaluate the behaviour of other participants according to their own cultural and communicative norms. This is a continual and ongoing process, in mono-cultural and multi-cultural contact situations.

However, in the latter, because the behaviour of participants is likely to reflect more divergent underlying communicative and sociocultural norms, misunderstandings and miscommunication are more frequent (cf. Gumperz 1982a). Yet in many cases, interactants tend not to be cognizant of the fact that their evaluative behaviours are rooted in culturally-based 'ways of talking', concluding instead that their interlocutors are 'difficult', 'awkward', or the like. This is particularly so in the case of discord deviance. It would appear that discourse analysts, with their interests in uncovering the micro-details of the negotiation process, are particularly well placed to examine how evaluative behaviour is manifest in the discourse of actual, real-life negotiations.

SECTION IV

NEGOTIATIONS IN PROFESSIONAL-LAY INTERACTIONS

CHAPTER 11

NEGOTIATING CATEGORIES IN TRAVEL AGENCY CALLS

HARRIE MAZELAND

MARJAN HUISMAN

MARCA SCHASFOORT

1. INTRODUCTION

Analyzing eight phone calls to a travel agency,[1] we observed that one of the things participants 'negotiate' over in this type of exchange is how *categories* may be described. One of the problems both the person who calls the travel agency and the call-taker have to solve is the delivery of a description of a holiday that is appealing to the caller. This description has to meet the interests of both parties. Customer and employee have to agree upon a description that not only fits the wishes of the former, but also enables the latter to select a particular holiday from the agency's assortment. In other words, the selection of an appropriate category description is a collaborative achievement of both parties.

This chapter focuses on how participants of sales calls to a travel agency negotiate over the categories they use to describe the holiday or excursion of interest to the

We thank the editor of this volume, Alan Firth, for his detailed comments and useful suggestions.

customer. We try to demonstrate that in the calls studied participants use different methods to negotiate categories. We describe category transition by the parties' deployment of two procedures, here referred to as the 'scaling-up operation' and 'attribute transfer'.

For our analysis, Harvey Sacks' (see, e.g., Sacks 1992a, [Fall 1964, Spring 1965, Lecture 6]) work on membership categorization proved to be very useful. Sacks describes how people use orderly procedures to select 'categories'. He not only demonstrates how such categorization devices are used to constitute social order by making observable correct and appropriate descriptions of persons and their actions, he also shows that these devices provide orderly procedures for the constitution of sequential coherence and the making of socially reasonable inferences. In section 3 of the chapter we present a brief characterization of Sacks' work on categorization. However, in order to demonstrate the relevance of categorization work in sales talk, we first discuss a fragment of a call in section 2. In sections 4 and 5 we describe two methods by which category transition is achieved in our data material. Section 6 describes a principle through which participants accomplish cross-sectional coherence with respect to category selection: the principle of *level consistency*. In section 7 the core of our argument is summarized.

2. THE RELEVANCE OF CATEGORIZATION WORK IN SALES TALK: AN EXAMPLE

In the following exchange the caller has asked the employee of the travel agency what it would cost if a group of eleven persons — six adults and five children — were to book a holiday at a particular apartment complex on the Spanish coast. After the Sales woman mentions a first net total price (line 183 in fragment 1a) the caller inquires about the possibility of *reduction for children* (lines 184-186). The call-taker answers this question negatively by informing the customer that there is no reduction for children on the type of holiday she wants to book (*with apartment trips no, there isn't* line 188):

(1a) [lstraat/a/hm] *(simplified translation into English)*[2]

```
176  A      we ┌ ll when I'm going to calculate the pric ┌ e (.) five hundred
177  B        └ m:m                                       └ m:m:
178  A      eighty-five times eleven ┌ :
179  B                               └ m:m
180         (0.3)
181  A      tha ┌ t will be::
182  B         └ (and-)
183  A      six thousand four hundred thirty-five guilders=
```

```
184  B→   =er yes and for the children
185        (0.5)
186    →   so to say er- 'cause is there reduction for children with it or
           whatever:
187        (0.2)
188  A     with apartment tri:ps no, there isn't
189        (.)
190  B     o:h y ⌈ es.
191  A→          ⌊ (e:) reduction for children only applies up to
192        six year((s old)) twenty percent with hotel: tri:ps
193        (0.2)
194  B     o: ⌈ h yes
195  A        ⌊ but it doesn't apply to apartment trips
196        (0.5)
197  B     oh:
```

Following the rejection of the caller's suggestion, the call-taker accounts for this dismissal by relating the matter of reduction for children in several ways to different types of categories: accommodation and transport.

* She first informs the caller that *reduction for children only applies up to six year((s old)) [...] with hotel trips, [...] but it doesn't apply to apartment trips* (lines 191-195). Here the category of the accommodation the caller wants to book is used to account for the non-relevance of a categorical distinction between adults and children. The relevance of price reduction for children is simply presented as a matter of category-bound features of different sorts of accommodation. Moreover, the exclusive attachment of the feature 'reduction for children' to the category 'hotel trips' is treated as something that may be unilaterally defined on the part of the travel world and is put forward as a non-negotiable matter.

* Although the topic of reduction for children could have been closed at this point the call-taker continues to address the subject by asking how old the children are (line 198 in fragment (1b)). After the caller's answer that there are *three children of eight year((s old))* (line 200), *one of [...] about three* (lines 203-204) and *one of fifteen* (line 208) the employee again concludes that there is *unfortunately no reduction for children* (lines 212-213). The subsequent accounts for that conclusion make clear that the Sales woman now addresses the possibility of reduction for children with respect to the transport costs, cf. *eight year((s old)) need a whole bus seat* (lines 213-215; earlier in the exchange the caller has already informed the Sales woman that they want to travel by bus):

(1b)   [lstraat/a/hm] ((*continuation of fragment 1a*))
    188 A   with apartment tri:ps no, there isn't
    189   (.)
    190 B   o:h y ⌈ es.
    191 A→   ⌊ (e:) reduction for children only applies up to
    192   six year((s old)) twenty percent with hotel: tri:ps
    193   (0.2)
    194 B   o: ⌈ h yes
    195 A   ⌊ but: it doesn't apply to apartment trips
    196   (0.5)
    197 B   oh:
    198 A   how old are the childr ⌈ en ⌈ at the date of depar ⌈ ture
    199 B   ⌊ e: ⌊ :h   ⌊ let's see.
    200   there are: three children of eight year((s: old))
    201   (0.2)
    202 A   eight year((s old)) ⌈ yes,
    203 B   ⌊ y:es, ·hh and e::r there's one of e::r
    204   let's see of e:r about three year:((s old))
    205   (0.2)
    206 A   y:es
    207   (0.3)
    208 B   and one of: e:r fifteen,
    209   (0.4)
    210 A   y:es, ·hh
    211   (1.2)
    212 →   no. (0.2) there e::r is unfortunately er nho reduction
    213 →   for children going anymore. ·h ⌈ h eight year((s old))
    214 B   ⌊ o:ah.
    215 A   nee:d a whole bus seat anyway,=
    216 B   =yes:y ⌈ es
    217 A→   ⌊ (and) they cannot go together e::r
    218   for instance two seats- ·hh or one seat
    219   and then two children on it
    220   (.)
    221 B   yes ⌈ :yes,
    222 A→   ⌊ hHH (.) and: er fifteen year((s old))
    223   is an adult person with us:
    224   (.)

```
225  B        o:h yes yes, yes of course
226           no that is: er true indeeh:d heh ·hi:hh
227           yes that is: true ind ⌐ eed.
228  A                          └ so you really get eleven times
229           e::r five hundrede:h ⌐ eighty-five guilders ·h ⌐ h
230  B                            └ eighty-five guilders    └ mm
```

The rejection of the possibility of reduction for children and the account for this non-application are thus divided over two separate steps. First the 'accommodation' component of the costs of the trip is addressed, and subsequently the part of the price that consists of the 'transport costs'.

Particularly interesting in the second step is the fact that the reasons the Sales woman gives for the non-applicability of reduction for children are partially different. Following the caller she partitions the group of children into different age groups and treats these groups in a specific way by relating them each to a different aspect of the travel business (lines 213-219 and 222-223). In lines 213-215 the Sales woman says that children of eight years old need a whole bus seat. She explains this further by stating that they cannot share one seat (lines 217-219). Subsequently she simply states that *fifteen year((s old)) is an adult person with us* (line 222-223).[3]

In the case of the fifteen years old the Sales woman does something that is comparable with the way she previously accounted for the applicability of reduction for children on the accommodation part of the costs. She legitimates the rejection by the delivery of an explicit, unilateral definition of what is an 'adult person' for the travel agency. However, in the case of the eight year old the employee accounts for the rejection by giving a functional[4] description of the way children of this age might be distributed over bus seats. Instead of the formalist, definitional treatment of the applicability of reduction for children on both apartment trips and the transport costs of fifteen year old persons, the account for the non-applicability is now presented as the result of everyday reasoning about a category-bound feature of children of a particular age group, i.e. their possible capacities for seatsharing.

One may conclude that in these fragments the Sales woman uses three methods to account for the non-applicability of reduction for children.

* In the first method, the *relevance* of the category 'child' is made dependent on the applicability of the category 'hotel trip', i.e. on the applicability of one specific member out of another collection of task-relevant categories. The fact that reduction for children is not a possible trait of this particular category from the collection of accommodation-describing categories explains why reduction does not apply. It is only through the

selection from the situation-bound collection of categories for different kinds of accommodation (hotel, apartment) that the relevance of the category 'child' can be determined.

* In the second method it is not the relevance of the category 'child' that is at issue but the *applicability* of this category. The feature of being 15 years old is treated as a sufficient condition to determine the inappropriateness of the category 'child' for an individual of this particular age. So, the accounting is accomplished by formulating a rule of category application which establishes the inappropriateness of the category 'child' for a person who is fifteen years old (who *is an adult person with us*). Contrary to the former method of accounting, a particular feature of one of the members of the group of customers is assigned a category-excluding potential, independent of its relation to other collections of situation-bound categories.

* In the third method it is again the *relevance* of the category 'child' that is under discussion: here the feature of 'not being able to share seats' is used as a sufficient condition to determine the non-relevance of the category 'child'. As opposed to the unilateral definitions and rules used in the first two methods, here the non-consequentiality of category incumbency is the result of situated everyday reasoning. Whereas the first two methods of accounting explain the non-applicability of reduction for children by membership exclusion from particular categories (15 year old persons are *not* a 'child', it is *not* a hotel trip), the third method deletes the applicability of reduction by attribute-specification of a subset of the members of the category 'child' (cf. Jayyusi 1984:28).

All these different accounts for the non-applicability or the non-relevance of the category 'child' have at least two things in common: (a) they are all triggered by the use of the term 'reduction for children' in a specific sequential position (after the Sales woman mentions the total price[5]); (b) different features of persons of a particular age or that age itself are made relevant dependent on the category or task to which they are related. The accounts all display a way of reasoning about the applicability or the relevance of the category 'child' relative to categories from categorization devices that are specific for the organization the caller speaks with (is it a hotel trip, or an apartment trip; is the person in question able to share his bus seat with someone else with that same capacity) or of which the application rules are specifically and unilaterally defined by this organization (persons of fifteen are adult persons for us).

It is also remarkable that the customer — at least at the level of what she displays explicitly — accepts and agrees with these situation-bound methods of categorization and the ways in which they are accounted for. In other words, there seems to be asymmetry in the possibilities the participants have to classify persons of a certain age at that particular point in the exchange. Incumbents of the category 'customer' do not have the same rights to determine how categories from the stage-of-life (child, adult) device may be applied as an incumbent of the complementary category of the relational pair (customer, Sales person).[6]

3. THEORETICAL BACKGROUND: SACKS' WORK ON CATEGORIZATION

The preliminary observations in the preceding section show that the examination of categorization work of participants is relevant for the analysis of negotiations in at least some kinds of sales talk. They also suggest the usefulness of conversation analytic and ethnomethodological work on categorization. Especially Harvey Sacks' work on *membership categorization devices* (Sacks 1972a,b) and the way Jayyusi (1984) elaborates central aspects of the apparatus developed by Sacks, has been conducive for the analysis we develop in this chapter.

Sacks' analysis of membership categorization devices (MCDs) is a detailed attempt to spell out the informal logic that the members of a culture use to describe persons and the way this logic is intertwined with sequential organization. MCDs are collections of categories plus rules of application. The use of a category in a particular context locates at least one collection of categories of which that category is a member — e.g. the use of a term 'child' might identify a *stage of life* collection of categories, including children, adolescents, adults, and elderly people. In selecting a particular category a speaker displays an orientation to a set of *application rules* that not only govern the contextually appropriate pairing of population members and collection members, but also provide guidelines for methodical everyday reasoning.

Contrary to the hierarchies constructed in lexical semantics (e.g. Cruse 1986), collections of categories may be assembled on a basis other than a taxonomic one. Which set of categories constitutes a collection, or what is oriented to as a categorization device, may be the result of situated and task-oriented interactional work of conversationalists. Categories are grouped together relative to the relevancies of the task at hand (cf. Jayyusi 1984:82). Schegloff points to the possibility of *classes whose co-members are grouped together for a single attribute, and hence may be a class for a single (or limited range of) topic* (Schegloff 1972b:124). The assembly of a collection is thus observably provided for in the talk itself; e.g. the relevant collection in the case of the discussion of the category 'child' in the fragment above seems to be confined to the pair {child, adult}.

An example of a rule of application which also proved to be relevant for the present analysis is the rule which Sacks called the *consistency rule*. According to this rule, categories may be interpreted as 'second items' (cf. Sacks 1992a:150 ff.): *if you can hear a second category as coming from the same device as the first, then hear it that way* (Sacks 1972a).[7] Thus the use of the category 'adult' in the above fragment (line 223 in fragment (1b)) accomplishes in that particular context the instruction that it is to be interpreted as coming from the collection {child, adult} and not from a collection such as {juvenile, adult}, which might be relevant in talk on, for instance, income policy or delinquency.

MCDs also deliver a basis for making accountable inferences. Categories carry with them clusters of related features. Not all these features have the same relation to their category, nor do they have to be exclusively associated with only one category from a particular collection. Some features may be criterial or — in Jayyusi's terminology — *constitutive* for the determination of category membership. Others may be expectable or *category-bound*, as Sacks called it.[8] Yet the relevance of other features may have to be established in the discourse itself. The selection of a category or the assertion of category-bound or category-relevant features[9] allows for situated inferences with respect to the relevancy and applicability of other associated features.

Moreover, conversationalists may *negotiate* the relation a feature has to a category, as is demonstrated in the discussion of fragment (1a/b). Such negotiations may not only result in the exclusion of population members from a category. Jayyusi (1984) analyzes how discussion of categorization may also lead to phenomena such as the deletion of possible inferences, the transfer of attributes to other categories, the transition from one category to another one, or the methodical transformation of categories.

Sacks' work has given an initial impetus to a very promising kind of 'empirical semantics'; that is to say, to an analysis of the procedures that enable conversationalists to produce sense as a situated, methodically ordered and interactionally-based achievement.

In the remainder of this chapter we will try to show how Sacks' work is useful for the description and analysis of the methods by which members of a culture reason about, describe and constitute non-human objects — in this particular case some of the methodical ways through which caller and call-taker deliver a description of the trip the caller wants to make. We describe how negotiation takes place via the collaborative achievement of category transition by the 'scaling-up operation' (section 4) and by 'attribute transfer' (section 5).

4. CATEGORY TRANSITION BY THE 'SCALING-UP OPERATION'

As noted in the introduction, customer and employee have to agree upon a description that meets the wishes of the former and the possibilities of the latter. However, callers are not equally precise in describing their wishes. On some occasions a caller may have a precisely circumscribed idea of their holiday; on other occasions a caller may be less precise. Call-takers, on the other hand, may also be vague about what the agency has to offer, even if the caller is able to provide a precise characterization of a holiday. Therefore, one of the tasks of the participants is to achieve collaboratively a description that satisfies the interests of both parties.

In sections 4 and 5 we look at a negotiation in which the outcome is unclear. In the closing phases of the call the customer only promises to discuss the proposals made by the employee; she does not choose a particular holiday and we would not be surprised if this caller did not call back to the agency. However, somehow the 'unsuccessfulness' of the call yields rich material for the investigation of negotiations on categorizations — possibly precisely because of the problems customer and employee have to cope with in finding a description that satisfies *both* parties. We discuss how the agency employee deals with restrictions of the assortment of the travel organization in a case in which this particular assortment appears to be only partially compatible with the wishes of the caller.

In fragment (2a) the Sales woman asks a mother calling on behalf of her daughter where in Italy this daughter wants to go (line 108). The mother answers that her daughter has a preference for Venice and Florence (lines 110-111), and adds a formulation of a consequence of this preference: *so [..] it should be situated in the vicinity* (line 113). The Sales woman then translates this consequence by saying *then you get something on the Adriatic coast* (line 117):

(2a) [xdrecht/f/hm/ms] ((*mother calls on behalf of her daughter*))

```
108   A      and er where she- where in Italy did she want to go to:
             (...)
110   B      what she 's talking about mostly that is e:r
111   →      Venice and Florence. that's where she would like to go to.=
113          =so yes, ·hh ⌜ it should be situated in the vi ⌜ cinity er
114   A                  ⌊ it should be si-             ⌊ in the vicinity
115   B      ⌜⌜yes
116   A      ⌊⌊·hh yes: and then you get Florence
117   →      yes then you get something on the Adria:tic coa:st
118          (0.4)
119   B      yes
```

By translating the criterion 'in the vicinity of Venice and Florence' into 'something on the Adriatic coast', the Sales woman does not select a place between Venice and Florence; neither does she provide the name of a region between these two cities, nor the name of a region adjacent to one of these cities, nor, for that matter, the name of a region including one of them. Instead the possibilities are moved into a far more eccentric direction: to a non-adjacent zone geographically below and beside these cities. In other words, the destination of the travel is dislocated.

This dislocation is made possible by the addition *in the vicinity* the customer made to her description of the destination. The employee uses the resources provided by this particular way of describing, to interpret *in the vicinity* as a rather large vicinity: she 'scales up' the target region. We shall call this operation the 'scaling-up operation'.

However, a consequence of such an up-scaling is that the customer must be willing to 'stretch' her requirements in such a way that the offer of the agency is still compatible with them. It is not until the Sales woman refers to actual towns in the dislocated and scaled-up region that the customer starts to negotiate the acceptability of this dislocation. The following data extract shows this negotiation and the accounts the Sales woman gives. These accounts provide some indication about the possible rationality behind the scaling-up operation.

(2b) [xdrecht/f/hm/ms] *((call-taker has just retrieved some documentation material))*

```
168  A     e::r to: Italy. so that should
169  →     for instance Cattolica I'll just mention first:
170        a e::r:- ┌ a:-
170  B             └ yes but that's ra:ther far: from there
171        I belie ┌ ve
172  A             └ m:yes the nearest by: is the-
173  →     yes Ravennah, but there are no- ·hh yes
174  →     Rimini ┌ :      ┌ then is closest by: you know
175  B            └ (m    └ :)
176  A     ·h ┌ h              ┌ yes
177  B        └ really Rimini  └ :
178        (0.3)
179  A     Rimini: hh 'cause well you actually are e::r
```

Fragment (2b) opens with the mentioning of a city which is located about one hundred kilometres south of Ravenna, Cattolica[10] (line 169). When the caller subsequently makes the comment that this city is rather far from *there* (line 170), the Sales woman mentions Ravenna as a next possibility, a city which is slightly more concentric to the line Venice-Florence. However, she also immediately makes a remark from which one might infer that this is not an appropriate alternative (line 173 *but there are no-*).[11]

After the mentioning and the subsequent discarding of Ravenna, the Sales woman proposes a third alternative: *Rimini then is closest* (line 174). Rimini is still situated at a considerable distance from Florence as well as Venice and it is at least less concentric than Ravenna. Of the possibilities of the travel organization, however, this seems to be the best compromise which the Sales woman has to offer to meet the wishes of her customer.

Important for the present analysis is the conclusion that one of the obvious reasons why the Sales woman dislocates the travel destination is that this company does not seem to have a travel destination available which fits more concentrically. The necessity of dislocation might have motivated the scaling-up operation. By describing the domain within which the travel destination may be found with a category from a collection of terms for geographical entities of a much larger scale than the cities mentioned initially, the Sales woman has created an intermediate level by which the transition can be made to other collections of city-names which only a very benevolent observer would still call 'in the vicinity'. Through the extension of the search domain the Sales woman has created a latitude that allows for a possible overlap between the possibilities of the assortment of her agency with the preferences of the customer.

The employee is bound to the more or less 'absolute and categorical restrictions' of the assortment of the organization she works for. Within the borders of the current conversation, these restrictions constitute the more or less 'objective' limits of the proposals she is able to make to the prospect. In response to that, the wishes, preferences or demands of the customer are treated not only as 'subjective' criteria, but also as criteria that might be modified, adapted, extended or enlarged. The employee tries to create an overlap between the possibilities of the agency and the preferences of the customer by interpreting the categorization *in the vicinity* of the customer in such a way that it contains categories that satisfy both.

5. CATEGORY TRANSITION BY ATTRIBUTE TRANSFER

In the previous section we discussed one method by which the Sales woman achieves transition to another category. In this section we describe another method: the operation of *attribute transfer*.

In the conversation discussed in the previous paragraph the caller opens the talk by asking about a *brochure for coach trips to Italy* (cf. line 1 in fragment 3a):

(3a) [xdrecht/f/hm/ms] *((recording starts at this point))*

1	B→	·hh do you have a: brochure for coach trips to Italy and
2		then: it should be the tee tee (.) travels. is that possible
3		(0.8)
4	A	tee tee
5		(1.4)
6		and what- what should that stand for as abbreviation.

Within an extended repair sequence that is occasioned by troubles with the identifiability of the particular travel brochure (cf. lines 2 and 4-6 respectively in 3a), the employee asks what kind of trip the caller wants to go on (cf. line 30 in 3b):

(3b)[xdrecht/f/hm/ms]

```
30   A→ 'cause what kind of trip did you want to go: ⌈ on
31   B                                             ⌊ hh=
32        =well it (act) is essentially actually
33   →   a teenager tri:p( ⌈ b:)      ⌈ =and: e:r ⌈ (to Ita-)
34   A                    ⌊ yes ·h= ⌊          ⌊ I do have:
35        very nice travel brochures for teenagers:
```

In response to and consistent with the employee's question, the customer now modifies the description of the object she is interested in from a *brochure for coach trips to Italy* to a *teenager trip*.[12] The questioner reacts to this answer by confirming that 'she' (*I*, not *we*) has *very nice travel brochures for teenagers*. Thereby she not only continues to make 'travel brochures' the current topic of the talk,[13] she also modifies the description of the object the caller inquires about in two ways:

(i)   from *trip* to *travel brochure* ('reis' to 'reisgids' line 33-35);
(ii)   from *teenager trip* to *very nice travel brochure for teenagers* ('jongerenreis' to 'hele leuke reisgids voor jongeren').[14]

The way the original modifier 'teenager' is reformulated (from *teenager trip* to *travel brochures for teenagers*) affects the status that is assigned to this specification. At least in Dutch, a speaker has the possibility to build a compound noun construction such as 'teenager travel brochure' (*'jongerenreisgids'*). However, the Sales woman does not use this possibility. Instead she postpones the 'teenager'-part of the description, presenting it as a subsequent prepositional noun phrase. As a consequence the descriptor *teenagers* is deprived of the functional equivocality it would have had in the description 'teenager travel brochure'. In the latter case 'teenagers' would not only specify the class of intended recipients of the brochure, but also the agent of the travels. In a description such as *travel brochure for teenagers* the 'agent' aspect of the meaning of *teenagers* not only has disappeared, but the class of intended recipients is now specified *after* having described the type of the brochure.

This difference might be relevant. When a speaker describes an object through a series of three nouns,[15] the speaker still categorizes the object as an exemplar of a 'type' that is constituted through the ordered collocation of these three descriptors. By decoupling the specifier 'teenager' from the ordered series of 'type descriptors' and moving it to a postponed prepositional phrase the Sales woman removes the type-constitutive force of this category. She somehow downgrades its descriptive power to a mere description of the group of intended recipients. Instead of a *category-constitutive feature* of travel brochures the property 'addressed to teenagers' is presented as a *category-relevant* feature of this class of brochures.

These kinds of subtle modifications are not as irrelevant as they may appear to be at first glance. On the contrary, a large part of the negotiations customer and Sales persons accomplish exist out of such 'minor' changes in the description. Through these changes the caller and call-taker may arrive at an acceptable characterization of the travel arrangements. The description itself is assembled out of several categories or descriptors and, in the course of the interaction, is changed by substitution, modification, or changes in the hierarchy of its parts. Each party not only makes a particular, specifiable contribution to the accomplishment of such modifications; each party also appears to play a specific role in the particular modification.

But the Sales woman not only has to find out which categories are essential for or constitutive of the wishes of the customer. When she has discovered them she may also try to adapt them to the possibilities the agency has in its assortment. That is to say, she has to change the categories the customer uses into other, somehow related, categories. One of the ways she may accomplish this is by first determining which attributes of a category are the most relevant for the customer. She then may try to find another category (or a combination of other categories) that fits the relevant attributes of the category used by the caller in such a way that there is some form of reasonable overlap of the attributes of both categories. The overlap of attributes then allows for the transition to the new category.

In the following fragment, later in the talk, the Sales woman proposes a shift in categories and accounts for this shift by informing her co-conversationalist of the transferability of the relevant category-attributes:

(4) [xdrecht/f/hm/ms]

```
65  A→ but: e:r it should specifically be a teenager trip,
66       'cause you ⌈ know it-                        ⌈ often is:.
67  B                ⌊ well: that 's not necessary e:r ⌊ (fe- )
68  A   when you go for example to Italy
```

```
69  →    and ┌ you just take a e:r shuttle ((trip:))=you know
70  B        └ yes,
71  A    so that me ┌ ans ·hh e:r the transport back and forth:
72  B              └ yes:
73  A→   and over the:re e:r accommoda:tion either an apartment
74       or a hotel: ·h ┌ h you know then: there will be of course also
75  B                   └ yes,
76  A    a lot of young people am ┌ o:ngst ((them)) of course right?=
77  B                             └ ye:s
78  B→ ┌ =so that ┌ doesn't make any difference
79  A  └ ·hh     └ ri:ght so those real ·hh you know where you do have
80  →    more older people joining eh that are
81       those e:r excursion trips ┌ you know which ev- ·hh
82  B                              └ yes,
```

In line 65 the Sales woman asks the customer whether it 'specifically' has to be a *teenager trip*. Here the modifying category *teenager* is brought up for discussion.[16] The customer answers with *well: that's not necessary e:r* (line 67). Thus the customer — possibly reluctantly — accepts the Sales woman's discussion of the category. The Sales woman subsequently reformulates the category 'teenager trip', which was used by the customer, by proposing two new categories in combination: *a shuttle ((trip))* and *accommodation* (lines 69 and 73, respectively).[17] She then tells her customer that there *of course* will be 'a lot of young people' amongst the travellers on a trip characterized by such a combination (lines 74-76).

In fact the Sales woman takes the attribute *young travellers* of the category *teenager* and replaces the category with two categories in combination. She then accounts for this substitution by mentioning a feature that overlaps with the specifying category of the description 'teenager trip'. This overlap of attributes thus allows for and is presented as accounting for the transition to the alternative categories. In the present case this transition seems to be successful. The customer herself formulates a consequence of this shift of categories: *so that doesn't make any difference* (line 78). She thereby appears to accept the transition.

It is remarkable that the attribute 'young travellers' here is reduced in status, as was the case with the shift in the description of 'teenager trip' to 'travel brochure for teenagers'. In both cases the attributes are changed from defining, constitutive attributes, to relevant, self-evident, but nevertheless non-defining, non-constitutive properties. We shall call this type of modification *reduction of attribute status*. In this conversation the off-record reduction of attribute status seems to facilitate the transition to an other category.

It is worth noting that the Sales woman gives yet another account for the plausibility of the category transition she accomplishes. She contrasts the list of new categories ('shuttle' and 'accommodation') with the category 'excursion trips' by opposing the attribute 'young travellers' of the 'shuttle-and-accommodation' trip to the attribute 'older travellers' of the category 'excursion trips' (lines 79-81).[18] By this contrast the Sales woman seems to give her combination of new categories a higher 'value'. She suggests preference for this product by contrasting it with a product the customer definitely does not want. Thus, the transition to another description of the object the customer is interested in is at least doubly accounted for.

6. CONSISTENCY OF CATEGORY LEVEL

Thus far we have described two methods by which category transition is achieved in our material. We return now to Sacks' work on categorization (see section 3) and propose an extension of his consistency rule.

In the interaction of fragment 2a (see section 4) it is remarkable that both customer and employee immediately agree that the residence of the daughter should not be located in Venice or Florence itself, but in the vicinity of these cities. There are obviously reasons known to both of them — though not necessarily identical for both — why a stay in these cities is not negotiable. Indeed, later in the exchange the Sales woman says something from which one could infer one of the reasons why this is so:
(5) [xdrecht/f/hm/ms]

```
180  A→   Venice is way up in the North. over there you have
181        excursions organized which go there=
182  B    =y ⌈ es,
183  A       ⌊ hh you know i- but then: it still is:-
184        she really wants to go to there more o:ften. or not
185        (0.7)
186  B    w ⌈ ell:
187  A→      ⌊ 'cause there are of course no holidays in-
188     →   at ⌈ least no e:r ⌈ trips to you know
188  B →       ⌊ (n:)noh.    ⌊ no: I know that no
189        (.)
190  B    no: but she likes to-
191        yes, well, have seen it once
```

In line 187 the agency employee mentions as a reason for the exclusion of Venice as a possible residence, that *there are of course no holidays* in this particular city. She subsequently corrects herself and substitutes *holidays* by *trips* (line 188). 'Holiday' somehow seems to be a more encompassing category than 'trip'. It might be used in a more general sense so that it also may refer to activities called 'trip' elsewhere. Nevertheless, in the present context the Sales woman prefers the category 'trip'. She thereby seems to allude to the possibility that people surely may have their 'holidays' in Venice, but that 'there are no trips' — in her organization — to this city. So 'trip' is used in a situated, institution-bound sense, whereas 'holidays', contrastively and retrospectively, is redefined as either referring to self-organized trips or trips organized by other organizations than the current one.

In this case at least one of the reasons why Venice is excluded as a relevant destination seems to be its non-availability in this travel agency's assortment of travel-destinations. Moreover, both participants appear to know this — as is clear from the response the caller gives: *no I know that* (line 188). This might explain why the caller also presupposes and accepts the transition to somewhere in the vicinity of these cities.

There might yet be another principle of ordered social reasoning which plays a role in the self-evidence with which Venice or Florence are excluded as candidate residences. Sacks has formulated a powerful and insightful rule which participants orient to in selecting categories: the *consistency rule*. It states: 'if you can hear a second category as coming from the same device as the first, than hear it that way' (cf. Sacks 1972a).

Conversationalists do orient to such a principle, both while selecting categories and while interpreting them. For instance, the fact that the Sales woman in the fragments discussed in section 2 eventually returns to the selection of city names to characterize candidate destinations might be the result of an orientation to the consistency rule (cf. Cattolica, Ravenna and Rimini in fragment 2b). After the customer's first characterization of the destination through city names the employee also selects members of collections of city names to describe candidate-destinations. She does not propose names from, for example, collections of region names, tourist beaches or apartment complexes. Which categories are treated as a collection, or what is oriented to as a categorization device, may be sensitive to the task-oriented interactional work of the conversationalists.

However, besides orienting to a consistency-rule that operates on separate devices, participants also seem to orient to consistency principles that operate *across* collections of different devices. One may conclude this from the way this customer initially describes the trip she is interested in:

(3a) [xdrecht/f/hm/ms] *((detail))*

1   B → ·hh do you have a: brochure of coach trips to Italy

(3b) [xdrecht/f/hm/ms] *((detail, simplified))*
    32 B   =well it (act) is essentially actually
    33 →   a teenager tri:p(b:) (...) and: e:r (to Ita-)

The caller not only informs the call-taker that she wants to go to Italy, but also that she wants to go by *bus* (line 1, (3a)) and that it should be a *teenager trip* (line 33 in (3b)). Through the use of these latter two categories, the customer has not only provided a complex description of her demand (a *teenager trip/by bus/to Italy*), she has also provided information that allows for category-bound inferences to be made. The category 'teenager trip' not only specifies the class of agents of that type of travel, but also has as a category-relevant — perhaps even category-constitutive — feature that it is inexpensive. Also the assertion of the choice of a bus trip excludes more expensive ways of transport. So, in the present setting the inference might be that this customer requires a trip that is cheap.

Hence, in the assemblage of the description of the desired type of trip, the customer is also consistent in the categories she selects from different collections. All these categories share the feature that they are relatively cheap alternatives compared to the other options that might make up the co-selected, relevant other collections.

Relative to the task at hand the relevant collections may be partially ordered with respect to task-relevant properties; such as, in this case, an ordering with respect to the price dimension. Selections of several categories from different collections that together accomplish a specific task — such as the description of a trip — may be governed partially by a consistency principle that operates across these collections. Each particular category selected from one of the relevant collections has to share or somehow has to be compatible with the feature that also governs the selection of the categories from the other relevant collections. We shall provisionally call this mechanism the *principle of level consistency.*[19]

The principle of level consistency might be one of the rationalities behind the self-evidence with which a 'holiday' in Venice itself is excluded (cf. fragment (5)). That kind of holiday is usually rather expensive and does not fit with the level constraints that are implied by the categories the customer has chosen to describe her trip.

The principle might also explain how this customer is persuaded to consider 'regular' trips instead of 'teenager trips'. In the phase of the call in which employee and customer accomplish the transfer of attributes from teenager trips to regular trips (see section 3), the employee also says that the customer could take another, *regular* travel brochure *for the same money* (lines 81a-5 and 87):

(6) [xdrecht/f/hm/ms]

```
81a A→ ·h b ⌈ ut for the same money- you can
82  B         ⌊ yes,
83  A    also say well I take an other travel brochure=
84       =which maybe does have something nice of Italy
85       in it ·hh ⌈ a:nd
85  B              ⌊ (yes)
86       (0.3)
87  A    from a regular travel brochure,
88       (0.2)
89  B    yes, yes, yes,
```

The expression 'for the same money' is equivocal in Dutch in that it could mean 'for the same price' as well as the more general 'it makes no difference'. Although it is mostly used in its non-literal, 'metaphorical' sense, in this context it could also be heard literally. In the literal sense it may imply that the shift to 'regular trips' has no or almost no financial consequences. Part of the method through which the employee accomplishes the shift from 'teenager' to 'regular' trips is via the assertion of level consistency with respect to the price dimension. It is said or at least implied that this feature will not change as a consequence of the transition to the other category.

The principle of level consistency appears to be a more global, cross-sectional device by which the negotiations in sales talk are governed. We think that it might play a substantial role in the negotiation of category transformations and the transfer of attributes to other categories.

7. CONCLUSION

In this chapter we have attempted to show how negotiations between a travel agency employee and her customer are, at least partially, realised by categorization work. What seems to be clear from our analysis is that participants, by subtly negotiating categories, collaboratively try to arrive at descriptions — and thus holiday bookings — that satisfy both parties.

We attempted to demonstrate the 'scaling-up' operation and the operation of 'attribute transfer', two methods by which employee and customer collaboratively achieved transition from one category to another and thereby negotiated a description that could satisfy the wishes of the customer and the possibilities of the employee. We described how the Sales woman tried to dislocate the customer's destination in order to be able to offer her a trip. To be able to realize this dislocation, the Sales woman had to 'scale up' the target region of the customer's destination. By means of the scaling-up operation the Sales woman could realise the transition to another category out of the collection of city names.

With the operation of attribute transfer we described how the Sales woman convinced the customer that she might as well take a 'shuttle-trip with accommodation' instead of a 'teenager-trip' because both categories have the attribute 'young people'. Here the overlap of attributes allowed for the transition to the other categories. We also noticed that in the sales person's description the status of the attribute was reduced from category-constitutive to category-relevant. It might very well be that this reduction of attribute status facilitates the transition to the other category.

In the final part of the chapter we proposed an extension of Sacks' 'consistency rule': the 'principle of level consistency'. This principle seems to be a more global, cross-sectional device restricting and governing the margins of the negotiations. In the negotiations we described the participants seemed to orient to the restriction that the holiday had to be relatively cheap.

The principle of level consistency also confirms a very central observation Sacks (1972b) has made: members organize knowledge in a 'categorically localized' way. They orient to the position a category occupies in task-ordered collections as an aspect of the meaning of that category.

Future research needs to examine how and in what way a description, which is agreed upon by both participants, is connected to the successfulness of the negotiation as a whole: whether a deal is agreed upon which satisfies both parties. It might also be interesting to study categorization work in other contexts and to examine which methods participants use there; because the methods we discovered in our material of travel agencies are task-related and context-bound, it may very well be that participants in other contexts orient to specific other methods.

NOTES

1. Our data consist of transcriptions of 8 unsolicited telephone calls to a travel agency. The recordings were made by employees of the travel organization itself in three branches in three different Dutch cities. The aim of the recordings was to obtain materials for an internal examination of the effectiveness of telephone calls with customers. The call-takers knew their conversation was recorded; the customers were not informed of this.

Five of the transcribed conversations lasted between 5 and 10 minutes; the other three were relatively short (between 1 and 3 minutes). Not only because of the restricted size of our corpus, but also because of the limited time we had to prepare the current chapter, our analysis has to be regarded as a preliminary exploration of the richness of this kind of material.

2. The appendix contains the original Dutch versions of the transcripts.

3. One may ask how it is possible that the employee at one moment asks how old 'the children' are and thus is able to refer unproblematically to such a group of persons, whereas a few moments later she declares that one of the individuals so characterized cannot be classified as such. Obviously the same categories may be used with different senses on different occasions, or, to be more precise, these categories are submitted to different rules of application on different occasions. Moreover, not only the ways in which a selection of a specific sense is accomplished, but also how such a variation in selection methods is accounted for, may vary across occasions.

Also noticeable in this particular case is the fact that the sales woman does not say anything about the three year old child. The functional account she gives for the eight year old children might not hold for this child. Without discussing this type of child she simply concludes that her client has to pay full amounts for all members of the group (cf. lines 228-30). The client does not object to this.

4. Cf. Wygotski's distinction between 'functional' and 'scientific' concepts (Wygotski 1969:119 ff.).

5. Price announcements may constitute distinctive sequential slots in sales talk. Pinch and Clark (1986:171ff.) e.g., describe how price announcements constitute 'Sales Relevance Places' in the sales routines of market pitchers. That is to say, in this type of sales talk they establish a point where buying actions occur.

6. Differences in the distribution of rights to apply categories in specific, situated ways also account for the use of 'institutional' participant categories such as 'customer' and 'Sales woman'. These characterizations appear to be 'procedurally consequential' in the present context (cf. Schegloff 1991). For example, the fact that the call-taker speaks of 'us' when she tells the caller that fifteen years old count as 'adults' in her organization (see line 223 in fragment (1b)) probably is not accidental. The call-taker stresses her membership of the organization that defines this distinction precisely on a point where the everyday and the institutional use of the category is distinguished.

7. Jayyusi gives the following 'relevance version' of the consistency rule: *If the hearable task or concern at hand can be fulfilled or accomplished by following a first category with a second drawn from the same device, then do so* (Jayyusi 1984:81).

8. Originally, Sacks (1972a) has described the relation of category-boundness only with respect to activities (category-bound activities). Jayyusi (1984:35ff.) proposes an extension to category-bound *features*.

9. The distinction between category-*relevant* and category-*constitutive features* is also based on Jayyusi (1984).

10. Cattolica is at least 200 kilometres south of Venice and about 150 south-east of Florence.

11. The fact that call taker does not finish the comment in line 173, but withdraws its completion before she has explicitly said that 'there are no trips to Ravenna' is probably a methodically motivated withdrawal. 'There are no trips to Ravenna' would have meant that her firm does not cater for trips to Ravenna. The call-taker might avoid the delivery of information that would allow for the making of inferences pertaining to restrictions or deficiencies of the company she represents.

12. In the original Dutch version the participants use the word 'jongeren' which is etymologically related to the English 'youngsters'. However, in Dutch 'jongeren' is normally used to refer to adolescents and young people up to twenty or twenty-five years. 'Teenagers' might thus be a partially appropriate equivalent.

13. This persistence in making the 'travel brochure' the primary topic might be encouraged by an equivocality in the talk of the caller. In line 33 it is unclear whether the caller only says 'teenager trip', or that the '*g*' that follows 'trip' is the initial consonant of the Dutch word for 'brochure' ('*gids*'). In the latter case the caller might have been providing a kind of 'leakage'-self-correction (cf. Jefferson 1987): without actually saying 'teenager trip *brochure*' she gives a cue that might work as a kind of recognition point of the planned-but-observably-withdrawn delivery of the noun for 'brochure'.

14. The modification from *trip* to *travel brochure* ('reis' to 'reisgids', ln.33-34a), is a change from a:
　　(i) [single noun] to a [noun + noun] format.
Whereas the modification from *teenager trip* to *very nice travel brochure for teenagers* ('jongerenreis' to 'hele leuke reisgids voor jongeren') goes from a:
　　(ii) [noun + noun] format to the format [[adjective + [noun + noun]] + prepositional noun phrase].
The reason for the second transformation could in part be semantical-grammatical. By the first transformation the single noun *travel* is assigned the function of a subject specifying description of the class of objects described in the newly added head noun:
　　(ia) from *trip* to *travel brochure*:
　　from an [activity describing noun^1] format to a [subject specifying noun^1 + class noun^2] format (identical indexes indicate identity of the lexeme used).
The new primary specifier *travel* pushes away the original agent-specifying noun *teenager*:
　　(iia) from *teenager trip* to *travel brochure for teenagers*:
　　from an [agent-type specifying noun^3 + class noun^1] format to a subject specifying noun^1 + class noun^4 + class of recipients specifying prepositional noun^3 phrase] format.
　　The rationale behind this kind of displacement probably is that in the case of multiple pre-specification of nouns describing reading material (such as 'brochure') the subject-describing specifier usually requires the position of primary specifier (thereby downgrading the position-possibilities of the other competing specifications). 'Travel teenager brochure' sounds strange, whereas 'teenager travel brochure' seems to be more natural from a common sense perspective.

Note also that when the category *teenager* specifies *trip* it is characterizing teenagers as the agents of the activity formulated in the head; however, when *teenager* specifies *travel brochures*, it rather seems to characterize the target group of the brochure. So depending on which category is made the head of the description, the feature 'teenager' is 'transformed' with respect to its semantical-functional status/implications. With a variation on the notion 'category-transformable features' as developed by Jayyusi (1984:107ff.), one could call this kind of changes in 'sense' 'category-dependent transformation of features'.

15. In such a series of three nouns the first functions as a kind of secondary specifier, the second as the primary specifier and the third as the head that describes the set of objects of which the foregoing specifiers cumulatively delineate a more restricted subset. Starting 'backwards' from the head, each following specifier delineates a smaller subset of the subset delineated by the foregoing specifier.

16. Note that in the question 'does it *specifically* have to be a *teenager* trip' (lines 65-66), the questioner makes the specifying category *teenager* the problematic item by such procedures as the use of the adverb 'specifically' and the contrastive stress on *teenager*.

17. The Sales woman proposes these two new categories *shuttle trip* and *accommodation* in the format of a short two-part list ('and you just take a shuttle trip, you know, that means the transport back and forth and over there accommodation, either an apartment or a hotel', lines 69-74). The receptionist clarifies each item of this list by the embedding of either an explanation of the meaning of the previous item, or the specification of the alternatives contained in the collection indicated by the device category. Such 'multiple embedding' of item within item not only seems to work as 'practical translations' of the categories proposed by the Sales woman (cf. Jayyusi 1984:96ff.); as a translation it might also have a function in the interactional constitution of an expert/lay-relationship between called and calling participant. By observably taking a 'didacticizing' stand to the terminology she uses the Sales woman displays herself as the 'insider', the one who knows what these expressions amount to. Meanwhile she puts the caller in the complementary position of an outsider to whom these terms presumably are not familiar.

18. Cf. Atkinson (1984:73ff.) for the use of contrasts.

19. The principle of level consistency might be oriented to as a *'preference* for level consistency' if preference organization is regarded as a ranking order of a set of more or less preferred alternatives. In fragment (6) we encounter an indication that the principle of level consistency works as a kind of preference organization. There the travel agency employee has to do extra 'work' to accomplish the transition to a possibly less preferred alternative (cf. line 81a). However, because more work has to be done before the difficult concept of 'preference' can be appropriately used to characterize the current mechanism, we prefer the more neutral and more cautious notion of 'principle'.

Note also that the principle of level consistency might be seen set-theoretically as the intersection of all these subsets of categories from the relevant collections that are oriented to, and may be seen as falling within the constraints of the level that might be inferred from the participants' selections of categories.

APPENDIX

Original Dutch versions of the transcripts

(1a) [lstraat/a/hm]

```
176   A         no ⌐ u als ik de prijs ga uitreken ⌐ e (.) vijfhonderd
177   B            └ m:↑m                          └ m:↑m:
178   A         vijfentachtig maal elf ⌐ :
179   B                                └ m:↑m
180             (0.3)
181   A         da ⌐ t is dan::
182   B            └ (°en-)
183   A         zesduizend vierhonderd vijfendertig gul↑deh=
184   B →       =ehj↑ah ·h >en voor de kinder↑eh
185             (0.5)
186   B →       zeg maar eh- >want is 'r kinderkorting< bij °of zo↑:°
187             (0.2)
188   A         bij appartementsrei:zen ↓niet ↓nee:
189             (.)
190   B         o:h °j ⌐ ah.°
191   A →              └ (a:) kinderkorting geldt alleen twe↑e tot en
192   A         met zes jaar twintig procent bij hotel:↓rei:zeh
193             (0.2)
194   B         o: ⌐ h jah
195   A            └ maar: >appartementreize nie↓:t
196             (0.5)
197   B         °o↓:°
```

(1b) [lstraat/a/hm]

```
188   A         bij appartementsrei:zen ↓niet ↓nee:
189             (.)
190   B         o:h °j ⌐ ah.°
191   A →              └ (a:) kinderkorting geldt alleen twe↑e tot en
192   A         met zes jaar twintig procent bij hotel:↓rei:zeh
```

```
193            (0.2)
194   B        o: ⌈h jah
195   A           ⌊ ma̲ar: >appartementr̲eize nie↓:t
196            (0.5)
197   B        o↓:
198   A        hoe o̲ud zijn de ki̲nder ⌈↑eh ⌈op vertrekdat ⌈↑um
199   B                                 ⌊ e:  ⌊:h            ⌊eve kijken.
200            d'r zijn: dri̲e kindere van a̲cht ja↑ar: d'rbi̲j↑:
201            (0.2)
202   A        acht jaar ⌈: °jah,°
203   B                  ⌊j:↑ah, ·hh en e::h d'r is ée̲n van e::h
204            even kijkeh ↓hoor van e:h ongeveer dri̲e ja̲ar: d'rbi̲j↑:
205            (0.2)
206   A        j:↑ah
207            (0.3)
208   B        en ée̲n van: e:h >↓vi̲jftien,
209            (0.4)
210   A        j:a̲h, ·hh
211            (1.2)
212   →        nee. (0.2) da̲ar e::h zit he̲lahasheh ghee̲hn
213   →        kinderkorting meer bi̲j. .h ⌈h >a̲cht jaar hebbe
214   B                                    ⌊°oo:ah.°
215   A        sowieso 'n hele bu̲splaats no:dig,=
216   B        =°ja↑:°↓j ⌈ah
217   A   →              ⌊(en)> die ku̲nne niet bij elkaar e::h
218            >bevoobeeld twee sto̲eleh- .hh >of ée̲n stoel
219            en dan twe̲e kindere d'r ↑op
220            (.)
221   B        °ja ⌈:jah,°
222   A   →        ⌊.hHH (.) en: eh >vijftien jaar
223            is 'n volwa̲ssen iemand bij↓ons:
224            (.)
225   B        o:h jah °ja° ja̲h natu̲urlijk.
226            ne̲e dat is: eh inderda̲ah:d ↓zhoh heh·hi:hh
227            ↓jah °>dat is: inderdaad z ⌈o.°<
228   A                                   ⌊dus u krijgt e̲cht e̲lf keer
229            ij̲fhonderde:h ⌈vijfenta̲chtig gul↑deh ·h ⌈h
230   B                      ⌊vijfenta̲chtig guldeh      ⌊m↑m
```

(2a) [xdrecht/f/hm/ms]

108	A	→	en eh waar ze- waar in Italië wilde ze naar toe gaan:
			(...)
110	B		>waar ze 't meest over heeft dat is e:h
111		→	Venetië en Florence. daar wil ze graag naar toe.=
113			=dus jah, ·hh ⌈ 't zou daar in de bu ⌈ urt eh moete
114	A		⌊ 't moet dar- ⌊ in de buu:rt moete
115	B		zij↓:n: jah
116	A		zijn: °·hh ja:° en >dan krijg je Florence
117		→	>jah dan krijg je iets aan de adra:tische ku↑:st
118			(0.4)
119	B		jah,

(2b) [xdrecht/f/hm/ms]

168	A		e::h naar: >Italië. °dat moest dus°
169		→	>bevoorbeeld Cattolica< ↓ik noem zo maar eerst even:
170			'n e::h:- ⌈ °'n:-°
170	B		⌊ ja maar dat ligt daar vrij: ↑ver: vandaan:
171			↓>geloof ⌈ ik
172	A		⌊ m:jah 't dichtste bij: is de-
173		→	↑jah Ravennah, maar daar worden geen- ·hh jah
174		→	Rimi↑ni ⌈ : ⌈ is dan 't dichtste bij: ↑hè
175	B		⌊ (°m↑° ⌊ :)
176	A		·h ⌈ h ⌈ jah
177	B		⌊ toch Rimini ⌊ :
178			(0.3)
179	A		Rimini: ·hh want jah je zit dus eigelijk e::h

(3a) [xdrecht/f/hm/ms]

1	B	→	·hh heeft u ook 'n: >gids van busreizen naar Italië
2			>en dan:< moet 't zijn de tee tee (.) reizeh. kan ↑dat
3			(0.8)
4	A		tee TE↑e
5			(1.4)
6			en wat- wat moet dat z↑ijn voor ↑afkorting.

(3b) [xdrecht/f/hm/ms]

```
30   A        >want wat voor soort reis wilde u ma:k ⌈eh
31   B                                              ⌊·hh=
32            =nou 't gaat (aan) principe eigenlijk om
33   →        'n jongerenreisz:( ⌈g:)      ⌈=en: e:h ⌈(°naar Ita-°)
34   A                          ⌊jaↄ.h= ⌊          ⌊'k heb wel:
35            hele leuke reisgidseh voor jongereh:,
```

(4) [xdrecht/f/hm/ms]

```
65   A   →   maar: >e:h< 't moete:h specↄiaal 'n jongerehreis
66           zijn, want w ⌈eet je wat 't wel:-      ⌈>vaak is:.
67   B                    ⌊nou: >dat hoeft niet e:h ⌊fe- )
68   A       als je bijvoorbeeld naar Italië gaat
69   →       en ⌈u neemt gewoon 'n e:h pendelre↓is:=hè
70   B          ⌊ah,
71   A       dus dat be ⌈tekent ·hh e:h 't vervoer heen en trug:.
72   B                  ⌊jaↄ.h
73   A   →   en daar: e:h accomoda:tie >hetzij 'n appartement
74           of 'n hotel: ·h ⌈h hè dan: >zit daar dus natuurlijk
75   B                       ⌊jah,
76   A       ook veel jongelui daar ⌈tusse:h ↓natuurlijk hè=
77   B                              ⌊ja: wel:
78   →       ⌈=dus dat ⌈maakt nie uit
79   A       ⌊·hh     ⌊hè: dus die echte ·hh e:h weetje waar je
80   →       dus meer oudereh mense meehebt. eh dat zijn dus
81           die e:h >excursiereizeh< ⌈hè die dus el- ·hh
82   B                                ⌊jah,
```

(5) [xdrecht/f/hm/ms]

```
180  A   →   >Venetië is helemaal in 't noordeh. daar worden
181          wel: excursies dan: naar toe gemaaↄ:kth=
182  B       =j ⌈ah,
183  A          ⌊·hh hè i- >maar dan:< is nog wel:-
184          >ze wil 'r echt ↑va:ker toe. °of nie↓:t°
185          (0.7)
```

```
186   B         n ┌ou:
187   A    →      └want daar zijn natuulijk geen vakanties na-
188        →    >°ten° ┌ minste geen e:h ┌ reizeh naar toe ↑hè
188   B    →           └(°n:)neeh.°      └nee: >dat weet ik. nee.
189             (.)
190             nee: maar >ze wil dat-
191             jah, >toch wel 'n keer gezien hebbeh
```

(6) [xdrecht/f/hm/ms]

```
81a   A    →   ·hh >ma ┌ ar voor 't zelfde geld- kunt
82    B              └ ah,
83    A        u ook zeggeh nou ik neem 'n andereh reisgids=
84             =>waar misschien< wel iets leuks van Italië
85             insta↓at ·hh ┌ en:
85    B                     └ (°jah°)
86             (0.3)
87    A        uit 'n gewoneh reisgids,
88             (0.2)
89    B        jah, jah, jah,
```

CHAPTER 12

NEGOTIATING TERMS IN SOCIAL WELFARE OFFICE TALK

PER LINELL

ERIK FREDIN

1. INTRODUCTION

This chapter is concerned with the work of street-level bureaucrats in their dealings with clients seeking social welfare subsidies. It focuses on how people use language to handle problems of immediate concern to them, in the micropolitics of sorting out social problems (Maynard 1988) in dialogues between social workers and their clients at social welfare offices.[1] More generally, the chapter deals with what Zimmerman and Boden (1991) call "structure-in-action":

> Social structure, on this view, is not something 'out there' independent
> of members' activities, nor are the structures of social action located at
> the unobservable level of Durkheim's collective. Rather, they are the

---

This chapter is a revised version of a paper read at the conference "Negotiations in the Workplace", Aalborg, Denmark, May 11-13, 1992. Research was supported by grants from The Bank of Sweden Tercentenary Foundation (RJ 83/137 awarded to Karin Aronsson and Per Linell) and The Swedish Council for Social Research (B87/99:1 awarded to Erik Fredin). The data used were collected within another project conducted by Lars-Christer Hydén. We wish to thank Elisabet Cedersund, Alan Firth and Doug Maynard for comments on previous versions of the chapter.

practical accomplishments of members of society. Members can and must make their actions available and reasonable to each other and, in so doing, the everyday organization of experience *produces* and *reproduces* the patterned and patterning qualities we have come to call social structure. (Zimmerman and Boden 1991:19)

The more specific perspective to be adopted in this chapter is that of trying to view the discourse between professionals and clients at social welfare offices as a *negotiation of terms*. We ask: In what sense do the parties negotiate? Is the interaction an example of negotiating services and future commitments, and, if so, how is this accomplished?

2. THE CONCEPT OF NEGOTIATION

According to the Concise Oxford Dictionary, to negotiate is "to confer (with another) with view to compromise or agreement". It involves some sort of (usually verbal) interaction with the goal of reaching some kind of a deal. The original meaning of Latin *negotiari* (from *negotium* "not leisure", i.e. "business") had to do with the bartering and bargaining in the market-place. Later, the term has established usages in the realms of political or diplomatic negotiations, business negotiations (among companies), workplace and labour-market negotiations, etc. (see, e.g., Bell 1988).

We usually understand by 'negotiation' some sort of give-and-take process in interaction. Some things are, at least perfunctorily, put at stake, and the parties give, take, or withhold information, bids, and offers of various kinds. Negotiation theorists also stress that parties have opposed goals and interests; from this basis they engage in interaction to reach a mutually satisfactory outcome (e.g. Sawyer and Guetzkow 1965). The competition involved in negotiation takes place within the confines of a coordinated interaction involving reciprocities and mutualities. Of course, any kind of communicative interaction presupposes *reciprocity*, the exchange of actions with respect to one another (*do-ut-des*) (Schutz 1964). It is also reasonable to argue that various kinds of *mutualities* must obligatorily be present in communication (for a discussion of the concepts of reciprocity and mutuality, see Graumann 1994). But we are always faced with a web of *partial* mutualities in communication and negotiation; in the latter case, there might be a shared interest in reaching an agreement, but apart from this, as was just pointed out, parties most often have (at least partly) opposed, rather than shared, interests. Yet, at the same time, for negotiation to take place, there must be some kind of common ground, including a *mutually held* understanding that there are *differences* of interest. Beyond this, parties may entertain shared, complementary, or conflicting (perhaps even contradictory) goals. It is important to note, however, that reciprocity does not necessarily presuppose symmetry or equality (cf. Linell and Luckmann 1991). For example, the kinds of interactions we are going to investigate in this chapter do not involve equally strong parties; they differ in their abilities and opportunities to influence the interaction as such, as well as in their access to social power (status, authority, recourse to sanctions, etc.) (Fredin 1993).

If negotiation is defined as any kind of reciprocating exchange of actions leading (potentially) to some kind of outcome, the notion is so broad that it virtually covers any kind of verbal or nonverbal communication. Hence, there is a possible stance which amounts to saying that any conversation, or talk-in-interaction, includes a ubiquitous *dimension* of negotiation; this may then concern either participation framework (positions in the interaction as such, cf. Goffman 1981) or knowledge and understanding of matters talked about (topics, perspectives, interpretations, and labellings) (cf. Linell and Luckmann 1991). Another position is that the term 'negotiation' be confined to certain communicative *genres*, e.g. primarily political, business and labour-market negotiations. In this chapter, we will adopt something of a middle position, looking at negotiating interaction as a process and as an institutionalized activity in social welfare discourse. In our case, we will be concerned with a genre which is not negotiation in the everyday sense, and we would of course not argue that any strip of discourse in social welfare office talk (or in other kinds of conversation) is negotiation in any interesting sense. The term must have more substance than that; hence, we require some focus on, or thematization of, the relevant outcomes (services, esp. financial assistance on the part of the welfare organization, and commitments for future conduct on the part of the client), or on some major concepts or categories which are relevant in the process of approaching a solution to the problems which the encounter is concerned with. It seems quite obvious that ordinary social welfare office talk includes such moments, and interviews with the participants reveal that they do see parts of their interactions as (at least) resembling 'negotiations'.

3. SOCIAL WELFARE OFFICE TALK

In this chapter, we will not be concerned with discourse in social work at large, nor will we deal with the societal system for social services in general. Rather, we will be interested only in (some kinds of) conversations taking place in social welfare offices between social workers and clients who seek financial assistance. This business, where street-level bureaucrats meet with clients in their offices, is quite considerable in Sweden, and presumably in other Western countries too.[2] Our data are derived from a corpus of about twenty social worker-client interactions observed and tape-recorded in various districts in Stockholm in 1986-87. Information pertaining to the corpus, and analyses thereof, have been presented elsewhere (Hydén 1988, 1991, 1994; Fredin 1993).

At face value, it might be possible to conceive of the allocation of social welfare subsidies as a purely administrative business, as a matter of mechanically applying bureaucratic rules and norms to the various cases of client problems. However, if we care to look at the actual practices, we will find that there are many moments of negotiation involved, i.e. the outcomes are far from entirely clear at the outset (cf. Hydén 1991:1). There is often a negotiation of the exact amount of money to be given out, in many cases also whether certain kinds of subsidies can be offered or not at all, and research has shown that there is considerable variation among administrators in how, in practice, they cope with the (politically decided) norms for financial assistance (Hydén 1990).

However, there is more involved than variation in the content of agreements and outcomes. The process of bargaining involves negotiating the concepts that are being applied (e.g. Putnam and Holmer 1992), and "the processing of people" in e.g. social work has to do with labelling and categorizing clients and their circumstances (Prottas 1979). Such labellings build upon implicit (or sometimes explicit) moral categorizations. For example, if you do not have resources to support yourself economically, i.e. if you are poor, then there has been for a very long time in social work (e.g. from the English Poor Act Law of 1834) and still is a moral distinction between those who are "legitimately poor", e.g. due to illnesses or involuntary unemployment, and those who are "illegitimately poor", e.g. due to laziness or abuse (Hydén 1988, 1994). Some of the central practices of today's social agency work concerns the circumstances which have led to the social problems of the clients, and among the social workers' primary tasks are those of determining the legitimacy of the clients' demands and the credibility of their statements. Thus, Hydén (1988, 1991, 1994), in his studies of the discursive practices of Swedish social welfare agencies, claims that the level of financial aid (amounts of money) is often a rather peripheral topic, while the clients' moral characters remain central. Categories are no longer as openly moralistic as they used to be ("illegitimately poor"); rather, they are concealed by other linguistic usage (Cedersund 1992a,b). Modern welfare institutions, it would appear, prefer "veiled moralities" (Bergmann 1992).

We noted above that any negotiation builds upon a web of partial mutualities. For example, in social worker-client interaction, there are shared conceptions of responsibility for certain actions. Clients know and understand that they must fulfil certain requirements and commit themselves to certain future actions in order to qualify as recipients of assistance. The negotiation is partly concerned with the exact substance of these commitments. The clients also know that they are dependent on society, on its ultimately limited resources and on its norms for providing help, and they grant (at least in practice) social workers with rights, sometimes obligations, to make moral comments and challenges, and to classify demands as legitimate or not. And indeed, the social workers, for their part, usually take it for granted that they can freely do so. Yet these verbal exchanges between professionals and clients often develop into arguing from two different positions, the norms and categorizations of the social welfare and the rationalities of the clients' everyday life world (Maynard 1988; Cedersund 1992a,b). Similar perspectival conflicts have been observed and explored in many other professional-lay interactions, e.g. within health care (e.g. Mishler 1984; Beck and Ragan 1992) and judicial procedures (e.g. Linell and Jönsson 1991, on police interrogations).

4. NEGOTIATING CATEGORIES AND ARGUING FOR LEGITIMACY

In our data corpus, a fair number of different topics are dealt with (Fredin 1993). However, we will only be concerned here with matters that pertain to financial assistance. The clients who appear at the welfare offices claim to be eligible for assistance on several kinds of grounds. Many of those who are unemployed, can get no subsistence from the unions' unemployment funds; they therefore need financial support. One central issue is the reasons and causes behind their unemployment. In particular, the rules state that no regular assistance can be gained if one is not actively seeking a job, which means, in practice, that one has to register regularly at the public employment agency. Whether this condition is actually met in the individual case is a point of dispute in some of the talks.

One part of the economic aid is specifically intended to cover (parts of) the clients' costs for housing (rent). This then presupposes that the individual client either owns a house, for which (s)he cannot carry all costs (this case, however, does not occur in our corpus), or (s)he must have a valid rent contract with a landlord. In many cases, clients do not unequivocally meet this requirement, which gives rise to negotiations about how to understand and label their particular circumstances. In this chapter we will select a few interactional episodes in which these two different points concerning legimacy of demands and eligibility for social welfare, i.e. the points having to do with active job seeking and genuine costs for housing under valid contracts, are disputed and negotiated.

Most institutional discourses can be analytically divided into 'phases' with different goals and interactional patterns (Agar 1985); this applies to lessons in school, police interrogations (e.g. Linell and Jönsson 1991), business negotiations (Firth 1991, this volume), etc. An ordinary encounter between a social worker and a client at the agency can also be seen as structured in a few major phases of interaction. First, there is a (usually fairly long) sequence, in which the client presents his or her problems, the social worker collects certain personal data and probes the circumstances forming the background of the problems, and this leads to specifications and negotiations between the two parties. The excerpts to be discussed here are drawn from this 'diagnosing phase' (cf. Agar 1985). This is usually followed by another 'phase', in which the social worker formulates a decision and calculates sums. In some cases, the latter episodes involve more negotiations between the parties, and sometimes no decision can be taken during the encounter itself. After the 'decision phase' there is often some talk on practical matters, such as how to make payments and when (if at all) to have the next meeting between the two. In some encounters, the boundaries between phases are naturally rather blurred.

Let us now turn to our first example. It is drawn from a meeting between S(andra), a 33-year-old social worker, and C(lara), a 20-year-old client, who claims that she needs economic help. It turns out that that it is not altogether clear how to describe her terms of tenancy:[3]

(1) (Tema K: E100:63-76)

63   S   eh as a boarder you have a norm of subsistence of 2170 kronor every month (C: mhm) and that is based on the calculations of the national consumers' institute of what it costs to live and (C: mhm) within this subsistence you should eat, buy clothes, pay electricity bills (C: oh) such like

64   C   because the thing is that it depends on what you call boarder, this is, you know, a collective that I live in (S: yes) and it is a five-room flat, we are five people (S:mm), it is only one, so far not me who is on the contract (S: mm) but since I am on the big contract then it is no longer boarding but it is then a second-hand re- (S:mm) well, what do you say (S: mm) I don't know if there is any difference among them=

65   S   =no, subsistence for a single-living person who lives single in the flat (C: mm) is 2260 kronor per month (S: mm) and if you share food as well

66   C   but you see we don't share food ⌈ but

67   S   ⌊ no but if you share food and live in a family then you get 1840 kronor (C: mm) 'cause then you expect it to be cheaper with grocery shopping (C: mm) and laundry and such like (C: mm) and for you it will be 2170 (C: oh) and then you have

68   C   even if as a matter of fact I live in principle alone only that it is a

bigger flat 'cause we have, you know, separate households

69 S yeah, how do you do with electricity bills and such like

70 C eh electricity we share but no food and nothing such but it it is included in the rent, it (S: mm) telephone we share

71 S mm lemme see, well it is still that norm which is valid then because since you share such things you get it a little cheaper

72 C yes but we don't get it cheaper, food and such

73 S yes but telephone no, but it is just reduced by 90 kronor

73a C ⌈⌈yes about

73b S ⌊⌊it should cover electricity and telephone 'cause the telephone only costs a subscription, ⌈you have no telephone of your own?

73c C   ⌊yes exactly

74 C no I haven't (S: no) that we share

75 S mm and then you add the rent then to this then, 750 kronor, do you have any tenant's contract or piece ⌈of paper on what you pay

76 C   ⌊it's that one

Prior to this sequence, Clara has stated that she is a boarder (Swedish: *inneboende*)[4] with a contract (Sw. *inneboendekontrakt*). The problem is that things are not quite straightforward, as is shown in (1). Sandra explains the norm of subsistence for boarders (turn 63), whereupon, in turn 64, Clara discloses that "actually" she is living in a collective, which implies that she may share costs with the others with whom she divides up the living quarters. Sandra explains (turn 67) that the entitlement, what social workers refer to as 'the norm', for "single-lodgers" (Sw. *ensamboende*) is higher than for those who run a household together with others. Clara then counters with a claim that "in principle" she lives on her own and should be treated as a one-person household (turn 68). Then, there follows a negotiation, in which the parties try to determine to what extent costs are shared and in what sense Clara is a "single-lodger". The category which is found applicable will have practical consequences for the level of allowance, i.e. the sum of money the client can expect to receive.

In (1), and the subsequent discourse (not cited here), the parties negotiate a solution in a cooperative manner. Clara provides information that is consequential for the categorizations made, but she accepts the social worker's interpretations. When we move on to (2), we will find a case where conditions of accommodation and social relations are rather more difficult to determine. The social worker S(am) is middle-aged (48), while the client C(hristian) is a 26-year-old man, who has had drug problems (now claimed to be surmounted) and who appears to lack a tenant's contract:

(2) (Tema K: E201:1-26, from the very beginning of the recording)

1	C	this lass who I'm lodging in with is an old mate and she helps me out then with... I'm homeless ((Sw. *bostadslös*)) she's struggling with the housing agency for a priority right, I feel I'm entitled to social priority
2	S	you're homeless?
3	C	yes, very much homeless
4	S	and you live at present where then?
5	C	on in Miller's Lane in Belbury (2.0) a two-roomed one ((i.e. a flat with two rooms))
6	S	have you sort of- have you some sort of a tenant's contract or something such
7	C	yes sure (10.0) ((searching among papers))
8	S	mm
9	C	'cause it is after all so=
10	S	=that Anna Svensson you know (C: yes) have you any is she somebody you know (C: mm) or your girlfriend
11	C	no definitely not (3.0) but she helped me out and lends me a room like but she has she has ren- she has helped me she has children you know whom she has joint custody of (S: yes) and she said that if you in that case want to stay here then you'll have to help me with grocery bills I didn' didn't know that there should be some documentation for that
12	S	no that which what the documentation lacks is how much rent you have=
13	C	=you see I pay no rent
14	S	you pay no rent? ((surprised tone))
15	C	no but I pay in kind I pay for the food and she pays the rent
16	S	mm but it'll be very difficult so to speak to have if it gets.. if it's so that we must see here then if you'll get money from here in order to give to a person or two persons
17	C	of course
18	S	well in fact it's better if we do it the other way so to speak that you decide so to speak how much rent you should pay (C: mm) and then supplementary benefit is paid out for it

19	C	yes but I ⌐counted on
20	S	⌐I mean that that if I count then.. I can't count with her or else (C: no sure) or else so.. that is, you are completely sure that you aren't cohabiting
21	C	mm I'm not
22	S	that you're sure of, then I can rely on that
23	C	yes of course
24	S	because if you're cohabiting then we must also count with, start out from that norm anyway
25	C	no we aren't cohabiting, right?
26	S	you're not cohabiting ((assertive tone))

Christian starts out by stating that he has nowhere to live (turns 1 and 3). Yet, as is subsequently revealed, he does indeed live somewhere (4-5), which makes Sam ask for the contract (turn 6). In spite of Christian's initial affirmative answer (7), it later becomes clear that he has no contract, while, as a matter of fact, he stays with a young woman (Anna) and her two children in a small flat. This of course raises the question of Christian's and Anna's relationship: is Anna his girl-friend (10), which would imply that the two cohabit (Sw. *sammanboende*)? Christian emphatically denies this (11). Now, cohabitation (in Swedish colloquial usage (*sambo*) as well as in official terminology and regulation (*sammanboende*)) implies basically two things: (a) living together under marriage-like conditions (usually implying sexual relations) and (b) sharing a household. Christian denies the former (although Sam has difficulties in being convinced, cf. turns 20-26; the same doubts reappear later in the interview), but on the other account (b), one might speak of a shared household; Anna pays the rent and Christian pays for the food (16). Christian wants help from the social security system. He could receive money, if he had a valid contract, but he has not, and moreover, he pays no rent at all. Hence, the regulations, the 'norms' (cf. 24), of the social welfare do not fit the life-circumstances of the client, and this situation sparks off a negotiation between the social worker and the client. In the excerpt cited, the parties are, in effect, concerned with how to categorize Christian's residence status, and later in the encounter, the two negotiate a solution, which in fact would give Christian some money, if he transforms his contribution to the living costs into a rent. Accordingly, he should present a piece of paper showing that he has an agreement, an informal contract as it were, with Anna amounting to this. (Incidentally, as revealed later, Anna receives an allowance for housing in her own right, so this new arrangement might jeopardize that allowance. The exact relations of Christian and Anna never become clear during the recorded interview, in spite of the fact that Sam returns to the topic several times. In a parallel case (E202), which we will introduce presently, the social worker also mentions the written documentation required, pointing out that she must "know in which way you are living together, for the sake of the allowance", whereupon the client replies "yes yes, oh no, it's not a mistress or something" although he too shares a flat with the woman involved.)

In effect, the negotiations between Christian and Sam take place both at the discursive level (as labellings etc.) and at the official level of rule-application and social welfare expenditures. Christian is recategorized from a (kind of) cohabiter into a boarder possessing a (kind of) written contract. While his situation is thereby at least perfunctorily assimilated to the norms of the social welfare, these norms themselves hardly remain unaffected; they are accommodated to the specific case, accepting an arrangement which is probably not according to the letter of the law (cf. Button and Sharrock this volume).

Sam, in (2), appears to be prepared to take Christian's perspective at least partly and temporarily. This perspective meets the rationality of the social welfare partly *within* Sam's own discourse (turns 16, 18, 20), where he tries to fit rules to reality, and/ or vice versa. Christian is of course participating in the collaborative sense-making, yet he is himself fairly passive in this sequence, where the social worker engages in a 'thinking-aloud' problem-solving activity. The same phenomenon can be seen in a similar case, with a social worker (Sally, 45), voicing two, partly contradictory perspectives in probing the case of Christopher (40):

(3) (Tema K: E202:204-212)

204 S okay, so then then you ((*ni*, 2nd person plural)) have.. you ((*du*, 2nd pers. singular))[5] live in a room there then?

205 C yes

206 S how did you ((*ni*)) agree upon electricity an' such things, how you ((*ni*)) should.. you ((*du*)) pay I guess part of the electricity bill when it comes, supposedly

207 C electricity is included I think
        (2.0)

208 S mm

209 C she has to pay the rent tomorrow so I can check up on that but I think it is included

210 S yes

211 C it's Peter Ström who owns the flat ⌜ you see

212 S   ⌞ mm but probably it does since she has written it that way (C: yes) an' telephone and such, you'll ((*ni*)) probably have to make an agreement on that in another way then,

'cause the norm will be as you ((*du*)) understand lower then,= you ((*du*)) will <u>not</u> get the full norm for singles like when one ((*man*, 3rd pers. sg. indef.)) lives alone in a flat (C: no) but it will be, you know, 1840 ((i.e. Sw. kronor)) per month plus the rent part

We can see here how the social worker switches from information-seeking into a sort of advice-giving within a sequence in which he appears to think aloud (especially 212). Note Sally's vacillation in the use of pronouns in this turn. First, she uses *ni* (2nd pers. plural), which here unambiguously refers to Christopher and his "partner", meaning 'the two of you', and then he switches to *du* (2nd pers. sing.) first in "you understand" and then, more interestingly, in "*you* will not get the full norm for singles". Incidentally, 'norm' is here a shorthand expression, commonly used by the social workers, for 'financial assistance (i.e. a certain sum of money) according to the 'norm' (i.e. the regulations)'. After this, there is a switch to *man*, 'one', the indefinite (and impersonal) pronoun, which more clearly points to the abstract rule relevant in this case. The (second) interjacent *du* here seems to be vague with respect to two possible interpretations. One is the 'half-personal', or contingently personal, 'you', used in explaining a *general* rule that is potentially applicable to the present addressee. This kind of 'you' does not unequivocally refer to the addressee directly, but can of course be heard as relevant to him or her. The other interpretation of *du* in the passage at issue is of course the personal 'you' referring directly to the individual person addressed. The use of 'half-personal' *du* 'you' is quite common with professionals, e.g. social workers, addressing clients or customers; it is a discursive device which allows the professional to allude to the generality of a rule, while at the same time implicating its relevance for the recipient in the interaction.[6]

While the circumstances under which you pay (or do not pay) for housing are one recurrent topic for negotiation in social welfare interviews, the requirement of "actively seeking jobs" is another one. We noted above that, for the bureaucracies, this is specified as "having regular contacts with the public employment agency". There are several vaguenesses (and ambiguities) involved here; just how "active" must "active job seeking" be? what does "regular contacts" mean precisely? We will look at one episode, in which this issue becomes a matter of dispute. In (4), a female social worker (S(tella), 35) meets with C(arl), 25, who has run a small business but has now been unemployed for a number of months:

(4) (Tema K: E101: 28-42)
28 S mhm (2.0) when you were in Newtown, didn't you apply for jobs then?
29 C no, I was forced to sort things out round that firm I had earlier,

going to the bank and such like
30   S   mm
         (2.0)
         I see
         (2.0) ((shuts the door))
         (3.0)
         then it'll of course be difficult I think to receive supplementary
         benefit for that time
31   C   in October you mean?
32   S   yes, well exactly the time when you were in Newtown then
33   C   I was as a matter of fact unemployed then too
34   S   yeah but the requirement is that you must seek jobs and keep
         contact with the employ- the employment agency, now=
35   C   =yes but now I've been you know in contact with the employment
         agency anyway. these are such things which I have to clear up see
         (S: mm) it's okay if it's difficult to be seeking jobs meanwhile (S:
         mm) that's such a thing which has to be cleared up in any case
36   S   mm, what kind of job was it you had in Newtown then?
37   C   in Newtown?
38   S   yes, what was it you cleared up?
39   C   no, that was in the bank 'cause I have bank debts you see (S: I see)
         so I went down to talk to them there and talked about how we shall
         plan this thing now when I have y-know claims, I'm behind with
         instalments
40   S   mm but, you see, there is time between the 18th of September and
         the 2nd of ⌈ October
41   C   ⌊ yes but I- I was away for those days, I should have been
         there later, and I was anyway-
42   S   mm how many jobs have you applied for then?

It appears that Carl has failed to register at the employment agency for some time; he
states that he had to leave Stockholm to visit Newtown, and Stella wants to know if he
applied for jobs during that period (turn 28). Carl claims that he had to clear up economic
matters with a bank (29), which was necessary (35). This, however, meant that he was
unemployed all the time (33), which presumably implies that he considers himself
entitled to financial assistance. Stella now counters by repeating the requirement to
contact the employment agency (34), and later (36, 38) she asks whether Carl's visit to
Newtown had anything to do with his jobs. She also points out that they are talking

about a fairly long period of time (40), implying that Carl had opportunities to look for jobs. His answers are apparently not considered satisfactory to her concerns, since she persists in asking about how many jobs Carl applied for (42). Evidently, the logics of the two parties are at odds with one another. Stella's argument seems to be that, given that one is entitled to subsistence only if one applies for jobs continuously, Carl has spent too long a period doing other things to be so entitled. In her view he appears not to have been seeking jobs diligently enough. Carl, on the other hand, seems to argue that he needed to clear up his business with the bank, in order for him to be able to move on to new jobs. His personal 'everyday rationality' does not square with the norms of the social welfare and their underlying rationalities; perspectives conflict. (In this case, Stella does not give in, although she gives a vague promise that she would speak to her boss concerning Carl's time in Newtown.)

As a final example, let us consider a case in which both lodging conditions and the job-seeking requirement are at issue at the same time. Here, we have S(usan), 34, talking with C(lark), 26, who has drug problems (claimed by him to be overcome), is unemployed and appears to have rather unclear living conditions:

(5) (Tema K: E106: 102-120)

102	S	so you know also that in order to get allowance for rent you have to present a valid second-hand contract
103	C	mm but I haven't got that, I've said that all the time ((irritated tone)) I haven't got hold of it you see
104	S	no but that it ⌈ was you
105	C	⌊ what the hell can I do, I must have somewhere to stay, right?
106	S	mm but then you have to fix that if you want an allowance from here ⌈ to-
107	C	⌊ mm but then, now it's like this, I got two thousand one ((i.e. 2100 kronor)) from the insurance last Friday and then I've paid the rent and such out there
108	S	okay, then you've chosen to pay the rent and so
109	C	yeah, what the hell can I do then? damn it I can't live on the street if I get a job, right? (3.0)
110	C	you know that yourself, don't you?
111	S	what is it I know myself, that=
112	C	=yeah, if you don't have anywhere to stay, how could you be at the job?
113	S	this is something I hear very often, these circular arguments

114 C   this isn't a circular argument
115 S   well, I think it is
116 C   I think not actually
117 S   but if you apply if you apply for an allowance for rent, that was
         what it was all about (C: yes) then you need a valid second-hand
         contract
118 C   ⎡⎡yes but I won't⎤
119 S   ⎣⎣also such a   ⎦ fundamental thing
120 C   yes but I won't get that (S: no) you know, since it's not known
         whatchamacallit that they don't know, the landlord doesn't know I'm
         renting there, you see

Clark needs money to pay the rent. Upon Susan's demand for a contract (turn 102), he
says that he has not been able to get a flat (103). Nevertheless, he does live in a flat,
where, he disclosed earlier in the interview, he stays without a contract, without, as it
transpires (120), the landlord knowing it (the contract belongs to somebody else).
However, he has paid a rent, using up money he has received from the social insurance
(Sw. *Försäkringskassan*) (107). Now, he needs money from the social welfare to
compensate for the sum he has in fact spent on the rent (107). Susan's reply (108)
seems to imply that it is his own business, if he chooses to use his money in this way.
This sparks off an irritated remark from Clark, which alludes to a prior accusation that
he has not been active in seeking a new job (109). In what is fairly exceptional for our
corpus, the parties now get into an argument, and the rest of the meeting is conducted
in a rather hostile atmosphere. Susan cannot accept Clark's implicit reasoning and
accuses him of circular reasoning (113, 115). Several interactional episodes later, their
different logics are spelled out. We will cite one passage, where Clark argues his point:
(6) (Tema K: E106: 131-138)

131 C   in order to get something for the rent, that I know, then I need a
         second-hand contract (S: yes) or something, now I can't get that you
         see, but this is only a temporary way out for me, right (S: mm) if I'm
         gonna fix a job for me, if I have nowhere to stay, I will have to keep
         moving around and then there's no point in carrying on seeking a
         job, right?
132 S   mm hmm
         (2.0)
133 C   how the hell can I get up in the mornings if I don't know, well
         maybe I have to sleep in a doorway, can you explain that?
         (2.0)

I have no alarm clock in my pocket you see.

(4.0)

that's it.

(3.5)

134　S　but I don't really think that's it

135　C　isn't it? where the hell should I live then (S: well, that) if now I
　　　 don't- if I hadn't got hold of this second-hand... where should I stay
　　　 then= lemme hear now, if I say I'm sleeping in a doorway (S: mm)
　　　 how could I go to a job then?

　　　 (2.0)

　　　 shall I sleep there and have dirty clothes and everything

136　C　but you have no job to go to now

137　S　but it'll come any day (S: mm) I can tell you that.

　　　 (2.0)

　　　 it will.

138　　but what it is still all about is this thing with the allowance for (C:
　　　 mm) this thing with the rent

This encounter creates a sharp inconsistency between the social welfare logic and the client's everyday 'common sense' rationality. Susan's argument is fairly simple: first, one is not entitled to financial assistance unless one has clearly demonstrated a motivation to seek, accept and sustain employment, and secondly, one cannot get an allowance for rent without a valid contract, and if one is without a contract yet still paying for a flat, that is entirely irrelevant. Clark's argument starts out from the fact (or assumption) that he cannot get a contract. Yet, he must have money to pay for his living quarters, and he has to have somewhere to live, or else he is not in a position to apply for or accept a new job. Thus, he claims that the precondition for getting financial assistance cannot be set up, unless he first gets some money, and hence it should not be a precondition. This is the rhetoric or argumentative strategy dubbed by Susan as a 'circular argument' (113). Her own final remark, in episode (6), is that Clark's argument that he needs somewhere to live in order to work is invalid, because he has no job anyway (speaking of circular reasoning!). (This encounter does not lead to any rent allowance, though Susan tells Clark that some of his other demands will be considered. Incidentally, Clark discloses towards the end that he has a jail sentence (for drug selling and assault) pending.)

In the social welfare office talks there are recurrent negotiations of the meaning of words, norms and descriptive categories. Similarly, the customer and the travel agency employee negotiate modifications in descriptive categories (cf. Mazeland,

Huisman and Schasfoort this volume), in order to bridge the gap between the customer's wishes and the agency's alternatives. There is an intrinsic, and highly significant, relation between outcomes and category definitions in negotiation activities. That is, if certain decisions are taken in an encounter, this presupposes at least implicit contextual (or situated) interpretations of relevant categories. Conversely, if you can agree on definitions and applications of relevant categories, then the outcomes largely follow from these agreements. (In the rather exceptional case of (6), Susan and Clark apparently fail to agree upon and resolve the issues.) The negotiation of outcomes is largely an issue of getting one's linguistic and situated definitions accepted, of determining the terms in which phenomena should be understood (Cedersund 1992b).

5. DISCUSSION

5.1. Negotiating terms

As we noted in the introduction, almost any kind of verbal (or non-verbal) interaction, in speaking or through the exchange of written texts, amounts to doing work in and through language, and this may be called negotiating. However, there are cases where the concept of negotiation is used in a more significant sense. These may involve diplomacy, business, employer-employee negotiations, and many kinds of institutional interaction: court trials, police interrogations, job interviews, doctor consultations etc., and, as in our case, social welfare office talk.

Given that negotiations are carried out in linguistic interaction, we find that the objects negotiated are of at least two different kinds. First, we negotiate *outcomes*. In the case of social work, this concerns first and foremost matters like levels and kinds of financial assistance, decisions on therapy and medical or other treatments, future contacts between the parties, and so on. Second, in the process of accomplishing this, there are other kinds of negotiating going on: we negotiate *means* for making progress in the tasks of achieving results. These means, in turn, may be said to fall into two major analytic categories, those concerning social relations and those concerning descriptive and administrative categories used in the interpretation and evaluation of matters talked about.

Parties deploy discursive resources to coordinate the interaction itself, and at the same time they also reconstruct social organization in the micropolitics of interaction. In Goffmanian terms, this would involve both face-work and, more generally, participation framework and participant roles, and the negotiation of these may lead to redefinitions of more long-standing social relationships. In the encounter between the social worker and the client, the latter's moral character is collaboratively constructed (Hydén 1992, Cedersund 1992b:77ff.). We will return to this issue presently.

On the other hand, parties negotiate the *linguistic categories and concepts* to be used in the discourse. In interaction and negotiation, definitions are created and recreated. The Oxford Latin Dictionary cites as one (of many) meanings of *negotium* "the action or business of negotiating or making terms with others" (cf. Bell 1988:234). We now see, with an apt turn of the phrase, that parties are *making terms* together in several ways and senses; the social worker and the client agree, or are made to agree, on certain outcomes, but, before that, they also engage in *defining meanings* of words, categories and the client's circumstances. Indeed, the latter aspect is much more salient in the interactions.

5.2. Negotiating participation

An interaction, most clearly perhaps a professional-lay interaction, involves the enacting of both an institutional order and a participation structure in the interaction itself (Zimmerman and Boden 1991, Wilson 1991). On the one hand, the institutional mooring pertains to (the reproduction of) power structures, authority, expertise, and sanctions. On the other hand, there is an 'interactional bedrock' consisting of, among other things, dominance patterns; the parties interact so as to allow one another more or less 'interactional space'. Fredin (1993) has shown that the social welfare interviews under study vary considerably in terms of who governs and who is governed interactionally in discourse; there is variation across dyads and topics, though usually with a considerable interactional dominance on the part of the social worker. This asymmetry is regularly enhanced, when the parties treat topics of immediate importance for the eventual outcomes of the encounters (Fredin op cit.). But the interaction is always a collective accomplishment; not only are outcomes and labellings negotiated in the discourse, so is the participation structure of floor-holding, speaking rights and social relations. With yet another twist of the word, we can say that the parties also negotiate on what kinds of speaking terms they are and should be.

There is often, it seems, a tacit presupposition that a ("real") negotiation involves equally strong parties. Similarly, there is an often entertained idea that a ("real") dialogue is basically symmetrical. We believe that there should be no conceptual relation between equality and symmetry, on the one hand, and negotiation or dialogue, on the other (cf. Linell and Luckmann 1991). Empirically, it turns out that many negotiations take place under conditions of asymmetry; asymmetry with regard to participation, knowledge, status and authority. In many ways, the social worker, representing the system and 'society', has a dominant position in meeting the client; (s)he has measures and sanctions at her/his disposal, (s)he has the professional expertise and knows the rules as well as other clients' typified needs and rights. Nevertheless, no professional can dictate the terms and conditions. For one thing, clients have rights to services according to the law, and professionals may be sanctioned for abuse of authority or misapplication of rules. Furthermore, (s)he is dependent on the client for providing the information necessary for diagnosing the case. There is a moment of negotiation, even if the client is extremely passive or incapable of explaining his or her case; the social worker still has to cope with the problem of how to make the categories and the specific circumstances in the individual case fit together.

The point just alluded to could perhaps be given a slightly different twist: irrespective of whether the client him- or herself indulges in an overt negotiation, it may be that the social worker as a person embodies a negotiation between different identities of his or her self (Taylor 1989) or between different voices within his or her own mind and discourse (Wertsch 1990). For example, Sally in (3), in part takes the client´s perspective and argues with the norm-dependent social worker perspective in a short, polyvocal monologue. It is obvious that the social worker has to cope with different roles, e.g. both that of a listening, possibly empathetic, fellow human being, thus partly and temporarily adopting the client´s everyday life-world perspective, and that of an author/animator voicing the perspective of the social welfare system. Indeed, this system in itself may appear as multi-voiced (Hydén 1988, Fredin 1993).

5.3. Negotiating rules and realities

In social welfare interviews, the parties negotiate both how the client's life circumstances should be properly understood and how the systems of rules and norms, the administrative categories, are to be applied and accommodated. It is not a question of simple subsumption of cases under general rules (Cicourel 1972). Just as in the negotiation of outcomes, the process involves compromises. Potentially, the negotiation involves opposed interests and perspectives. Sometimes, clients claim that an orthodox application of the rules would lead to absurd consequences; Clark, in (5, 6), argued this without getting Susan to concede. In other cases, social workers go along with some rather specific accommodations of the rules; Sam seemed to do this in Christian's case (2). Assimilation of specific conditions to rules and categories and accommodation of rules to the almost endless variation in reality might sometimes appear as tampering with the "facts" and gerrymandering the norms. But it is important to realise that there is always and necessarily a reflexivity involved even in the most exemplary applications.

Rules are always indeterminate in their application (Zimmerman 1971); abstract categories have to be contextually interpreted, and in categorizing realities, one must select some properties as decisive and disregard others. This, in fact, is the essence of language use (e.g. Garfinkel 1967).

When people negotiate definitions in professional-lay interaction, this may consist both in choosing among different words (e.g. professional jargon vs. everyday colloquial language) and in specifying or selecting different interpretations of the *same* words. For example, notions like 'boarder' (*inneboende*), 'cohabiter' (*sammanboende*), 'seek jobs' (*söka arbete*) are used both in mundane contexts and in the administrative language of lawyers and administrators. The technical senses may well be specifications or redefinitions of the mundane ones, but the precise nature of these reconstructions are often partly opaque to the lay people. This constitutes part of the background for negotiating these terms. Another aspect of the problem is, as we noted, how to apply the technical terms to the individual cases.

The negotiation of definitional terms obviously pertain to specific applications of the categories involved. But does it also affect the concepts themselves? Given that there is an inherent reflexivity between language and its situated use, it seems to us that one can hardly exclude an affirmative answer to the latter question either. Even if redefinitions of administrative categories are not always codified in new (versions of) regulations, they do sediment into routinized practices of individual professionals or collectives of professionals (local cultures). For the life of institutions and their clients, these practices are of course at least as important as the black-letter norms and regulations. Therefore, following Maynard (1988), Zimmerman and Boden (1991), and many others, we contend that the actual social practices are important to study for anyone who wants to understand institutions, and representatives of institutions, and their treatment of social problems.

NOTES

1. There are a number of Swedish bureaucratic terms used in this sector of society, and these do not always have self-evident English equivalents. In this chapter, we will usually employ the following translations: *socialtjänst*: social (welfare) services, *socialbidrag* :financial assistance (or supplementary benefit), *socialbyrå*: social welfare office (or agency), *social förtur*: social priority, *arbetsförmedling*: (public) employment agency, *bostadsförmedling*: (local) (public) housing agency, *försäkringskassa*: (local) social insurance (office). For some additional terms, see note 4.

2. Hydén (1988) claims that there are more than 100,000 such encounters yearly in Stockholm alone.

3. All names appearing in the excerpts are fictionalized. Social workers are given pseudonyms beginning with S, and clients names beginning with C. Excerpts have been transcribed verbatim and are given here in a rough English translation of the Swedish originals, though it has proven hard to do justice to some nuances of colloquial conversational Swedish. Basically the same transcription conventions as elsewhere in this book have been used, but note the following point:
(S: yes) etc: such parentheses contain back-channel items uttered by the speaker not holding the floor and are placed approximately at the position in the current speaker's flow of speech where they occur.

4. There are a number of Swedish terms pertaining to different categories of accommodation, which are crucial to our discussion but seem hard to translate appropriately into English. These words are compounds formed from the verb *bo* "to live, stay, lodge", the present participle being *boende* "living, staying, lodging", which, when nominalized, is used both about the way, or circumstances, of living (e.g. def.sg. *sammanboendet*), and about the person living under these circumstances (def.sg. *den sammanboende*) The three most important compounds are:
inneboende, literally "living/staying/lodging (with)in (i.e. somebody else's flat or house)", meaning (as an agent noun) approximately 'boarder' (though the sharing of a household is usually not included), and here translated simply as *boarder;*
sammanboende "living/staying/lodging together (with somebody)", "co-habiting", as an agent noun corresponding to colloquial *sambo*, here translated as *co-habiter;*
ensamboende, "living alone or single", i.e. in a separate flat (or house), the agent noun here translated (very awkwardly) as *single-lodger.*

5. There are two regular 2. person pronouns in Swedish, *du* (2.sing.) and *ni* (2.plur.), both translated into English as "you". In addressing a person who is not one's intimate, either *du* or *ni* can be used in present-day Sweden; *du* is more informal but quite wide-spread. (*Ni* is used also when addressing two or more persons at the same time, or when addressing a single person but referring to both him/her and some other person(s) associated with him/her.) In addition *du*, but not *ni*, can be used in a more generic sense, corresponding to English 'you' when used as a generic pronoun; this is the use called 'contingently personal' below in the text (*á propos* excerpt 3, turn 212).

6. Given that excerpt 3, turn 212 can be heard as (a kind of) advice-giving, compare the use of generic *you*, often followed by an instance of personalization, in English institutionalized advice-giving contexts (see, e.g., Heritage and Sefi 1992).

CHAPTER 13

DISPOSAL NEGOTIATIONS IN GENERAL PRACTICE CONSULTATIONS

PAUL TEN HAVE

1. INTRODUCTION

I take *negotiations* to be those interactions in which parties at the outset take a stand that differs one from the other, after which they put forward various alternatives, together with assessments of the acceptability of those alternatives, which may lead to a settlement when one aligns with the other or when they agree on a compromise. Negotiations can be explicit, as in various kinds of bargaining, or implicit, as in conversational 'negotiations' about the course of the conversation, versions of 'what happened' or implied identities.

In this chapter I explore some issues regarding negotiations in medical settings, i.e. GP (General Practitioner) consultations focused on decisions regarding case disposals.[1] The substantive 'negotiations' of doctors and patients are mostly carried on implicitly, almost furtively, while only sometimes assessment, advice and treatment is given the form of a bid in a 'negotiation'. This suggests important but difficult analytic issues of 'form' versus 'content'. For participants, the interaction in consultations is 'framed' by the fact that it occurs in that particular institutional setting. And specific interactional episodes are for them, in addition to that, situated in their common history, including specifically the course of the consultation so far.

To begin, I will use Maynard's (1984) study of plea bargaining as a primary resource. He offers a sequential model of negotiation or bargaining that could serve as a baseline for any treatment of negotiation as an interactional phenomenon. Examining fifty-two cases in which the parties had to agree some disposition, he found that:

> This is not done haphazardly, but in an orderly fashion by means of bargaining sequences consisting of (1) a turn in which speaker exhibits a position, and (2) a next turn where recipient displays alignment or non alignment with the initially exhibited position (Maynard 1984:78).

Between an 'opener', which may take the form of a 'proposal' or a 'position-report', and a (final) alignment, many things can happen, including insertion sequences, third party mediations, silences or counters, with various kinds of elaborations following from that (Maynard 1984:91-100). Preceding the basic sequence, one can find introductory material, such as Solicits and Announcements followed by Go-Ahead's (Maynard 1984:85-90). One also can have recyclings of various components and sequences. In short, negotiations can get quite complicated, but they are claimed to be similar in their basic structure, which can be, and often is, elaborated in systematic ways.

As noted, my explorations of negotiations in the medical consultation focus on the 'disposal', the final decision on what should be done with the case presented. In GP consultations, this disposal is often decided 'on the spot', brought forward at a certain moment, based on what went before and proposing what shall be done next. The literature presents quite variant pictures of medical disposals as interactional events, ranging from authoritarian order to more or less egalitarian bargaining. This chapter explores some of the formats that are used in four quite ordinary 'natural' consultations.[2]

2. PROPOSAL/ACCEPTANCE SEQUENCES: ANALYSIS OF A CASE

My interest in the topic of disposal *negotiation* was raised by the following utterance by a GP:

> maar vind je 't een ↑goed ↑voorstel? om het ↑zo te doen?
> *but do you think it's a good proposal to do it like that*
> (case 1: line 162)

In this, the GP refers to his own previous utterance as a 'proposal' and requests his patient to give his opinion on it, whether he thinks it is a 'good proposal'. The 'but' suggests that this assessment has not yet been given although it is due.

When we look at the larger episode from which this was taken, the utterance to which the GP refers as his 'proposal' seems to be the one starting in line 138 of the transcript given below:

.h en nou (z) wat ik je nou wilde ↑v<u>oo</u>rstellen is om een
↑p<u>ij</u>nstiller te nemen (.) tegen de p<u>ij</u>n
and well what I would like to propose to you is to take a
sedative to counter the pain

In this utterance the GP explicitly formulates his action as 'proposing', and it is this proposal that he invites the patient to assess in line 162, suggesting that this should already have been done but hasn't. Excerpt 1 (below) presents the episode under discussion in full.

Excerpt 1, disposal episode

```
125      (1.8)
126 D→  ik denk dat het ↑t<u>o</u>ch eh die dat 't iets ↑is met ↑sp<u>iere</u>↓
        I do think that after all uh that that it's something in your
127     ⌈ wat je daar ↓h<u>e</u>bt hè? die ↓p<u>ij</u>n ·hh dat 't een soort e::h
        muscles what you have there that pain that it's a kind of
128 P   ⌊ (merkwaardig)
        strange
129 D   ↑sp<u>ie</u>rpijn is,
        muscular pain
130     (.)
131 P   ⌈ 't zit echt ↑<u>o</u>nder m'n schouder (↑hi ⌈ e-) °dus hie ⌈ r°
        it's really under my shoulder here so here
132 D   ⌊ ·hh                        ⌊ j<u>aa</u>        ⌊ ja
                                        yes            yes
133 P   ↓en ↓hier. ⌈ (recht er voo ⌈ r.)
        and here right in front
134 D              ⌊ aan je        ⌊ in je ↓flank ja ja .hh want 't ↑is allemaal
                   in your          side yes yes      because it's all
135     het ↑v<u>oe</u>lt allemaal en het ↑h<u>oo</u>rt allemaal normaal ↑<u>aa</u>n, .hh dat
        it feels all       and it sounds all     normal        that
136     <u>a</u>demen.
        breathing
137 P   nou ben ↑bl<u>ij</u> toe.
        well I'm happy about it
138 D→  .h en nou (z) wat ik je nou wilde ↑v<u>oo</u>rstellen is om een ↑p<u>ij</u>n-
        and well what I would like to propose to you is to take a
139     stiller te nemen (.) tegen de p<u>ij</u>n
```

sedative   to counter the pain
140 P   °↓hm↑hm°
141 D   dat je in ↑ieder geval je (.) laten we maar zeggen alles d'r
         so you in any case you   let's say   can do everything
142   mee kan ↑doen.
         with it
143 P   (°°hmhm°°)
144 D   .hh (.) en dat moet je niet langer als een week gebruiken,
                    and you shouldn't take it for more than a week
145 P   (°hahhm°)
146 D   en dan zullen we kijken hoe het in die tijd ↑gaat,
         and then we will consider how it is after that
147 P   (°jha°)
148 D   en zodra je (.) ↑toch niet eh tevr↑eden bent, .hh ⌈ ( )
         and the moment you are still not satisfied
149 P   ⌊ 't is e:h
                                                           it is uh
150   'sn↑achts is 't 't ↑ergste °hè°
         during the night it is at its worst huh
151 D   ja
152 P   want dan ja dan ↑wil je slapen normaal als (.) 'k in ↑bed stap,
         because then you want to sleep normally when I go to bed
153   nou e:h dan ↑slaap ik al.
         well I sleep immediately
154 D   ja
155 P   (wa-) meestal nog wel eh of moe of eh .hh
         bec- mostly well either tired or uh
156 D   jaja ⌈ .hh
         yeah yeah
157 P   ⌊ (pft)
158   (.)
159 D   nou=
         well
160 P   =(w) daar word je gek van.
              that makes me crazy
161   (.)
162 D→   maar vind je 't een ↑goed ↑voorstel? om het ↑zo te doen?
         but do you think it's a good proposal to do it like that

```
163 P   ja nat↑uurlijk, ┌ als (°'k 'r ma- van↑af ben°).
        yes of course     as long as I'm rid of it
164 D                    └ eh dan e:h
                            uh then uh
165 D   .hh dan eh (.) ↑hoop ik dat het in deze week dus afzakt, als je
        then eh          I hope        it will come down this week when you
166     dus minder pijn hebt hoef je ook minder tabletten te nemen,
        have less pain          you can take less tablets
167     .hh je begint met vier (.) per dag,
        you start with four        a day
168 P   ja
        yes
169 D→  en dan e:h zo minder, .hh en dan zal ik je voor die ↑neus zal ik je
        and then uh less and then for that nose I will give you some
170     nog wat ↑neusdruppels geven dan kan je tenminste
        nosedrops so you can in any case breath
        ┌ door je ↑neus  weer ↑ade men.
        through your nose again
171 P   └ ja
          yes
172 P   enne (.) ben ik daar ↑ook gelijk vanaf.
        and        will I be free from that too
173 D   ja
        yes
174     (.)
175 P   en ik gebruik altijd die eh die redax↑on, die die vitamines (.)
        and I always use      those uh redaxon those those vitamins...
```

When we look at the interactions that follow the 'proposal' to take a sedative, we see that the patient produces some soft and unarticulated acknowledgements, like '*hmhm*', in lines 140, 143 and 145, switching to a clearer '*ja*' (yes) in 147. These acknowledgements, following the various 'components' of the proposal, do not seem to show a strong commitment to what is proposed, rather they indicate that the patient 'understands' the doctor's words. The patient seems to constitute himself as a 'passive recipient' of the doctor's 'orders', rather than as a party to a negotiation. His switch to the somewhat more active '*ja*' (yes) in 147 may be seen as a way to prepare an incipient shift to a more active participation, which indeed follows in line 149 (cf. Jefferson 1984, Mazeland 1992). This contribution, however, is not easily seen as a response to the proposal in progress, rather it seems to be a re-affirmation of previous complaints, possibly 'triggered' by 'satisfied' in the previous utterance by the physician (Ten Have 1989:121).

In short, the GP is seen to remind his patient in line 162 that, from 138 onwards, he is expecting a clear reply to his proposal which he has not as yet received, since the patient has only acknowledged receipt of the proposal and its elaborations, shifting to reinforced complaints afterwards. This physician, then, makes it clear that the patient should assess his proposal for a disposal in an explicit manner. The patient, on his part, suggests in his response that such an acceptance is to be taken for granted, with a relatively soft:

> ja nat↑uurlijk, als (°'k 'r ma- van↑af ben°).
> *yes of course   as long as I'm rid of it*
> (case 1: line 163)

In this consultation, then, the disposal is enacted by the physician in the format of a proposal-acceptance sequence. By pursuing an acceptance, the physician shows that he considers his proposal to be in principle negotiable, providing for a non-aligning response, such as a refusal, a complication, or a counter-proposal; but the patient seems to evade negotiation of any kind. By his insistence on an acceptance, the GP does 'work' to put the patient's acceptance firmly 'on record', as an interactionally-established fact. It might be part of a more or less deliberate strategy by the doctor to have the patient confirm his 'satisfaction' with the disposal, and with the consultation as a whole. Apart from its local benefits, it might be seen to add to the patient's motivation to comply with the prescription later on.

3. DISPOSAL FORMATS

Let us now inspect a small number of other GP consultations to see whether proposal/ acceptance sequences involving disposals are to be found there, or, possibly, how disposals are formatted alternatively. Here follows the disposal episode from my Case 2.

Excerpt 2 (transcribed by Gail Jefferson)
```
196   D→   .t.hhh ( ) get your chest X-rayed at the:, just at the
197           mass X-ray unit Missiz: Murphy
198           (2.8)
199           ↑How old are you?
```

```
200          (0.3)
201    P     .t.hh T̲wenty sev̲e̲n,
202          (0.3)
203    D     ((soft whisper)) °°(          )°° ·hhh
204          (2.2)
205          .t.hhhhh
206          (5.1) ((writing))
207          .t.hhhhhhhh
208          (4.0) ((writing))
209    P     ekhh-heh .hh e̲khh e̲khh
210          (0.5)
211    D     :pt.h̲h̲h̲
212    P     e̲khh
213          (2.7) ((paper being handled))
214    D     .t.hhhhhh
215          (5.0) ((paper being handled))
216    →     Just a simple precau̲t̲ion this .hhhh (.) uh:m,h te̲n til
217          twelve thirty tw̲o̲ thirty till four thirty in the ma̲ss X-ray
218          jh (.) department at the General.
219    P     Uh-h̲u̲h,
220          (0.9)
221    D     (Y'c'd) belt along n̲o̲w'n get it done straight away there's
222          n̲o̲ waiting you just (.) they just take you straight away=
223    P     = ⌜Yeh
224    D     = ⌊.hhhhhhh
225    P     (M ⌜m)
226    D→         ⌊ And (0.3) th̲a̲t's just a s̲imple c̲o̲ugh bottle.
227          (0.3)
228    P     U̲h-huh,
229    D→    Nothing very c̲lever about it at a̲:ll. :hhhh (0.2) I th̲i̲nk
230          this'll settle down without doing anything very much it-
231          about it
232    P     ⌜ Yeah
233    D     ⌊ .hmhh If it d̲o̲esn't,hh will you come back'n se̲e̲ me
234    P     Yes:
235    D     if you're not happy with the way it's going on.
236    P     Right. ⌜Th̲a̲nk you,
237    D           ⌊Okay?
```

```
238   D      ↓°Right.°
239          (0.6)
240   D      ↑Bye bye no ┌ w
241   P                  └ Bye bye:.
```

In line 196-197 the doctor simply announces his disposal: further examinations by X-rays:

> .t.hhh ( ) get your chest X-rayed at the:, just at the
> mass X-ray unit Missiz: Murphy

He leaves a (2.8) pause, but there is no vocal reply from the patient. Then he engages in some administrative questioning, evidently writing the reference for the X-ray examination (lines 199-215). Having handled the referral form, he reassures the patient and instructs her on how to proceed (lines 216-225). In line 226 the physician announces another part of the disposal:

> And (0.3) that's just a simple cough bottle.

The pronoun 'that' in the announcement probably refers to a prescription being written or handed over to the patient. The medicine is described as a rather simple one: 'just a simple cough bottle.'. The announcement is acknowledged by the patient with an 'Uh-huh,' (line 228). Then a physician adds another kind of 'mitigation' of the medication:

> 'Nothing very clever about it at a:ll.' (line 229).

Added is a kind of forecast that the disorder will pass quite easily, which is, in a way, another mitigation to the medication. This is accepted with a 'Yeah' (line 232). Then the physician adds a right to return if the disorder doesn't clear up to the patient's satisfaction (lines 233-235). The patients accepts this rather strongly, confirmed by the doctor (236-238). Following that, the patient 'thanks' the GP and departs.

In this case, then, the double disposal was 'announced' rather than 'proposed'. No formal acceptance was provided or requested in the first instance, but the patient cooperated fully in the further processing of the disposal, including 'yeah'-receipts to the instruction. The second disposal was acknowledged rather than accepted as such. But the disposals as a set, and the consultation as such, seem to have been accepted through a 'spontaneous' 'Right. Thank you,', followed by an 'Okay? ↓°Right.°' from the physician.

Although the two parts of the disposal were announced rather flatly, they were, as noted, both followed by what I have called 'mitigations':

216   D   Just a simple precaution this .hhhh (.) uh:m,
        ...
226   D   And (0.3) that's just a simple cough bottle.
        ...
229   D   Nothing very clever about it at a:ll.

So although this GP gave his disposal an 'announcement' format, he took the trouble to belittle its importance in various ways.

The next case to be considered, Case 3, is again from the Netherlands.

Excerpt 3 a, (transcribed by Chris Driessen and Heidi van Mierloo)

116   kan ik die rooie lamp d'rop ⌐ -
           can I put the red lamp on it
117   D   L ehhhn ((hoest))
                                ((cough))
118   P   d'r op ⌐ doen?
           on it? ⌐
119   D→   L ja maar u krijgt er nog wat bij:.
           yes but you get something with it
120   (1.1)
121   van mij.
           from me
122   (0.7)
123   ook nog.
           also
124   (0.4)
125   om in te nemen.
           to take
126   (2.2)

This first fragment from the consultation starts when the patient asks whether it makes sense to continue to expose her muscles to a 'red lamp'. The physician approves that, but announces that she will get something to take with it. Then he starts to question her on her work, after which he examines her feet. There is no reaction from the patient to this, although she had a chance to do so (2.2 pause in line 126).

Excerpt 3 b (transcribed by Chris Driessen and Heidi van Mierloo)

228 D→ ja u moet toch maar=
          yes I think you should

229   =(ik weet nie of) als u weer 's aan schoenen t<u>oe</u>:bent,
          I don't know when you need shoes again

230   (0.3)

231 P   ja ja dan k<u>oo</u>p ik 'n paar <u>a</u>ndere 's
          yes yes then I buy another pair

232   om in me w<u>e</u>rk te lopen
          to walk on at work

233   (.)

234 D→ probeer 't 's
          try it once

235   (.)

236   ↓ja
          yes

237   (.)

238   't ligt soms ↑f<u>ou</u>t aan de- aa ⌐ n het ↑v<u>oe</u>t(bed)
          sometimes it's wrong with the with the footbed

239 P   ⌐ en ↑m<u>oe</u>t ik-
                                   and do I have

240   (.)

241   dit is me ↑<u>e</u>nige paar schoene met 'n ↓h<u>a</u>k
          this is my only pair with a heel

242   hoor dokter,=
          doctor

243   =want ik heb ⌐ (altijd) sch<u>oe</u>ne me 'n
          because I always wear shoes with a

244 D   ⌐ uhuh ((hoest))
                          ((cough))

245 P   platte h<u>a</u>k.
          low heel

246   (0.7)

247   want ik kan ↑sl<u>e</u>cht op deze schoene,-
          because it's hard on these shoes

248   of sl<u>e</u>cht↑, maar-=
          or hard but

249 D→ =U m<u>a</u>g geen eh-

```
              you're not allowed to uh
250   U       ↑moet met hakke.
              you must wear heels
251           (0.7)
252   P       ↑Moet met hakke?
              must wear heels?
253           (.)
254   D       ↓ja↑:
              yes
255           (.)
256   P       ik loop ammel op hele ↓platte schoene dokter.
              I always wear very low heels doctor
257           (1.9)
258           is dat kwaa,-
              is that bad
259           i- ⌈ kan dat soms ↓kwaa:d↑
              can that be be harmful
260   D         ⌊ mwo:
261           (1.1)
262   P       ik heb ⌈ ammel van die-
              I always wear those
263   D               ⌊ ↑ja:↓a:↑
                        yes
264           (.)
265   P       platte schoene met een ↓ve:↑ter.
              low heeled shoes with laces
266           (.)
267   D→      n::↓ee: m'r d'r moeten hakken onder.
              no but you need heels with it
268           (0.6)
269           ⌈ .hhh        kijk⌉
              look
270   P       ⌊ dus ik kan dez⌋ deze ↑hoogte beter ↑hou↓den.=
              so I should rather keep this height
271   D       =↑ja:↓↓ja
              yes yes
272           (0.4)
```

```
273    →      ⌈ja pro↑beer 't 's          ⌉
              yes try it once
274  P        ⌊en ↑ik maar denken ⌋ dat 't ↑slecht is
              and I was thinking that it's bad
275           (.)
276  D→       pro↑beer 't 's
              try it once
277           (.)
278           't is ↑net ↑net anders↓om.
              it's just the other way around
279           (0.6)
280  P        oh (daa:'om) doe ik ⌈ ↑dat!
              oh therefore I will do that
281  D→                           ⌊ pro↑beer 't 's
                                    try it once
282           (0.5)
283           ja:
              yes
284           (0.6)
285  P        Dus ↑dit hoe f'k ma ↓in te neme,=
              so this I just have to take it
286  D→       =Ja:: en nog 's
              yes and also
287           en nog 'n eh-
              and also a
288           (0.5)
289           zo'n
              such an
290           (.)
291           sz:alf er↓bij.
              ointment with it
292           (0.4)
293  P        ↑oké↓ ik dank u wel=
              okay thank you very much
294           =Da::g
              bye
295  D        Nou↓
              well
```

296		(.)
297	→	pro↑b<u>ee</u>r 't 's ja.
		try it once yes
298		Da:g
		bye
299		((deur))
		((door))

We re-enter this consultation when the doctor completes the examination of the patient's feet. He suggests that, when she is going to buy another pair of shoes, she might buy shoes of a different kind (228-229). It seems that what the patient considered 'healthy' kinds of shoes, i.e. flat-heeled, are not what the doctor would suggest. The patient shows her surprise at this, but is willing to 'try' (280). She then refers to the earlier announced medication, probably referring to a prescription ('this' in 285), but the doctor announces that she will get an ointment with it (286-291). She accepts all of this with a joyful 'Okay, thank you very much' (293) and a salutation. The physician re-states his suggestion that she should 'try'.

In this case, a *triple* disposal is produced. The two medications are presented in a straightforward manner and apparently accepted in a non-vocal way. The third element, however, the suggestion that the patient should buy a different kind of shoes, is brought forward rather tentatively. It is suggested four times that she should 'try it once' (234, 273, 276, 297). But as regards the kind of shoes, he formulates his preference rather strongly, in terms of 'must' (249-250, 269). One might think that the difference in 'force' of the two medications on the one hand, and the buying of shoes on the other, as well as the fact that the buying itself is suggested as a trial, while the kind of shoes to be bought is announced strongly, might be connected to the fact that the strong formulations are related to the doctor's claimed competence, while the suggestion to buy new shoes is expressly left to the patient's discretion, i.e. her own budget considerations (cf. line 229).

In these two cases, then, both the doctors and the patients seemed to follow an announcement/acknowledgement format, rather than a proposal/acceptance one, although the acknowledgements were often 'absent' vocally and the announcements might be mitigated.

The next case to be presented, case 4, displays yet another format, let us say one of 'deliberate alternatives'.

Excerpt 4 a (transcribed by Chris Driessen and Heidi van Mierloo)

```
416  D      ⎡ .hhh
417         ⎣ (0.4)
418         ehm hhh
419         (3.4)
420  →      .ik denk aan ↑twee dingen.
            I am thinking of two things
421         (.)
422  →      't ene is
            the first is
423         (0.8)
424         dat u 'n
            that you have
425         (0.3)
426         'n 'n voet hebt die-
            a a foot which-
427         (0.5)
428         normaal gesproken wordt 'n voet ↑zo afgewikkeld
            normally a foot is unrolled like this
429         (maar bij) u
            but in your case
430         (0.3)
431         overdreven gezegd ↑zo=
            formulated exaggeratedly like this
432         =dat u dus as 't ware te veel op de
            that you therefore as it were too much on the
433         (0.5)
434         onderkant van uw ↓tenen↑=
            bottomside of your toes
435         =dus eh: ⎡ :
            so uh   ⎣
436  P               ja=
                     yes
437  D      =aan de onderkant van de ↑voet gezien
            seen from below the foot
438         (.)
439         ⎡ .hhh
440         ⎣ (0.5)
```

441		en dit de t<u>e</u>nen zijn,
		and these are the toes
442		(.)
443		dat die h<u>ie</u>r drukt=
		that it pushes here
444		=en dat h<u>oo</u>rt niet=
		and that's not right
445		=want je hoort namelijk
		because you should
446		(0.4)
447		↑h<u>ie</u>r↓ op te lopen
		walk on this
448		(.)
449		op de z<u>ij</u>kant ⌈ en
		on the sides
450	P	⌊ ↑ja↓
		yes
451	D	⌈ .hhh
452		⌊ (0.4)
453		(0.3)
454	→	en dat zou ↓w<u>ij</u>↑zen op 'n beetje een ↑ingezakte
		and that could be an indication of a bit of a collapsed
455		voorvoet.
		forefoot ((front underside of the foot))
456		(1.1)
457		⌈ .hhh
458		⌊ (0.6)
459	→	't is ↑n<u>ie</u>t over↓t<u>ui</u>gend.
		it is not convincing
460		(0.5)
461	P	nee=
		no
462	D	=as ik er zo naar kijk.
		when I look at it like this
463		(.)
464		⌈ .hhh
465		⌊ (0.4)
466	→	't tw<u>ee</u>de waar ik aan denk=

the second I am thinking of

467 → =en dat is een beetje atypische ↓pl<u>aa</u>ts↑,=
and that is a bit atypical location

468 =dus niet helemaal de plaats waar je 't zou ver↓wachten↑,=
so not altogether the location where you would expect it

469 =is aan ↓j<u>i:</u>cht
→ *is gout*

470 (0.6)

471 ⌜ .hhh
472 ⌞ (0.4)

473 → 't enige ↑r<u>a:</u>re daarvan is dat u n<u>ie</u>t-
the only strange thing is that you don't

474 (.)

475 dat u dat mee-=
that you most-

476 =dat je dat meestal n<u>ie</u>t hebt
that you mostly don't have that

477 ⌜ .hhh
478 ⌞ (0.4)

479 en dat de d<u>a</u>g daarna weer alle sympt<u>o</u>men weg zijn=
and that the day after all symptoms have disappeared again

480 =dat is heel r<u>aa</u>:r.=
that is very strange

481 =dat ↑kl<u>o</u>pt eigenlijk helemaal ⌜ niet
that doesn't seem to fit really

482 P   ⌞ nee
                                                   no

483 (.)

484 nee.
no

485 (.)

486 D ⌜ .hhh
487 ⌞ (0.4)

488 → dus e- en 'n d<u>e</u>rde mogelijkheid ↑z<u>ie</u> 'k↓ gewoon niet.
so an- and a third possibility I just don't see

489 (0.6)

490 → da ↑w<u>ee</u>t <u>i</u>k n<u>ie</u>t.=
I don't know another

```
491            =<laat ik 't zo maar zeggen.
               let me put it that way
492            (.)
493   P        °ja:h.
               yes
494            (0.7)
495            'k weet ook niet
               I don't know either
496            (0.8)
497            daarom kom ik bij u
               that's why I come to you
498            (0.7)
499            den ⌈ k ik (dat de) dokter raad ⌉ weet
               thinking that the doctor will know
500   D            ⌊ ja: dat is prima, dat- ⌋
               yes that is alright that
501            (.)
502            dat is uitstekend
               that is excellent
503            (0.3)
```

In this case a woman patient has a complicated complaint regarding her foot, which tends to swell in a certain spot on the front part of the sole. After many descriptions and an examination, the physician states his opinion in terms of two alternative possibilities: :hh ik denk aan ↑twee dingen. (*I am thinking of two things*; line 420). He starts by describing the first, an abnormal unrollment of the foot, which could be an indication of a bit of a collapsed forefoot (lines 422-455), but he declares that it is not a convincing possibility (line 459). The second alternative (lines 466-469) is gout, but the location is 'atypical' (467) and the timing of the symptoms does not fit this diagnosis either (473-481). The physician says he is not able to think of a third possibility (488-491). The patient reacts by saying that she doesn't know either and that she is consulting the physician in the hope that he would know (493-499).

One might speculate that the doctor, faced with a diagnostic dilemma, one in which the alternatives he considers are both not very strong, has elected to 'play' this situation out loud, so to speak. Rather than choosing one alternative and acting on it as if he were convinced himself, he shares his doubts publicly, and takes the risks that go with such an action. In this way he keeps his options open for trying either alternative and switching to the other if the first fails. The patient, however, seems to refuse to

enter the debate; if she knew the diagnosis, she wouldn't be there.
Excerpt 4 b presents a later episode:

559		((schrijven))
		writing
560		(4.4)
561	D→	ik schrijf hier 's <u>o</u>p,
		I am writing here
562		(.)
563		p<u>ee</u> <u>e</u>(m)
		p.m.
564		(0.7)
565		dat ik eventjes
		that I have to
566		(0.5)
567		over n<u>a</u>denk,
		think about it
568		(.)
569		of althans dat we dat 's in g<u>a</u>ten houden,
		or at least that we keep an eye on it
570		laat 'k 't z<u>o</u> maar zeggen,
		let me put it that way
571		⌈ .hhhh
572		⌊ (0.7)
573	→	om dokter P<u>e</u>reboom toch 'ns te laten kijken=
		to have doctor P. take a look at it
574		=de ortho ⌈ pedische chirurg=
		the orthopedic surgeon
575	P	⌊ oh
576	D	=dat ie gewoon 's kijkt van ↑h<u>ee</u>
		that he just take a look like well
577		(.)
578		i ⌈ s-
		is
579	P	⌊ °jah,°
		yes
580	D	is die ↑v<u>oo</u>rvoet niet te veel doorgezakt,
		is that forefoot not collapsed too much
581		(.)

582	P	(°ne ⌈ e°)
		no
583	D	⌊ ik:< >v:<u>oe</u>l 't n<u>ie</u>t Ømaar:
		I don't feel it but
584	→	>ik ben wat dat betreft 'n l<u>ee</u>k.
		I am a layman in that area
585		(2.3)
586	P	(°n↑ou!°)
		well
587		(1.1)
588		(ik weet niet)
		I don't know
589		u zegt ('t maar wat u't ⌈ beste vindt)
		you can say what you think is best
590	D	⌊ ja↑A:, dat lijkt me 't b<u>e</u>ste,
		yes that seems best to me
591		⌈ .hHh
592		⌊ (0.5)
593	→	maar ik ga u w<u>e</u>l e:hm:
		but I will give you uhm
594		(0.4)
595		ik gaat:-
		I will
596		(0.2)
597		<u>ee</u>n ding nog probere,
		try one more thing
598		(0.6)
599		of 't dat inderdaad is,
		whether it's that really
600		(.)
601		en as dat <u>oo</u>k niet helpt,
		and if that doesn't help either
602		⌈ hhhh
603		⌊ (0.6)
604		dan=
		then
605	→	=<en daarom zet ik (dat) hier op de kaart<=
		and that's why I'm putting that on this card

606   =dan wil ik graag dat u toch 'n keer naar
           that I would like you to go one day to
607   dokter Pereboom gaat.
           doctor P.
608   (.)
609   P   ja
           yes
610   (.)
611   maar
           but
612   (.)
613   u wilt <u>ee</u>rst nog wat anders ⌐ proberen?
           you want to try another thing first?
614   D   ⌐ ja
                                                 yes
615   (0.4)
616   ja
           yes
617   (.)
618   P   goed.
           alright
619   (0.5)
620   en as d<u>a</u>t niet helpt,
           and if that doesn't help
621   (.)
622   D   ja
           yes
623   (.)
624   dan d<u>a</u>cht ik d'rover om do ⌐ kter P<u>e</u>re ⌐ boom te vragen
           furthermore I am considering asking doctor P. about it
625   P   ⌐ ja   ⌐ ja
                                               yes   *yes*
626   (3.1)
627   maar d<u>a</u>t spreken we dan later af.=
           but in that case we will arrange that later
628   D   = ⌐↑ja↓:↑
             yes

629 P ⌊we handelen <u>ee</u>rst d<u>i</u>t af ⌈ (hè)
        we will settle this first

630 D   ⌊↑ja prec<u>ie</u>s↓
                                                yes exactly

631   ⌈(18.1)
632   ⌊((schrijven))
        ((writing))

633 →   en dat (de volgende) w<u>ee</u>k of drie vier,=
        and the the next week or three four

634   =en as u dan zegt 't helpt me eigenlijk ≠n<u>i</u>ks,
        and if you say it doesn't help me really at all

635   (.)

636 P   ja
        yes

637   (0.4)

638 D   dan eh:
        than uh

639   (0.4)

640   gaan we dokter Pereboom inschakelen.
        we are going to enlist doctor P.

641   (.)

642 P   j ⌈ a
        yes

643 D   ⌊ja?=
          yes?

644 P   =krijg ik daar tabl<u>e</u>tten voor?=
        do I get tablets for that?

645   =of-
        or

646   (0.5)

647 D   eh:: j<u>a</u>
        uh yes

648   (.)

649   tw<u>ee</u> per dag.
        two a day

650   (0.5)

651 P   tw<u>ee</u> per dag.
        two a day

```
652        (.)
653  D     ja=
           yes
```

In this episode, the physician again plays an 'open game' by telling the patient explicitly what and why he writes on her record card (lines 561-580). He considers asking a specialist to look at the case, with a mind to the first-mentioned alternative. He goes as far as saying that he is a "layman" in that area (584). The patient, again, claims ignorance and says she leaves it all to him (586-590). But before referring her, he wants to try one other thing — he does not explain what or why, nor even from which of the alternatives considered it follows, just that it involves tablets, two a day — and if that doesn't help, he will consider referring her to the specialist (lines 593-624). After this there follows some repetitions and instructions (not quoted for reasons of space), but the treatment as such is no longer discussed. Again we see in this case a combination of 'announcement' and 'proposal'-like formats, related, so it seems, to 'strong' or 'weak' positions, taken by the physician. But, as we saw, the patient refuses quite explicitly to 'join' in the consideration of the 'weak' possibilities, i.e. by taking stands in the debate of the alternatives. In other words, in these episodes the physician seems to start a 'debate' on diagnostic possibilities and disposal alternatives, displaying his inability to make up his mind on the case. The patient, however, refuses to take a stand on either issue, she just accepts what the doctor ends up proposing.

4. DISPOSALS AS MOVES IN EXTENDED NEGOTIATIONS

Until now I have at least implicitly suggested treating disposal negotiations as relatively isolated episodes, starting with a proposal by the physician. And I have been rather unsuccessful in discovering anything resembling 'negotiations' as ordinarily conceived. In case one, the patient had to be reminded of his 'duty' to react to the proposal, or of the fact that it was a 'proposal' in the first place. In the second and third cases, the announced disposal was simply acknowledged by the patient. And in the last case, the physician presented the patient with alternatives to which the patient showed herself to be reluctant to respond. One might suggest that the physicians who took a 'weak' position, bidding for acceptance or presenting alternatives and displaying insecurity, had special motives for suggesting that the disposal was negotiable. Let us now re-examine the cases to explore where those motives might have their origins.

Taking 'negotiation' in a broad sense, one might say that it starts the moment the patient enters the consulting room. That act already 'proposes' that the patient is in a state that deserves medical attention in one way or another, that he or she is a legitimate patient. In many cases, of course, the story the patient tells the doctor, and additional elements brought forward later, often only loosely connected to the physician's questions or completely unsolicited, can be seen as a case presentation, as an elaboration of the proposal stated by entering. When we accept this argument, the disposal proposed or announced later by the physician is not a 'first' act, but a 'subsequent' one, in sequential terms. For this reason, we should look at the pre-disposal episodes to discover the 'sequential environment', in a large sense, of the disposal, to explore sequential reasons for the choice of one or another of various disposal formats.

Space prohibits a detailed inspection of all four pre-disposal episodes, so I will have to summarize. In case 1, the patient's story,[3] and especially the many elements he adds to it, suggest that he has entertained two alternative possibilities, some kind of muscle disorder and a persistent cold. He has reported that he has had a patent medicine applied to relieve his muscle ache, but without success.[4] The announcement of the doctor's findings in lines 126 etc. seems to be designed to display its relevance to that earlier hypothesis, which is recovered, so to speak, because the alternative, a strong cold, could not be confirmed by the physical examination. So the proposal is to attack the muscular pain directly, in the implied expectation that when the patient moves easier, the muscular pains will heal automatically. And an additional prescription for nose drops might at the same time relieve some of the symptoms of the 'minor' cold.

Subsequent to the episode cited, the parties discuss the patient's eating habits, triggered by his question about vitamins in line 175. And when the physician writes the prescription and gives his instructions, the patient asks another question, suggesting the air conditioning in the place where he works — a bar — is the real source of the trouble. The physician agrees that this may very well be the real cause of both the persistent cold and the muscular pain. After that, they exchange some rather hilarious complaints about air conditioning generally, and ways to counter its effects at the patient's workplace in particular. Then the consultation ends.

The way the physician 'proposed' his disposal may be seen as a subsequent move in a progression of a rather vague presentation of a complaint, with additional information that suggest two alternative hypotheses, one of which had to be rejected in its strong form, leaving the other as an unexplained problem. That proposal is to cure the symptoms, rather than the disease which is as yet unaccounted for. The 'proposal' strategy may function as a way to co-opt the patient's acceptance of this less satisfactory solution. It is only after the patient himself, in a pre-closing episode, has suggested the basic cause, that the cognitive puzzle can be solved, or at least that a plausible solution is found. So we have a case here where it is the patient who brings in, in a delicate fashion, material that enables the physician to construct his disposal. The latter's role thus seem to be that of an 'arbiter' for a debate that has been going on in the patient's life world, and a provider of medication. The format of the consultation (Ten Have 1989), however, requires that this game be played furtively, under the cover of an ignorant lay person consulting a professional specialist. As for the other cases, their pre-disposal course is somewhat less complicated.

In case 2 the disposition follows a rather explicit consideration of two alternative diagnoses, on the one hand a cold with coughing, on the other an allergy with wheezing. The first alternative was suggested by the symptoms presented on entering, the second came up somewhat accidentally, when the patient mentioned that her coughing was worse at bedtime. The first alternative was explored by looking into the patient's throat and listening to her lungs, the second by a verbal examination of symptoms and circumstances. The first possibility seems rather weak, but the second is firmly rejected by the doctor (Well I- uhhhhhh I don't think that that's: (1.2) a specific enough: .hh relationship if you really are allergic dust'n feathers .hhhhh it (0.2) It really is a very noticeable thing. (0.4) Th' dut- tih- you (.) byou: the dust flies'n you really- You start to wheeze rather than to cough. — patient's contributions omitted). So the decision is to follow the cough/cold argument, although the complaint does not seem to be taken too seriously. The disposal, in this way, is a kind of 'just for sure' closing of the case. In no way has the patient expressed any opinions or recounted experiences that might be a basis for disagreement with the physician's disposal.

Case 3,[5] starts with the patient requesting an examination of her leg. The leg is examined and it is concluded that it is a muscular complaint (misschien geforceerd 'n keer — *maybe strained one day*, line 99). After the first episode quoted above in excerpt 3a, the patient is questioned on her experiences during her work, after which she refers to various circumstances that seem to be connected with a worsening of the complaints. This leads to an examination of the patient's feet, which results in 'ja hij is niet alleen dik maar hij is ook ontzettend doorgezakt' (*yes it is not only swollen but it is also terribly sagged*, lines 213-214). It is after this diagnosis that the episode about buying shoes, quoted as excerpt 3b, starts. In short, this is a rather straight-forward 'complaint-examination-diagnosis-advice' sequence. The only complications are the phases in the examination, i.e. a physical examination of the leg, a verbal inquiry about symptoms and circumstances, and again a physical examination of the feet, and the 'social' complications of the advice to buy a different kind of shoes, as discussed earlier. The patient is anxious to have the doctor find a solution to her problem (and to be able to continue her work) and she seems quite happy with the outcome.

In case 4,[6] finally, the patient has consulted the doctor about another, acute complaint. The moment that case is settled, she mentions that her foot is causing discomfort. She continues for quite some time to explain how she suffers from it, while the physician displays his recognition from earlier occasions. At a certain moment he reads from the patient's record card: '.hhh ik heb vorige keer, (0.7) hier gezet op vijfentwintig oktober, (0.7) is dit toch niet een ra:re vorm van ji:cht.' (*I have last time written here on 25 October isn't this after all a strange kind of gout*, lines 250-255), and recounts that he had written something similar. So he 'shares' his hypotheses with his patient, who seems unwilling to enter this 'game', as she comments on the just-mentioned statement with a '.hh ik kan 't nie zeggen.' (*I cannot say so*, line 258). After that, she alternates between 'locational' and symptom/circumstances descriptions. The doctor participates briefly in this and examines her feet. It is after some writing that he starts the disposal episode discussed earlier. Again, the pressure from the patient is for a solution to stop the suffering, but she in no way claims any non-experiential knowledge. In fact, she rejects, both earlier and in the episode discussed before, the possibilities offered by the physician to participate cognitively in the 'debate'. She makes it clear that she is willing to accept anything he proposes, refusing to 'negotiate' what she seems to consider his prerogative and responsibility.

5. CONCLUSION

The four cases explored in this chapter offer examples of some of the ways in which case disposals in GP consultations may be formatted. Three formats were found, in various combinations: Proposals, Announcements and Debates. The patients in these data seemed rather reluctant to join in a more active way in the disposal episodes, i.e. to *negotiate* proposals and debates. This is in line with Heath's (1992) findings concerning the diagnosis. Heath comments on "an extraordinary 'passivity'" of patients "in receiving news or information concerning their illness" (260-261).

The choice of the formats was shown to be responsive to case characteristics, in sequential terms, concerned with the earlier contributions by the patients, and in terms of whether the disposals were 'strong' or 'weak' decisions, and whether they were strictly medical or had some social implications. Further research is needed to elaborate this framework, and especially to see whether 'real', explicit disposal negotiations can be found and how they are socially organized through discourse action.

NOTES

1. The disposal of the case, deciding what should be done should be distinguished from the diagnosis, the medical assessment of the current medical condition. On the latter, see Heath (1992). His analysis is compatible with the one presented in this chapter.

2. Cases 1, 3 and 4 concern GP consultations recorded in the Netherlands; below the transcript lines in Dutch, rough 'glosses' in English are provided in italic. Case 2 was recorded in the U.K.

3. Quoted in ten Have (1991b:144).

4. Quoted in ten Have (1991b:147).

5. Aspects of this consultation were examined in ten Have (1991a:57-59).

6. Aspects of this consultation, including the 'lamenting' way in which the patient offered unsolicited information, were examined in ten Have (1991a).

CHAPTER 14

NEGOTIATING 'ADVICE' IN A CALL TO A CONSUMER HELPLINE

BRIAN TORODE

1. INTRODUCTION

The telephone helpline of the Office of Consumer Affairs, Dublin, has taken calls from the public since the passing of the 'Sale of Goods and Supply of Services Act' (Government of Ireland 1980). During 1988, in the course of some two hundred and fifty working days, "nearly 19,000 complaints about unsatisfactory goods and services were received" (Government of Ireland 1990:29). During the Spring of 1990, two hundred and twenty eight of these calls, representing three days' work, were recorded. This chapter examines call 02, the first to be recorded, of five minutes' duration. The caller is a consumer who experienced a problem, contacted the store to complain, but was dissatisfied with the response. She seeks to discover whether she has grounds to return again to the store.

According to Gulliver (1979:3), "the picture of negotiation is one of two sets of people, the disputing parties or their representatives, facing each other across a table". On this view, a call to a consumer helpline might seem to be not a *negotiation* but rather an *adjudication* by the helper between two parties, consumer and store, either of whom may "address ... information, opinion, and argument" to him, enabling him to "eventually ... pronounce his decision on the issues". Helper resembles an adjudicator in that he is not a party to the dispute, and either party may seek his advice. But he differs from an adjudicator in that he hears only one side of the dispute — usually the consumer's — and he has no power to enforce a decision. He can only advise caller how to pursue her case, in further *negotiation* with the store. He may encourage her to seek more or less than she had proposed, and he may add to or subtract from her arguments in support of her case.

In its sequential organization, the call also differs from adjudication as described by Gulliver (op. cit.). It begins with an exchange of initial positions, hers based on the perceived 'facts' of the case, his on relevant legal provisions. Rather than concluding the proceedings, his initial recommendation — expressed partly in technical terms somewhat unfamiliar to caller — completes only the first part of the call. It is followed by talk in which both parties search for agreement as to the practical course of action which caller can best pursue, on which basis the call can be closed. This search is a *negotiation* in Gulliver's sense. "They exchange information and opinion, engage in argument and discussion, and sooner or later propose offers and counter-offers relating to the issues in dispute between them, seeking an outcome acceptable to both sides" (op. cit.:3).

2. CALLER AND HELPER

In a recent paper, Wilson (1991) compares emergency telephone calls with courtroom deliberations between a Judge, a Public Defender and a District Attorney. Like emergency calls, most consumer calls can be characterized as 'complaints', and the parties to the call identified as 'complainant' and 'complaint-taker', respectively. However, just as Wilson notes that "we cannot argue that complaint-takers *command deference* in a way we might be willing to concede for judges" (op. cit.:32, emphasis added), so we cannot argue that consumer complaint-takers are *empowered to act* in a way we might concede for both emergency complaint-takers and judges. Whereas the emergency complaint-taker is *immediately* able to "send someone out to see you", and the judge is *immediately* able to "sentence you to ninety days", the consumer complaint-taker can only recommend action to be taken by caller after the call is over: *Call 02/24-26.*

        24   H   hhh so what you should do is (0.1) contact the store hhh (0.1)
        24a   explain your com<u>plain</u>t to: them hhh and see (.) if you can
                    ne<u>go</u>tiat:e
        24b   one (.) of thos:e (.) sol<u>u</u>tions
        25   C   yeah
        26   H   either to the repair replacement or refund

Whereas legal counsel who say what they want are *negotiating* with the judge, who may or may not give it to them, and emergency line complainants who show what they want are *negotiating* with complaint-takers, who may or may not give them what they want, it seems that callers to the consumer helpline are engaged initially in something preliminary to a negotiation, as is indicated in the phrase "see (.) if you can negotiat:e (.)" (line 24a). Whereas the respective actions of the judge and of the emergency complaint-taker bring negotiations to a natural close, the OCA helper's inability to *act* can lead to difficulty in closing such sequences; it is not until much later in the call that caller appears willing to accept the advice offered:

Call 02/52-54b

```
52    C    Yes. (0.2)
53          Th↑at's f↑air=en↑ough
54a         th↑at's what I wanted to clarify
54b         °before I go back into: them°=
```

It therefore seems best to characterize the parties simply as 'caller' and 'helper' on the understanding that part of the research purpose is to describe what kind of 'help' it is that is being provided.

3. REQUESTING ADVICE

The call begins with a reference to "advice":

Call 02/1-2

```
1     H    er (.) yes?
2     C    I want to get your advi:ce: (0.2)
```

"Advice" is caller's category for a kind of help. It is not yet actually requested; instead, the remark is a kind of 'story preface' (Sacks 1992b:222ff), seeking the floor to tell a 'story' to show what advice is required. The preface tells what it will take for the story to be over, namely, a request for advice will have been made.[1]

Ethnomethodological conversation analysis (hereafter, CA), the turn-by-turn study of the accomplishment of order in talk (Sacks, Schegloff and Jefferson 1974), has paid particular attention to 'adjacency *pairs*' of turns (Schegloff 1968, emphasis added), whereby a first pair part — e.g. a question, or an invitation — constitutes a 'conditional relevance' such that the following talk will be searched for an appropriate second pair part - an answer to the question, an acceptance or declining of the invitation. The next turn will be heard if possible as such a second pair part, or otherwise as *relevant* to the later production of such a second pair part. When completed, caller's request for advice, anticipated but not yet delivered in line 2, will serve as such a first pair part, and helper's delivery of such advice will become conditionally relevant. It will be for caller to determine whether and when that advice has been acceptably delivered, at which point the call can terminate.

Caller's first remark thus anticipates call completion when three moves have been made:

1 Caller requests advice
2 Helper offers advice
3 Caller accepts advice

Of these, the first and second moves seemingly constitute an adjacency pair: the first is a request for an item to be delivered in the second, which delivery is relevant immediately on completion of the first. The second and third moves seemingly constitute another adjacency pair of which the first part is an offer of advice to be accepted in the second part which is relevant immediately on completion of the first. It seems the second move must have a complex structure whereby it can serve at once as the second part of one adjacency pair, and the first part of another.

By her use of the word "advice", caller announces at the outset a criterion by which to determine what it will take for the whole call to be over. When caller uses the word again it is to move directly into closing:

Call 02/61-66

61	C	=>thanks for your ad<u>vice</u><
62	H	o: <u>ka:y</u>?=
63	C	>↑ok↑ay< (.)
64	C	[>b↑ye=b↑ye<
65	H	[right] ho (0.1)
66	H	bye now

At each earlier point which could have concluded the call, caller raised additional questions, showing she wanted more from helper, and helper provided more. We will seek to show what further help was provided on each of these occasions.

4. THE FIRST ADJACENCY PAIR

The first move of the call's three-part structure is fulfilled by lines 2-6, as follows:

Call 02/2-7a

2	C	I want to get your advi:ce: (0.2)
3		on a jacket I bought hhh
4		now the jacket's >a hundred and twenty< pou:nd::s
		(0.1)
5a		a:nd (.) hhh when I washed=it>following=the=
		=instructions<the=jacket=ran
5b		now the shop want it ba:ck to send it to their lab
		or whatever hhh (0.2)
6a		What am I entitled to:: for (.) the jacket (0.2)
6b		they're now (0.1) half pric::e hhh (0.2)
7a	H	hhh o::ka::y (.)

At lines 3 to 6, caller tells a story which - as anticipated in the preface, line 2 - constitutes a request for "advice". At line 7, helper's "o::ka::y" shows that he has so heard it. But his delivery of advice does not begin until line 14:

Call 02/14

14	H	ok well first thing he::re I'll go through the legislation give you a
		guideline as to what rights: are invo:lved hhh

Following his acknowledgement of the request, but before beginning to deliver the advice, he directs three questions to caller (lines 7, 9 and 12):

Call 02/7-13

7	H	hhh o::ka::y (.) you were returning the:: jacket to the store? (.)
8	C	ye:s=
9	H	=and what (0.2) were they accepting respons:ibility? hhh
10	C	we::ll (0.1) she said >send it in< that it was a mess and that (0.1)
		they'd s(.)send it to whatever department they'd send it to:
11	H	rr:ight (0.1)
12		but they haven'actually accepted that the jacket was faulty at the
		moment?=
13	C	=no: (0.1) no: (0.1)

Each question and answer comprises an adjacency pair in its own right. Thus the completion of the 'outer' adjacency pair is postponed while a chain of 'inner' adjacency pairs understood to be relevant to that completion is pursued. Schegloff (1972b) calls this an 'insertion sequence'.

4.1. Insertion sequences in sequential structure

Wilson (op. cit.) shows that the local logic of insertion sequences accounts for many features which might be misleadingly ascribed to the institutional context in which talk takes place. As an instance of such a phenomenon Wilson cites a Judge's (J) deliberations (in interaction with the Public Defender (PD) and District Attorney (DA)) before sentencing a defendant already found guilty:

Mather 1973/1-14[2]

1	PD	Your Honour, we request immediate sentencing
2		and waive the probation report.
3	J	What's his record?
4	PD	He has a prior drunk and a GTA [Grand Theft Auto].
5		Nothing serious. This is just a shoplifting case.
6		He did enter the K-Mart with the intent to steal.
7		But really all we have here is a petty theft.
8	J	What do the people have?
9	DA	Nothing either way.
10	J	How long has he been in?
11	PD	Eighty-three days.
12	J	I make this a misdemeanor by P.C. Article 17 and
13		sentence you to ninety days in County Jail, with
14		credit for time served.

Although (lines 3-11) a series of questions is directed by the judge to other parties, and the floor returns to the judge each time, we do not need to account for this in terms of judicial authority in the court room. It is simply an 'insertion sequence', understood by co-participants as preliminary to the completion, by the questioner, of another adjacency pair, which he is accountable to them to do. That adjacency pair is initiated by the public defender's utterance, "Your Honor, we request immediate sentencing" (line 1), a turn explicitly built as a 'request'. So although the party (who happens to be the presiding judge) has authority to conduct this sequence, in collaboration with his co-parties, his authority is not that of 'judge' but of 'projected second pair part completer', and his conduct is ongoingly monitored by the co-parties for its relevance to this project. Although both are 'membership categorisations' in Sacks' (1972a) terms, 'judge' is an *institutional* identity ongoing negotiated by the parties in the specific setting, whereas 'projected second pair part completer' is a *discourse* identity available as part of the "fundamental mechanisms of interaction" (Wilson 1991:36).

Wilson also notes *institutional* features of the sequence. A request for sentencing "cannot be directed to just anyone"(op. cit.:34). The judge directs his first question (line 3) to the Public Defender (PD) who draws a "contrastive formulation" between shoplifting and burglary (lines 6-7). This distinction "is not a sequential matter, but rather has to do with the institutional structure of the criminal justice system" (op. cit.:35). To make it the PD employs "devices generally found in disagreement sequences (Pomerantz 1984b)", but there is no actual disagreement with any prior talk. There is *potential* disagreement with possible future talk by the DA (who is invited to speak next by the judge), and also by the judge (if he should be inclined to decline the request). It seems that the PD's turn is designed to discourage either occurrence by rehearsing the potential disagreement ("intent to steal", line 6, indicates burglary but, despite that, "really all we have here is a petty theft", line 7), rendering it unnecessary for either of them to do so.

4.2. The call's first insertion sequence

The first insertion sequence in the helpline call resembles Wilson's insertion sequence in that helper's questions pursue a contrast between two possible cases, that store *have* or *have not* accepted that the product is faulty. As narrated by caller, this contrast had a sequential aspect. Both her original story (line 5) and her retelling of it (line 10) propose that at one point in time store might not accept fault, whereas at a later time, they might do so:

Call 02/5

5a	C	a:nd (.) hhh when I washed=it>following=the= =instructions<the=jacket=ran
5b		now the shop want it ba:ck to send it to their lab or whatever hhh (0.2)

Call 02/10

10	C	we::ll (0.1) she said >send it in< that it <u>was</u> a mess and that (0.1) they'd s(.)send it to whatever department they'd send it t<u>o:</u>

But in the insertion sequence, helper secures caller's agreement to a formulation which eliminates this aspect:

Call 02/12-13

12	H	but they haven' actually acce<u>p</u>ted that the jacket was <u>faul</u>ty at the moment?=
13	C	=no: (0.1) no: (0.1)

Potential disagreement between speakers (whether store are likely to accept fault in the future) is avoided by discovering an area of actual agreement (that store have not *yet* accepted fault). This process of mutual discovery is facilitated by caller's way of responding to helper's second question: rather than answer affirmatively and risk disagreement, she resorts to narrative story-telling (line 10) in an elaboration or 'unpacking' (cf. Jefferson 1985) of her original story (line 5) to provide helper with the means to make out an answer to his question. When he proposes a negative answer, she accepts it.

Whilst this insertion sequence exhibits certain features of 'negotiation' as described by Gulliver (information and opinion are provided, there is discussion, an offer is proposed and an agreed outcome is achieved), there is no *exchange*. The sequence is explicitly one-sided. Questions are put by helper inviting caller to "address...information, opinion, and argument" to him, to clarify the position she is proposing, enabling him to "eventually ... pronounce his decision on the issues". In this sense, the insertion sequence and the first adjacency pair as a whole could be said to resemble 'adjudication', as defined by Gulliver.

But we do not need to account for this one-sidedness by appealing to institutional processes in this specific social situation. Rather, a feature stressed by Wilson (1991) enables us to account for it as the outcome of a social process. In effect, any 'inner' insertion sequence is controlled by the party due to deliver the second pair part in the 'outer' adjacency pair, to whom the floor repeatedly returns, on the proviso that he or she is accountably pursuing preliminaries relevant to the closing of the insertion sequence, and the delivery of that outer second pair part. Here, helper's question-answer chain at lines 7 to 13 is recognisably an 'insertion sequence' in Schegloff's terms, which helper 'controls' in Wilson's terms.

4.3. Completing the first adjacency pair

Having received answers to his three questions, helper's 'ok' at line 14 marks the beginning of his response to caller's request, i.e. the second pair part of the adjacency pair begun by the request, and the second of the 'three moves' in the call structure. According to CA's account of the "fundamental mechanisms of interaction" (Wilson 1991:36), caller should be attending to helper's remarks from line 14 for two distinct purposes: first, and most fundamentally, to see when they are over so she can resume the floor; second, less fundamentally, to see when he has given her the "advice" she seeks. Caller does indeed monitor helper's remarks at lines 14-24, responding to each

with a continuer ("ye::es", "ye::ah", "mmh yes", etc.).
Call 02/14-26

14	H	ok well first thing he::re I'll go through the legis<u>l</u>ation give you a guideline as to what rights: are inv<u>o</u>:lved hhh
15		now hhh th<u>e</u>:: act is what's called the:: Sa:le (.) of (.) Goods=Act hhh
16	C	ye::es
17	H	now that states that when you purchase goods:(2.0) those goods should be:: (.) fit for their <u>p</u>urpos:e (0.2) of (0.1) merchantable (0.2) quality and (0.2) hhh as desc<u>ri</u>:bed hhh
18		now (.) if a fault develops in the jacket widin an un<u>rea</u>sonable le:ngth of ti::em hhh you have a right (.) to seek <u>r</u>edress:: fr<u>om</u> the shop hhh
19	C	yeah
20	H	now that <u>r</u>edress can be to a re<u>p</u>air (0.2) a re<u>p</u>lacement:: (0.2) or (0.1) a <u>r</u>efund of money (0.1)
21	C	ye::ah
22	H	now (.) the normal rule is (0.1) if the fault is <u>min</u>or your rights are to a re<u>p</u>ai:r hhh where if the fault is <u>maj</u>or (0.1) your rights are to a re<u>f</u>und (.) or re<u>p</u>lac<u>e</u>ment
23	C	mmmh yes
24	H	hhh so what you should do is (0.1) contact the store hhh (0.1) explain your com<u>pl</u>aint to: them hhh and see (.) if you can ne<u>g</u>otiat:e one (.) of thos:e (.)sol<u>u</u>tions
25	C	yeah
26	H	either to the repair replacement or refund

By prefacing his delivery of advice with "first thing here" (line 14), helper announces a departure from caller's immediate concerns into discussion of certain legal technicalities. Some of these sound obscure (e.g. "merchantable quality", line 17) and are mentioned once only, early and briefly. Some are familiar everyday expressions (the two varieties of 'fault', and the three forms of 'rights' to 'redress' available): these arc mentioned repeatedly and discussed in some detail.

With "hhh so what you should do" (line 24) helper shows he has concluded his summary of the legislation and is now doing a second thing, namely making a practical recommendation for caller's conduct of her case, in a way which makes reference to the legislation just described, thereby showing the relevance of the "first thing". His recommendation (line 24) comprises a three-part list, namely:

    1. contact the store;

    2. explain your complaint to them;

    3. and see if you can negotiat:e one of those solutions.

In a 'tag', in 'monitor space' (Davidson 1984:119ff), he repeats for a third time his mnemonic "three R's" list of remedies (line 26).

Atkinson (1983) has shown how, in speeches, three-part lists function as "claptraps", which the audience can hear as a natural break in the monologue and an opportunity to take a turn, by applauding or otherwise. At this point helper might be heard to have given the advice requested. Given, as earlier noted, his inability to *act* decisively in the manner of a judge or an emergency dispatcher, he can nonetheless be heard to have completed the adjacency pair in at least three senses. Most importantly, the structure of his elaborate turn has a recognisable completeness to it, in that having departed from practicality to legal technicality it has returned to practicality with a positive use of the legal knowledge gained. Secondly his repetition of the "three R's" list appears designed to show that he has concluded his delivery and is merely summing-up or reminding his listener of what she has already heard. Finally, his remark "so what you should do is contact the store" (line 24) has the quality of making *arrangements*, an activity which is often "specifically used to place conversation on a closing track" (Button 1991:251).[3] Here it reminds caller that her real business is with store, with whom she should "see if you can negotiat:e" (line 24). But caller does not treat his remarks as yet complete. Somewhat contrary to his advice she begins to 'negotiate' with *him*, here and now.

5. THE SECOND ADJACENCY PAIR

Just as caller's request for advice constitutes the first pair part of a first adjacency pair, expecting helper's delivery of advice as its second pair part, so helper's delivery of advice constitutes the first pair part of a *second* adjacency pair, expecting caller's acceptance of advice as its second pair part. Naturally there can be cases when advice requested is not delivered, or when advice delivered is not accepted. However these are exceptional, and as such accountable. In the unexceptional case, delivery and acceptance both occur. But neither need occur immediately. In either case, the expected delivery of the second pair part of the adjacency pair may be deferred by an insertion sequence, prototypically a question-answer chain, understood by all parties concerned to be relevant to the task of producing the second part.

Following helper's initial delivery of advice (ending at line 26), caller's *acceptance* of his advice does not begin until line 52:

Call 02/52-54b

52	C	Yes. (0.2)
53		Th↑at's f↑air=en↑ough
54a		th↑at's what I wanted to cla̱rify
54b		°before I go back i̱nto: them°=

It is deferred by her insertion sequence of two questions (lines 27-36, and line 46) and helper's answers to them. In this sense, the two ISs are similarly organised. But in another sense, their organization is different. Whereas the first merely clarifies caller's position, and is of minor significance in relation to the call as a whole,[4] the second is the major component of the whole call. It is a negotiation in the full sense between two distinct positions, of which one ultimately wins and the other loses the argument.

Call 02/27-36

27	C	but what my point is]
28		like it's a red ja̱cket and (.) and whi̱te
29		and the red is all gone through the whi̱te hhh erm
30		the jacket was a hundred and twe̱n:ty
31		they're now si̱xty erm
32		one hundred and ni̱neteen
33		they're now fifty ni̱ne whatever (.)
34		so > say one hundred=and=twe̱nty
35		they're now sixty hhh < ERR (1.0)
36		IF THEY GIVE ME A NEW JACKET >VALUED AT SIXTY POUNDS < AM I EN̲TI̲TLED TO SIXTY POUNDS AS WELL?

As in response to helper's questions in the first insertion sequence, Caller here resorts to narrative story-telling.[5] But then she avoided disagreement by allowing helper to provide the upshot of her story (line 12). Now she draws her own conclusion from her stories. Her candidate answer to her original question concerning entitlement (line 6) is a new jacket "valued at sixty pounds" and "sixty pounds as well" (line 36).

5.1. Disagreement sequences

How is it possible for caller to commence *negotiation* at this point in the call, if helper's advice-giving (lines 14-26) has completed the adjacency pair begun by her request for advice (lines 2-6)? One way to understand caller's intervention from line 27 is as a 'third turn', described by John Heritage as a general feature of the turn-taking system:

> one 'third turn' option which is open to the first speaker is the explicit correction or repair of any misunderstanding which was displayed in the second speaker's turn (Heritage 1984a:257).

He extends this observation to the following "very general phenomenon":

> [A]fter any 'second action', the producer of the first has a systematically given opportunity to repair any misunderstanding of the first action that may have been displayed in the second (op. cit.:258).

Heritage's 'three action' model is similar to the 'three move' model for the call as a whole implied by caller's initial request for 'advice'. However, whilst it may be generally applicable, it does not arise in the 'institutional' interaction discussed by Wilson: his court-room transcript concludes with the judge's completion of the adjacency pair.

It might be claimed that in this case the institutional authority of the speaker was such that, in this context, his decision was final. Further, it might be noted that the decision sought was granted, so there was no need for negotiation. These explanations complement one another: as noted earlier, the judge is in a position to act. He need not be understood to have 'authority' over the *interlocutor* (to prevent the asking of further questions), but he is understood to have 'authority' over relevant *third parties* so that when he pronounces "ninety days in County Jail, with credit for [eighty-three] days served", the prisoner will be released within seven days.

Helper lacks such practical authority. Nothing he says will take immediate effect. His advice in this sense is theoretical. Its practical enactment is for caller to undertake. This being so, an apparent difficulty is that if caller should fail to accept the advice, and begin to negotiate, then she might never accept the advice, and negotiation between them need never cease.[6] This predicament has been discussed in an institutional context by Judy Davidson (1978:124), citing a lecture by Harvey Sacks delivered on 10 May 1971 (see Sacks 1992b:391ff.). Davidson notes that — for institutional rather than for fundamental reasons, in Wilson's terms — in the case of a client-advising organization there is a preference that clients should *accept* advice given. Client can then use this preference as 'leverage' to negotiate a form of advice which she will accept. However this presupposes the existence — for fundamental rather than for institutional reasons — of the 'third turn' slot within which client (here, caller) can indicate acceptance or otherwise of the advice given.

In a subsequent discussion, Davidson (1984) has proposed a four turn-position sequence for doing disagreement. When a speaker offers an *assessment* this constitutes a first pair part [turn position 1] inviting an *evaluation* of that assessment in second part [turn position 2] with a preference for *agreement* with the assessment. Helper's advice (lines 14-26), the second of our 'three moves', is an assessment which can constitute turn position 1 in this sequence. Then if caller *agreed* with the assessment, a single turn [turn position 2] would suffice to express it. Such a turn would comprise our 'third move,' the 'third action' in Heritage's general account. But, Davidson points out, when second speaker does *disagreement*, matters become more complex. It is commonly done not in a single turn, but over three turns [turn positions 2, 3, 4] in collaboration with first speaker, as follows:

Turn position 1: A	Initial Version	Assessment
Turn position 2: B	Weak Agreement[7]	
Turn position 3: A	Subsequent Version	Reassessment (Upgrade/Downgrade)
Turn position 4: B	Response	Strong Dis/Agreement

This structure is not limited to four positions. When second speaker passes over successive possible response points, or responds in other than the desired way, successive subsequent versions may be produced by first speaker, in an attempt to elicit a desired response.

To do disagreement with helper's assessment (lines 14-26) [turn position 1], following Davidson's model, caller should pause before delivering a brief "weak agreement" turn [turn position 2], inviting helper to upgrade or downgrade his assessment [turn position 3]. But this is not what happens. At line 27 caller takes the floor early, in overlap with line 26, to extend and upgrade the version of events (lines 27-36) which she stated more briefly in her original request for advice (lines 2-6). But her intervention *is* recognisable as part of a disagreement sequence comprising the call so far as a whole, beginning with her initial request for advice:

Turn position 1: C	Q	Initial Version	(lines 2-6)
	{first insertion sequence (lines 7-13) ommitted from this analysis, see below}		
Turn position 2: H	A	Weak Disagreement	(lines 14-26)
Turn position 3: C	Q	Subsequent version:	
		Upgraded to strongly positive	(lines 27-36)

When presented, her original story did not appear to *assess* her position, nor did helper's advice appear to *agree* or *disagree* with a prior assessment. But she responds to helper's

358   *B. Torode*

"advice" by returning to that story, providing details previously glossed (the colours which "ran" and the exact price changes). The upshot is her *candidate answer* (line 36) to her question regarding "entitle"-ment (line 6). This "subsequent version" of her request for advice (lines 27-36) [turn position 3] shows that her original story [turn position 1] provided enough information to make out what her assessment was. Her *upgraded* assessment of her situation is one which differs from what helper has said is available by the "normal rule" namely replacement *or* refund (lines 22, and 24-26) [turn position 2]. In the special circumstances of her case, she seeks *both*: "if they give me a new jacket valued at sixty pounds am I entitled to sixty pounds as well?" (line 36).

Helper now responds to caller's 'subsequent version':

Call 02/37-45

37a	H	hhh what you're generally entitled to (.) would be (.)
37b		if they ac<u>cept</u> that the item is fau<u>lt</u>y (.)
37c		would be to a re<u>fund</u> or rep<u>lac</u>ement: hhh
38		now if they rep<u>lace</u> it with an i<u>dent</u>ical jacket=
39	C	=yeah
40	H	and you're willing to ac<u>cept</u> that
41	C	mmmh
42	H	then your rights would generally be t<u>o:</u> that hhh
43		if (.) you're (.) talking about a <u>refund</u> of money (.) you would be talking about a refund on the pri<u>c::</u>e (.) that you actually (0.2) hhh er (.) pai:d <u>for</u> the jacket:
44	C	yes::
45	H	that would be the the: full refund ⌈of m⌉ oney

This evaluation (lines 37-45) [turn position 4] is upgraded to strongly-negative in response to caller's strongly-positive upgraded proposal (lines 27-36) [turn position 3]. Its precision matches hers. Just as her re-telling is designed to show that the relevant facts had already been provided, so his re-telling is designed to highlight its repetition of his previous points.

Turn position 4: H   A   Response:
                                 Upgraded to strong disagreement   (lines 37-45)

Caller's response to this (line 46) is not one which employs "devices generally found in disagreement sequences" (Wilson 1991:35 such as delay, appreciation, or excuse. Rather it is an early and direct statement, in overlap with helper's prior turn:

Call 02/45-46

```
45   H      that would be the the: full refund ⌐ of m ¬ oney
46   C                                        ⌊ yes ⌡ yes but if I take a
            half=price jacket a similar jacket at half price [(am I still)
```

This is not a complete sentence. Rather it is a proposed *repair* which amends helper's "full refund" (line 45) to "half price jacket", and his "identical jacket" (line 38), to "similar jacket", then allows him to continue his turn. It seeks to undermine the precision achieved by helper [turn position 4] in response to caller [turn position 3], rather than to constitute a turn position in its own right. If accepted, this would blunt the disagreement which is now apparent and — she claims — would address specific aspects of her case which his "general" case neglects, especially the feature that the jacket is "now half price", which she stated in each of her turn positions. But helper replies in kind:

Call 02/46-48

```
46    C                            ⌊yes ⌡      yes but if I take a half=price
             jacket a similar jacket at half price ⌐ (am I s ¬  till)
47a   H                                           ⌊ If it's a⌡ =if it's an identical
             replace ⌐ ment ¬ jacket (.) you know
48    C             ⌊ yes ⌡
```

He repairs her phrase "a similar jacket at half price" to "an identical replacement jacket", showing that her loss of precision was unwarranted and, further, that the price issue was irrelevant.[8] In accepting his repair immediately (her line 48 overlaps with the word "replacement" in his line 47a), caller accepts that helper's stance [turn position 4] has not been weakened but remains strong.

Call 02/47a-52

```
47a   H                                    ⌊If it's a⌡ =if it's an identical
             replace ⌐ ment ¬ jacket (.) you know
48    C             ⌊ yes ⌡
47b   H      that's all you would be generally entitled ⌐ to ¬ you know would be
49    C                                                 ⌊ yes⌡
47c   H      an identical replac:ement and that (0.1)
50    C      yes
51    H      because you would be receiving li:ke for li:ke
52    C      Yes. (0.2)
```

He explicitly repeats his confirmed strong terms "generally entitled" (lines 37a and

47b) and "id̲e̲ntical replacement" (lines 47a and 47c), gaining caller's immediate acceptance for each of these as he does so (lines 49 and 50). His "you know" response to each acceptance reminds her that these terms are already known to her. He rounds off his statement with the proverbial, "li:ke for li:ke" (line 51), a device which is an especially appropriate way to "tell one's co-participants what they already know" (Sacks 1972c:139), which also gains immediate acceptance (line 52).

5.2. Completing the second adjacency pair

After some delay caller responds with an appropriate though distinct proverbial of her own, "that's fair enough" (line 53), and an appreciation which formulates the call as a 'pre' sequence to her return to store:

Call 02/52-54b

52	C	Yes. (0.2)
53		Th↑at's f↑air=en↑ough
54a		th↑at's what I wanted to cla̲rify
54b		°before I go back i̲n̲to: them°=

At this point, helper's advice appears to be accepted, completing the second adjacency pair. Two kinds of sequential structure are at work in the call up to this point. The first is implied by caller's own way of requesting "advice", and receives confirmation both from "fundamental" considerations due to Heritage and Wilson, and from "institutional" considerations due to Sacks and Davidson. On this model, the call comprises *three moves* (Caller requests Advice, Helper offers Advice, Caller accepts Advice). Both the first and second taken together, and the second and third taken together constitute adjacency pairs. Each can receive insertion sequences under the control of the party due to deliver the second pair part, namely helper in the first case, and caller in the second.

The second is implied by caller's way of responding to the advice given, which closely matches Davidson's account of a disagreement sequence, encompassing the whole call as a sequence of *four turn positions*. In this sequence, the first and second positions are caller's request for advice and helper's initial offer of advice. The third is caller's restatement of her request for advice, within the second insertion sequence. The fourth is helper's restatement of his advice, also within the second insertion sequence. Further talk within this sequence was designed to repair and restate the fourth position, which was finally accepted by caller.

It is the second of these accounts which reveals the character of the second insertion sequence as a *negotiation*, within which the work of the call as a whole (requesting, offering, and accepting advice) is repeatedly re-worked, closely matching Gulliver's (1979:3) description of negotiation as involving "exchange" of "information and opinion", "argument and discussion", "offers and counter-offers relating to the issues in dispute between them, seeking an outcome acceptable to both sides". However it is the first account which reveals the framework within which the negotiation occurs. Negotiation is systematically possible in an insertion sequence embedded within an adjacency pair. Party B, due to complete the pair, may defer doing so in order to raise matters of concern. Since party A, the initiator, seeks completion of the pair, party B can treat resolution of these matters as a *condition* of completion of the pair, thereby exercising the "leverage" identified by Davidson.

In a conversation comprising a sequence of adjacency pairs, party B can re-open in the second pair matters which had apparently been resolved in the first, treating re-consideration of the matters as a *condition* of completion of the second pair. This is especially salient in a two-party conversation when the first pair was initiated by party B, but the second pair is initiated by party A, since it provides systematically for B to reopen matters which A had closed. In the second adjacency pair in the present call, caller is due to complete the pair by accepting the advice. But she defers doing so in order to reopen matters addressed in the first adjacency pair. She restates her request, and helper restates his advice. The parties use the insertion sequence in the second adjacency pair to *repair* the first adjacency pair.

This analysis leaves two questions unanswered. First, if in fact any insertion sequence may have the character of a negotiation, then why does the first insertion sequence (lines 7-13) not have this character? Second, how can helper's advice (lines 14-26) serve both as second part of the first adjacency pair, and first part of the second? These questions will be addressed below.

6. TOPICS IN THE CALL

Caller's remarks at lines 52-54b apparently constitute an adequate acceptance of helper's advice, and might be appropriately followed by a closing sequence (such as occurs at lines 62-66). But in mid-turn (line 54c), caller 'interrupts' herself to mention another matter.

Call 02/54a-55

54a	C	th↑at's what I wanted to cla<u>ri</u>fy
54b		°before I go back <u>into</u>: them°=
54c		=NO THEY'RE THEY'RE QUITE NICE A<u>BOUT</u> IT YOU

KN↑OW AND THEY'LL TAKE THE JACKET IN WHICH IS
SOMETHING
(0.2)
55   H   yea:h

This matter involves store in the context of caller's return visit. In this sense it is
continuous with her immediately prior remark. But it is discontinuous with helper's
prior remarks. It refers not to the matter of "entitlement" which has been - at her
instigation - the main topic of discussion between them but to the matter of "acceptance"
of fault by store. This matter was first mentioned by caller but thereafter repeatedly
pursued by helper.

There has been a division of topics throughout the call. The *major* topic,
"entitlement" — which caller vigorously pursued at the outset — is the one in which
helper has professional expertise, namely the Sale of Goods and Supply of Services
Act (Government of Ireland 1980) and its relevance to consumer complaints according
to "the normal rule" (line 22). It is a technical topic, discussed by means of special
terminology ("merchantable quality", "redress", etc.) or else in everyday terms which
are made to carry specially precise but restricted meanings ("entitle", "accepting
responsibility", "fault", "reasonable time", "repair, replacement or refund"). The
discussion of this topic aspires to *objectivity* but — as the negotiation at lines 37-51
shows — this can be achieved only in relation to a "general" case (line 37) which may
not quite correspond to the specific case at hand.

The *minor* topic, "acceptance" — which helper vigorously pursued at his first
available opportunity (first insertion sequence, lines 7-13) — is one in which his
competence is that of an informed layman. Through the practice of helping callers he
has accumulated a wealth of experience greater than that of any particular caller: in
particular, he has learned in detail of their experiences in negotiation with stores.[9] This
is a practical topic, discussed in everyday terms whose meanings are overtly *indexical*
("a mess", "like for like", "fair enough", "quite nice about it").[10]

By line 54b in the call, caller had graciously accepted helper's advice with respect
to the major topic, and it seemed that call closing was immanent. Instead she now
reopens discussion of the minor topic just as, at lines 27-36, she reopened discussion
of the major topic. She had earlier provided narrative accounts of this matter (lines
5-13, see section 4.2). There she produced a 'strong' agreement (Pomerantz 1984b)
which helper relied upon throughout the subsequent call up to this point. But now (line
54c) she revises that strong agreement.

She does not directly disagree with his earlier formulation (line 12), but her
"which is something" (line 54c) strongly disagrees with an *upgraded* version of that

formulation, namely "they haven't actually accepted anything at the moment?" (line 12). This amounts to a (relatively) weak disagreement with what helper actually said. Her pause (0.2) invites his response. He offers a weak agreement (line 55). She prompts for a further response (line 56), which he provides (lines 57-59):

Call 02/56-59

```
56   C      you know?
57a  H      well it'(.)be a matter of discussing that and see
57b         will they conce::de  that there is a fau:lt ┌ then ┐
58   C                                                  └ yeah ┘
59   H      i:n (0.1) the actual jacket=
```

His response avoids a direct answer to her question. Instead, like her response (line 10) to his question on the same topic, it is a story enabling her to *make out* his reply. He proposes that the matter raised (store's acceptance of fault) is for further discussion not with him but with store. That this discussion will take the form of a "negotiation" (his term at line 24 above) is shown by his requirement that "they conce::de that there is a fault".

7. NEGOTIATION IN AND OUT OF THE CALL

In proposing this division of labour, helper attends to caller's division between topics of the call: the *major* topic, about which he is willing to offer his own independent "general" assessment (notably his formulation of caller's "entitlement", lines 37-45), and the *minor* topic, about which he is not. (His candidate assessment at line 12 was based on the information which he had elicited from caller, and was immediately offered back to her for approval, which she gave.) In proposing this division of labour here, helper also proposes the end of the call. His rationale is precisely that which Wilson notes in the monitoring of the judge's questioning by other parties in the court room:

> [E]ach turn in the Insertion Sequence displays understanding of two matters: first, what was said in preceding turns, and second, that a request is still pending so that each present turn is understood to be relevant to providing a response to that request (Wilson 1991:35-36).

The "request that is still pending" here is no longer caller's request for advice, for helper indicates that that has been satisfied. It is helper's request to caller: "see (.) if you can negotiat:e(.)" with store. This request, made as part and parcel of his advice in response to her request to him, displays understanding that each turn in the present conversation between caller and helper is understood to be relevant to her future provision of a response to that request. In short, both parties understand that the helpline call is itself an 'insertion' within the conversation between caller and store, which preceded and will follow it.

'Advice' is preferably followed by 'acceptance' of advice, and it appeared that this had been straightforwardly achieved by line 54a. But, for a third time within this conversation, a prior turn unit is reassessed. Caller's 'acceptance' of advice at lines 60-61 is prompt, direct (briefly stated, it repeats the core component - the proverbial - of her prior version) and includes an explicit reference to her preface which opened the call as a whole:

Call 02/60-61

60	C	=yeah FAIR ENOUGH=
61		=>thanks for your ad<u>vice</u><

This is a *strong* acceptance. Retrospectively it reveals her prior version to have been *weak*, delivered late, with a pause, an appreciation, and an excuse:

Call 02/52-54b

52	C	Yes. (0.2)
53		Th↑at's f↑air=en↑ough
54a		th↑at's what I wanted to cl<u>a</u>rify
54b		°before I go back <u>into</u>: them°=

These are characteristic features of dispreferred second pair parts (Heritage 1984a:266-267) reflecting the fact that the advice was not what was hoped for.

7.1. The call as an insertion

In her role of 'projected second pair part completer', by virtue of the expectation that she should accept advice given to her, caller initiated the second insertion sequence to reopen matters closed in the first adjacency pair and so renegotiate both her own request for advice concerning "entitlement", and helper's advice in response to that request, in a disagreement sequence. This nonetheless ended in her apparently accepting his advice. Now by interrupting herself — more strictly, by repairing her apparent acceptance, which would be call-closing implicative — caller initiates a third insertion sequence. She uses it to reopen the issue of store's "acceptance" of fault. This was a matter closed in the first insertion sequence (lines 7-13), and not reopened since (though mentioned at line 37b). She thereby pursues negotiation of "acceptance" through a disagreement sequence in an insertion sequence much like the one through which she earlier pursued negotiation of "entitlement".

In that negotiation we found that the disagreement sequence of four turn positions did not fit the insertion sequence in isolation (treating helper's response as first turn position), but did fit the call as a whole (treating caller's request for advice as first turn). In the present negotiation we have noted the following sequence of exchanges between caller and helper:

Turn position 1:	C	The shop want it back	(line 5b)
Turn position 2:	H	Were they accepting responsibility?	(line 9b)
Turn position 3:	C	Narrative story	(line 10)
Turn position 4:	H	They haven't actually accepted that	
		the jacket was faulty at the moment	(line 12)
	C	No no	(line 13)

This sequence does not follow the expected pattern for disagreement. H's intervention in second position, though it is interrogative, is strong. C's response in third position, being a narrative story rather than a formulation, is weak: it neither upgrades nor downgrades her first, but merely provides more detail. H's fourth position is strong, but it only restates without interrogative what was already a strong second position. We seem here to have only two positions, not four: one is weak, and gives way to the other which is strong. These observations confirm our earlier conclusion that this talk has the character of an *adjudication* rather than a *negotiation*.

The third insertion sequence is as follows:

Turn position 1:	C	No they're quite nice about it you know and	
		they'll take the jacket in which is something.	(line 54)
Turn position 2:	H	Yeah	(line 55)
Turn position 3:	C	Ye know?	(line 56)
Turn position 4:	H	Well it would be a matter of discussing that and	
		see will they concede that there is a fault.	(lines 57-59)

This sequence does not follow the expected pattern for disagreement. Turn position 1 contains an assessment, and turn position 2 a weak agreement, but there is no revised assessement in turn position 3, and turn position 4 remains weak. Here we seem to have only one weak position, confirmed by both parties.

From the separate standpoints of the two parties, there are clear reasons why this should be so. From caller's standpoint, her assessment in line 54 is - as argued above - a weak (dis)agreement[11] with helper's assessment in line 12, a repair of her previous agreement in line 13. From her perspective line 54 invites helper to engage in a disagreement sequence, within which to "negotiate" whether or not the shop will accept responsibility for fault. Helper does not dispute that such a negotiation can appropriately occur - but not with him. Whereas he negotiated with caller concerning "entitlement", he will not do so concerning "acceptance". He has consistently maintained that this is a matter for her to negotiate with store.

But if this has been helper's consistent orientation to the matter of "acceptance", then the talk between helper and caller about this issue should be considered in a different light. Rather than regarding it as a disagreement sequence (a negotiation) between helper and caller (as we have regarded the discussion of "entitlement"), we should perhaps regard it as a *report* of a disagreement sequence (a negotiation) between caller and store.

7.2. The call as a report of a disagreement sequence

In this light, the following *disagreement sequences* become apparent:

Turn position 1: Caller   C's assessment   (lines 2-5a)
            [regarded as report of C's complaint to store prior to calling H]
Turn position 2: Store   Store's weak response [present-oriented] (line 5b)
                               restatement of same   [past-oriented]   (line 10)
Turn position 3: Caller   C: what am I entitled to?   (line 6a)
            [regarded as report of question put to store]
Turn position 4: Store   H: they haven't actually
                               accepted the jacket was faulty   (line 12)
            [regarded as report of store's present position]

This talk reports an actual disagreement sequence between caller and store, preceding the current call. It begins with (1) caller's assessment, presumably in the same terms as reported to helper. Then follow (2) store's weak agreement, (3) caller's upgrading of her assessment, and finally (4) store's strong disagreement at least *for the present*.

Turn position 1: Caller   H's assessment   (lines 47b-51)
            [regarded as report of C's complaint to store after calling H]
Turn position 2: Store   C: Store's weak response [future-oriented] (line 54)

	C: ye know?	(line 56)
Turn position 3: Caller	H: well it would be a matter of discussing that	(line 57a)
	[regarded as a report of caller's pursuit of complaint]	
Turn position 4: Store	H: and see will they concede that there is a fault	(line 57b)
	[regarded as report of store's hoped-for future response]	

This talk reports an anticipated disagreement sequence between caller and store, following the the current call. It begins with (1) caller's assessment of her entitlement, following H's advice. Then follow (2) store's weak agreement, (3) caller's upgrading of her assessment through "discussion", and finally (4) store's hoped-for strong agreement (i.e. "concession") in the future.

7.3. Bargaining sequences

The "disagreement sequences" achieved by way of insertion sequences in this call may be compared with the "bargaining sequences", also achieved by way of such sequences, in plea-bargaining between PD and DA. According to Maynard' (1984) study of a California courtroom, the sequence is based on a single adjacency pair in which party A makes either a firm proposal or a tentative 'position-report' to which party B makes a 'reply' (acceptance or rejection). This sequence may be elaborated "externally" or "internally" (op. cit.:91). External elaborations are relationships between successive bargaining sequences resulting in what Maynard terms a "discourse system". When B accepts, the negotiation is closed in a single adjacency pair ("Unilateral Opportunity"). When B make a counter-offer, one party may relinquish and align with the other ("Bilateral Opportunity") or the parties may compromise on an intermediate position ("Compromise Opportunity").

In these terms, the major negotiation in the present call may be mapped as follows: (1) helper offered one of repair, refund *or* replacement (line 20, repeated at line 22, repeated at line 26); (2) caller offered refund *and* replacement (line 36); (3) helper offered replacement *or* refund (lines 37 to 45); (4) caller offered "half price jacket" or "similar jacket at half price" (line 46); (5) helper offered "identical replacement" (lines 47a to 51), which caller accepted. In this call, helper and caller each essentially proposes a single position. The outcome is that helper's proposal is accepted unaltered. The call involves no compromise but it involves both a bilateral aspect (caller advanced a counter-position) and a unilateral aspect (caller ultimately accepts helper's initial position).

It might be suggested that the present call does not involve bargaining, being perhaps more akin to Maynard's exceptional instance in which overlapping talk and factual disagreements appear to violate mutuality (op. cit.:117) so that the public defender proclaims "this isn't plea bargaining" (op. cit.:116). But in the present call, helper's "unilateral" stance — his precisely worded repetition of the same proposal throughout - is achieved *with* mutuality. Although at one point (lines 26-27) overlapping occurs, it is momentary, and he subsequently gives her case a hearing, if only to reject it. By the end of the call, caller appreciatively endorses his reasoning.

8. CALL CLOSING

Helpline calls which do not receive advice in the form requested still achieve appreciation and acceptance. Every one of 228 calls recorded closed with an appreciation and acceptance of helper's advice. It is a matter of common courtesy that they should do so. The mechanism by which it is achieved is clear in the final IS of the present call. Caller has received bad news: her case for refund *and* replacement has been rejected. But she declares that an objective of her call has been achieved (" th↑at's what I wanted to cl<u>a</u>rify °before I go back <u>into</u>: them° =", line 54) and thanks helper for that ("thanks for your advice", line 61).

In contrast to this, Maynard's bargaining sequences frequently conclude without acceptance by one party present of what the other proposes. The two main devices which achieve this are *continuances* (cf. Maynard op. cit.:183-184), i.e. deferal to a future meeting between these parties, and *commital* for trial. Parties to plea bargaining can continue their conversation at a later date, so they need not reach agreement here and now. Parties to the helpline conversation cannot continue at a later date, so they must reach agreement on this single occasion.

9. CONCLUSION

Helper proposes and Caller counter-proposes. Helper identically repeats the same formula in response to her various restatements of her case. From her point of view, bargaining is in progress: she can take his time before she accepts. She can see what he will offer. From his point of view, however, she can be made accountable, within the call, for the time she takes. If his position remains unchanged, she can be seen to be making no progress. Then she has no grounds for continuing to take his time.

What is at issue here is not the *content* of the call, for instance whether or not there is 'really' disagreement between caller and helper, or whether it is rather a matter of clarification by helper of truths which are as non-negotiable as the laws of geometry. What is at issue is the *form* of the talk. Although, in the call, caller is being instructed in how to converse with store, she has had no prior instruction in how to converse with helper. The devices she uses are everyday devices. She initiates an adjacency pair to request his advice. This enables him to insert a sequence to clarify the acceptance issue. She hears his offer of advice as inviting her acceptance. This enables her to initiate an insertion sequence in which to renegotiate her request and his advice. Yet the premise on which she initiates this sequence is that she will conclude it by agreeing with him and accepting his advice.

The devices he uses are also everyday devices, but differently chosen. In the course of their disagreement sequence he is at pains to precisely repeat his wording from turn to turn. It is even possible that his repetition of the term "identical" (lines 47a and 47b) can highlight the fact that his *words* are identical from turn to turn. In this way, helper ensures that he can be heard as clarifying a position which remains unchanged throughout his talk. By contrast, while pursuing disagreement caller was obliged to continually rephrase her points ("a new jacket", "a half-price jacket", "a similar jacket") in order to justify taking each additional turn.

The contrast with Maynard's cases is revealing not only as to the distinct forms of dialogue which occur in the two settings, but also as to the distinct knowledge claims made in each. Plea bargaining is intrinsically adversarial in form, reflecting the assumption that there may be no single agreed view as to the facts or their interpretation.[12] Helpline calls are not. Helper is at pains not to take sides (his advice may be sought by stores or their customers). He seeks to uphold a single agreed view, grounded in the idealised world of the Sale of Goods and Supply of Services Act: if store accept fault, then *one* of repair, refund or replacement is the consumer's right.

But relations between consumer and store *are* intrinsically adversarial, insofar as these relations are represented in calls to the helpline: if they were not, no call would have been made. It would be impractical to seek to prevent these adversarial relations (disagreements) being aired on the helpline. Yet they do not belong at the core of helper's work, as he conceives it. Therefore a paradox arises. Given that adversarial relations (disagreements) are being aired, helper could keep them at bay by confining himself to the "mathematical" (non-negotiable) explication of caller's rights under the Act, excluding the "contingent" (negotiable) question of store's acceptance of fault.[13] But then there would be nothing for caller and helper to discuss (nothing to disagree or negotiate about) since that discussion is for caller and store. This paradox is resolved practically by the sequential organization of the call. Crucial to that organization is the way in which helper's response serves as a pivot between the two APs, each of which addresses the mathematical/contingent aspect in a distinct way.[14]

Helper is able to accomplish the transition from the first AP to the second because he has *two* competences. So far as technical solutions to technical problems, are concerned he is a trained expert. Caller is a novice: she may not even know the *relevance* of these technicalities, until she learns about them in the course of the call. So far as the relevance of the technical solutions to everyday problems is concerned, helper is not an *expert*, but he is *experienced*. In terms of the distinction drawn by (Wilson 1991) this is in large part the *institutional* result of his extended practical experience of dealing with callers on the helpline; but it also reflects the fundamental fact that, whilst being legally trained, he is also a competent member of society. In contrast caller, whilst being a competent member of society, is not legally trained.

Helper's ability to manage the call substitutes for his inability to resolve the dispute between consumer and store. Instead of resolving the dispute, he shows how caller can resolve the dispute. To do so he plays two parts. In the first insertion sequence (lines 7-13), to reveal caller's predicament, he plays store, casting doubt on her case: his words at line 12 report the way the store can deny that it yet accepts fault. In the second (lines 27-59), to resolve caller's predicament, he plays consumer, asserting her rights: his words at line 47 report the way caller can claim her entitlement.

In consequence of its two special features namely that helper cannot act but can only advise, and that caller must ultimately accept his advice despite its inefficacy, the call is unavoidably doing two things. In part it is *reporting* on a negotiation between caller and store. In part it is actually *negotiating* between caller and helper. It is not merely that these are separate matters which ought not to be confused. They are not entirely separable: any aspect of the reporting can given rise to re-negotiation, likewise any aspect of the negotiation can raise the relevance of report. The relation between them is *reflexive* in this sense: in the way they actually practice negotiation together on the helpline, they display to one another how the negotiation with store may have been done in the past and might be done differently in the future. They show one another that they understand 'negotiation' in that way.

NOTES

1. In practice this task proves to be complex. Caller's first telling (lines 3-6) does not achieve this objective to her full satisfaction, and she later re-tells her story (lines 27-36) to state more explicitly what advice she seeks. In the call as a whole, each of lines 6b, 13, 36, 46, and 56 is a possible completion point for this story.

2. Quoted by Wilson (op. cit.: 28) from Mather (1973).

3. Button (1990) reviews discussion of *making arrangements* as a closing-implicative activity in the CA literature. The issue was first broached by Schegloff and Sacks (1973). These discussions refer to parties arranging to speak again at a later date. In the helpline situation this does not arise. There is no way caller can be sure to reach helper again, or indeed to reach the helpline again at all, given the pressure of calls. The arrangements proposed are for caller to speak again with store.

4. It comprises only lines 7-13, out of 66 lines of the call as a whole.

5. Lines 28-29 comprise an unpacking (Jefferson 1985) of "the=jacket=ran", line 5. It has the two-aspect structure [I thought] (I bought) "a red jacket and white" but [then I realised] (after I washed it) "the red is all gone through the white" which Sacks (1992b:229ff.) finds characterize story-telling. Lines 30-35 unpack "they're now (0.1) half pric::e hhh (0.2)", line 6b in caller's original story. This talk has the distinctive three-part organization which (Sacks 1992b:222ff) finds characterizes the overall sequential organization of story-telling, namely (i) a preface (lines 30-31) which tells what it will take for the story to be over, (ii) a story exhibiting the two-aspect structure noted above (lines 32-33) and (iii) a response synonymous with the preface to say, the story is over (lines 34-35). Here each of these three parts exhibits the two-aspect structure, thus "I thought" (I bought a jacket worth) [one hundred and nineteen] but "then I realised" [they were on sale for fifty nine], and so on. The precise detail provided in the story tests what is "claimed" in the preface. The claim passes the test and is repeated as "proven" in the response (Sacks 1992b:249ff).

6. The fundamental difficulty here is that "given the utterance by utterance organization of turn-taking, unless close ordering is attempted there can be no methodic assurance that a more or less eventually aimed-for successive utterance or utterance type will ever be produced" (Schegloff and Sacks 1973:297).

7. Many distinct items can play the part of "weak agreement", including hesitation markers, a pause, or simply the absence of early ("strong") agreement, by second speaker. First speaker can hear such items, and may produce components designed to fill this 'monitor' space.

8. Caller seems to be as aggrieved by the cut in price subsequent to her purchase as by the alleged fault in her jacket. However the Sale of Goods and Supply of Services Act does not address the price of goods, and helper consistently disregards the "price" issue in this case. The legislation informing his work concerns "faulty" products. The fact that goods have been reduced in price is not considered grounds for consumer complaint. Indeed other legislation *requires* that goods said be to be "reduced" in price have previously been on sale at a higher price. In the present case, it is noteworthy that, were caller to seek and obtain a "full refund" (line 45) of the price she "actually paid" (line 43), i.e. £120, this would enable her to purchase a new jacket at "half price", i.e. £60, and keep the balance of £60, so fulfilling her objective (as stated at line 36). But neither party pursue this possibility.

9. Nearly every caller has discussed the problem with store, and narrates this experience during the call.

10. Garfinkel and Sacks (1970) discuss the distinction between *objective* and *indexical* expressions. The distinction is a 'design feature' but in practice — according to Garfinkel and Sacks — all expressions are indexical.

11. It is in the nature of a 'weak' response that it is ambiguous as between agreement and disagreement.

12. Maynard explicitly shows that resolution of plea and sentence do <u>not</u> presuppose such agreement.

13. Helper would then be performing the same task as the brief illustrated pamphlets for consumers, such as Office of Consumer Affairs, 1988, which explain the Act in general terms. The negotiation which takes place in the call is the way the helpline attends to the contingencies of specific cases, which the literature cannot do.

14. The first AP addresses the mathematical, and the second the contingent aspect. The insertion sequences in each case reverse this focus: the first addresses acceptance; the second, entitlement.

CHAPTER 15

LOCATING NEGOTIATION ACTIVITY WITHIN DOCUMENT DESIGN PRESENTATIONS

JOHN WHEATLEY

1. INTRODUCTION

This chapter is concerned with the linguistic enactment of presentations by small teams of professional people involved in producing business documentation. The chapter attempts to show a regular, generic pattern to the way this task is carried out. This will then allow for discussion on the way 'negotiation activity' occurs as part of the routine way in which the presentations are performed. The location, function, and pattern of onset of the negotiation activity will de demonstrated and described.

The document in question is a brochure being produced by Birmingham University, U.K., in order to interest industry in 'using' Birmingham University as a research and consultancy partner. For this reason it is a document aimed at a wide audience, and aimed to stimulate initial interest. It is thus light on words and heavy on visuals and design. This makes the presentation of this design to interested parties crucial to the progress of the project. Three instances of such presentations provide the data for this study.

I would not want to label the activity examined here a negotiation 'activity type' (Levinson 1979) or a negotiation 'genre' (Swales 1990), nor a negotiation 'speech event' (Hymes 1972). The social activity occurring here is *document design*, and the stage that this process has reached is called a *presentation*. This is a term used by the parties themselves in at least two of the three interactions, which provides some evidence that the participants are oriented to the stage of the process and, furthermore, that they are aware of what is and is not 'usual' or 'acceptable' behaviour in such a stage. The consequences of this are that unexplicated 'norms of conduct' — the implicit 'rules of the game', so to speak — are not those of a negotiation, if indeed such rules exist, but those of the particular work activity taking place.

Different work activities allow different types of interaction to occur. Some are verbal, some are not. Some are monologic, some interactive. Some will use text types such as narrative and exposition and will facilitate an information flow from one party to another; a 'briefing' is such an event. Some will be built around question-and-answer sequences and the use of directives; negotiation speech events, it seems, can be like this (Donohue and Diez 1985). Presentations permit, and are designed to allow, the flow of information largely in one direction. Additionally, this stage of the document design process calls for an evaluation of what is presented before further stages of the document design process can be undertaken. It is this feature of the social situation that allows for negotiation to take place. The way in which it occurs is due to the nature of the presentation and the working practices of this group of people.

Some definitions of negotiation activity, however, do fit this data. Let us briefly examine some instances where this applies:

1. *Verbal communication between two or more parties which is at least ostensibly aimed at reaching joint agreement on some course of action or verbal formulation* (Pruitt 1969:2). The expected outcome of these presentation events is all-party agreement. Indeed the event exists largely to allow that agreement to be voiced. In the case of document design it is agreement on a course of action; how to design a brochure, and less on verbal formulation than visual, the latter being the jurisdiction of the designer who undertakes the presentation.

2. *Negotiation involves more than a decision to confer:* "there must be an operative desire to clarify, ameliorate, adjust or settle the dispute or situation" (Morley and Stephenson 1977:22). What is going on in these data is not a dispute that needs settling, but the construction of an activity recognizable as a *presentation*. Clearly more is going on than conferral, and as my analysis shows, this includes the sharing of information, the clarification of that information and, where necessary, the agreement on changes to be instigated. All this is done in order to move the work towards the goal of producing a document to specification.

Morley and Stephenson (1977:23) also propose some "defining characteristics" of negotiation which are apposite to the data examined here. These 'characteristics' are as follows:

1. *Negotiators must engage in a process of joint decision making.*
This is true for my data, although it is not the main activity taking place. The main action in these meetings is the presentation of design features; in itself this is not decision making, although it does provide substance upon which decisions can be made.

2. *Negotiations are mixed motive situations.*
This may be a convenient description of a negotiation event, but as I have already indicated, the event is not being approached by the analyst or by the participants as a negotiation; it is a stage in the process of document design in which some of the verbal activity that occurs fits many of the definitions put forward for negotiating activity. The data do not meet the requirements of a formal negotiation situation.

3. *Negotiation involves strategic decision making.*
In these data this may be the case. The analysis to follow will show a structured, organized pattern to the decision making that occurs in this meeting. It will be shown to occur in well defined ways and in characterisable sequential positions; whether this counts as 'strategic' is debatable. Certainly the participants are not competing against one another in order to achieve their individual conflicting objectives. There is a shared objective to produce as good a brochure as possible for the client. The client-designer relationship is the working condition for this interaction, and does not allow for the kind of negotiation between two parties over the price or delivery of goods (cf. Firth, this volume). Rather it allows for *team* negotiations. All members are clearly working cooperatively towards a shared goal; and each brings different sets of skills and knowledge to bear on the operation. No one party knows how the brochure will look at the outset of the project. The public relations officer (pro) knows the kind of text he might write; the industrial liaison officer (ilo) knows what must be said to appease university departments, and the designer (des) has a repertoire of styles she works with.

There have been numerous calls in the management communication literature for micro analysis of negotiation and decision making (Poole 1985, Putnam 1985). Until now, however, very little that has been done to focus on the micro communicative practices of institutional activities (see, though, Drew and Heritage 1992). Within business communication research there has been a focus on a specified type of activity, though much of this occurs in unspecified situations. A great deal of research has uncovered 'phases' in small group behaviour (e.g. Bales 1950, Fisher 1974, Tuckman 1965), or patterns of decision making (Brandstatter, Davis and Stocker-Kreichgauer

1982 for a review). What these studies do not do is focus on the communicative and interactive nature of naturally-occurring, socially situated tasks. Social psychologists set up experiments that fail to mirror any real-life activity, and small group theorists largely ignore specific activity in the search for general features of small group operations.

Poole (1985 and passim) recognized the importance of the task dimension. His research showed how 'phase' theories of decision making ignored the task dimension. He hypothesised that task would be the key variable in small group interaction (Poole 1985). Poole also saw the applicability of Giddens' structuration theory to understanding group interaction, and indeed, the notions of system and structure in Giddens' work (Giddens 1979) inform this chapter. This theory asserts that members of a community have at their disposal 'systems' of behaviour and thus ways of constructing discourse that will accomplish a known task, a task such as a presentation. The pattern of discourse is enacted and can change and develop to take account of contingent features of the task. It is this approach to social action that the analysis in this chapter seeks to highlight.

The activity under consideration here is not an example of a negotiation event. It is a recurring type of work situation for all the participants: the presentation of document design. It is this task and the work environment that constitute the parameters of what can and cannot be done. I argue that it is by understanding the task at a micro level that will allow for an improved understanding of negotiation as a communicative activity. 'Negotiation', that is, as it occurs outside formal negotiation settings — the type of activity prevalent in all the many workplace and family environments where decisions are made and agreements on courses of action are reached.

Various researchers have shown basic patterns of discourse that can embody the activity of reaching agreement (Jackson and Jacobs 1981, D. Murray 1987). The nub of decision making is not necessarily problematic, indeed it may be a rather dull exchange. What is needed is to understand the kinds of 'activity types' (Levinson 1979) within which negotiational work can be embedded. It is these larger patterned practices that we use, invent and restructure that researchers need to investigate. One such activity, a document presentation, comes under scrutiny in the sections that follow.

2. THE DATA

There are three participants involved in the work activity examined here. They are the university's public affairs officer — referred to as 'pro' hereafter. He is responsible for the university's public relations and is the main brochure copywriter. The Director of

Industrial Liaison (ilo) at the university; it is his job to interest industry in what the university can do and to help establish research projects. He is the client for this brochure, and the brochure is being paid for out of his budget. He will be the main user, handing out copies at presentations and arranging a direct mailshot to likely collaborating companies. Lastly a designer is involved. This person works for a private design company and is employed on a regular basis at Birmingham to do brochure and prospectus design work.

The transcripts analysed are each 'framed' parts of longer meetings. By this it is meant that work is done in each of the meetings to demarcate the presentation from other activities. The way this is done will be discussed later. The sections under consideration are presentations of design work to other members of the team. Recording A occurs at a fairly early stage, at least some four months before recordings B and C. Here the pro presents the designer's rough sketches to the client. Recording B and C occur within a week of each other. Recording B is a presentation of a mock-up brochure by the designer to the pro. Recording C is a presentation of the same brochure in the same state of development by the designer to the client, with the pro also present and participating. No work is done on the brochure between recordings B and C. In fact there is no contact at all between the parties in the intervening time. Recording B can be seen as a 'dry run' for the following important meeting where the client must be content with what he sees.

3. INTRODUCTION TO THE ANALYSIS

Professional documents such as this are designed through a process that necessitates some negotiation. Stages such as briefings, draft checks and presentations seem to be the key interactive elements of the process, interspersed with more individual stages of the process such as designing the spreads and writing the copy. These interactive stages allow other members of the group to evaluate and seek clarification on what it is that group members have accomplished individually. 'Briefings' allow the designer to reach a common understanding with her client on the job specification being set. 'Draft reviews' allow realignment between client and text producer on wording. 'Presentations' allow the client to evaluate the product of the designer's work, which he had a hand in specifying at the briefing. It is at these points of the interaction, across all three presentations under consideration here, that negotiation occurs. It is negotiation that is invariably linked to the client's negative evaluation, or failure to understand what he is shown.

The aims of the ensuing analysis are to show :

1. Features of a kind of *talk at work*: a presentation, that distinguishes itself from other forms of talk.

2. Common interactional features that belong to this kind of presentation and distinguish it from other interactive stages of the document design process.

3. The points in presentation stages as defined by the analysis that allow for negotiation to occur and the regular forms that negotiation takes.

The chapter will examine types of interactional sequences and, in particular, the way these sequences are enacted in Recordings B and C. Some attention will be paid to the way the *participants themselves* orient to the kind of activity in which they are collaboratively engaged. The analysis will impose a *coding scheme* on the data in order to categorise sections of the interaction in a manner that may be referred to as *etic* rather than *emic* (Pike 1967). By 'etic' I mean that analysis will focus on features of the discourse that are not necessarily orientated to by the participants. However, the concept of a 'presentation' is *emic*: that is, the *participants themselves* use the term and one can — as an analyst/observer — rely upon this orientation to discover organizational goals that the parties perceive as relevant to participation in this kind of talk-activity.

The detailed linguistic analysis of the data is in terms of *acts* (Sinclair and Coulthard 1975) and *topic types* (Davies 1985, 1986). These too are 'etic' (i.e. analyst) terms and constructs, not directly oriented to by participants but nevertheless useful for showing that what counts as a complete activity — the presentation — has a regular, patterned, sequential structure throughout its construction. These units then are *etic*, not necessarily verbally accounted for by the participants but essential as the basic 'building blocks' of the activity. They provide an analysis of the entire activity and enable the analyst to locate generic features of this talk-activity.

Because the units identified *do* recur and form a structured sequential pattern for the talk, one may argue that this provides evidence for the fact that the participants themselves construct the social activity in a recognized and mutually oriented-to manner. The means by which this evidence is gathered and analysed however do not depend on participant recognition of each act he or she performs in the discourse. For this reason the analysis adopts both emic and etic perspectives.

3.1. Analytical Framework

The outer framework of this analysis is in two parts. It consists firstly of a coding scheme that is based on categories of 'acts' and 'moves' as found in Sinclair and Coulthard

(1975), Ventola (1987), and Lampi (1986). No attempt yet has been made to establish an 'exchange structure', or to prepare a closed list of items for coding all the moves in the interaction. Nevertheless, as I hope to demonstrate, coding of most utterances need not be particularly problematic, if done in broad terms. The point of the analysis, following Hasan (1984) and Ventola (1987), is to describe a generic pattern in the unfolding social activity in each of the three transcripts.

The second element is *topic-type analysis*. Above the coding system, the data have been categorized in terms of topic type. Francis (1986:55) claimed that "there are constraints upon topicality in negotiation talk which are not operative for ordinary conversation". In these data such constraints are categorised in terms of topic type rather than topic per se.

Traditionally topic has been analysed to show a coherence of content in a stretch of discourse. Researchers have tried to recognize 'topically coherent units' (Francis 1986) by recognizing points at which new topics are introduced (Button and Casey 1984, B. Crow 1983), or the way topics 'drift' from one to another (e.g. Sacks 1992a:535-46 [Lecture, March 9, Winter 1967]). 'Topic' was initially a candidate analysis for this data; however it did not prove a useful unit for the data. Almost the only topic discussed is the brochure or, at a more delicate level, each page of the brochure or each item on a page as it is brought to the attention of those receiving the presentation details. There is however a regular way in which these topics are oriented to by the participants, which clearly shows organization and sequential patterning in the talk. Each topic is presented, evaluated and clarified rather than, say, questioned or directed. This allows the adaption of the category of 'topic type' for the categorisation of the recurring types of activity that are performed on each topic. This is a text framework developed by Davies (1985, 1986). It works on the principle that while there may be an unlimited number of 'topics' there is a limited number of 'topic types'. Davies' approach was originally applied to scientific texts; however, with a change of 'topic types' the approach appears to equally applicable to the presentation data. The fact that there are so few of these types in the data makes the analysis particularly suitable.

By focusing on topic type I am attempting to define a different unit of talk to topic: one that shares some of the attributes of Levinson's *activity types* (Levinson 1979). It is, in fact, a hybrid of 'activity type' and discourse 'topic'. It is likely that what Levinson calls an activity type would equate with a whole presentation from the data, though the analysis shall be restricted to a smaller unit of discourse. This unit bears some relation to 'talk episodes'. This is a unit below 'speech event' on a rank scale. Thus a 'speech event' is composed of a number of 'talk episodes'. While this holds true for the unit here entitled 'topic type', I think the way 'talk episode' is conceived is as a recognizable part of the whole social activity, such as the discussion of grades in a school counselling session. 'Topic type', on the other hand, is a category of discourse unit, rather than a social action per se, and has something in common with what Sinclair and Coulthard (1975) call a 'transaction' and what Lampi (1986) calls a 'phase'. Lampi equates 'phase' with Sinclair and Coulthard's 'transaction' (1986:51). However, she uses it to distinguish 'bargaining sections' from 'discussion sections' in her data. Her 'bargaining phases' are claimed to be self-contained units of activity, which is not the case for my 'topic types', since they are only constituent parts of such a unit. Sinclair and Coulthard's own description of 'transactions' for classroom activity does seem more in keeping with the units I am describing (Sinclair and Coulthard 1975:56-57). However, as their definition of a transaction is in terms of a number of 'exchanges', and as this analysis recognizes no unit between 'move' and what I am calling 'topic type', I would argue that to call them 'transactions' would be misleading. I do, however, see this chapter as an attempt to construct a meaningful structural analysis at a level above the exchange, at a level where Sinclair and Coulthard left off, so to speak.

4. THE ANALYSIS

4.1. Topic Types

All three interaction sequences contain no more than five distinct *topic types*. This, I argue is a distinguishing feature of this kind of discourse, distinguishing it, one suspects, from everyday conversation, where such a narrow range of topic types would perhaps not be expected, and clearly separating 'presentation' interaction from other stages of the document design process, such as briefings, where a wider set of topic types occur (Wheatley forthcoming). The topic types in question are as follows:

VISUAL PRESENTATION
NEGATIVE EVALUATION
POSITIVE EVALUATION
CLARIFICATORY
PROCEDURAL.

All the data fit felicitously into these five categories. This topic type listing does not tell us what the participants were talking about at any particular stage, but it does, I want to propose, inform us *what* they were doing. Whatever topic arose in the course of the presentation did so to achieve one of the above five types of interaction. Here is a breakdown of the levels of occurrence of these topic types in the three recordings under consideration.

	Tape A	Tape B	Tape C
Visual Presentation	9	16	14
Negative Evaluation	5	-	5
Positive Evaluation	3	3	2
Clarification	7	2	9
Procedural	7	3	5
Others	2	-	1
Totals	33	24	36

Here is a selection of typical examples of the five topic types. For clarity, only the key moves have been labelled. A glossary for the move types can be found in appendix 1. Following that a description of the key constituents of the most common topic type — visual presentation — will be given.

VISUAL PRESENTATION TOPIC

Designer	VIS PRES	the cover
		is a generic cover but erm
		obviously we're falling in line with the bio technology
Client	ACK	yes yes
Designer	POS EV	so it all follows through
	VIS PRES	erm obviously heading across the centre. The whole cover, the way that it would be printed is erm working on textures, a matt cover ...
	POS EV	we're very simple sophisticated
Client	ACK	yes

'Visual presentation', not surprisingly, is the most common topic type. It is invariably the presenter who initiates these topics, the designer in recordings B and C, the pro in recording A.

Negative Evaluation

Client	NEG EV	I was just wondering if you think that 'among them are researchers and scholars of high distinction' is a bit is a bit mealy mouthed
	ALT DP	whether we should ⌜ simply make a statement
Pro		what does it say? ⌞ there are can I see that a sec
Cl		We should just make a statement of er you know our staff are researchers and scholars of high distinction
Pro		we're not the kind of I mean I know that's giving you
Pro		yeah
Cl	NEG EV	but it's just 'among them are' [cont]

These negative evaluation topics only occur in client meetings, not in recording B where the presentation is made by the designer to the pro. Furthermore it is invariably the client who initiates them. Their function in the discourse highlights differences in client and pro roles as presentation *receiver*. It is through the initiation of negative evaluation sequences that the client can bring about decision making in the presentation. The sequence opening shown above, instigated by the client, leads into decision making, a negotiated activity. Without the initiation of this topic type the presentation would continue and the client's best chance of making a negative evaluation of this item would have been by-passed. If negative evaluation is not offered in this meeting, indeed at this *point* in the meeting, it becomes increasingly more difficult for the client to engineer another space for himself to express his lack of approval. Silence here appears to stand for positive evaluation. Indeed, the negative evaluation move is immediately followed by a decision proposal. This is now an issue that has to be negotiated to a satisfactory conclusion before the designer can return to her presentation. The sequence ends as follows:

F	Dp sugg	I think I'd suggest we just put there are
J	acc	mmm
B	acc	⌜ yes
F	cont	there ⌞ are researchers and scholars of high distinction
		effect then that leads across here they are ⌜ is this
	(pos ev)	where they are
J	acc	⌞ yeah yeah
B	acc/ pos ev	yes yes that's good that ⌜ is good

F   align   ⌊ yeah

The pro picks up on the client's proposals and makes a more specific suggestion on the wording. He supports his own proposal and this then receives positive evaluation from the client. Thus the negotiation can end. The team are in agreement again and talk can revert to enacting the presentation. The client has made a negative evaluation of what the designer has presented and followed this up with his own proposal. This *negotiation activity* within a presentation had to end with either the client's own proposal being accepted by the others or, as in this case, the client accepting another modified proposal.

Positive Evaluation

Client	POS EV	I mean this couldn't be more timely now you know I mean
Pro		no with the research thing
Client		=with the news last night ⌈ about
Pro		⌊ oh last night
Cl	CONT	=about the universities
	ELAB	did you they interviewed some polytechnic director
Pro	ACK	mmm
Client		=who said he thought the big shock was going to be for those universities that dropped off the end.
Pro	ACK	mmm
Client		He said the polys were well used to this world of having to fight for every penny
Pro	ACK	mmm
Client		but some universities who weren't going to make it
Client	POS EV	and erm so this couldn't be more ⌈ timely I think
Pro	AGREE	⌊ yeah

Positive evaluation is, to the presenter, a supportive element within the visual presentation sequence and not a disruptive one. Whereas negative evaluation, as explained above, cannot be left untreated by the other participants, positive evaluation can. The presenter here provides no verbal response to what the client says and the Pro offers acknowledgement and agreement. The client's voiced positive evaluation is, I propose, welcomed by the other two participants but as a discourse unit it has no consequences. Once it can be 'closed down', the designer can return to her presentation. Occasionally positive evaluation is judged to form a topic type of its own and is then initiated by a participant other than the presenter. Evaluation and clarification can either be topic types in their own right or handled within another topic type, normally the visual presentation. This is dependent on how the participants themselves orient to the handling of the issue. If the clarification request can be dealt with promptly and allows swift return to visual presentation then no purpose is served in the analyst labelling it a separate topic. If however a visual presentation has to be lengthily interrupted in order to deal with, say, a positive evaluation sequence — as is the case with the example above, then it seems reasonable to label it separately. Thus the labels 'positive evaluation', 'negative evaluation' and 'clarify' are both names of topic types and names of moves that occur as parts of the enactment of a topic. Visual presentation too is both a topic type itself and a move within a visual presentation topic.

Clarification

Client	FRAME	Now
	CLFYR	what's the small print
Designer		you said you weren't going to use the atom bomb
Client		yes quite
	CLFYR	What's the small print?
Des	CLFY	The small print is the Cobuild erm dictionary
	REPAIR	I mean these are things that have been used
Cl	REFORM	ahh so it's a visual
Pro	CLFY	just a few of the twenty million words
Cl	ACC	some of them yeah
Des	JUSTIFY	We felt obviously you know it's important really in a publication that it's not all words and that you know you need to supplement with some diagrams
Cl	CLFYR	what words can be visual as well
Des	CLFY	yeah and

A clarification request interrupts the ongoing sequence of events; it is an element of the discourse with consequences, and therefore has to be dealt with. Once the clarification request has been successfully dealt with, events can revert to where they left off, to the 'default' activity of visual presentation. Here the client is simply seeking clarification of an item — the small print on the designer's page. There are other clarification sequences however that do not fall into this simple type, and they function as 'pre-sequences' that establish that for the client at least there is a problem with the presentation. They thus operate as a starting point from where negotiation sequences can develop.

Like negative evaluation, 'seeking clarification' is a procedure open to the client for introducing more interactive talk than is the case with visual presentation or positive evaluation topics. It is a legitimate way for the client to interrupt the presentation process and to negotiate some change in current thinking on the brochure, ahead even of the current presentation. The format of a presentation, its turn-taking mechanisms and the way it discoursally unfolds all indicate the issues raised by the client require resolution not only in this meeting but at *this point* in the presentation.

Finally there are PROCEDURAL TOPICS:

Recording C

Pro	FRAME	so erm I've had I've had this prior knowledge of what of what Juliana's done so best if
Des	OFFER	would you like me to present it =
Pro		=you pre- you present to Bob =
Des		=yeah sure
Pro		yeah
Des		=sure very happy to.
		Right
		erm quite a challenge
Pro		[laugh]
Des		a fair challenge . .

In all three cases the presentation is bounded, or 'framed', by procedural topics. This seems to be an essential part of the presentation process. Procedural topics thus function as opening 'boundary markers' (Sinclair and Coulthard 1975). The following is another example from Recording B:

Recording B

Pro	FRAME	right
	DIR	Do you want to you lead off ⌈ Juliana cos
Des		⌊ well yes
Pro		you know where we are
Des	ACC	yeah sure.

Recordings B and C also mark the presentation sequence end with very similar procedural topics. In Recording C we find:

| Des | OFFER | Did you want to go back through it? |
| Cl | ACC | yes through it again |

Pro		well we perhaps ought to rehearse what we said as well
Des		yeah actually I'll just try and
Pro		Have you got your notes Juliana that I seem to remember insisting that you made some

And in Recording B:

Pro	REQ	Can we go through it again
Des	ACC	yeah
Pro		and I can make some more detailed
Des		mm
Pro	POS EV	I mean overall I think it's smashing
Des	ACC	oh good
Pro	POS EV	I'm really very excited by it
Des	ACC	hmm good oh good ⌈ thankyou
Pro	POS EV	⌊ it's great

In both presentations a request or offer of a 're-run' clearly marks the end of the presentation stage. The visual presentation topic is almost entirely lacking from the second run through. It is a strange enough event to have something visually present pointed out once without this being required a second time. These procedural framing topics demarcate a section of talk wherein topic choice is restricted and a pattern of turn taking exists that is different to both conversation and other stages of the document design process. Clearly, re-runs create a second 'slot' for negotiation on the same issues, this time without the weight of new information obstructing the client's responses. Taking care of staging and other procedural matters is a task handled almost single-handedly by the pro throughout the whole design process. Not surprisingly, then, all the procedural topics in both presentations are initiated by him.

4.2. Sequencing Patterns Within the Topic Types

Before looking for pattern in the sequential ordering of the social interaction constituted by these topic types, I want to indicate the regularity and orderliness of topic enactment itself. In order to justify the initial placing of such an analytical framework over the data, I want to show that there is a common development to visual presentation topics that clearly groups them and separates them from, say, negative evaluation topics. There should also be enough variation in this pattern between the recordings to highlight differences in the interaction sequences due to varying participant roles.

Hasan (1984) has done work on the genre of service encounters and nursery tales in terms of 'optional' and 'obligatory' elements occurring with sequential restriction. She suggested that "the crucial properties of a genre can be expressed as a definite range of possible textual structures" (Hasan 1984:74). It seems possible to see some such pattern for visual presentation topics in recordings B and C and, to a lesser extent — due to its weaker genre membership — in recording A also. There are a number of reasons for seeing recording A as less of a presentation than B or C. Firstly it is not performed by the producer of the work being presented. Secondly it occurs at an early stage of project development. This means that what is being presented is nowhere near final copy but is only a set of alternatives for the client to assent or dissent to. This means that whereas negative evaluation needs to be resolved in recordings B and C, and, typically in presentations, is the site of negotiation activity, this is less the case in recording A, where a choice between kinds of approach is looked for rather than a final assessment. The client's negative evaluation of a possible design merely leads to its rejection in favour of other available alternatives. In recordings B and C, however, there is no other alternative and changes to the design need to be resolved between the participants. Therefore the analyses to follow will focus on recordings B and C.

Ventola's work (1987) on service encounter genres, following Hasan's, has questioned whether in fact there are any obligatory elements — after all in some instances it is possible to shop without saying anything and without this seemingly 'marked' behaviour. I suspect that a silent visual presentation in a professional setting, though possible, would be highly 'marked' and at some stage commented on. I will try to maintain an obligatory / optional distinction between elements with the proviso that 'obligatory' in this context means slightly less than 100 per cent and that the absence of such an element would appear marked and would need to be accounted for.

4.2.1. *Visual Presentation Topics*

Both presentations are heavy on visual presentation topics. They account for 66% of all topics on recording B and 40% on recording C where the presence of the client occasions negative evaluation topics and far more clarificatory work. In both presentations nearly all the topics open with a 'page shift' move. Exponents of this in recording C include:

the cover
then go onto the informative part
this one of course
we then go onto another spread
and then we have

we then go onto
next spread
and then we go onto the last spread

The first task the presenter (the designer) undertakes, in both these meetings, is to direct the attention of her addressee to the appropriate page or part of the page. The visual presentation topics that lack this page shift mechanism are either 'topic returns' after an evaluation or clarification topic or presentations of design features in general such as "what we have done is to produce the visual in book form", or "all of the spreads are designed differently". Every other visual presentation topic opens with a page shift marker. The same is true of recording B. Here the range of exponents is:

when we open
we then go onto
this is one of the spreads
and then we go onto
this here
and then we get another page
and then obviously
and then we get onto our back page
and then obviously on the back

Again, page shift markers are only absent for the same reasons as in recording C. So far, then, we have recognized the opening and obligatory element of a visual presentation topic. This is followed again in both recordings, without exception, by the visual presentation element itself. As explained earlier, the topic 'visual presentation' includes within it a visual presentation move. These are of two basic types:

A) A simple listing of visually present features. Such as, in recording C:
   The cover is a generic cover,
   the heading across the centre,
   working on textures, a mat cover generally overall with a corner of it in high
   gloss, not giving them any visual on the front cover at all,
   the introduction, the large picture of the campus
   the main message is obviously that there,

B) An indication of what has been done by the design team, as in the following examples also from recording C:

We've looked in typographic terms we've looked at different ways of actually putting all the copy together,
Typographically again, two messages in one,
We've tried obviously to echo the feeling of the cover,

The pattern is repeated in Recording B. These are simple visual presentations:
    saw the front cover as being very plain
    that message coming across very strongly
    keeping the corporate blue
    in terms of overall finish this would obviously be a matt varnish,
    again using just a spot gloss varnish . . .this follows through on the bio tech, And ways of showing what has been done.
    we've tried to add an element to it that runs throughout and it's this headline that we have on all of the pages I think what we have tried to do is produce a brochure that has an element of surprise to it
    we've tried to treat all these elements ... and we've tried therefore to make it very different

Both presentations therefore contain the same two openings:
obligatory elements. P. SHIFT — VIS PRES

The third element is that of POSITIVE EVALUATION. This occurs in 11 out of 14 visual presentation topics in recording C and 13 out of 15 in recording B. In visual presentation topics it is overwhelmingly given by the designer herself; in 9 out of 11 instances in recording C, and 12 out of 13 in recording B, although here the pro often also provides positive evaluation within the visual presentation topic. In everyday talk 'positive evaluation' of one's own work may be regarded as strange; however, its regular occurrence here, with no uptake, indicates its ordinariness and suggests one more distinguishing characteristic of this genre of talk. Positive evaluation by the presenter is an integral part of a design presentation as the data show, allowing for the smooth ongoing of the presentation process. Negative evaluation, on the other hand, never occurs within a presentation sequence. When it does occur it is not produced by the presenter. It routinely develops into a topic in its own right and occasions the occurrence of a different range of acts. Designer's own positive evaluation can occur in two ways in the presentation sequence: either inextricably linked to the visual presentation itself or as a free-standing act. Here are examples of both kinds from recording C:
A) As a separate act.

it all follows through.

we're very simple sophisticated

we want to entice them to go inside.

so that there is a liveliness to the brochure.

the way that this works we think is quite nice.

again creating, erm using our white space to effect.

B) Inextricable from the visual presentation act.

Then go on to the informative part of the brochure so to speak .

.. the whole of the brochure, the principle of the brochure and the layout works on erm the juxtaposition of type, of sizes of type...of areas of type together

we tried to obviously echo the feeling of the cover...of the cover as the centre spread

In the first example, juxtaposition of type is positively evaluated as being present in the design and as a feature that makes the brochure 'work'. In the latter, that the centre spread echoes or in some way links up with the front cover as a design-positive feature. Clearer examples of type B occur in recording B. There are similar free-standing positive evaluation acts there too.

A) As a separate act

but this one we felt very clean in terms of layout

Little elements like this —— just to add that little bit more interest

B) The inextricable examples

that message coming across very strongly, erm keeping the corporate blue that we have that works quite well

when we open very strong statement about the university

This is a very very strong statement, the main statement on that page we felt.

Whether designer 'positive evaluation' is a near obligatory act or an optional one is a moot point. In recording C, only as the presentation draws to an end is the positive evaluation provided by the client. Preceding that, every topic has a positive evaluation element provided by the designer unless, as in topic 15, it is a return to a previously discussed and positively evaluated spread; or because the topic meets serious interruption — in the form of important clarification-initiated-topics from the client. Thus it seems there is a tendency for the designer to produce positive evaluation of everything she shows of her near final work. It is interruptable however in a way that the visual presentation element is not and is, to some degree, optional. However, the interrupting clarification topics must themselves be resolved and group alignment regained before the visual presentation can continue. Furthermore, it must be remembered that all the clarification topics effect and depend on the current presentation spread. It could be said then that either positive evaluation is an obligatory part of each presentation element or the removal of a client problem with the topic must be achieved. There is no other outcome in either recording B or C.

4.3. Optional Presenter Moves

4.3.1. *Qualification*
An optional designer move in the presentation sequence is that of qualification. This might be seen as the designer countering the need for negotiation even before it is initiated. Here are some examples. First from recording C:
> Nothing is in a final stage at the moment
> but it will give you an impression of what the publication should look like.
> but where we come to the listing, again at the end of the day, we may slightly you know do this very slightly differently — but the overall idea is to get this fanning out of the different faculties.

And from recording B:
> Well there are elements in this that we feel obviously we will possibly go through change modify — but it might give you a feel, ... what the brochure is going to look like at the end of the day we might actually space these out rather differently once we spend more time on that

The function of this move in a presentation sequence is to stress the non-finality of the mock-up, or to emphasize possible or likely changes still to be made. By allowing the possibility of change, these moves function to head-off negative evaluation of the mock-up and to replace it with positive suggestions. This move indicates the presenter's awareness that what she presents is to be evaluated, and that if this evaluation is negative that changes to the design will have to be decided upon. The 'qualification' move changes the status of the information being presented from generally negotiable to negotiable on grounds other than those covered in the qualification. These moves also emphasize the designer's orientation to the staging of the process; to what kind of evaluation or criticism is justifiable at a particular stage. This is unequally distributed knowledge at least in this document design process, and can be used by some participants to control acceptable and unacceptable discourse contributions.

> Thus far we have a genre enactment that reads;
> p shift* — vis pres* — pos ev (*) — qualify
> [where * = obligatory]

4.4. Addressee Moves in Presentation Topics

All these elements are performed by the designer. The visual presentation topic is largely presenter dependent and may be carried out with no verbal assistance from the addressee — as one or two examples in recording A indicate. In recordings B and C the role of client and pro, within the visual presentation topic, is to seek clarification, to offer acknowledgment of what is presented and/or to positively evaluate it. Negative evaluation leads to a new topic type. Sometimes positive evaluation and clarification requests also lead to new topic talk.

The range of exponents that function as acknowledgment markers is very limited, especially considering that they occur in every visual presentation topic in recording C and recording B. The list does not extend beyond YES, RIGHT, NO, THAT'S RIGHT, MMM, YEAH. They occur widely within and around all the other moves made by the designer, after the visual presentation element, or within it, after or during evaluation, and after or during qualification. One other available move for the addressee is to 'other-complete'. This too shows alignment (Nofsinger 1990) with what the presenter presents, thus indicating that what is being shown is comprehensible and acceptable.

In accounting for this, the largest topic type in both recordings, we have also accounted for the action that moves the whole process of a visual presentation towards closure. Nearly all the other topics are linked to the ongoing or just-completed page presentation. An adjoining clarification topic only concerns items of current interest, as do negative evaluation topics. This will be shown more clearly in the following section.

Only visual presentation topics, then, in a visual presentation sequence, advance the discourse by introducing new topics for consideration. Other topic types such as clarification requests and negative evaluation are used to initiate negotiation on a range of issues that are relevant to the current topic.

4.5. The Sequential Pattern of Topic Type Occurrence in Visual Presentation Sequences

Having outlined the components of the visual presentation sequence and of the visual presentation topic in particular, I now wish to illustrate how these topic types co-occur and thereby highlight some important features of a presentation sequence. In this section I want to concentrate on how these units co-occur, move from one to the other and back again; throughout I shall focus on the orientation of the participants themselves to enact a presentation sequence in a particular way.

Once the visual presentation is underway — marked by the 'procedural topic' as outlined in the previous section — then all talk by the participants orients to the ongoingness of the presentation — until it reaches a conclusion, again as marked by a procedural topic as described previously. One can say that although the presenter has no special right to an extended turn he/she does have the right to complete the presentation and that, failing an immediate need to perform other functions relevant to the presentation, the speaking turn will revert to the presenter. There are severe constraints on what the presenter can do with her extended speaking rights in that all topics initiated by her are presentation topics. So this appears to be a feature that distinguishes this kind of professional talk from conversation, where it is highly unlikely for there to be one participant to whom speaking rights consistently revert.

Within the document design process this is certainly one of very few sequence types where the speaker who consistently regains the speaking turn is not the pro, the procedural organizer of the interaction. This is how topic development for the two presentation sequences appears:

TOPIC LINKAGE for Recording C:
      1. PROCEDURAL
      2. PROCEDURAL
3. PRESENTATION
4. PRESENTATION
5. PRESENTATION
6. PRESENTATION — 7. CLARIFY
8. PRESENTATION
9. PRESENTATION — 10. CLARIFY
11. POSITIVE EVALUATION
      12. NEGATIVE EVALUATION
      13. PROCEDURAL
      14. (12) — REFORMULATE
15. PRESENTATION RETURN (9)

16. PRESENTATION — 17. CLARIFY
18. PRESENTATION — 19. NEGATIVE EVALUATION
20. PRESENTATION — 21. CLARIFY — 22. CLARIFY
    23. PROCEDURAL
    24. CLARIFY
    25. BONDING
    26. POSITIVE EVALUATION
    27. NEGATIVE EVALUATION
28. PRESENTATION — 29. CLARIFY— 30. NEGATIVE EVALUATION
31. PRESENTATION — 32. CLARIFY — 33. CLARIFY
34. PRESENTATION
35. PRESENTATION
    36. POSITIVE EVALUATION
    37. PROCEDURAL

TOPIC LINKAGE for Recording B:
    1. PROCEDURAL
    2. PROCEDURAL
    3. PROCEDURAL
4. PRESENTATION
5. PRESENTATION — 6. CLARIFY
7. PRESENTATION
8. PRESENTATION
9. PRESENTATION
10. PRESENTATION
11. PRESENTATION
12. PRESENTATION — 13. POSITIVE EVALUATION
14. PRESENTATION
15. PRESENTATION
16. PRESENTATION — 17. POSITIVE EVALUATION
18. PRESENTATION
19. PRESENTATION
20. PRESENTATION
21. PRESENTATION
    22. POSITIVE EVALUATION
    23. PROCEDURAL

Presentation topics are listed down the left margin. Non presentational topics linked to the current presentation issue are place adjacent to the relevant presentation topic. Most other topics do orient to the current visual presentation. Once any issues of concern, disagreement, dissatisfaction have been negotiated, and in recordings B and C they must be dealt with to an adequate conclusion for all parties, only then does talk revert to visual presentation.

In recording B, once the procedural matters have been dealt with, topic progression is as follows:

Topics 1-3 are procedural and once the visual presentation boundary has been established then Topic 4 covers presentation of the brochure in general terms. The topic ends with pro acknowledge moves ('yeah' . . . 'yeah'). This I take to indicate satisfaction with what has been presented so far or at least preparation to hear more and let the presentation reach completion before making detailed comments. Topic 5 is the cover visual presentation. Pro initiates a clarifying topic on the colour being used, and once this is settled and alignment between pro and designer reestablished, then Topic 7 is a 'return-to-cover' presentation by the designer. This pattern continues throughout the presentation but not beyond its procedural boundaries.

Recording C progresses with more hold ups and more expansion at a number of points, but the orientation of participants to progress from spread to spread, dealing with problems with the current page, is retained.

One finds a similar orientation to allowing the designer to continue the presentation of her work unless there is a pressing need to do otherwise, namely to negotiate changes. The presence of the client, looking at near-complete final work does however change the range of issues likely to interrupt the designer's progress. Still, all interruptions can be dealt with in terms of the five topic types listed earlier, but of those five there was no negative evaluation topic in recording B, whereas there are four occurrences in recording C. Additionally, in recording C some clarification topics also led to negotiation activity. Consequently, realignment between participants to a discourse consisting largely of presentation topics initiated by only one speaker, was not so easily achieved in recording C as it was in recording B.

The sequence of topic development was as follows: Topics 1 and 2 are procedural, the second setting up the opening frame of the presentation. Topic 3 is the opening general presentation of design team work. It ends with a client 'accept' move ('right, right, right') and is followed by Topic 4. This opens with a 'page shift' move to direct attention to the cover. The designer's own 'positive evaluation' of it follows ('we're very simple sophisticated'). This is 'acknowledged' by the client, and then topic five directs attention to the first spread. Designer 'positive evaluation' of the first half of the spread ('very clean layout') receives no response from the client; this seems tantamount to acceptance at least for the time being, and appears to be an orientation to an understanding of the work laid before him. This is borne out by the designer's topic progression to the other half of the spread. Topic 6 ends with a client 'request for clarification'. Once alignment has been reestablished, talk reverts to a visual presentation topic in Topic 8. This pattern continues to the end of the presentation. There are larger gaps in the delivery of presentation topics here than in recording B. This is due largely to the 'negative evaluation' that client gives that needs to be dealt with and removed there and then — as the work nears completion there is no room left for any party, especially the client, to be dissatisfied with what is being done. Earlier recordings show a greater readiness to accommodate higher levels of uncertainty.

5. CONCLUSION

It is a distinguishing characteristic of these presentation activities that the talk is organized around five recurring topic types. This seems unlikely to be a feature of other types of discourse. These topic types do not occur in an unstructured way either. There is a pattern to the way they unfold that can be seen as constitutive of doing a presentation as part of the document design process. Visual presentation functions as a 'default' topic. Once any problems have been dealt with it is this topic that will occur; and it is the presenter who will initiate it and be allowed a lengthy turn for this purpose, but for no other purpose. Thus there is a distinct turn-taking mechanism for enacting this kind of data that, because it is linked to the occurrence of certain topic types, is another defining features of this kind of presentation.

In presentation talk negotiation occurs at well-defined points in the discourse. Issues for negotiation are raised through clarification and negative evaluation topics. Only the client initiates negative evaluation and this can be seen as one indicator of his role as *negotiation-instigator* within these proceedings. The client raises issues for negotiation through 'negative evaluation' and 'clarificatory' moves. The way the negotiation proceeds is dependent on the stage at which the presentation occurs. In recording A matters can be left unresolved, to be dealt with in later discussions; by recording C, realignment of participants on nearly all the issues is striven for and largely achieved as they occur. Once dealt with, the talk reverts to a non-negotiative 'visual presentation' sequence. This pattern holds until all the spreads have been shown.

The sequencing of topic types and of the moves within them across all three presentation episodes indicates a generic quality to the enactment of this task. The differences between recordings B and C highlight in structural terms that it is largely the presence of the client that leads to negotiation activity. Moreover, it is through his production of negative evaluation and clarification sequences that this negotiation work is initiated.

APPENDIX

Act types recognized in the data

Acc	Accept
Ack	Acknowledge
ALt DP	Alternative Decision Proposal
Clfy	Clarify
ClfyR	Clarification Request
Dir	Directive
DP	Decision Proposal
Inf	Inform
Neg Ev	Negative Evaluation
Offer	Offer
Pos Ev	Positive Evaluation
Req	Request
Vis Pres	Presentation of Something Visually Available

BIBLIOGRAPHY

Abelson, H., Sussman, G. J. and Sussman, J. (1985). *Structure and Interpretation of Computer Programs*. The MIT Press, Cambridge, MA.

Adler, N. J., Graham, J. L. and Gehrke, T. S. (1987). Business negotiations in Canada, Mexico, and the United States. *Journal of Business Research*, **15**, 411–429.

Agar, M. (1985). Institutional discourse. *Text*, **5**, 147–168.

Anderson, R. J., Hughes, J. A. and Sharrock, W. W. (1989). *Working for Profit: The Social Organization of Calculation in an Entrepreneurial Firm*. Avebury/Gower, Aldershot, U.K.

Angelmar, R. and Stern, L. W. (1978). Development of a Content Analystic System for Analysis of Bargaining Communication in Marketing. *Journal of Marketing Research*, **XV**, 93–102.

Arthurs, H. (1985). Understanding labour law: The debate over 'Industrial Pluralism'. *Current Legal Problems*, **38**.

Asaoka, T. (1987). *Communication Problems Between Japanese and Australians at a Dinner Party*. Working Papers of the Japanese Studies Centre, 3. Japanese Studies Centre, Melbourne.

Atkinson, J. M. (1983). Two devices for generating audience approval: A comparative study of public discourse and texts. *In*: Ehlich, K. *et al*. (eds), *Connectedness in Sentence, Text, and Discourse*, pp. 199–236. Tilburg Studies in Language and Literature. Tilburg, Katholieke Hogeschool.

Atkinson, J. M. (1984). *Our Masters' Voices. The Language and Body Language of Politics*. Routledge and Kegan Paul, London and New York.

Atkinson, J. M. and Drew, P. (1979). *Order in Court: The Organization of Verbal Interaction in Judicial Settings*. Macmillan, London.

Atkinson, J. M. and Heritage, J. (eds) (1984). *Structures of Social Action: Studies in Conversation Analysis*. Cambridge University Press, Cambridge.

Auer, P. and di Luzio, A. (eds) (1992). *The Contextualization of Language*. John Benjamins, Amsterdam.

Austin, J. L. (1961). *Philosophical Papers*. Oxford University Press, London.

Bacharach, S. B. and Lawler, E. J. (1981). *Bargaining: Power, Tactics, and Outcomes*. Jossey-Bass, San Fransisco.

Bachrach, P. and Baratz, M. (1970). *Power and Poverty*. Oxford University Press, New York.

Bales, R. F. (1950). *Interaction Process Analysis: A Method for the Study of Small Groups*. Addison-Wesley, Cambridge, MA.

Barbaux, M. -T. (1991). The so called "non-linguistic": A facilitator for foreign language acquisition. Paper presented at the 16th Applied Linguistics Association of Australia Congress, September–October 1991, Townsville, Australia.

Barley, S. R. (1991). Contextualizing Conflict: Notes on the anthropology of disputes and negotiations. *In*: Bazerman, M. H., Lewicki, R. J. and Sheppard, B. H. (eds), *Research on Negotiation in Organizations, Vol. 3. Handbook of Negotiation Research*, pp. 165–199. JAI Press, Greenwich, CT.

Beardsley, R. K., Hall, J. W. and Ward, R. E. (1959). *Village Japan*. University of Chicago Press, Chicago.

Beck, C. S. and Ragan, S. L. (1992). Negotiating interpersonal and medical talk: Frame shifts in the gynaecologic exam. *Journal of Language and Social Psychology*, **11**, 47–61.

Bell, D. V. J. (1975). *Power Influence and Authority: An Essay in Political Linguistics*. Oxford University Press, New York.

Bell, D. V. J. (1977). Political linguistics and political education. *Teaching Politics*.

Bell, D. V. J. (1988). Political linguistics and international negotiation. *Negotiation Journal*, **4**, 233–246.

Berger, P. and Luckmann, T. (1967). *The Social Construction of Reality*. Allen Lane, London.

Bergmann, J. (1992). Veiled morality: notes on discretion in psychiatry. *In*: Drew, P. and Heritage, J. (eds), *Talk at Work: Interaction in Institutional Settings*, pp. 137–162. Cambridge University Press, Cambridge.

Bilmes, J. (1981). Proposition and confrontation in a legal discussion. *Semiotica*, **34**, 251–275.

Bilmes, J. (1985). Freedom and regulation: An anthropological critique of free market ideology. *Research in Law & Economics*, **7**, 123–147.

Bilmes, J. (1986). *Discourse and Behavior*. Plenum Press, New York.

Bilmes, J. (1988). The concept of preference in conversation analysis. *Language in Society*, **17**, 161–181.

Bilmes, J. (1992a). Dividing the rice: A microanalysis of the mediator's role in a Northern Thai negotiation. *Language in Society*, **21**, 569

Bilmes, J. (1992b). Mishearings. *In*: Watson, G. and Seiler, R. M. (eds), *Text in Context: Contributions to Ethnomethodology*, pp. 79–98. Sage, London.

Bilmes, J. (1993a). Ethnomethodology, culture, and implicature: Toward an empirical pragmatics. *Pragmatics*, 3(4), 387–409.

Bilmes, J. (1993b). Accounting Practices as an Ethnomethodological and Linguistic Pragmatic Concern: The Case of Response Priority. Paper presented at the 1993 meeting of the International Pragmatics Association, Kobe, Japan.

Bilmes, J. and Woodbury, J. (1991). Deterrence and justice: Setting civil penalties in the federal trade commission. *Research in Law and Economics*, **14**, 191–221.

Boden, D. (1994). *The Business of Talk: Organizations in Action*. Polity Press, Cambridge.

Boden, D. and Zimmerman, D. (eds) (1991). *Talk and Social Structure: Studies in Ethnomethodology and Conversation Analysis*. Polity Press, Cambridge.

Brandstatter, H., Davis, J. H. and Stocker-Kreichgauer, G. (eds) (1982). *Group Decision Making.* Academic Press, London.

Brehmer, B. and Hammond, K. R. (1977). Cognitive Factors in interpersonal conflict. *In*: Druckman, D. (ed.), *Negotiations: Social Psychological Perspectives*, pp. 79–103. Sage, Beverly Hills, CA.

Brenneis, D. (1988). Language and disputing. *Annual Review of Anthropology,* **17,** 221–237.

Brooks, P. F., Jr (1982). *The Mythical Man-Month: Essays on Software Engineering.* Addison-Wesley, Philippines.

Brown, B. R. (1977). Face-Saving and Face-Restoration in Negotiation. *In*: Druckman, D. (ed.), *Negotiations: Social Psychological Perspectives*, pp. 275–299. Sage, Beverly Hills, CA.

Brown, P. and Levinson, S. C. (1987). *Politeness: Some Universals in Language Usage.* Cambridge University Press, Cambridge.

Burton, D. (1980). *Towards an Analysis of Casual Conversation.* Routledge and Kegan Paul, London.

Buttny, R. (1993). *The Social Accountability of Communication.* Sage, London.

Button, G. (1990). On varieties of closings. *In*: Psathas, G. (ed.), *Interaction Competence*, pp. 93–147. University Press of America, Washington, D.C.

Button, G. (1991). Conversation-in-a-Series. *In*: Boden, D. and Zimmerman, D. (eds), *Talk and Social Structure: Studies in Ethnomethodology and Conversation Analysis*, pp. 251–277. Polity, Cambridge.

Button, G. and Casey, N. (1984). Generating topic: the use of topic initial elicitors. *In*: Atkinson, J. M. and Heritage, J. (eds), *Structures of Social Interaction: Studies in Conversational Analysis*, pp. 167–190. Cambridge University Press, Cambridge.

Button, G., Drew, P. and Heritage, J. (eds) (1986). Interaction and language use. *Special issue of Human Studies*, **9**.

Button, G. and Sharrock, W. W. (forthcoming a). The mundane work of writing and reading computer programs. *In*: Ten Have, P. and Psathas, G. (eds), *The Social Organization of Talk and Embodied Activities*. The University Press of America, Washington, D.C.

Button, G. and Sharrock, W. W. (forthcoming b). Occasioned practices in the work of software engineers. *In*: Jirotka, M., Bickerton, M. and Goguen, J. A. (eds), *Requirements Engineering*. Academic Press, New York.

Button, G., Sharrock, W. W. and Anderson, R. J. (1990). Talking through the software design. American Association for Artificial Intelliegence, *Proceedings of the Workshop on Complex Systems, Ethnomethodology and Interaction Analysis*, Boston.

Candlin, C., Coleman, H. and Burton, J. (1983). Dentist-patient: Communicating complaint. *In*: Wolfson, N. E. and Judd, E. (eds), *Sociolinguistics and Language Acquisition*, pp. 56–81. Newbury House, Rowley, Massachusetts.

Carnevale, P. J. D. (1986). Strategic choice in mediation. *Negotiation Journal*, **2**(1), 41–56.

Casse, P. (1981). *Managing Intercultural Negotiations.* Society for Intercultural Training and Research.

Cedersund, E. (1992a). *Talk, Text and Institutional Order.* (Diss.) (Linköping Studies in Arts and Science, 78). University of Linköping.

Cedersund, E. (1992b). *Från personligt problem till administrativt beslut: Att söka om ekonomiskt bistånd.* (From personal problems to administrative decisions: Applying for financial assistance) (Studies in Communication, 33). Linköping: Department of Communication Studies.

Chastain, K. (1980). Native speaker reaction to instructor-identified second-language errors. *Modern Language Journal,* **64,** 210–215.

Chatman, J. A., Putnam, L. L. and H. Sondak (1991). Integrating communication and negotiation research. *In:* Bazerman, M. H., Lewicki, R. J. and Sheppard, B. H. (eds), *Research on negotiation in Organizations, Vol. 3. Handbook of Negotiation Research,* pp. 139–164. JAI Press, Greenwich, CT.

Cicourel, A. V. (1973). *Cognitive Sociology.* Penguin Books, Harmondsworth.

Cicourel, A. V. (1992). The interpenetration of communicative contexts: Examples from medical encounters. *In:* Duranti, A. and Goodwin, C. (eds), *Rethinking Context: Language as an Interactive Phenomenon,* pp. 293–310. Cambridge University Press, Cambridge.

Cohen, R. (1987). Problems of intercultural communication. *International Journal of Intercultural Relations,* 29–47.

Cohen, R. (1990). *Culture and Conflict in Egyptian–Israeli Relations: A Dialogue of the Deaf.* Indiana University Press, Bloomington.

Cole, S. G. (1972). Conflict and cooperation in potentially intense conflict situations. *Journal of Personality and Social Psychology,* **22,** 31–50.

Collins, R. (1981). On the microfoundations of macrosociology. *American Journal of Sociology,* **86**(5), 984–1014.

Connolly, W. (1974). *The Terms of Political Discourse.* Lexington, Boston.

Corder, S. P. (1967). The significance of learner's errors. *IRAL,* **4,** 161–170.

Corder, S. P. (1981). *Error Analysis and Interlanguage.* Oxford University Press, Oxford.

Cross, J. G. (1969). *The Economics of Bargaining.* Basic Books, New York.

Crow, B. (1983). Topic shifts in couples' conversations. *In:* Craig, R. and Tracy, K. (eds), *Conversational Coherence.* Sage, Beverly Hills.

Cruse, D. A. (1986). *Lexical Semantics.* Cambridge University Press, Cambridge.

Davidson, J. (1978). An instance of negotiation in a call closing. *Sociology,* **12**(1), 123–133.

Davidson, J. (1984). Subsequent versions of invitations, offers, requests, and proposals dealing with potential or actual rejection. *In:* Atkinson, J. M. and Heritage, J. C. (eds), *Structures of Social Action: Studies in Conversation Analysis.* Cambridge University Press, Cambridge.

Davies, F. (1985). Toward a methodology for identifying information structures based on topic type. *In:* Ulijn, J. M. and Pugh, A. K. (eds), *Reading for Professional Purposes: Methods and Materials in Teaching Languages.* ACCO (Contrastive Analysis series), Leeuwen, Belgium.

Davies, F. (1986). Structure and language of textbooks across the curriculum. *In:* Tickoo, M. L. (ed.), *Language in Learning. Selected Papers from the Twentieth SEAMEO Regional Language Centre Seminar on Language Across the Curriculum.* RELC, Singapore.

Day, R. and Day, J. (1977). A review of the current state of negotiated order theory: An appreciation and a critique. *The Sociological Quarterly,* **18,** 126–142.

Donohue, W. A. (1981). Analyzing negotiation tactics: Development of a negotiation interact system. *Human Communication Research*, **7**, 273–287.

Donohue, W. A. and Diez, M. (1985). Directive use in negotiation interaction. *Communication Monographs*, **52**, 305–318.

Donohue, W. A., Deiz, M. E. and Stahle, R. B. (1983). New directions in negotiation research. *Communication Yearbook*, **7**, 249–279.

Donohue, W. A., Diez, M. E. and Hamilton, M. (1984). Coding naturalistic negotiation interaction. *Human Communication Research*, **10**, 403–425.

Donohue, W. A., Ramesh, C. and Borchgrevink, C. (1991). Crisis Bargaining: Tracking relational paradox in hostage negotiation. *The International Journal of Conflict Management*, **2**(4), 257–274.

Dore, R. P. (1978). *Shinohata, A Portrait of a Japanese Village*. Pantheon Books, New York.

Dore, J. and McDermott, R. P. (1982). Linguistic indeterminacy and social context in utterance interpretation. *Language*, **58**, 374–398.

Douglas, A. (1957). The peaceful settlement of industrial and inter-group disputes. *Journal of Conflict Resolution*, **1**, 69–81.

Douglas, M. (1962). *Industrial Peacemaking*. Columbia University Press, New York.

Drew, P. (1984). Speakers' reportings in invitation sequences. *In*: Atkinson, J. M. and Heritage, J. (eds), *Structures in Social Action: Studies in Conversation Analysis*, pp. 129–151. Cambridge University Press, Cambridge.

Drew, P. (1990). Conversation Analysis: Who needs it? *Text*, **10**(1/2), 27-35.

Drew, P. (forthcoming). Interaction sequences and anticipatory interactive planning. *In*: Goody, E., *Social Intelligence*, Chapter 4. Cambridge University Press, Cambridge.

Drew, P. and Heritage, J. (1992). Analyzing talk at work: An introduction. *In*: Drew, P. and Heritage, J. (eds), *Talk at Work: Interaction in Institutional Settings*, pp. 3–65. Cambridge University Press, Cambridge.

Drew, P. and Heritage, J. (eds) (1992). *Talk at Work: Interaction in Institutional Settings*. Cambridge University Press, Cambridge.

Druckman, D. (1973). *Human Factors in International Negotiations*. Sage, London.

Druckman, D. (1977). Social-psychological approaches to the study of negotiations. *In*: Druckman, D. (ed.), *Negotiations: Social Psychological Perspectives*, pp. 15–44. Sage, Beverly Hills, CA.

Duranti, A. and Goodwin, C. (1992). *Rethinking Context: Language as an Interactive Phenomenon*. Cambridge University Press, Cambridge.

Edmondson, W. (1981). *Spoken Discourse: A Model for Analysis*. Longmans, London.

Ehlich, K. and Rehbein, J. (1986). *Muster und Institution. Untersuchungen zur schulischen Kommunikation*. Tübingen: Narr.

Ehlich, K. and Wagner, J. (eds) (*in press*), *The Discourse of Negotiation*. Mouton de Gruyter, Berlin.

Eisentein, M. (1983). Native reactions to non-native speech: A review of empirical research. *Studies in Second Language Acquisition*, **5**(2), 160–176.

Fairclough, N. (1992). *Discourse and Social Change*. Polity Press, Cambridge.

Fant, L. (1989). Cultural mismatch in conversation: Spanish and Scandinavian communicative behaviour in negotiation settings. *Hermes*, **3**, 247–267.

Ferraro, G. P. (1990). *The Cultural Dimension of International Business.* Prentice Hall, Englewood Cliffs, New Jersey.

Festinger, W., Abel, R. and Sarat, A. (1980–81). Transforming of disputes: Naming, blaming, claiming. *Law & Society Review,* **15**(3–4).

Firth, A. (1990). 'Lingua franca' negotiations: Towards an interactional approach. *World Englishes,* **9**(3), 269–280.

Firth, A. (1991). Discourse at work: Negotiating by telex, fax, and 'phone. Unpublished doctoral dissertation. Dept. of Languages and Intercultural Studies, Aalborg University, Denmark.

Firth, A. (1993). Presentation to Negotiation Workshop, York University (May).

Firth, A. (1994). 'Accounts' in negotiation discourse: A single-case analysis. *Journal of Pragmatics* **23**(2).

Firth, A. (*in press*). Multiple mode, single activity: Telenegotiating as a social accomplishment. *In:* ten Have, P. and Psathas, G. (eds), *Situated Order: Studies in the Organization of Talk and Embodied Activities.* University of America Press, Washington, D.C.

Fisher, A. S. (1991). *CASE Using Software Development Tools.* John Wiley, New York.

Fisher, B. A. (1974). *Small Group Decision Making: Communication and the Group Process.* McGraw-Hill, New York.

Fisher, R. and Ury, W. (1981). *Getting to Yes: Negotiating Agreement Without Giving In.* Hutchinson Business, London.

Foucault, M. (1971). *The Archeology of Knowledge.* Tavistock Publications, London.

Francis, D. W. (1982). Some features of accounts in industrial conflicts. Unpublished PhD thesis, University of Manchester, U.K.

Francis, D. W. (1986). Some structures of negotiation talk. *Journal of Language and Social Psychology,* **15**, 53–80.

Francis D. W. (*in press*). Negotiation, decision making and formalism: The problem of form and substance in negotiation analysis. *In:* Ehlich, K. and Wagner, J. (eds), *The Discourse of Negotiation.* Mouton de Gruyter, Berlin.

Fredin, E. (1993). *Språk i socialt arbete.* (Language in Social Work) (Diss.) (Studies in Communication, 36). Linköping: Department of Communication Studies.

Friedrich, C. (1941). *Constitutional Government and Democracy.* Little Brown, Boston.

Garcia, A. (1991). Dispute resolution without disputing: How the interactional organization of mediation hearings minimizes argument. *American Sociological Review,* **56**, 818–835.

Garfinkel, H. (1967). *Studies in Ethnomethodology.* Prentice-Hall, Englewood Cliffs, NJ.

Garfinkel, H. (ed.) (1986). *Ethnomethodological Studies of Work.* Routledge and Kegan Paul, London.

Garfinkel, H. and Sacks, H. (1970). On formal structures of practical actions. *In:* McKinney, J. C. and Tiryakian, E. A. (eds), *Theoretical Sociology,* pp. 338–366. Appleton-Century-Crofts, New York.

Garfinkel, H. and Wieder, D. L. (1992). Two incommensurable, asymmetrically alternate technologies of social analysis. *In:* Watson, G. and Seiler, R. M. (eds), *Text in Context: Contributions to Ethnomethodology,* pp. 175–206. Sage, London.

Garfinkel, H., Lynch, M. and Livingston, E. (1981). The work of a discovering science construed with materials from the optically discovered pulsar. *Philosophy of the Social Sciences*, **11**, 131–158.

Gibbons, P., Bradack, J. J. and Busch, J. D. (1992). The role of language in negotiations: threats and priorities. *In*: Putnam, L. L. and Roloff, M. E. (eds), *Negotiations: Threats and Promises,* pp. 156–175. Sage, London.

Giddens, A. (1979). *Central Problems in Social Theory: Action, Structure and Contradiction in Social Analysis*. University of California Press, Berkeley.

Goffman, E. (1974). *Frame Analysis*. Harper and Row, New York.

Goffman, E. (1981). *Forms of Talk*. University of Pennsylvania Press, Philadelphia.

Goodwin, C. (1986). Audience diversity, participation and interpretation. *Text*, **6/3,** 283–316.

Goodwin, M. H. (1990). *He-Said, She-Said: Talk as Social Organization Among Black Children*. Indiana University Press, Bloomington, IN.

Goodwin, C. and Duranti, A. (eds) (1992). *Rethinking Context: Language as an Interactive Phenomenon*. Cambridge University Press, Cambridge.

Goodwin, C. and Harness Goodwin, M. (1990). Interstitial argument. *In*: Grimshaw, A. D. (ed.), *Conflict Talk: Sociolinguistic Investigations of Arguments in Conversations*, pp. 85–117. Cambridge University Press, Cambridge.

Goodwin, C. and Heritage, J. (1990). Conversation analysis. *Annual Review of Anthropology*, **19**, 283–307.

Government of Ireland (1980). *Sale of Goods and Supply of Services Act*. Vol. 16 of 1980 of Dublin, Ireland. Stationery Office.

Government of Ireland (1990). *Annual Report of the Director of Consumer Affairs and Fair Trade for 1988*. Stationery Office, Dublin, Ireland, 80 pp.

Graham, J. L. and Sano, Y. (1984). *Smart Bargaining: Doing business with the Japanese*. Ballinger, Cambridge, MA.

Graumann, C. F. (1994). Commonality, reciprocity, mutuality. *In*: Graumann, C. F., Foppa, K. and Marková, I. (eds), *Mutualities in Dialogue*. Cambridge University Press, Cambridge.

Gray, B., Purdy, J. and Bouwen, R. (1990). Comparing dispositional and interactional approaches to negotiating. *University of Pennsylvania Center for Research in Conflict and Negotiation, Working Paper*.

Greatbatch, D. (1988). A turn-taking system for British news interviews. *Language in Society*, **17**, 401–430.

Griffin, T. and Daggart, W. R. (1990). *The Global Negotiator: Building Strong Business Relationships Anywhere in the World*. Harper Business, New York.

Grimshaw, A. D. (1987). Disambiguating discourse: Members' skill and analysts' problem. *Social Psychology Quarterly*, **50**(2), 186-204.

Grimshaw, A. D. (ed.) (1990). *Conflict Talk: Sociolinguistic Investigations of Arguments in Conversations*. Cambridge University Press, Cambridge.

Grindsted, A. (1989). Distributive communicative behaviour in Danish and Spanish negotiation interaction. *Hermes*, **3**, 267–279.

Gronn, P. C. (1983). Talk as the work: the accomplishment of school administration. *Administrative Science Quarterly*, **28**, 1–21.

Gronn, P. C. (1985). Committee talk: Negotiating 'personal development' at a training college. *Journal of Management Studies*, **22**, 245–268.

Groth, B. (1992). Negotiating in the global village: Four lamps to illuminate the table. *Negotiation Journal*, **July**, 241–257.

Gudykunst, W. B. and Kim, Y. Y. (1984). *Communicating with Strangers*. Addison-Wesley, Reading, Massachusetts.

Gulliver, P. H. (1979). *Disputes and Negotiations: A Cross-Cultural Perspective*. Academic Press, New York.

Gulliver, P. H. (1988). Anthropological contributions to the study of negotiation. *Negotiation Journal*, **4**(3), July.

Gumperz, J. J. (1982a). *Discourse Strategies*. Cambridge University Press, Cambridge.

Gumperz, J. J. (ed.) (1982b). *Language and Social Identity*. Cambridge University Press, Cambridge.

Hadden, B. L. (1991). Teacher and non-teacher perceptions of second language communication. *Language Learning*, **41**(1), 1–24.

Hall, E. (1959). *The Silent Language*. Doubleday, New York.

Hargie, O. (ed.) (1986). *A Handbook of Communication Skills*. Croom Helm, Kent.

Harré, R. (1993). *Social Being*, 2nd edn. Basil Blackwell, Oxford.

Harris, Z. (1951). *Methods in Structural Linguistics*. University of Chicago Press, Chicago.

Hasan, R. (1984). The nursery tale as genre. *Nottingham Linguistic Circular*, **13**, 71–102.

Hasegawa, R. (1985). Politeness strategies in a Japanese conversation. Unpublished paper.

Heath, C. (1992). The delivery and reception of diagnosis in the general-practice consultation. *In*: Drew, P. and Heritage, J. (eds), *Talk at Work: Interaction in Institutional Settings*, pp. 235–267. Cambridge University Press, Cambridge.

Heller, M. S. (1982). Negotiations of language choice in Montreal. *In*: Gumperz, J. J. (ed.), *Language and Social Identity*, pp. 108–118. Cambridge University Press, Cambridge.

Heritage, J. (1984a). *Garfinkel and Ethnomethodology*. Polity, Cambridge.

Heritage, J. (1984b). A change-of-state token and aspects of its sequential placement. *In*: Heritage, J. and Atkinson, J. (eds), *Structures of Social Action: Studies in Conversation Analysis*, pp. 299–345. Cambridge University Press, Cambridge.

Heritage, J. (1985). Analysing news interviews: Aspects of the production of talk for an overhearing audience. *In*: van Dijk, T. (ed.), *Handbook of Discourse Analysis Vol. 3, Discourse and Dialogue*, pp. 95–117. Academic Press, London.

Heritage, J. and Atkinson, M. J. (1984). Introduction. *In*: Atkinson, J. M. and Heritage, J. (eds), *Structures of Social Action: Studies in Conversation Analysis*, pp. 1–15. Cambridge University Press, Cambridge.

Heritage, J. and Sefi, S. (1992). Dilemmas of advice: Aspects of the delivery and reception of advice in interactions between health visitors and first time mothers. *In*: Drew, P. and Heritage, J. (eds), *Talk at Work*, pp. 359–417. Cambridge University Press, Cambridge.

Heritage, J. and Watson, D. R. (1979). Formulations as conversational objects. *In*: Psathas, G. (ed.), *Everyday Language*, pp. 123–162. Irvington, New York.

Hinkle, S., Stiles, W. and Taylor, L. A. (1988). Verbal processes in a labour/management negotiation. *Journal of Language and Social Psychology*, **7**(2), 123–136.

Holmes, M. E. (1992). Phase structures in negotiation. *In*: Putnam, L. L. and Roloff, M. E. (eds), *Communication and Negotiation*, pp. 83–108. Sage, Newbury Park, CA.

Hopmann, P. T. and Walcott, C. (1977). The impact of external stresses and tensions on negotiations. *In*: Druckman, D. (ed.), *Negotiations: Social Psychological Perspectives*, pp. 301–323. Sage, Beverly Hills, CA.

Hosking, D. and Morley, I. (1991). *A Social Psychology of Organizing: People, Processes and Contexts*. Harvester Wheatsheaf, Hemel Hempstead.

Hydén, L. -C. (1988). *Fredagsarbete: Scener från en socialvårdsbyrå*. (Friday work: Scenes from a social welfare agency). FoU-rapport nr 82. Stockholms socialförvaltning.

Hydén, L. -C. (1990). Handläggare om socialbidrag. (Administrators on financial assistance.) *FoU-rapport*, nr 136. Stockholms socialförvaltning.

Hydén, L. -C. (1991). Moral och byråkrati: Om socialbidragsansökningar. (Morality and bureaucracy: On applications for financial assistance.) *FoU-rapport*, 1991:7. Stockholms socialförvaltning.

Hydén, L. -C. (1994). The social worker as moral worker: Applying for money — the moral encounter between social workers and clients. *In*: Gunnarsson, B.-L., Linell, P. and Nordberg, B. (eds), *Text and Talk in Professional Contexts* (ASLA's Skriftserie, No. 6). Department for Advanced Studies in Modern Swedish, Uppsala University.

Hymes, D. H. (1972). On communicative competence. *In*: Pride, J. B. (ed.), *Sociolinguistics*, pp. 269–293. Penguin, Harmondsworth.

Hymes, D. H. (1974). *Foundations in Sociolinguistics. An Ethnographic Approach*. University of Pennsylvania Press, Philadelphia.

Ikle, F. C. (1964). *How Nations Negotiate*. Harper and Row, New York.

Ikuta, S. (1980). Ethnography and Discourse Cohesion: Aspects of speech level shift in Japanese discourse. M.A. Thesis. Cornell University.

Ikuta, S. (1983). Speech level shift and conversational strategy in Japanese discourse. *Language Sciences*, **5**(1), 37–53.

Inglehart, R. (1990). *Culture Shift in Advanced Industrial Society*. Princeton University Press, Princeton.

Jackall, R. (1988). *Moral Mazes: The World of Corporate Managers*. Oxford University Press, Oxford.

Jackson, S. and Jacobs, S. (1981). The collaborative production of proposals in conversational argument and persuasion: A study of disagreement regulation. *Journal of the American Forensic Association*, **18**, 77–90.

Janosik, R. J. (1987). Rethinking the culture–negotiation link. *Negotiation Journal*, October, 5–13.

Jayyusi, L. (1984). *Categorization and the Moral Order*. Routledge and Kegan Paul, Boston and London.

Jefferson, G. (1972). Side sequences. *In*: Sudnow, D. (ed.), *Studies in Social Interaction*, pp. 295–338. Free Press, New York.

Jefferson, G. (1984). Notes on a systematic deployment of the acknowledgement tokens "Yeah" and "Mm hm"'. *Papers in Linguistics*, **17**, 197–206.

Jefferson, G. (1986). On the interactional unpackaging of a 'gloss'. *Language in Society*, **14**, 435–466.

Jefferson, G. (1987). On exposed and embedded correction in conversation. *In*: Button, G. and Lee, J. (eds), *Talk and Social Organisation*, pp. 86–100. Multilingual Matters, Clevedon.

Johansson, S. (1975). Papers in contrastive linguistics and language testing. *Lund Studies in English*, **50**.

Johansson, S. (1978). *Studies of Error Gravity: Native Reactions to Errors Produced by Swedish Learners of English*. ACTA Universitatis Gothoburgensis, Sweden.

Jones, K. (1990). Conflict in Japanese conversation. Unpublished Ph.D. Dissertation. University of Michigan.

Jones, K. (1992). Ratifying conflict in Japanese interactions. Paper given at the Annual Meeting of the Association of Asian Studies, Washington, D.C.

Jorden, E. and Noda, M. (1987). *Japanese: The Spoken Language, Part 1*. Yale University Press, New Haven and London.

Kelley, H. H. and Schenitzki, D. P. (1972). Bargaining. *In*: McClintock, C. G. (ed.), *Experimental Social Psychology*, pp. 298–337. Holt, Rinehart and Winston, New York.

Kendon, A. (1992). The negotiation of context in face-to-face interaction. *In*: Duranti, A. and Goodwin, C. (eds), *Rethinking Context: Language as an Interactive Phenomenon*, pp. 323–334. Cambridge University Press, Cambridge.

Khalil, A. (1985). Communicative evaluation: Native speakers' evaluation and interpretation of written errors of Arab EFL learners. *TESOL Quarterly*, *19*(2), 335–351.

Knapp, K., Enninger, W. and Knapp-Potthoff, A. (eds) (1987). *Analyzing Intercultural Communication*. Mouton de Gruyter, Berlin.

Kochran, T. A. (1980). Collective bargaining and organizational behavior research. *In*: Staw, B. M. and Cummings, L. L. (eds), *Research in Organizational Behavior, Vol 2*, pp. 129–176. JAI Press, Greenwich, CT.

Kolb, D. M. (1985). To be a mediator: Expressive tactics in mediation. *Journal of Social Issues*, **41**(2), 11–26.

Kotthoff, H. (1993). Disagreement and concession in disputes: On the context sensitivity of preference structures. *Language in Society*, **22**, 193–216.

Krauss, E. S., Rohlen, T. P. and Steinhoff, P. G. (eds) (1984). *Conflict in Japan*. University of Hawaii Press, Honolulu.

Kulick, D. (1992). Anger, gender, language shift and the politics of revelation in a Papua New Guinean village. *Pragmatics*, **2**, 281–296.

Labov, W. (1972). Rules for ritual insults. *In*: Labov, W. (ed.), *Language in the Inner City: Studies in the Black English Vernacular*, pp. 297–353. University of Pennsylvania Press, Philadelphia.

Labov, W. and Fanshel, D. (1977). *Therapeutic Discourse: Psychotherapy as Conversation*. Academic Press, New York.

Lampi, M. (1986). *Linguistic Components of Strategy in Business Negotiations*. Helsinki School of Economics, Helsinki.

Landsberger, H. A. (1955). Interaction process analysis of mediation of labour-management disputes. *Journal of Abnormal and Social Psychology*, **57**, 552–558.

Lemke, J. L. (1989). Semantics and social change. *Word*, **40**, 37–50.

Levinson, S. C. (1979). Activity types and language. *Linguistics*, **17**, 356–399.

Levinson, S. C. (1983). *Pragmatics*. Cambridge University Press, Cambridge.

Levinson, S. C. (1992). Activity types and language. *In*: Drew, P. and Heritage, J. (eds), *Talk at Work: Interaction in Institutional Settings*, pp. 66–100. Cambridge University Press, Cambridge.

Lewicki, R. J. and Litterer, J. (1985). *Negotiation*. Irwin, Homewood, IL.

Lewis, S. A. and Fry, W. R. (1977). Effects of visual access and orientation on the discovery of integrative bargaining alternatives. *Organizational Behavior and Human Performance*, **20**, 75–92.

Lindstrom, L. (1992). Context contests: Debatable truth statements on Tanna (Vanuatu). *In*: Duranti, A. and Goodwin, C. (eds), *Rethinking Contest: Language as an Interactive Phenomenon*, pp. 101–124. Cambridge University Press, Cambridge.

Linell, P. and Jönsson, L. (1991). Suspect stories: perspective-setting in an asymmetrical situation. *In*: Marková, I. and Foppa, K. (eds), *Asymmetries in Dialogue*, pp. 75–100. Harvester Wheatsheaf, Hemel Hempstead.

Linell, P. and Luckmann, T. (1991). Asymmetries in dialogue: Some conceptual preliminaries. *In*: Marková, I. and Foppa, K. (eds), *Asymmetries in Dialogue*, pp. 1–20. Harvester Wheatsheaf, Hemel Hempstead.

Livingston, E. (1986). *The Ethnomethodological Foundations of Mathematics*. Routledge and Kegan Paul, London and New York.

Longabaugh, R. (1963). A category system for coding interpersonal behaviour as social exchange. *Sociometry*, **26**, 319–344.

Lynch, M. (1985). *Art and Artefact in Laboratory Science: A Study of Shop Work and Shop Talk in a Laboratory*. Routledge and Kegan Paul, London and New York.

Lynch, M., Livingston, E. and Garfinkel, H. (1983). Temporal order in laboratory work. *In*: Knorr-Cetina, K. and Mulkay, M. (eds), *Science Observed: Perspectives on the Social Study of Science*. Sage, London and Beverly Hills.

Magenau, J. M. and Pruitt, D. G. (1979). The social psychology of bargaining. *In*: Stephenson, G. M. and Brotherton, C. J. (eds), *Studies on Behaviour in Organisations: A Research Symposium*, pp. 101–134. University of Georgia Press, Athens, GA.

Manusov, V., Cody, M. J., Donohue, W. A. and Zappa, J. (1994). Accounts in child custody mediation sessions. *Journal of Applied Communication Research*, **22**, 1–15.

March, J. G. (1988). *Decisions and Organizations*. Blackwell, Oxford.

March, R. M. (1988). *The Japanese Negotiator: Subtlety and Strategy Beyond Western Logic*. Kodansha, New York.

Marková, I. and Foppa, K. (eds) (1991). *Asymmetries in Dialogue*. Harvester Wheatsheaf, Hemel Hempstead.

Marriott, H. E. (1989). The Japanese negotiator (book review). *Asian Studies Association of Australia Review*, **13**(2), 185–187.

Marriott, H. E. (1990). Intercultural business negotiations: The problem of norm discrepancy. *Australian Review of Applied Linguistics Series S*, **7**, 33–65.

Marriott, H. E. (1991a). Native speaker behaviour in Australian–Japanese business communication. *International Journal for the Sociology of Language*, **92**, 87–117.

Marriott, H. E. (1991b). The development of Japanese business communication research. *Unesco ALSED-LSP Newsletter 31*, **13**, 3, 12–28.

Marriott, H. E. (1993). Politeness phenomena in Japanese intercultural business communication. *Intercultural Communication Studies*, **3** (1), 15–37.

Marriott, H. E. (forthcoming). The management of discourse in international seller-buyer negotiations. *In*: Ehlich, K. and Wagner, J. (eds), *The Discourse of Business Negotiations*. Mouton de Gruyter, Berlin.

Marsh, P. D. V. (1974). *Contract Negotiation Handbook*. Gower Press, Epping.

Mastenbroek, W. (1989). *Negotiate*. Basil Blackwell, Oxford.

Mather, L. M. and Yngvesson, B. (1980–81). Language, audience and the transformation of disputes. *Law and Society Review*, **15** (3/4), 775–822.

Mather, L. M. (1973). Some determinants of the method of case disposition: Decision-making by public defenders in Los Angeles. *Law and Society Review*, **8**, 187–217.

Maynard, D. W. (1984): *Inside Plea Bargaining. The Language of Negotiation*. Plenum, New York.

Maynard, D. W. (1988). Language, interaction, and social problems. *Social Problems,* **35**, 311–334.

Maynard, D. W. (1982a). Person-descriptions in plea bargaining. *Semiotica,* **42,** 195–213.

Maynard, D. W. (1982b). Defendant attributes in plea bargaining: Notes on the modeling of sentencing decisions. *Social Problems*, **29**(4), 347–360.

Maynard, D. W. (1984). *Inside Plea Bargaining: The Language of Negotiation*. Plenum, New York.

Maynard, D. W. (1985). How children start arguments. *Language in Society*, **14**(1), 1–29.

Maynard, D. W. (1989). On the ethnography and the analysis of talk in institutional settings. *In*: Holstein, J. and Miller, G. (eds), *New Perspectives on Social Problems*, pp. 127–164. JAI Press, Greenwich, CT.

Mazeland, H. (1992). Vraag/antwoord-sequenties. Ph.D. dissertation, University of Groningen. Stichting Neerlandistiek VU, Amsterdam.

McDonell, D. (1986). *Theories of Discourse: An Introduction*. Basil Blackwell, Oxford.

Mey, J. (1993). *Pragmatics: An Introduction*. Basil Blackwell, Oxford.

Mishler, E. (1984). *The Discourse of Medicine: Dialectics of Medical Interviews*. Ablex, Norwood, NJ.

Moeran, B. (1989). *Language and Popular Culture in Japan*. Manchester University Press, Manchester and New York.

Moerman, M. (1988). *Talking Culture: Ethnography and Conversation Analysis*. University of Pennsylvania Press, Philadelphia.

Molotch, H. and Boden, D. (1985). Talking social structure: Discourse, dominance and the Watergate hearings. *American Sociological Review*, **50,** 273–388.

Morley, I and Stephenson, G. (1977). *The Social Psychology of Bargaining*. Allen and Unwin, London.

Mulholland, J. (1991). *The Language of Negotiation*. Routledge, London.

Murie, A. (1976). Communication problems in Australia-Japan business relations. Unpublished honours dissertation, Monash University.

Murray, D. (1987). Requests at work: Negotiating the conditions for conversation. *Management Communication Quarterly*, **1**(1), 58–83.

Nakata, T. (1992). The role of repetition in conversations involving complaints. Paper given at the Annual Meeting of the Association of Asian Studies, Washington, D.C.

Neu, J. (1988). Conversational structure: An explanation of bargaining behaviors in negotiation. *Management Communication Quarterly*, **2**(1), 23–45.

Neustupny, J. V. (1973). Sociolinguistics and the language teacher. *In*: Rado, M. (ed.), *Language Teaching: Problems and Solutions*, pp. 31–66. Bundoora, La Trobe University, Australia.

Neustupny, J. V. (1983). Nihongo kyooiku to nijuubunka kyooiku (Japanese language teaching and bicultural education). *Nihongo Kyooiku*, **49**, 13–24.

Neustupny, J. V. (1985a). Problems in Australian-Japanese contact situations. *In*: Pride, J. B. (ed.), *Cross-Cultural Encounters: Communication and Mis-Communication*, pp. 44–64. River Seine, Melbourne.

Neustupny, J. V. (1985b). Language norms in Australian–Japanese contact situations. *In*: Clyne, M. C. (ed.), *Australia, Meeting Place of Languages*, pp. 161–170. Pacific Linguistics, Canberra.

Neustupny, J. V. (1988). Problems of English contact discourse and language planning. Paper presented at the 1988 Regional Seminar on Language Planning in a Multilingual Setting: The Role of English, National University of Singapore.

Neustupny, J. V. (1989). *Strategies for Asia and Japan Literacy*. Japanese Studies Centre, Melbourne.

Neustupny, J. V. (1991). Atarashii nihongo kyooiku no tame ni (Towards new developments in Japanese language teaching) *Sekai no nihongo kyooiku* (Japanese language education around the globe) **1**, 1–14.

Noda, M. (1990). The extended predicate and confrontational discourse in Japanese. Ph.D. Dissertation. Cornell University.

Noda, M. (1992). Relation maintenance in discourse of disagreement in Japanese. Paper given at the Annual Meeting of the Association of Asian Studies, Washington, D.C.

Nofsinger, R. (1990). *Everyday Conversation*. Sage, Newbury Park.

O'Donnell, K. (1990). Difference and dominance: How labor and management talk conflict. *In*: Grimshaw, A. (ed.), *Conflict Talk: Sociolinguistic Investigations of Arguments in Conversation*, pp. 210–240. Cambridge University Press, Cambridge.

Office of Consumer Affairs (1988). *Your Rights as a Consumer: A Guide to the Sale of Goods and Supply of Services Act 1980*. Office of Consumer Affairs and Fair Trade, Dublin.

Oishi, T. (1985). A description of Japanese final particles in context. Ph.D. Dissertation, University of Michigan.

Pharr, S. (1990). *Losing Face: Status Politics in Japan*. University of California Press, Berkeley and Los Angeles.

Piazza, L. (1980). French tolerance for grammatical errors made by Americans. *Modern Language Journal*, **64**, 422–427.

Pike, K. (1967). *Language in Relation to a Unified Theory of the Structure of Human Behavior*. Mouton, The Hague.

Pinch, T. and Clark, C. (1986). The hard sell: 'Patter merchanting' and the strategic (re)production and local management of economic reasoning in the sales routines of market pitchers. *Sociology*, **20**(2), 169–191.

Pomerantz, A. (1975). Second assessments: A study of some features of agreements/ disagreements. Ph.D. University of California, Irvine.

Pomerantz, A. (1980). Telling my side: 'limited access' as a 'fishing' device. *Sociological Inquiry*, **50**, 186–198.

Pomerantz, A. (1984a). Pursuing a response. *In*: Atkinson, J. M. and Heritage, J. (eds), *Structures of Social Action: Studies in Conversation Analysis*, pp. 152–163. Cambridge University Press, Cambridge.

Pomerantz, A. (1984b). Agreeing and disagreeing with assessments: Some features of preferred/ dispreferred turn shapes. *In*: Atkinson, J. M. and Heritage, J. (eds), *Structures of Social Action: Studies in Conversation Analysis*, pp. 57–101. Cambridge University Press, Cambridge.

Poole, M. S. (1985). Tasks and interaction sequences: A theory of coherence in group decision making interaction. *In*: Street, R. L. and Capella, J. N. (eds), *Sequence and Pattern in Communicative Behaviour*. Arnold, London.

Poole, M. S., Shannon, D. L. and DeSanctis, G. (1992). Communication media and the negotiation processes. *In*: Putnam, L. L. and Roloff, M. E. (eds), *Communication and Negotiation*, pp. 46–66. Sage, London.

Power, R. J. D. and Del Martello, M. F. (1986). Some criticisms of Sacks, Schegloff, and Jefferson on turn-taking. *Semiotica*, **58**, 29–40.

Prottas, J. (1979). *People Processing: The Street-Level Bureaucrat in Public Service Bureaucracies*. Lexington Books, Lexington.

Pruitt, D. G. (1969). Indirect communication in the search for agreement in negotiation. Indirect Communications in Negotiations Project. Working Papers II.

Pruitt, D. G. (1971). Indirect communication and the search for agreement in negotiation. *Journal of Applied Social Psychology*, **1**, 205–239.

Pruitt, D. G. (1981). *Negotiation Behavior*. Academic Press, London.

Pruitt, D. G. and Lewis, S. A. (1977). The psychology of integrative bargaining. *In*: Druckman, D. (ed.), *Negotiations: Social Psychological Perspectives*, pp. 161–192. Sage, Beverly Hills, CA.

Putnam, L. L. (1985). Bargaining as task and process: Multiple functions of interaction sequences. *In*: Street, R. L., Jr and Cappella, J. N. (eds), *Sequence and Pattern in Communicative Behaviour*, pp. 225–242. Edward Arnold, London.

Putnam, L. L. and Holmer, M. (1992). Framing, reframing, and issue development. *In*: Putnam, L. and Roloff, M. (eds), *Communication and Negotiation*, pp. 128–155. Sage, Newbury Park.

Putnam, L. L. and Jones, T. S. (1982). The role of communication in bargaining. *Human Communication Research*, **8**, 262–280.

Putnam, L. L. and Poole, M. S. (1987). Conflict and negotiation. *In*: Jablin, F. M., Putnam, L. L., Roberts, K. H. and Porter, L. W. (eds), *Handbook of Organizational Communication: An Interdisciplinary Perspective*, pp. 549–599. Sage, London.

Putnam, L. L. and Roloff, M. E. (1992). Communication perspectives on negotiation. *In*: Putnam, L. L. and Roloff, M. E. (eds), *Communication and Negotiation*, pp. 1–17. Sage, London.

Read, S. J. (1992). Constructing accounts: The role of explanatory coherence. *In*: McLaughlin, M., Cody, M. J. and Read, S. J. (eds), *Explaining One's Self to Others: Reason-Giving in a Social Context*, pp. 3–19. Lawrence Erlbaum, Hilldale, NJ.

Rehbein, J. (1977). *Komplexes Handeln*. Metzler, Stuttgart.

Rehbein, J. (*in press*). International sales talk. On some linguistic needs of today's business communication in European settings. *In*: Ehlich, K. and Wagner, J. (eds), *The Discourse of Negotiation*. Mouton de Gruyter, Berlin.

Rosenthal, R. (1988). Interpersonal expectancies, nonverbal communication and research on negotiation. *Negotiation Journal*, July, 267–280.

Rubin, J. and Brown, B. (1975). *The Social Psychology of Bargaining*. Academic Press, New York.

Sachs, H., Schleghoff, E. and Jefferson, G. (1974). A simplest systematics for the organization of turn-taking for conversation. *Language*, **50**(4), 696–735.

Sacks, H. (1972a). On the analyzability of stories by children. *In*: Gumperz, J. and Hymes, D. (eds), *Directions in Sociolinguistics: The Ethnography of Communication*, pp. 329–345. Holt, Rinehart and Winston, New York.

Sacks, H. (1972b). An initial investigation of the usability of conversational data for doing sociology. *In*: Sudnow, D. (ed.), *Studies in Social Interaction*, pp. 31–74. Free Press, New York.

Sacks, H. (1972c). On some puns with some intimations. *In*: Shuy, R. W. (ed), *Report of the 23rd Annual Round Table Meeting on Linguistics and Language Studies*, pp. 135–144. Georgetown U.P., Washington.

Sacks, H. (1987). On the preference for agreement and contiguity in sequences in conversation. *In*: Button, G. and Lee, J. R. E. (eds), *Talk and Social Organization*, pp. 54–69. Multilingual Matters, Clevedon, U.K.

Sacks, H. (1992a). *Harvey Sacks: Lectures on Conversation*, Vol. 1. Blackwell, Oxford.

Sacks, H. (1992b). *Harvey Sacks: Lectures on Conversation*, Vol. 2. Blackwell, Oxford.

Sacks, H., Schegloff, E. A. and Jefferson, G. (1974). A simplest systematics for the organization of turn-taking in conversation. *Language*, **50,** 696–735.

Salacuse, J. W. (1991). *Making Global deals: Negotiating in the International Marketplace*. Houghton Mifflin, Boston.

Sawyer, J. and Guetzkow,. H. (1965). Bargaining and negotiation in international relations. *In*: Kelman, H. C. (ed.), *International Behavior: A Social-Psychological Analysis*, pp. 466–520. Holt, Rinehart and Winston, New York.

Schegloff, E. (1968). Sequencing in conversational openings. *American Anthropologist*, **70,** 1075–1095.

Schegloff, E. A. (1972a). Sequencing in conversational openings. *In*: Gumperz, J. J. and Hymes, D. (eds), *Directions in Sociolinguistics*, pp. 346–380. Holt, Rinehart and Winston, New York.

Schegloff, E. A. (1972b). Notes on conversational practice: Formulating place. *In*: Sudnow, D. (ed.), *Studies in Social Interaction*, pp. 75–119. Free Press, New York.

Schegloff, E. A. (1977). On some questions and ambiguities in conversation. *In*: Dressler, W. (ed.), *Current Trends in Textlinguistics*, pp. 81–102. Walter de Gruyter, Berlin.

Schegloff, E. A. (1979). Identification and recognition in telephone conversation openings. *In*: Psathas, G. (ed.), *Everyday Language: Studies in Ethnomethodology*, pp. 23–78. Irvington, New York.

Schegloff, E. A. (1982). Discourse as an interactional achievement: Some uses of 'uh-huh' and other things that come between sentences. *In*: Tannen, D. (ed.), *Analyzing Discourse: Text and Talk, Georgetown University Roundtable on Languages and Linguistics 1981*, pp. 71–93. Georgetown University Press, Washington, U.K.

Schegloff, E. A. (1986). The routine as achievement. *Human Studies, 9,* 111–152.

Schegloff, E. A. (1991). Reflections on talk and social structure. *In*: Boden, D. and Zimmerman, D. (eds), *Talk and Structure. Studies in Ethnomethodology and Conversation Analysis*, pp. 44–70. Polity Press, Cambridge.

Schegloff, E. A. (1992). On talk and its institutional occasions. *In*: Drew, P. and Heritage, J. (eds), *Talk at Work: Interaction in Institutional Settings*, pp. 101–136. Cambridge University Press, Cambridge.

Schegloff, E. A. (1992). Repair after next turn: The last structurally provided defense of intersubjectivity. *American Journal of Sociology, 97,* 1295–1345.

Schegloff, E. A. and Sacks, H. (1973). Opening up closings. *Semiotica, 7,* 289–327.

Schegloff, E. A., Jefferson, G. and Sacks, H. (1977). The preference for self-correction in the organization of repair in conversation. *Language, 53,* 361–382.

Schelling, T. C. (1960). *The Strategy of Conflict*. Oxford University Press, London.

Schiffrin, D. (1994). *Approaches to Discourse*. Basil Blackwell, Oxford.

Schutz, A. (1964). In *Collected Papers II: Studies in Social Theory*, Broderson, A. (ed.). Nijhoff, The Hague.

Scott, M. B. and Lyman, S. M. (1968). Accounts. *American Sociological Review, 33,* 46–62.

Searle, J. R. (1979). *Expression and Meaning*. Cambridge University Press, Cambridge.

Selting, M. (1985). Levels of style-shifting: Exemplified in the interaction strategies of a moderator in a listener participation program. *Journal of Pragmatics, 9,* 179–197.

Semin, G. R. and Manstead, A. S. R. (1983). *The Accountability of Conduct: A Social Psychological Analysis*. Academic Press, London.

Sharrock, W. W. and Button, G. (1991). Design in three dimensions. *Proceedings of the Institution of Electrical Engineers, Computing and Control Division Colloquium on CSCW: Some Fundamental Issues*, London.

Sharrock, W. W., Button, G. and Anderson, R. J. (forthcoming). Getting the design job done: Notes on the social organization of Technical Work, *Journal Of Intelligent Systems*.

Siegel, S. and Fouraker, L. E. (1960). *Bargaining and Group Decision-Making*. McGraw-Hill, New York.

Sinclair, J. McH. and Coulthard, R. M. (1975). *Towards an Analysis of Discourse: The Language Used by Teachers and Pupils*. Oxford University Press, London.

Smith, D. (1985). *The Conceptual Practices of Power: A Feminist Sociology of Knowledge*. University of Toronto Press, Toronto.

Smith, R. J. (1978). *Kurusu: The Price of Progress in a Japanese Village, 1951–75*. Stanford University Press, Stanford.

Smith, R. J. and Wiswell, E. L. (1982). *The Women of Suyemura*. University of Chicago Press, Chicago.

Stein, J. G. (ed.) (1989). *Getting to the Table*. John Hopkins University Press, Baltimore.

Stinchcombe, A. L. (1990). *Information and Organization*. University of California Press, Berkeley.

Stokes, R. and Hewitt, J. P. (1976). Aligning Actions. *American Sociological Review*, **41**, 838–849.

Strauss, A. (1978). *Negotiations: Varieties, Contexts, Processes, and Social Order*. Josset-Bass, London.

Strauss, A. L., Schartzman, L., Bucher, R., Erlich, D. and Sabshin, K. (1964). *Psychiatric Ideologies and Institutions*. Free Press, New York.

Streek, J. (1980). Speech acts in interaction: A critique of searle. *Discourse Processes*, **3**, 133–154.

Streek, J. (1983). *Social Order in Child Communication*. John Benjamins, Amsterdam.

Strong, P. M. and Dingwall, R. W. J. (1983). The limits of negotiation in formal organisations. *In*: Gilbert, G. N. and Abell, P. (eds), *Accounts and Action: Surrey Conferences on Sociological Theory and Method 1*, pp. 98–116. Gower Press, Aldershot.

Sunshine, R. B. (1990). *Negotiating for International Development: A Practitioner's Handbook*. Martinus Nijhoff Publishers, Dordrecht.

Swales, J. (1990). *Genre Analysis*. Cambridge University Press, Cambridge.

Szatrowski, P. (1992). Invitation-refusals in Japanese telephone conversations. Paper given at the Annual Meeting of the Association of Asian Studies, Washington, D.C.

Taylor, C. (1989). *Sources of the Self: The making of modern identity*. Harvard University Press, Cambridge, MA.

Taylor, T. J. and Cameron, D. (1987). *Analysing Conversation: Rules and Units in the Structure of Talk*. Pergamon Press, Oxford.

Tedeschi, J. T. and Rosenfeld, P. (1980). Communication in bargaining and negotiation. *In*: Roloff, M. and Miller, G. (eds), *Persuasion: New Directions in Theory and Research*, pp. 225–248. Sage, London.

ten Have, P. (1989). The consultation as a genre. *In*: Torode, B. (ed.), *Text and Talk as Social Practice*, pp. 115–135. R.I.: Foris Publications, Dordrecht/Providence.

ten Have, P. (1991a). The doctor is silent: Observations on episodes without vocal receipt during medical consultations. *In*: Conein, B., de Fornel, M. and Quéré, L. (eds), *Les formes de la conversation*, Vol. 2, pp. 55–76. CNET, Issy-les-Moulineaux.

ten Have, P. (1991b). Talk and institution: A reconsideration of the 'asymmetry' of doctor–patient interaction. *In*: Boden, D. and Zimmerman, D. H. (eds), *Talk and Social Structure: Studies in Ethnomethodology and Conversation Analysis*, pp. 138–163. Polity Press, Cambridge.

ten Have, P. and Psathas, G. (eds) (forthcoming). *Situated Order: Studies in the Organization of Talk and Embodied Activities*. University of America Press, Washington, D.C.

Tuckman, B. (1965). Developmental sequences in small groups. *Psychological Bulletin*, **63**, 383–399.

Tung, R. (1988). Toward a conceptual paradigm of international business negotiations. *In*: Farmer, R. D. (ed.), *Advances in International Comparative Management*, Vol. 3, pp. 203–219. JAI Press, Greenwich.

Tutzauer, F. (1992). The communication of offers in Dyadic bargaining. *In*: Putnam, L. L. and Roloff, M. E. (eds), *Communication and Negotiation*, pp. 67–82. Sage, Newbury Park.

Ulijn, J. M. and Gorter, Tj. R. (1989). Language, culture and technical-commercial negotiating. *In*: Coleman, H. (ed.), *Working with Language*, pp. 479–505. Mouton de Gruyter, Berlin.

van Dijk, T. A. (1985). *Handbook of Discourse Analysis (Vols 1-4)*. Academic Press, London.

Ventola, E. (1987). *The Structure of Social Interaction*. Frances Printer, London.

Volosinov, V. N. (1973). *Marxism and the Philosophy of Language*. (Translation by Ladislav Matejka and I. R. Titunik. First published in Russian 1930.) Seminar Press, New York.

von Nuemann, J. and Morgenstern, O. (1944). *Theory of Games and Economic Behavior*. Princeton, New York.

Walcott, C., Hopmann, P. T. and King, T. D. (1977). The role of debate in negotiation. *In*: Druckman, D. (ed.), *Negotiations: Social Psychological Perspectives*, pp. 193–211. Sage, Beverly Hills, CA.

Walton, R. E. and McKersie, R. B. (1965). *A Behavioral Theory of Labor Negotiations: An Analysis of a Social Interaction System*. McGraw-Hill, New York.

Watanabe, S. (1992). Japanese ways of carrying out group discussions. Paper given at the Annual Meeting of the Association of Asian Studies, Washington, D.C.

Weiss, A. (1988). Making negotiating demands: The concept and use of linguistic mitigation. Unpublished Working Paper.

Weiss and Stripp, W. (1985). Negotiating with foreign business persons. NYU Graduate School of Business Administration. Working Paper #85-86.

Weiss, S. (1993). *Negotiating with Romans: A Range of Culturally-Responsive Strategies*. Faculty of Administrative Studies, York University.

Wertsch, J. (1991). *Voices of the Mind*. Harvester Wheatsheaf, Hemel Hempstead.

Whalen, J., Zimmerman, D. H. and Whalen, M. R. (1988). When words fail: a single case analysis. *Social Problems*, **35**(4), 335–362.

Whalen, M. R. and Zimmerman, D. H. (1990). Describing trouble: Practical epistemology in citizen calls to the police. *Language in Society*, **19**(4), 465–492.

Wheatley, J. S. (forthcoming). *Briefings as part of the Document Design Process*.

Wilson, T. P. (1991). Social structure and the sequential organisation of interaction. *In*: Boden, D. and Zimmerman, D. H. (eds), *Talk and Social Structure: Studies in Ethnomethodology and Conversation Analysis*, pp. 22–43. Polity Press, Cambridge.

Wittgenstein, L. (1958). *Philosophical Investigations*. Blackwell, Oxford.

Wootton, C.A. (1989). Remarks on the methodology of conversation analysis. *In*: Roger, D. and Bull, P. (eds), *Conversation*, pp. 238–268. Multilingual Matters, Cleveland, U.K.

Wygotski, L. S. (1969). *Denken und Sprechen*. Fischer. Yamada, H. (1989). American and Japanese topic management strategies in business meetings. Ph.D. Dissertation. Georgetown University.

Young, O. (ed.) (1975). *Bargaining: Formal Theories of Negotiation*. University of Chicago Press, Chicago, IL.

Yourdon, E. and Constantine, L. C. (1979). *Structured Design: Fundamentals of a Discipline of Computer Program and System Design*. Prentice-Hall, Englewood Cliffs, NJ.

Zartman, I. W. (1975). Negotiations: Theory and reality. *Journal of International Affairs*, **9**, 69–77.

Zartman, I. W. (1989a). In search of common elements in the analysis of the negotiation process. *In*: Mautner-Markhof, F. (ed.), *Processes of International Negotiations*, pp. 241–255. Westview Press, Boulder, CO.

Zartman, I. W. (1989b). Prenegotiation: Phases and functions. *International Journal*, **XLIV**(2), Spring, 237–253.

Zeuthen, F. (1930). *Problems of Monopoly and Economic Warfare*. Routledge and Kegan Paul, London.

Zimmerman, D. H. (1971). The practicalities of rule use. *In*: Douglas, J. (ed.), *Understanding Everyday Life* pp. 221–238. Routledge and Kegan Paul, London.

Zimmerman, D. H. (1988). On conversation: the conversation analytic perspective. *Communication Yearbook II*, pp. 406–432. Sage, Newbury Park.

Zimmerman, D. H. (1992). The interactional organization of calls for emergency assistance. *In*: Drew, P. and Heritage, J. (eds), *Talk at Work: Interaction in Institutional Settings*, pp. 418–469. Cambridge University Press, Cambridge.

Zimmerman, D. H. and Boden, D. (1991). Structure-in-Action: An Introduction. *In*: Boden, D. and Zimmerman, D. (eds), *Talk and Social Structure: Studies in Ethnomethodology and Conversation Analysis*, pp. 3–21. Polity Press, Cambridge.

AUTHOR INDEX

SUBJECT INDEX